# THE ARMCHAIR
# MOUNTAINEER

# THE ARMCHAIR MOUNTAINEER

Edited by David Reuther
and John Thorn

Illustrations by Bob Carroll

MENASHA RIDGE PRESS
Birmingham, Alabama

*For Jacob and Kate*
*and Isaac and Jed*

# Contents

Introduction    ix

A. ALVAREZ: A Test of Will    1
*"It is like playing chess with your body."*

JEREMY BERNSTEIN: Needles and Pins    4
*Learning to climb, in the world capital of Alpinism.*

ALAN BLACKSHAW: Tackling the Climb    10
*Techniques and basic principles.*

CHRIS BONINGTON: Struggle for the Ice Ridge    14
*Annapurna South Face, a frightening climb on loose ice and snow.*

HERMANN BUHL: Nanga Parbat . . . Solo    20
*A forty-one-hour conquest of the peak that has claimed thirty-one lives.*

YVON CHOUINARD: Modern Yosemite Climbing    34
*A seminal and prophetic piece, written in 1963.*

RONALD W. CLARK: Mont Blanc and the Scientists    42
*Balmat, Paccard, de Saussure, and the primal myth of the mountains.*

SAMUEL L. CLEMENS: The Ascent of the Riffelberg    50
*A modest Alpine expedition, numbering 205.*

IAN McNAUGHT DAVIS: Drop, Plop, Fly, or Die    60
*"The pleasure center of climbing—falling off."*

CLINTON DENT: The First Ascent of the Dru    63
*A pioneering "modern" exploit: the challenge of smaller peaks.*

PHILIP C. GOSSETT: The Death of Bennen    70
*An avalanche on the Haut de Cry, 1864.*

ROBERT GRAVES: Climbing with Mallory    75
*A pupil's recollections; from* Good-by to All That.

PETER HABELER: Everest Without Oxygen    80
*Man against mountain: getting back to basics.*

WARREN HARDING: Reflections of a Broken-down Climber    85
*To bolt or not to bolt . . . was that the question?*

HEINRICH HARRER: The Tragedy of Toni Kurz    92
*A grisly death on the Eiger's North Face, 1936.*

MAURICE HERZOG: Back from Annapurna    101
*A harrowing bivouac in a crevasse, battling cold and despair.*

EDMUND HILLARY: The Final Assault    110
*The great prize attained—the summit of Everest.*

R. L. G. IRVING: Solvitur in Excelsis    119
*The truth of climbing: The physical and the contemplative quests are one.*

JOHN JEROME: Avalanches    128
*What accounts for their awesome and capricious destructiveness?*

CHRIS JONES: The Granite Crucible    133
*Yosemite and its climbing counterculture.*

MICHAEL LOUGHMAN: The Varieties of Climbing    145
*A comprehensive overview of rock climbing, by a veteran teacher.*

ARNOLD LUNN: My Last Climb    154
*It wasn't, of course, despite a crippling fall.*

JOE McGINNISS: The Mountaineer Despite Himself    158
*It was not a scree slope, he realized, but the side of a cliff.*

NORMAN MAILER: The Ledge    165
*"I can't go on, I can't"; from* The Naked and the Dead.

GEORGE LEIGH MALLORY: The Mountaineer as Artist    172
*Does a cricketer experience the sublime?*

PETER MATTHIESSEN: A Fine Chance to Let Go    179
*Looking for the snow leopard of the Himalaya.*

REINHOLD MESSNER: The Will to Survive    182
*Reflections on Nanga Parbat, with a look back to Hermann Buhl.*

ALBERT F. MUMMERY: The Pleasures and Penalties of Mountaineering    185
*Published in the year of his death on Nanga Parbat.*

ANTON NELSON: Five Days and Nights on the Lost Arrow    190
*A classic of Class-6 climbing, executed with Salathé in 1947.*

ERIC NEWBY: Mount McKinley    194
*Cook, the Sourdoughs, and the Reverend Stuck.*

JACK OLSEN: Rescue from the Eiger    202
*One was saved, three were lost.*

PIERS PAUL READ: Stranded in the Andes    208
*Which way lay survival—up or down?*

COLETTE RICHARD: Climbing Blind    216
*Sightless since the age of two, but happy in the heights.*

RICK RIDGEWAY: Bivouac on K2    219
*Just beneath the summit, at 40 below, without oxygen, food, or shelter.*

STEVE ROPER and ALLEN STECK: El Capitan, Salathé Wall    228
*Pioneering a new route.*

ARTHUR ROTH: Wall of Death    232
*Solving the last great problem in the Alps, the Eiger Direct.*

GALEN ROWELL: Rescue on the South Face of Half Dome    242
*"We cannot last another night!"—and then came a guardian angel.*

WOODROW WILSON SAYRE: Anti-Belaying    250
*How not to descend Everest.*

LESLIE STEPHEN: The Regrets of a Mountaineer    255
*A classic essay, from* The Playground of Europe.

JOE TASKER: The Way Down    264
*Retreat from Dunagiri, in delirium.*

LITO TEJADA-FLORES: Games Climbers Play    275
*The seven basic games, with the rules applicable to each.*

H. W. TILMAN: Kenya Mountain    283
*"A very good fortnight playing about on the mountain."*

TREVANIAN: "The Surface Was Moving Beneath Him"    288
*Snowslide on the Eiger; fiction.*

JOHN TYNDALL: Rescue from a Crevasse    291
*A stupefied porter, a theatrical guide, and yet the victim lived.*

JAMES RAMSEY ULLMAN: The White Tower    295
*"You have heard of a hand traverse, perhaps?"*

EVELYN WAUGH: Tricky Bits    305
*Trying to keep up with a man of action; delicious absurdity.*

H. G. WELLS: Little Mother Up the Mörderberg    309
*"Safe as Trafalgar Square. . . . Hop along, Mummykins."*

EDWARD WHYMPER: "But the Rope Broke"    318
*Surely the classic of mountaineering literature.*

GEOFFREY WINTHROP YOUNG: The Measure of Courage    331
*By one who would know; from Mountain Craft, the climber's Bible.*

FRANCIS YOUNGHUSBAND: Mallory and Irvine    333
*Their final hours, as nearly as we can know.*

Glossary    339
Permissions    341

# Introduction

The mountain is magic — the visible signpost to an invisible world in which men might be as gods. Threatening, alluring, exciting, soothing, this mass of contradictions draws one up short: presenting a supreme physical challenge, it confers rewards that are, nonetheless, spiritual. To mankind it poses profound questions; to the climber, it grudgingly yields answers. What are mountains for? Why climb them? What are men for? What is art? Sport? Beauty? Good?

Still, for all the majesty and mystery of the mountains, what sends men clambering up them is not the pursuit of understanding but simply that of pleasure. Games may be serious business, as students of any sport will testify, but if there is no elation, no expansiveness to them, then they are nothing at all. This volume exhibits the spirit, the struggle, even the *necessity* of mountain climbing to one who would live life to the fullest; above all, however, it conveys the freedom and joy of ascent.

*Why climb a mountain?* "Because it is there," said Mallory of Everest, in what has become a classic profundity or evasion. (Another, less celebrated answer by Mallory to this primal question of mountaineering was, "To struggle and to understand.") This view of climbing makes lemmings of men, driven by strange primordial forces to leave their natural element and assault the heavens. Risk is surely a prime component of climbing's appeal, but so is the need to rid oneself of mundane concerns — "to get above an atmosphere of doubt," in R. L. G. Irving's phrase — and confront life directly, without compromise. The elemental crucible on high, in which are bonded rise and risk, dream and dread, takes the measure of the man.

*Is climbing a sport?* Emphatically, yes—although in its glimpses of the infinite, its flashes of perfection, it enters the realm of beauty and art and so is more than sport. The impulse to make one's mark in the world by setting foot where no man has trod before is the trademark of an artist, the man or woman who would defy mortality. All the same, the daily-newspaper view of sport has intruded upon mountaineering. In the 1960s climbing became, unattractively, a competition between men (speed climbing, for example), or one between equipment and mountain in which the destination was all and the journey nothing. Today there is ample evidence of a return to the traditional perspective on climbing as sport—that the competition is between man and mountain and, at root, between man's hopes and fears.

*Why read about climbing?* It is not the next best thing to climbing—nothing is; rather, it is altogether different, and the pleasures of the armchair make for a splendid complement to the rigors of the crag. And being an armchair mountaineer is not a mean thing, Mummery notwithstanding, for the palms can sweat and the spirit soar even before a cozy fire with a brandy at one's side. No other sport except perhaps angling has been blessed with such a quantity of first-rate prose, and surprisingly little of it from the Hairbreadth Harry School of Sticky Situations. The editors could easily have compiled an anthology twice this size had they not been under the constraint that no author be represented more than once. Another principle guiding our selections was that the volume in the end reflect not only our estimates of the best that has been written about climbing but also that it afford the reader a panoramic view of mountaineering's history, lore, technique, literature, and, above all, those uniquely visionary misfits known as climbers. *The Armchair Mountaineer* presents a bouillabaisse of nationalities, literary genres, climbing types, calamities, and exultations. Evident in these pages is how far the sport has come in the 125 years since Europeans first made the Alps their playground. Next came the Himalayas and Karakoram; today the playground, or proving ground, is the Yosemite Valley; tomorrow it may be a "small is beautiful" sandbox, like free soloing on a modest peak.

Climbing has a copious and often confusing technical terminology. Even veteran climbers who know a jumar from a jump rope may find it useful to know that there is a glossary at the end of this book.

We wish to thank our friend and collaborator, Bob Carroll; Maron Waxman and Nancy Ackerman of Scribners; Elaine Chubb, our copy editor; and the knowledgeable people at the public libraries of New York and Saugerties. Special appreciation goes to Pat Fletcher, the superbly helpful librarian of the American Alpine Club of New York City, that great repository of mountaineering literature, and to Frances Miller, the consummate armchair mountaineer, who graciously permitted us the use of her extraordinary collection.

DAVID REUTHER AND
JOHN THORN

Through alphabetic luck this book opens with a splendid essay on the question central to mountaineering: Why climb? For Alvarez, the author of a book on suicide and another on that related phenomenon, gambling, the answer is risk—a risk not so great as to presume upon the benevolence of the fates, but one sufficient to require complete attention to the task at hand. Like a solo flight in an airplane, mountain climbing provides a certain clarity about whether one enjoys being alive or not.

# A. ALVAREZ

# A Test of Will

I started climbing in the summer of 1950, just before my twentieth birthday, hit my peak at the sport about fifteen years later, and have been on a gradually accelerating decline ever since. Yet I still try to get onto the rocks any Sunday when the weather is halfway decent, although my stamina and flexibility are sharply diminishing, and the rocks I usually go to—a little sandstone outcrop south of London—would fit comfortably into the foyer of the new A.T. & T. Building. These days, I climb mostly with my son. At fifteen, he is too young to know any better. Yet the fact is, whenever work or rain deprives us of our weekly fix of climbing, we exhibit identical withdrawal symptoms: restlessness, irritability, fretfulness, a glum conviction that our week has been spoiled. Climbing is an addictive sport that changes the psyche's chemistry as irredeemably as heroin changes the body's, and both of us are hooked.

When Mallory was asked why he wanted to climb Everest, he answered with a famous evasion: "Because it's there." I suspect that what he really meant was "Because you're here"—"you" being not only his aggrieved and aggressive questioner but also the town, the noise, the involvements, the problems, the routine. You climb to get away from all that, to clear the head, to breathe free air. Yet most weekend sportsmen—the fishermen and yachtsmen, golfers, even Sunday painters—do what they do in order to get away, without risking their necks in the process. Why, then, does climbing exert such a curiously addictive power?

First, because it is one of the purest, least cluttered sports, requiring a minimum of equipment: a pair of special boots, a rope, a safety helmet, a few carabiners (snap links), nylon slings, and artificial steel chockstones or pitons for protection. The whole lot costs very little, lasts for years, and hangs easily around your neck and from your waist. Unlike other sports, if something goes wrong, the fault is nearly always in you, not in your gear. Conversely, the reward, when a climb has gone well, is an intense sense of physical well-being. On those rare occasions when mood, fitness, and rock all come together and everything goes perfectly, you experience an extraordinary combination of elation and calm — tension dissolves, movement becomes effortless, every risk is under control — a kind of inner silence like that of the mountains themselves. No doubt every athlete feels that on his best days, but in climbing that style of contentment is attainable long after you pass, as I have, your physical prime.

It is also not a competitive sport, however much the top climbers vie among themselves for first ascents or ascents in the best style. The competition is not even with the mountain or the rock face. You are competing, instead, with yourself — with your protesting body, your nerves, and, when the going gets really tough, with your reserves of character.

In 1964, for example, a companion and I spent a night belayed to a small ledge — a couple of feet long and 18 inches wide — 1,300 feet up an overhanging face in the Italian Dolomites. We had been benighted on it by a sudden snowstorm and were soaked to the skin; but because this was August in Italy, we were climbing light, which meant we had neither protective clothing nor food. The route finished up a thousand-foot vertical corner, down which a waterfall of melted snow was pouring. It froze solid during the night, and privately both of us assumed that we would do the same. But neither of us mentioned the possibility, because to have done so would not only have undermined our confidence to complete the last 500 icy feet the next morning — if there was a next morning for us — it would also have been a violation of privacy. Our survival depended, as much as anything else, on tact. It was not just a question of being young enough and fit enough to withstand the cold, we also had to behave well and respect each other's feelings. Melodrama and self-pity would have done us in more surely than the freezing temperature.

I suspect that most men are secretly worried about how they will behave under pressure. Certainly I emerged from that night on the bare mountain with frostbitten fingers and a good deal more self-confidence than I had had before — a confidence that was quite apart from the pleasure of having got up a difficult climb in bad conditions. I had learned that the ability to sit quiet in a crisis and not fuss was more valuable than physical strength. I also discovered in myself an unsuspected, obstinate ability to survive and that, in some devious way, seemed to absolve me from the youthful need continually to apologize and explain. As the poet Thom Gunn wrote, "I was myself: subject to no man's breath." Perhaps I should also add that I have not felt the need to repeat the experiment; the Via Comici on the north face of the Cima Grande di Lavaredo was the last serious climb I did without checking the weather forecast beforehand.

"Life loses in interest," wrote Freud, "when the highest stake in the game, life itself, may not be risked." Those who cultivate risk for its own sake, however, are probably emphasizing only their own inner torpor, just as the people who talk most fervently about the beautiful emotions induced by drugs are those who have most difficulty in feeling anything at all. The pleasure of risk is in the control needed to ride it with assurance so that what appears dangerous to the outsider is, to the participant, simply a matter of intelligence, skill, intuition, coordination — in a word, experience. Climbing, in particular, is a paradoxically intellectual pastime, but with this difference: you have to think with your body. Each pitch becomes a series of specific local problems: which holds to use, and in which combinations, in order to get up safely and with the least expense of energy. Every move has to be worked out by a kind of physical strategy, in terms of effort, balance, and consequences. It is like playing chess with your body.

And, that, for me, is the final satisfaction. To be a professional writer is, in the end, a sedentary, middle-class occupation, like accountancy or psychoanalysis, though more lonely. For five or six days each week, I sit at my desk and try to get sentences right. If I make a mistake, I can rewrite it the following day or the next, or catch it in proof. And if I fail to do so, who cares? Who even notices?

On a climb, my concentration is no less, but I am thinking with my body rather than my weary, addled head, and if I make a mistake, the consequences are immediate, obvious, embarrassing, and possibly painful. For a brief period and on a small scale, I have to be directly responsible for my actions, without evasions, without excuses. In that beautiful, silent, useless world of the mountains, you can achieve at least a certain clarity, even seriousness of a wayward kind. It seems to me worth a little risk.

This delightful account of a physicist's initiation rites in the Aiguilles de Chamonix is taken from a book aptly titled *Mountain Passages*. The Haute-Savoie is the place where mountain climbing was born and the place where it still reigns, despite the increased accessibility of more exotic sites. For interesting counterpoint to this modern *monchu*'s relationship with his guide, see the nineteenth-century accounts of Philip C. Gossett, John Tyndall, and Edward Whymper.

# JEREMY BERNSTEIN

# Needles and Pins

There is no mountainous region on earth that provides a wider and more varied theater for climbing than the French Alps in the region near Chamonix. Mountain climbing and the mountain aesthetic were invented in Chamonix, and guides who have made hundreds of different climbs in the Chamonix Valley have told me that they have barely scratched the surface of what is available there. The publicity brochures about Chamonix advertise that it is the world capital of Alpinism, and they are right. In a real sense, "climbing" and "the Chamonix Valley" are practically synonymous.

I am neither a very distinguished climber, nor a very conventional one. I was first introduced to the high mountains, entirely by chance, in 1937, when I was eight—I have an ancient photograph that shows me clinging to a small rock and looking very worried. (I have a number of more recent photographs showing me clinging to *large* rocks with about the same expression.) Since then I have done some climbing in the western United States and elsewhere, but my climbing activities have largely been confined to the French Alps around Chamonix. I had the good fortune to stumble into Chamonix, and to meet the French alpine guide Claude Jaccoux, at a time when I could take advantage of it and at a time when I was in a position to write about it. Everything that has happened to me since in the way of mountaineering and travel has followed from this happy accident.

In September of 1959 I arrived in Paris with a two-year fellowship to do physics, only to learn that the academic year did not begin until November. I had a small car and decided to explore the country; knowing little about it in advance, I wandered into the Chamonix Valley. I was overwhelmed by the beauty of the place, but it certainly did not occur to me to climb anything; one look at the Aiguilles — needles — of Chamonix convinced me that they were not meant for the rational man. I recall taking a ride, with an elderly stranger, above the Vallée Blanche in a small gondola suspended from wires. As we swayed over the sickening void his seraphic smile never varied, and when, finally, I asked him about it, he told me that he had a literal and unwavering belief in the afterlife.

It is very unlikely that I would have returned to Chamonix except for two further twists of chance. The French physicists with whom I had been working in Paris had set up a summer school on the island of Corsica and, for its second summer, I was invited to join the faculty. I made friends with many of the French physicists, and especially with a young Parisian named Georges Bonnevay. He looked extremely frail and sported a long, narrow beard; I was surprised to learn that Bonnevay was a first-class Chamonix climber and that, moreover, most of my young colleagues at the school also climbed regularly in Chamonix. (Largely because of this, there is now at Les Houches, in the Chamonix Valley, one of the most distinguished physics summer schools in the world.) It seemed to me that the sheer lunacy of the climbing enterprise appealed to Georges's rather wild sense of humor. In fact, after he was married, the father of a young child, and the expectant father of a second, he gave up high climbing. In the summer of 1963 he was persuaded to go out one more time, and on the North Face of the Aiguille de Bionnassay, a beautiful peak near Les Houches, he was killed in a fall. It was just in the summer of 1963 that I began my own climbing in Chamonix.

From 1961 to 1966 I spent every summer at the gigantic nuclear laboratory CERN (Conseil Européen pour la Recherche Nucléaire) in Geneva, from which, on a clear day, one has a perfect view of Mont Blanc. On weekends I began going to Chamonix, which is about fifty miles by road from Geneva. In the beginning I had no intention of climbing anything. I was now past thirty — an age after which even many youthful climbing fanatics begin to calm down — and was, at least for a while, content to wander around the hiking trails in, or slightly above, the valley.

After two summers I simply ran out of trails and, if I were to continue to come to Chamonix, I had to learn to climb. I presented myself to Nicolau Barthélémy, who was then the *chef des guides* of the Compagnie des Guides de Chamonix. I tried to convince Barthélémy that, as a climber, I was a near-cipher. Perhaps I secretly hoped that if I painted a bleak enough picture, he would simply send me away and I could honestly say that I had tried without actually having to put foot to rock. But in 150 years the Chamonix guides have transported such an unlikely cargo of people into the mountains that my case was routine. That very afternoon I was presented to my first guide, Henri Dufour. We drove a short way out of town to the practice cliffs — Les Gaillands — which have been serving in that capacity for about half a century. The cliffs are about 300 feet high, which is not a lot by Chamonix standards, but they looked to me like the Empire State Building and about as vertical. Dufour assured me that abject fear—which is what I was feeling—was a perfectly normal survival instinct, and shot up the rocks like a cat. He had tied me to the other end of his climbing rope, and once he had settled into a comfortable belay stance he instructed me to come up using my feet and using my hands only for balance. I did as I was told and soon found myself several feet off the ground. When I reached Dufour, he took off again, and now I found myself even farther off the ground.

If I had an elderly aunt who wanted to learn technical climbing I would encourage her to begin with Dufour. He is about my age, short and agile, with the alert and amused face of certain hunting dogs. He is a master of what the French would call finding *trucs*—gimmicks—to make things as easy as possible. Some years ago, Dufour and I climbed the Couzy route on the Aiguille de l'M (named for its M-shaped twin peaks). The *Guide Vallot*—the four-volume climbing guide to the mountains around Chamonix—says of the Couzy, "TD"—meaning "very difficult"—and "very sustained with several passages of V and V superior" (rock climbers are classified from I to VI, with VI being the hardest). Somewhere near the top, my morale began to sag. Since I talk a lot while climbing, there is no doubt that Dufour sensed it. He slithered up a partially horrible-looking thin crack and vanished from view. I was left alone in my morbidity when, from above, I heard Dufour engaging in what appeared to be a lively conversation. He was saying things like, "Ah, madam, you have certainly found a lovely spot for a picnic. No, I don't think I *would* like one of your sandwiches since my wife is expecting me for lunch." "My God," I thought, "we are home free!" I shot up the crack in no time, only to find myself alone with Dufour and confronted by a short, blank wall which led to the summit.

In the summer of 1963, after I had managed to climb one of the practice cliffs, Dufour suggested that we next tackle the normal route of the Aiguille de l'M—a standard beginner's climb that is a perfect introduction to Chamonix climbing. First, it features a struggle with a couple of hundred fully equipped climbers and guides, at five in the morning, to get a place on the first *téléphérique* (aerial tramway) up to the Plan des Aiguilles, some 2,500 feet above Chamonix. From the upper station there is a comfortable path that leads to a small glacier that in turn leads to a steep couloir, or gorge, which debouches at the Col de la Buche, about a two-hour climb above the station. At this point Dufour suggested that we have some lunch while I took in the scenery. Looking over one side of the col, I saw a drop of what looked like miles. In front of us was another blank rock wall. I would have called it a day, but Dufour took off up the rocks. Finally we reached the summit and, it seemed, years later arrived back on the path below. I felt a wonderful sense of fatigue, relief, and satisfaction. I had forgotten how scared I had been and was even vaguely thinking about my next climb.

We did a few more easy classics that summer, and when I returned the next year I learned that Dufour had ruptured an Achilles tendon while skiing and would be out of action for the season. I went back to the Guide Bureau and Nicolau Barthélémy and entered the lottery that has matched climbers and guides almost since the founding of the company. One submits one's proposed climb to the Guide Bureau, and that evening, when the guides assemble, the list of proposed climbs is read out, sounding something like a fish auction: "I have two for the 'M' normal, six for the Mont Blanc (two guides), one Grépon Mer de Glace. . . . " All of the guides are on a roll, and each night the roll call begins where it left off the previous night; the first guide has the right to choose any of the climbs that have been requested. An established guide, during the season, will usually have a fixed clientele, and may never have to find clients through the *tour de rôle*. As it happened, I appeared in late June when the season had hardly started and, by chance, I drew Claude Jaccoux.

Dufour and Jaccoux, who are good friends, represent different colors in the social spectrum of Chamonix. Dufour is a *Chamoniard*—a native of the valley. As such he speaks with the somewhat flat accent of the Savoie and in the special patois of the mountains—the word *sarpé*, which is patois for "serpent," for example, is used by the guides to describe weak clients who cling to the rocks like lizards. Dufour lives with his wife and child and his parents in a sprawling house in the center of town. Chamoniards have the reputation of being rather *enfermé*—insulated. Dufour is one of the friendliest people imaginable, but it would never occur to me to drop in and visit him at home. Between Dufour and his clients—especially those of his generation or older—there is a certain reserve, a formal respect, which is, no doubt, a remnant from the days when the clients, mainly English, were very much the *monchus*—the "misters"—and the guides were expected to keep their place. When the nineteenth-century British heiress Isabella Straton married her guide, Jean Charlet, he took his *wife's* name. Dufour is a superb professional, and his life is in, and of, the Chamonix Valley.

Jaccoux, on the other hand, is an outsider, even though he was born in Sallanches, just a few kilometers from Chamonix. When Roger Frison-Roche, a Paris-born Chamonix guide and well-known journalist and novelist, compiled a list of Chamonix guides "foreign" to the valley, Jaccoux was on it. So were Lionel Terray, born in Lyons, and Gaston Rébuffat, perhaps the most famous of the guides still active, who was born in Marseilles. It took a special dispensation from the company to get these men admitted, one of the requirements of admission being that either the guide or his wife be valley-born. A dispensation is given only when an individual is of such merit as a climber that he would be of special value to the company. (Some of the young, non-native guides, resenting the exclusivity of the company, have formed their own company, Les Guides Indépendants du Mont Blanc.) Jaccoux's parents were both *lycée* professors, and Jaccoux had actually grown up in Paris, where, eventually, he went to the Sorbonne to study French literature. He did not begin climbing until he was eighteen—very late for a guide; the Chamonix guides usually begin climbing in the mountains when they are still practically babies.

When I first went climbing with Jaccoux in 1964, we tackled a fairly difficult practice rock climb in the Aiguilles Rouges, and afterwards Jaccoux asked me to join him
and his now ex-wife, Michèle, for dinner. (Some years later Jaccoux told me that he
had gone home and told Michèle that he had met a very funny American who spoke
argot.) The Jaccoux — both Jaccoux and Michèle, and now Jaccoux and his second wife,
Colette — have always had a rather Bohemian ménage. I can rarely remember a meal at
which there were less then ten people, with some of them coming and going all the
time. If the meal is at night, someone pops up every half hour or so to go outside and
look at the stars. If they are visible, the weather will usually be good the next day,
which means that anyone climbing will have to be up long before sunrise. During that
summer we did a number of climbs; I began to learn about the life of a guide and,
through Jaccoux, I met most of the great French guides and many of the best climbers
in Europe.

As climbers, Jaccoux and Dufour have contrasting styles. Dufour is not especially
powerful and relies on perfect technique and acrobatic elegance. Jaccoux, at about six
feet, is both taller and heavier than most guides. He is extremely strong and, like most
guides, has especially strong hands and fingers. Maneuvers with the rope can involve
a lot of hand strength since the rope is often under high tension when one is trying to
manipulate it. There are nonetheless limitations to what sheer physical strength can
accomplish in climbing. For example, belaying — protecting a climber who is held on a
rope — makes use of friction and mechanical advantage, and a guide like Dufour, who
is not extremely powerful but knows just how to use pitons as pulleys and the drag of
rock outcroppings, and how to react if someone begins to fall, can provide very safe and
solid belays. Belays from above are, by far, the safest. When I have fallen I have always
been belayed from above, which is why I have never fallen very far.

The riskiest belays are those involving traverses. Here the rope is stretched out horizontally and, unless there is a piton or a rock somewhere in the middle, a climber who
falls will go quite a long way. The main disadvantage of this — apart from the fact that
one can hit the rock pretty hard — is that one can land in a place from which it is very
difficult to extricate oneself. It is almost impossible for one person to pull another up
over an overhang. The friction on the rope is too great at the point where it makes
contact with the rock or snow.

My closest call involved an overhang. Jaccoux and I, along with another client and
another guide and his wife, also an excellent climber, set out to do one of the difficult
routes on the South Face of the Aiguille du Midi. This one is called the Cosmic Spur,
not for metaphysical reasons, but because there is an old cosmic ray laboratory at the
base of the ridge. The key passage on the route is an overhang that is ascended by
planting an *étrier* — a small rope ladder — near the top of it. To get to the rope ladder
requires some delicate negotiating of a couple of passages of V. Jaccoux had led, and
had planted his ladder. Above the ladder was a carabiner — a snap link — through which
two ropes were now running. One was attached to me and the second to his other client.

I was next and inched my way up to where the ladder was. These ladders swing in midair, and when one puts a foot on them, they move — not the world's most pleasant sensation, a couple of hundred feet above a glacier. I managed to get out on the ladder and to the top of it. The next task was to take the ropes out of the carabiner, since they were blocking all further progress. But there were two ropes, each under rather high tension, and blocking the gate of the carabiner, which I simply could not open. I was in no danger of falling, since Jaccoux had me from above, but I swung back and forth on the ladder for something like (I was told later) forty-five minutes, by the end of which (I was told) I was speaking nothing but English — a sure sign of trouble. Occasionally I would lean back and look at the glacier below, which seemed seductively tranquil. Finally, in a moment of desperation, I grabbed the ropes and the gate and somehow got everything detached. I was so exhausted that I fell backward, swinging the ladder into the rock so that my feet were on the rock. This was what Jaccoux had been waiting for, and the minute my foot hit the rock he pulled me up. I remember saying to him that I hoped that this was the hardest passage on the climb. He answered that for me it was since we were going back down. I then rappelled over the overhang while the climbers waiting below pulled me in like a fish. Later I asked Jaccoux what he would have done if I had not been able to detach myself. He said that he would have thought of something.

Too much writing about mountaineering technique communicates all the color of an auto repair manual or, worse, the strained jollity of a "user-friendly" computer training guide. Blackshaw's *Mountaineering: From Hill Walking to Alpine Climbing* is a model of its kind: balanced, sensible, clear, and, remarkably, entertaining. For many this book is in a clear line of descent from Geoffrey Winthrop Young's *Mountain Craft*, the climber's Bible.

# ALAN BLACKSHAW

# Tackling the Climb

*The climbing sequence.* When the leader is satisfied that he has found the start of the climb (it is often marked, by a cairn for example) the party should tie on to the rope. There should always be at least sixty feet of rope between each two climbers and the leader will need much more on most routes (the guidebook usually says how much rope is needed). If there is steep ground below, the second should belay, i.e., secure himself by tying himself to a spike, or other anchor, using the main rope, or a sling. The leader then leads the first pitch, perhaps protecting himself by putting on one or more running belays. When he reaches the ledge ("the stance") at the top of the pitch, he belays and takes in all the spare rope between himself and the second. He then passes the rope around his waist or over his shoulder in order to bring up the second, who has the moral encouragement of the rope from above but no direct assistance (unless he slips or asks for help). When the second reaches the ledge, he also belays, and takes the leader's end of the rope around his waist. He then puts on gloves so that the rope will not burn his hands in the unlikely event of the leader falling on the next pitch; this is in the interests of the leader as much as the second, since the latter will be able to arrest a fall much more effectively if he is wearing gloves. The leader then takes off his belay and goes on to tackle the next pitch, putting on running belays from time to time. When he reaches the top of this pitch the same process is repeated. Where both mem-

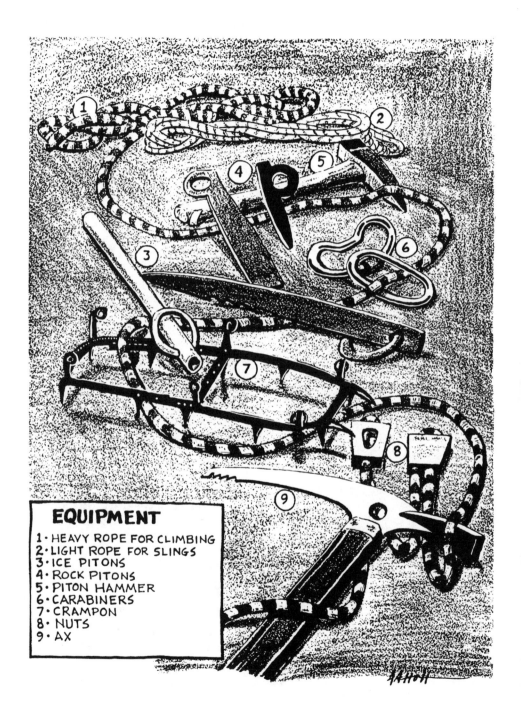

**EQUIPMENT**
1 · HEAVY ROPE FOR CLIMBING
2 · LIGHT ROPE FOR SLINGS
3 · ICE PITONS
4 · ROCK PITONS
5 · PITON HAMMER
6 · CARABINERS
7 · CRAMPON
8 · NUTS
9 · AX

bers are experienced and competent, it is normal to "lead through" (i.e., for number one to lead the first pitch and for number two to lead the second pitch), since this saves time in changing over belays. . . .

2. *Climbing technique*. The two essential principles are:

- planning ahead, so that you can anticipate the difficulties and work out the best way of solving them;
- conservation of energy, so that you can deploy your full strength when it is necessary to do so. It is best to stand upright, well away from the rock, and to take most of your weight on your feet, and not your hands.

In tackling each pitch:

- work out the general line, and note where it is possible to rest. When you reach each resting place calculate exactly how to do the next bit. Get the right sequence of holds — often a move will seem difficult because you are using your right foot where your left foot should be and vice versa (as second man, watch the way the leader does the pitch);
- try not to get held up for too long on any one move; but do not press on until you are sure you can do it. Slowness in working out the right combination of holds may be a sign that you are off form — recognize this;
- take care in finishing off the pitch; do it quickly but neatly and remember the footholds as you go over the top in case it is necessary for some reason to reverse it;
- if you decide to retreat, climb down with determination so that you reach safety before your strength gives out; wavering and lack of determination can lead to delay and exhaustion.

3. *The descent*. There are standard routes off the top of most of our cliffs, and it pays to identify these from the guidebook before you start, and to memorize them for future use. Take great care in the descent. It is very easy to relax when a difficult climb has been completed, and many accidents have occurred on the way down as a result of carelessness on easy but potentially dangerous ground. British climbers tend to neglect the art of climbing down because it is relatively simple to find an easy way down by the side of a cliff. There are, however, strong advantages in being able to descend almost anything that you can climb up, since this:

- greatly improves your all-around technique and understanding of holds;
- enables you to reverse difficult moves with safety should it not be possible to complete a pitch;

but once Martin climbed into it he found it was full of steep, rotten snow that slid away as soon as he put any pressure on it. It was much too nerve-racking at such an early stage of the climb.

He then tried to get around to the right of the tower where the way was barred by an overhanging ice wall. The only way to surmount this was to put in ice screws, and pull on these, but the ice was honeycombed and insubstantial, fracturing as the screw went in. There seemed little hope in this direction either. It was at this point that Martin noticed a hole that looked as if it might lead through the ridge. He took off his rucksack and plunged into it. The tunnel was about twenty feet long and only two feet high, running horizontally through the ridge. In places the way was part blocked by icicles which Martin had to clear out of the way. It was like potholing in a deep freeze, with a dim, greenish light filtering through the icy walls. He was hoping that the tunnel would lead right through onto easier ground, but it didn't. He could see its end, a glaring porthole of dazzling light, and eventually poked his head out to find himself looking onto a sheer ice wall that seemed to drop away to the glacier 2,000 feet below. The only hope seemed to be a traverse across the wall to where it went around the corner and the angle seemed to ease off. At least the ice here seemed fairly solid, and Martin was able to place a screw just beyond the exit of the tunnel and, swinging on this, hauled himself out onto the wall.

It was even steeper than it had appeared from the tunnel. He had to cut handholds in the ice to hold himself in balance, leaned out on the screw, and started hacking a line of foot- and handholds across the wall. He moved very slowly, yet very relaxed; this is Martin's style of climbing. You work out the sequence of steps and then cut them; you can't afford to waste energy on steep ice even near sea level, let alone at 21,000 feet. A few careful steps edging crabwise across the wall, the wall getting steeper, bulging above him so that he hangs on, arms, muscles aching; a step crumbles beneath his feet, but he adjusts his balance, fumbles with an ice screw with one hand, for he needs the other to cling on to the ice. It's difficult to get an ice screw started, rather like an ordinary screw in hard wood — you first have to tap out a little hole to allow the thread to get a purchase.

He gets it in, it bites, but then it's hard to turn just one-handed. He slots the pick of his ax through the eye of the screw, turns it this way, but can only manage a short fraction of a turn each time, for the ax keeps jamming against the ice, and his other hand is tiring. Eventually, the screw is right in and he is able to swing onto it, taking the weight off his arms. Time slips by imperceptibly, one hour, then two. He reaches the corner, pulls himself around. The angle eases off very slightly, but he is now in a repulsively steep gully encrusted with shreds of half-melted snow.

He lunged around and slightly down into the gully, but his footholds collapsed beneath him. He began a desperate swimming motion, digging elbows, knees, feet, ice ax into the bodiless wet sugar that just seemed to slip away from under him, until he managed to get himself precariously lodged on a slightly firmer layer below.

"I had been so frightened I had held my breath and now my lungs and heart were ready to burst," Martin admitted. "Only Nick will know how long I rested, but eventually I continued, feeling my way upward, expecting to be disgorged at any minute."

The rope behind Martin was dragging badly because of the friction caused by its passage through the tunnel and various piton runners. Toward the top the snow steepened, yet was as insubstantial as ever, and so he traversed out onto a vertical ice arête on the edge.

He was now fifty feet above his last running belay but had at last reached some ice that was sufficiently solid to take an ice piton. He hammered one in, clipped in the carabiner, but was so exhausted that he forgot to clip in the rope. He then continued up the ice arête, his renewed confidence based on the false premise that a fall would be quickly arrested by the running belay he thought he had placed. If he had fallen he would have gone a long way, for in actual fact he was fifty feet above his last running belay.

His arms were tiring from the incessant cutting and holding himself in to the full 150 feet of rope, though he was only fifty feet or so immediately above Nick Estcourt, so wide had been his diversion.

This was the hardest piece of ice climbing that Martin, who is among the best climbers in the country, had ever tackled, more difficult even than many Scottish winter climbs that have the reputation for being the toughest in the world.

The next problem was to get Nick up.

"I'll drop the rope straight down to you," Martin shouted. "You can jumar up it."

He threw the rope down, but it dangled about fifteen feet out from the base of the ice tower, because of the huge cornice that capped it. Nick eventually managed to rescue its end by climbing some distance down the slope below, but as soon as he pulled it tight the rope cut into the snow of the cornice. To climb it, Nick would have to tunnel up through the cornice with the ever present risk that the whole mass would collapse on top of him.

He therefore decided to follow in Martin's footsteps, safeguarded by the climbing rope. Even this, though, was a difficult undertaking, in some ways harder than Martin's original ascent. Beyond the tunnel the rope gave him no support, for it was running through a series of pitons on a slightly descending traverse leading around the corner. The steps had just taken Martin's weight but were now flaking away.

As Nick said afterward, "It was frightening enough on a rope; it must have been terrifying to lead."

It took him nearly two hours to repeat the pitch, it was so difficult, and in fact on the traverse he probably got even less help than Martin had done from the rope, which was running away from him slightly downward through the pitons. If he had slipped he would have spun into space on the end of the rope, the ice wall he was crossing overhung so much.

When he reached Martin on the ledge he was too tired to go through to lead the next pitch and so Martin, who was now well rested, continued in the lead.

He first tried to climb into the couloir on the left which they had first looked at, but it was appallingly loose and he very nearly fell off. Rebuffed, he returned to the arête and tackled a short ice wall that led onto another platform. From this he could see that the steep ice climbing probably finished about forty feet above; there was an obvious break in the ridge slightly to the right, but to reach it would have meant climbing a steadily overhanging ice wall. The arête to the left looked slightly easier, though it was still very steep, so he followed this, cutting a furrow in the honeycombed ice and then wriggling up to it. At least it enabled him to gain some height, though he was not at all sure where it would lead him.

It was just beginning to get uncomfortably steep when he pulled up onto a narrow shelf that had been completely invisible from below; overhung by the ice wall, it stretched horizontally across the face toward the break in the arête they had seen from below. He started along this, wriggling along on his stomach. Slowly the shelf grew narrower and the roof above lower, thrusting his body from out of its slippery grip. About twenty feet short of the corner it dwindled away completely. He now had to use ice pitons, but he had already used most of his stock on the lower part of the pitch. The rope had also got into a bad tangle and he was near exhaustion. He put in a couple of ice screws, then, having run out of these, hammered in ordinary rock pegs, which are much shorter than ice screws and not nearly as secure. He was still a few feet from the arête when the rope behind him jammed solid. By the time they had cleared it, it was nearly five o'clock and they retreated for the day. "He had got the ropes in an incredible tangle," Nick said later, "and in the end he stopped thinking and let me do the thinking for him. I lowered him back down to the ledge."

And then a quick abseil back to the box. It was amazing, having spent all day in climbing less than 300 feet up the ridge, to get back down again in a matter of minutes. The Ice Ridge obviously wasn't going to be easily cracked in spite of what Dougal [Haston] and Don [Whillans] had said when they first arrived at the site of Camp IV.

They returned to the fray the next morning, with Nick having his turn out in front. Even getting to the previous day's high point was difficult, for their rope was draped over a huge cornice and they had to burrow their way through it to get back up. From the end of the traverse that Martin had almost completed, Nick worked his way across the last five feet of wall, swinging in *étriers* suspended from ice pitons till he could pull up onto the corner.

He was back on frighteningly loose insubstantial ice; levering himself as high as he could from his last good ice screw, he managed to tap a long ice peg into a nose of rotting ice that jutted out from the profile of the arête. He then demolished all but the hard core of the nose to give him something to stand on and very, very gently transferred his weight onto it. As he pulled up onto the peg it came out in his hand. He very nearly teetered backward, but somehow readjusted his balance and hugged back onto the ice. He clawed for handholds but the ice crystals just broke away under his grip. Somehow keeping himself in balance, he pushed the ice piton back into place and edged around the corner into a gully very similar to the one that Martin had climbed the previous day. He climbed this to the crest of the ridge and then, finding no ice solid enough for ice pitons, dug a hole, buried a deadman in it, and sat on top of it to hold it down in the event of any strain coming onto it. The crest of the ridge was a frightening place, for the ice that comprised it was so insubstantial that he felt the entire mass could collapse without warning.

There was no queston of following the crest of the ridge, for it soared in a genuine knife-edge up to a fragile cornice. About a hundred feet to the right, however, rocks projected from the snow, a solid, safe-looking haven after all the insecurity of the Ice Ridge. It was now Martin's turn; he followed the crest of the ice arête for a short distance to where it steepened and then, digging a deadman into the insubstantial ice crystals, let Nick lower him into the gully which barred the way to the rocks on the right.

There was a terrifying moment when he first put his weight on the rope. He shot down for about three feet.

*God, I've had it*, he thought. Nick wasn't safely belayed, and it looked as if the deadman had pulled out.

But then he was abruptly brought to a halt. The deadman had been dragged deep into the crest of the arête until it bedded itself down. Martin was then lowered a further sixty feet or so into the bed of the gully, which was near-vertical and composed of hideously unstable snow, until it was possible to edge over to the relative safety of the rocks, using tension from the rope to do this.

At least he was now on stable ground, but his problems were far from over. The rock was near-vertical and sheathed in ice. There were plenty of piton cracks, but he couldn't use them, for this would have caused too many complications with his rope, as it would then have gone up through the deadman, down to a peg in the rock, then up to Martin like a letter Z tipped on its side. This inevitably would have caused the rope to jam.

He therefore had to climb without any protection from pitons, though if he had fallen off he would have had a punishing pendulum back into the gully, something that could have imposed an excessive strain on the deadman through which the rope was running. The higher he got up the rock rib, the fiercer would have been his fall, and the greater the likelihood of pulling Nick off his precarious belay.

The rock was plastered in ice, and though there were good holds underneath, it was very steep, tiring work, clearing away the ice and pulling up on the sheer rock blocks that seemed embedded in the ice. To make matters more difficult, Martin was wearing rubber vapor-barrier boots, which were very warm, but which were more like ordinary Wellington boots than climbing boots. The soles were flexible and even with crampons on were unpleasantly bendy for hard climbing. It was a superb but very nerve-racking lead.

Eventually Martin climbed the rib to a point slightly higher than the level of the deadman, put a peg in, and slid back along the rope to the col just above Nick.

It had been another punishing day, as much from nervous tension as from the effort of doing complex, high-standard climbing at altitude. They were still only 350 feet or so above Camp IV, but in those two days they had undertaken the most difficult ice climbing we encountered on the South Face, and I shouldn't be surprised if this was the toughest climbing ever tackled at this altitude.

In 1953, the same year in which Edmund Hillary and Tenzing Norkay captured world attention with their ascent of Everest, the Austrian climber Hermann Buhl recorded what may have been the outstanding achievement in the history of mountaineering: the solitary attainment, without oxygen, of Nanga Parbat's 26,620-foot summit. The world's seventh-highest mountain, the Terror of the Himalayas had claimed thirty-one lives and very nearly added Buhl's to its list of the vanquished. Buhl's incredible skill, courage, and dogged persistence won him worldwide fame but stirred controversy among his peers, some of whom felt that he was irresponsible in leaving his partner behind at Camp V. For the effect this turmoil had on Buhl's later mountaineering efforts, see Reinhold Messner's "The Will to Survive."

# HERMANN BUHL

# Nanga Parbat . . . Solo

We stamped the snow flat in a little hollow and set up the tent on it for our night's shelter. The sun soon disappeared behind the Silver Pinnacles on either side of the saddle and the evening chill drove us under our protecting roof. We packed the rucksacks and made the next day's tea, which took up the last hours of July 2. It was soon dark and the two of us crouched, huddled in our sleeping bags, over the hissing primus stove.

About eight o'clock I said to Otto [Kempter], "It's a waste of time our both hanging around. Do you mind if I lie down a bit? I'll fix breakfast in the morning to make up for it."

Otto agreed. I was very tired and tried to get to sleep before my cough could start racking me again, but I couldn't. In spite of everything I could do, my thoughts, which are always terribly active at night, weighed heavily on me. An hour later Otto blew out the candle. My spirit was up there on the summit again. Would we do it? I knew tomorrow must be the decisive day. We were still 4,000 feet below the top vertically, and nearly 4 miles from it as the crow flies. That was a tremendous distance; nothing like it had ever been done at such an altitude in the Himalayas, and it was wildly beyond reasonable hope of attainment. But what could we do? The porters wouldn't go any higher, and we had to make an effort without them. The two or three camps which would have been established in normal circumstances between us and the summit simply didn't exist.

Then I went over the whole route again in my mind's eye. I knew the snow ridge to the Silver Saddle; it steepened farther up, but I hoped not into polished ice, which would delay us. Aschenbrenner had once said that five hours was good time on it. Then the summit plateau, fearfully long, an unholy grind! We could only hope the snow up there wouldn't be too deep. But after that everything was guesswork, in unknown territory. What would the descent to the Bazhin Gap, and the ridge beyond it up to the shoulder be like? It had always been considered relatively simple. And the last bit from the shoulder on? Erwin Schneider had called it a "mown meadow, over which you could take anything from a pushcart to a light motorcar." So the whole thing might simply be a question of how we stood the altitude. The only thing that really worried me was the short rise to the subsidiary summit on the way back, an unavoidable matter of some 300 feet. The only way back to the camps lay over that subsidiary summit; that small ascent might be almost impossible if one were in an exhausted condition after one's labors. It would just *have* to be possible! Tomorrow was the decisive day, one way or the other — certainly the most important day in my life. . . .

Two o'clock was zero hour, so as to get as long a day as possible for the climb and avoid being overtaken by darkness at the end of it. . . . [It was] time to rout Otto out.

I called to him, "Otto — time to get up!" No reply, no reaction of any kind. He must be sleeping uncommonly well. I took more energetic measures, shaking him. "Do you hear?" I asked. "Almost two o'clock. Time to be going."

He mumbled something unintelligible. All I could get was "Much too early. We said three o'clock yesterday."

"Even if we *did*," I explained, "we need the time. It's a long way and we have to be back by nightfall." It was past two o'clock and still Otto wouldn't budge. I simply couldn't understand it.

I tried to goad him into activity, "Otto, haven't you got any willpower?" I asked. "Today of all days — and we're going for the summit?"

I heard a mumble from his sleeping bag: "No — I haven't any."

That settled it for me. I packed my little storm rucksack with things for an attempt on my own. I put in bacon, Dextro, Ovosport, and a few cuts of chocolate biscuit; I added warm clothing, my own Afga Karat camera — the expedition unfortunately didn't supply me with a Leica as supplementary equipment — then the little flask with Ertl's precious Cocatee, which he had brought all the way from Bolivia, and my crampons. Finally, a package of dried fruit and the Pakistan flag which Ertl had handed to me yesterday, and of course my Tirolese pennants, as Kuno and I had promised the members of our climbing club when they saw us off at Innsbruck Station. I had with me a few tablets of Padutin, a drug which stimulates the circulation and wards off frostbite, and a few pills of Pervitin for extra strength in case of extreme necessity. We had carried them ever since Base Camp.

Just as I was on the point of leaving the tent at two-thirty, I noticed that Otto was beginning to stir himself. I asked him if he meant to follow me and he said he did. So I gave him the bacon to put in his rucksack, so that I wouldn't have to carry everything.

As I left the tent I said, "You'll catch up with me somewhere. I'll go ahead and break the trail for a while."

The wind had almost died away; the sky above my head was brilliant with stars, but it was dreadfully cold. The slender crescent of the waning moon threw its ghostly light on the sharp snow crest tilting to the Silver Saddle. The curved ice edge between the dark heads of the Silver Pinnacles hung like a shining crescent of purest silver.

I stowed my ice ax through my rucksack straps and used only my ski sticks to support me, as I went on over the collapsing crust, always hoping it would give way to firm snow. But as I went on up the ridge I continued to find the same trying conditions. Suddenly I was aware of an immense shadow, the shadow of a snow wall the size of a block of buildings in front of me; it was the Whipped Cream Roll, a colossal cornice structure. There, in bygone years, fourteen first-class Sherpas had been in position, with another group of eleven up above on the Silver Saddle, and that expedition of outstanding mountaineers had nonetheless ended in a shattering tragedy. A sense of desolation swept over me. But you mustn't think of death or indulge in thoughts of horror when you are on your own. . . .

I went on up a steep funnel to the ridge, still on unusually deep snow, and, when eventually snow conditions improved, the ridge steepened considerably. I could sense the great drop to the right as I looked into a vast dark pit. The ridge had been blown firm, thank goodness; it soon became so hard that I had to strap on my crampons. The only sound in the world was the crunch of my ten-pointers. Soon a keen wind, this time blowing up the South Face, struck me. I turned my face away and worked over to the north side again, on steep slopes, passing enormous broken-off cornices. Here I met deep snow again, deposited by the wind, till I came to a steep gully falling away between the dark guardian shapes of isolated rock towers. I couldn't see very much, but I knew that the slightest slip here would land me at express speed many thousands of feet below. I no longer had the company of the moonlight, which was now cut off by the Silver Saddle, but I managed to find my way pretty well. I traversed steep slopes on the northern side and was well satisfied with my progress. I was taking only two breaths to a stride, which is pretty good going.

The ridge steepened and I drew nearer to the rocks of the left-hand Silver Pinnacle. A belt of light appeared to the northeast and slowly the sun's fiery globe rose over the ranges of the Karakoram, promising a glorious day. The sky was clear to its uttermost limits; down in the valleys, where no doubt they were still asleep, lay a transparent haze.

It was five o'clock. I sat down on the snow and ate a few crumbs while I watched the drama of day's rebirth. The magic world unfolded itself little by little. Things only dreamed of till now confronted my reeling eyes. That broad wedge of rock over yonder must be the Mustagh Tower, with a host of rock spires like Dolomites to the right of it. My eyes followed my own track downward. Right at the bottom I saw a small dot, which was Otto; he must be fully an hour behind me!

Soon the sun had enough strength to bring me comfort. The finely drawn curve of the Silver Saddle now seemed quite near, with bare ice glittering on it; I ought to be there in half an hour. I moved on over more crust with huge cornices above me, followed by wind whorls; compact snow followed with something hard underneath it, till I reached that shining strip of bare ice. I cut step after step in it, moving with extreme care. One careless movement, one small slip and I would certainly finish up 6,000 feet below in the neighborhood of Camp II.

What about my half hour now? I had been climbing for a full hour since then and the Silver Saddle seemed just as far away as ever. The thin air robs one of every means of measurement, makes a mockery of all one's estimates. It was two hours before there opened before me a vast snow plateau, seamed by wind drifts many feet high, with blue, bare ice between them—the gateway to the summit, the Silver Saddle. I pressed on upward, anxious to see how the way continued; but the slope hadn't flattened out yet. Somewhere at the back a slender snow spire raised its tip—the subsidiary summit. Then I could see the whole of the plateau, a gigantic expanse of level snow. I was on the sill of the Silver Saddle, at the rim of the summit snow plateau, 24,500 feet up. I sat down again in the snow and took a modest swig from my flask. Otto was only at the beginning of the traverse down below. To the right and left of me stood two tall pillars, the Silver Pinnacles; the western spike was quite sharp and the desire to climb it almost overwhelmed me. Beyond the furrow of the Indus, the Hundu Kush and Karakoram peaks ranged far and wide; indeed, I could see farther still—those mountains in the distance must be the Pamirs, in Russia!

I couldn't stay long; I had still far to go and mustn't waste a precious moment. I thought for a while: Ought I to wait for Otto? But surely he would catch up with me, for the way ahead was laborious to a degree, an endless undulating way, a kind of obstacle race over steps seven feet high. I knew there had been plenty of climbers who had found themselves fully capable of action at this altitude, even when, like myself, they had no oxygen. And I was fully acclimatized to the height. Yet I found it terribly difficult to make any progress, and I was breathing five times to each step I took. The sun was beginning to be unbearably hot, too. Could it be radiated heat? How extraordinary, I thought: the snow is dry, the air cold, yet the sun's heat is merciless, parching my body, drying out the mucous membrane, beating heavily on my whole being like a ton load! It grew more and more insupportable; I sat down again and tried to eat, but I couldn't swallow a morsel. If only I had the bacon with me, I thought; I could have gotten that to go down. But Otto had it in his rucksack. So on I went. . . .

Now the slopes tilted more steeply to the subsidiary summit. It was ten o'clock. I lay in the snow face downward on my rucksack, panting, panting, panting. This looked like the end. . . . Far away over there, on the Silver Saddle, I could see a dot—Otto. How glad I should have been to have him here with me, not just because of the bacon, either. I was so tired. Was it hunger, or thirst, or was I just feeling the altitude? I could now see almost horizontally across to the Bazhin Gap, no great distance away; but between me and it lay a vertical wall, with rocks in it: the South Face. To try to cross it alone would be suicide. I racked my brains how to circumvent the rise to the subsidiary summit. Perhaps I could do it on the northern side, and so be back by evening? Yes, but if I was going to try it, I should have to travel much lighter, for my rucksack was weighing terribly on my shoulders; true, it wasn't very heavy, but up here every extra ounce was an affliction. Food was useless, seeing that I couldn't force myself to eat, so that commodity could well be left behind. I looked over again at Otto; the dot was motionless. I could not wait for him.

I stowed the rucksack away in the hollow of a wind furrow, tied my parka around my middle, slung my ax sword fashion by my side, pushed my flask, spare clothes, summit flags into various pockets, hung my camera around my shoulders, with a spare film in the case, and started off again. Then I remembered that my heavy sweater was in my rucksack . . . But I hadn't the energy to go back those few yards for it. I tried to persuade myself that the thin one I had on would do, as I should certainly be back here by evening. For a few minutes I felt relieved, but very soon all the old sensations had set in again. One of the most painful efforts was getting on my feet again after rests; all I wanted to do was to stay on the ground and sleep. The dark background of the Indus Gorge, which now appeared over the Silver Saddle, gave some rest to my eyes; I should dearly have liked to remove those bothersome snow goggles, but that was against the rules, even when taking photographs — the light is too fierce and dazzling. There were occasional small crevasses, but they were quite easy to detect and avoid; then I reached a point about 25,600 feet up close under the subsidiary summit, whose northern flank I then traversed, plowing my lonely furrow over endless undulations in the snow. Looking back, I caught a glimpse of Otto, the size of a pin's head, this time below the Silver Saddle; he seemed to have given up, so I went on by myself. I could have bagged the subsidiary summit, quite a prize at 25,953 feet, but that would not have satisfied me. Crossing snow rib after snow rib, I reached a small saddle 120 feet below the subsidiary summit, at the very top of the plateau. I passed up the short slope leading to that peak, for I had to husband my strength.

Below me lay the Diamir Gap, easy to cross, but involving an infuriating loss of height. It must be possible to get across the Bazhin Gap somehow from here, across uncharted ground on which no man had ever set foot. A steep, rocky crag lay before me, with a steep snow slope at its foot and a sharp rock ridge opposite, a slabby face scored by countless gullies, and above it the shoulder. I found it exceedingly painful to contemplate so great a loss of height, and longed to be over there, across the gap. I climbed down a gully, crossed some boulders to the left, but soon found myself facing a vertical rock face, to climb which seemed to me a sheer impossibility. I was finding great difficulty now in keeping myself upright. I kept on sitting down on the rocks, wanting to go to sleep, overcome by a terrible feeling of lassitude. But I had to push on; the final prize glittered before me and some secret urge drove me on, its demonic energy planting one foot ahead of the other, endlessly.

I climbed back and tried higher up, where there seemed a better chance. Steep gullies full of ice led downward; I went on, asking myself the grim question, "Can I get any farther after the next corner of rock; if not, will I have the strength to come back this way?" I remembered the Pervitin, knowing its effects and also its reactionary afteref-fects, and fought a fearful battle with myself. My body wanted it desperately, but my mind wouldn't take it. I thought I could get as far as the Bazhin Gap without drugs.

I finally reached the gap at two o'clock and stood in that deep notch between the subsidiary and main summits at 25,658 feet. Completely exhausted, I fell down on the snow. Hunger racked me, thirst tortured me, but I knew I had to save the last drop as long as possible. Perhaps Pervitin was the answer? It couldn't be many hours before I got back again and the effects would last that long. Doubtfully, I swallowed two tablets and waited for them to take effect; nothing seemed to happen and I felt no benefit. Or was it that they had already done their work and that without them I would never have been able to get up again? You never know with tablets!

Once on my feet again, I clambered along an enormous chain of cornices and could soon see the rock ridge rising to the shoulder straight ahead of me. I had often looked at it from Camp IV and the Moor's Head, but had never been able to make up my mind definitely about it. I had remained skeptical about it; now my pessimistic views seemed to be confirmed. It was a sharp rock ridge that ran up in a series of saw-toothed crags, dominated by rock towers, and there was snow and ice all over it. Up above was a knife-sharp crest crowned with a rim of cornices; while to the right a slabby face fell hundreds of feet to the Diamir Gap. I could not guess what happened below that, but I knew that I had that terrific South Face on my left. Out of force of habit I searched the face on the right for possibilities and eventually detected some weak spots in it. If it wouldn't go by the ridge, that would be the only solution; but the last snow slope had a steep rock step above it.

I stood on the sharp-crested snow right at the foot of the rock ridge and looked out over my boots at the abysmal deeps of the Rupal Nullah 17,000 feet below. The awe-some sight hardly affected me, so apathetic had I become. Perhaps the climbing on the rock wouldn't be so bad after all. . . .

For a very short time on the first short pitch it wasn't; then exhaustion set in again. Completely breathless, I had to sit down on the next step and pant for a long time. Then I went on to the knife-edge, where, in order to avoid the slabby rock to the right, I had to tread on the snow cornice. Would it hold me? Through a crack I caught a glimpse of that horrific southward plunge, whose upper half was an Eiger Wall in itself. The delicate cornices arched from one rocky head to the next like carefully built bridges.

A vertical step lay ahead; I only hoped I had the strength to climb it. I got a few feet up it in a snow-filled crevice; with my last ounce of energy I pulled my body up over the rocky crest and lay prone for a long time on a flat slab, fighting for breath; then I sat up. There was the summit at last, but still a long way off. I felt quite desperate, but I couldn't give in now. I decided not to look and find each time that the summit had come no nearer. I would set myself my own target, fixing my eyes on some point only a few yards away, and that would by my target for the time being. I would look at the next step, the next ledge, the next spike on the ridge, and not until I got there would I look any farther ahead, and then only ten or twenty yards. I was no longer interested in the summit. I had stopped thinking about it; I had in fact stopped thinking altogether. I walked and walked, climbed and climbed, for hours and hours. My earlier climbs had taught me not to give in before I got to the top, and I had never given up or turned back on them just out of bodily weakness. But this was quite different; now it was an incredible, irresistible urge that drove my exhausted body onward.

After an age the shoulder loomed into my field of vision. The ridge grew flatter and more broken. Just when I thought I was over the worst, a sheer tower unexpectedly barred my way—a real gendarme. It is a habit of gendarmes to bar the way, but this one seemed to me to have put a final halt to my activities. It shot up nearly 200 feet above a quite insignificant indentation in the ridge. Did I really have to admit defeat so close to the end? It almost looked like it. I knew it couldn't be climbed direct, without a rope or any other climbing apparatus; in any case it would be crazy, seeing that I was alone. At first I didn't even consider the south side and tried the only possibility—to the north. I traversed across the broken rock of a rock scoop, in which a small vertical ice strip, equally brittle, interposed. There were lumps of loose rock hanging from the solid mountainside. I turned a rock edge and found myself after about 100 feet face to face with a projecting cliff; 15 feet below me there was a partly snow-filled gully leading straight up to the crest of the ridge. But how was I to get into the gully? It was protected above and below by overhanging crags. I was now prepared to risk anything. With my crampons still on my boots, I climbed the rapidly steepening face of friable, rusty-brown gneiss by a crack which gave me my only hope.

Once again I pocketed my gloves and jammed myself in the bottom of the crack, as I had so often done in my own native mountains; but now speed was of the essence. It was only about thirty feet, but my crampons got wedged in the narrow crevice, my fingers threatened to give up altogether. It was climbing of the severest order, comparable with the Salzburg route on the East Wall of the Watzmann. I had that horrible feeling in my fingers again; yet, only a few feet above me, I knew the way lay clear to the shoulder. It just had to be done, and presently I was safely in the gully. Those had been terrible minutes.

That put the tower behind me. A short, much less steep rock pitch and a steep, firm snow slope now lay before me; the tension relaxed. I was on Nanga Parbat again, and appallingly tired. I simply slumped to the ground and lay there fighting a desperate battle for that essential commodity, air. All the old altitude symptoms were there again, only worse — or was it just my raging thirst? I forced myself on again, struggling to gain every yard, and after a long time gained the crest of the shoulder. I was over 26,000 feet up, and it was six o'clock in the evening. The realization of that gave me a horrid fright; I had thought it would only take an hour from the Bazhin Gap. I was finished. For my eyes the summit was almost near enough over there for me to touch it; for my condition it was an eternity away. I took a last gulp from the flask; surely that would help!

Apparently the Cocatee had its effect. I felt a little fresher and, after laying everything I could dispense with on a boulder, I staggered to my feet again. I took nothing but my ice ax, the flags, and my camera. Indescribably wearily I dragged myself along a horizontal rock ridge. I realized that I was only obeying the dictates of a subconscious which had only one idea — to get up higher; my body had long since given up. I moved forward in a kind of self-induced hypnosis.

To the south the steep snow and ice slopes plunged away; to my surprise great bouldery rocks appeared to the north, rising steeply. I was astonished, and tried to think why. Did the gales up here sweep all the snow from the rock, so that it couldn't settle? I crossed some gullies and short patches of snow and stumbled laboriously over boulders to the foot of the summit structure; the highest thing I could see was a projecting rock, behind which the summit must be. But how far? And had I the strength to get there? That ghastly fear obsessed me. I could no longer stand upright; I was but the wreck of a human being. So I crawled slowly forward on all fours, drawing imperceptibly nearer to the rocky spur, toward which I was struggling with such grim doubts. . . .

To my joy and relief, there was nothing but a little crest, a short snow slope, only a few yards long, easier now, easier. . . .

I was on the highest point of that mountain, the summit of Nanga Parbat, 26,620 feet above sea level. . . .

Nothing went up any farther, anywhere. There was a small snow plateau, a couple of mounds, and everything fell away on all sides from it. It was seven o'clock. There I was on that spot, the target of my dreams, and I was the first human being since Creation's day to get there.

The sun went down behind a mountain range and in the instant the cold was penetrating. I suppose I had been up there half an hour, and it was time to be going down. As a sure sign of my ascent, for nobody could possibly have observed my movements, and as a symbol, too, I left my ice ax with the Pakistan emblem, the white half-moon and star on a green background, up there. I also carried a few stones to add to the summit rocks as a small cairn, but very soon found the effort too exhausting. It was sufficient, though; something built of man's hand now stood there.

I took a last look back, and turned to go. Then I remembered another promise I had given and went back those few yards to add a small stone for my wife, waiting at home so anxiously; then I started down for the shoulder. I immediately felt a change come over my body; I was suddenly much fresher, probably because I knew I had accomplished what I had set out to do. I moved quite quickly over ground where I had crawled on the way up and was soon back to where I had left my belongings at the shoulder. I knew well enough the difficulties of the rock ridge running down from there; it would be almost impossible to descend it. I had barely managed that last gendarme on the way up and I had no rope with me. So I had no choice but to find another way down.

There was a steep ice slope falling away below me, whose bottom part I could not see. There might be gullies running down from it, and it might do. I had taken a good look at the right-hand side on the way up and spotted a number of possible routes. If I could go down that way, I could easily climb the snow slopes to the subsidiary summit from the bottom of the rocks, 1,200 feet lower down. That must be the top of the rib by which Mummery, that great mountaineer, whose monument the glaciers and peaks of Nanga Parbat had become fifty-eight years before, tried to scale the mountain. And I had been granted the luck to be the first to reach its summit!

I couldn't yet grasp that fact. All I wanted was to get down to its foot again, back to people, back to life. . . .

So I went northward down the ice slope, losing height rapidly. The first part looked all right, but the rest was conjecture. I was very glad of my crampons, for ski sticks are no substitute for an ice ax; but I would far sooner do without the ax now than without the sticks later on. I still hoped to reach the Bazhin Gap before nightfall, so as to be able to cross the plateau by moonlight and so get down to Camp V without having to camp for the night in the open at such a height. Suddenly I felt something dangerously loose and wobbly on my left foot; I was startled to see the strap fastening of my crampon disappearing down below me. The crampon had come off and almost precipitated a disaster for me. I grabbed it quickly, but just in time; I had, however, no spare strap with me, not even a piece of string. And even if I had, how could I fasten the crampon again in so exposed a position?

I was standing on one leg, with my two ski sticks as my only support. To my right and left, above and below, there was nothing but snow and ice packed bone-hard by the winds. I tried to scrape a shallow dent with the points of my sticks; it wasn't so much a dent as a scrape, sufficient to give my smooth boot sole a moment's hold while I moved the foot that still had a crampon a step farther on, where the points could get a bite. . . . It was a most hazardous movement, but it was successful. In time I reached a snow rib, but found I could not proceed downward any farther; so I tried to get off the slope by the shortest possible way, traversing toward the ridge, balancing from one snow rib to another, until I felt rock under my rubber sole again. I moved like one walking in his sleep; there is no other way of explaining how I escaped from that slope. . . .

I got back into the gully behind the gendarme, and made swifter progress; the actual climbing occupied the whole of my attention to such an extent that I almost forgot how high up I was. The rock grew slabbier and I worked my way carefully down a smooth, fairly holdless rib. Then it suddenly began to get dark — could it be nightfall already? I had been so preoccupied that I had quite forgotten the time. I searched frantically for a better perch, for it was impossible even to stand where I was. In an astonishingly short time it was pitch dark; there is apparently no twilight in these parts. Where could I find a place in which to spend the night?

At last I found something firm beneath my feet, and immediately felt safe again. It was a stance with room for both feet on it, though it was too small to sit down on; I would have to spend the night standing up. Over there, toward the ridge, I could see a big, dark shadow thrown by a huge block; I could sit, or even lie down, over there, but the rock in between was polished and glazed with ice and to attempt the passage in the dark seemed too great a risk.

For better or for worse, I would have to make do with my perch. I put on everything I had with me, my woolen cap well over my ears, my balaclava well down over my head, two pairs of gloves, drew them all as tight as I could, and settled down to my long wait. I had a rock face, angled at from fifty to sixty degrees, as a backrest. I could have done with my heavy pullover, but that was far away, in the rucksack which I had left behind, down there. . . . Of course, I should have had a bivouac sack to protect me from the cold, and a rope to stop me from falling off the mountain, but somehow I viewed the prospect of the night which lay ahead of me without any great qualms. I was amazingly relaxed; everything seemed so normal. It had to be like this, all part and parcel of what I was doing. I almost faced that night at 26,000 feet with complete equanimity. I knew I would have been much better off higher up, where I could have lain down, but this is where I was, and that was all there was to it. Then I remembered the Padutin, a drug which stimulates the circulation and protects one against frostbite. I forced down five of the little pellets, which almost stuck in my throat. My left hand clutched the ski sticks; I hoped they wouldn't escape my grip, for I would need them, how I would need them! My right hand clung to that solitary hold. I looked at my watch again; it was nine o'clock. I prayed the wonderful weather would hold. . . .

Utter weariness came over me. I could hardly stay upright, and my head kept falling forward, my eyelids pressed on my eyes like lead, and I dozed off. . . .

I woke with a start, and straightened my head up. Where was I? I realized with a pang of fright that I was on a steep rock slope, high up on Nanga Parbat, exposed to the cold and the night, with a black abyss yawning below me. Yet I did not feel in the least as if I was 26,000 feet up and I had no difficulty with my breathing. I tried hard to keep awake, but sleep kept defeating me. I kept dozing off, and it was a miracle that I didn't lose my balance.

Oh, God, where are my sticks? Keep calm! You've got hold of them. I clutched them in a grip of steel. . . .

The cold grew more and more unbearable; I felt it on my face and, in spite of my thick gloves, on my hands, which were nearly numb, and worst of all in my feet. It crept farther and farther up my body; my toes had long ago gone dead, though at first

I had tried to keep them moving by trampling on my little stance, but I had to be careful, because it was loose. Never mind, I thought; I had often had cold, dead feet before without suffering serious frostbite as a result. . . .

Hunger and thirst asserted their needs, but I had nothing to give them. Time passed incredibly slowly, so slowly that I thought the night could never come to an end. Then, behind a toothy mountain range in the far distance, a streak of light broadened and rose gradually higher — the newborn day. For me, its light was the light of salvation. . . .

I leaned against my rock, motionless, my right hand still clinging to the hold, my left still gropping the sticks like a vise. My feet were like blocks of wood, my boots frozen stiff, my rubber soles clogged with rine. The sun's first rays fell on me with their blessed comfort, resolving my stiffness and immobility. I began to move again and got back into the gully. But now I really had to watch my step; everything was twice as dangerous under the smooth glaze of ice. I went down in the gully for ages, still wearing a crampon on one boot, while the other reposed in my parka pocket. . . .

I went on down, succeeded in getting into the snow gully and out of it again onto the rocks beyond. There on my right, almost level with me, was the Bazhin Gap; but I had to go still farther down, to the bottom of the rocks. . . .

There was one more steep pitch, an almost vertical crack, which took all the breath out of me; then at last I was on the snow. I had escaped from the clutches of the face, which now lay behind me. Steep snow slopes, hard as iron, led down to the rocks which plunged from the subsidiary summit. Here crampons were indispensable, and I tried to fasten the second one to my foot; I used the cord of my overall trousers to tie it to my boot, but after a few steps it was at right angles to the sole. Patiently I fastened it on again, only to find the spikes standing away from the sides of my boot very soon afterward, so that I had to repeat the dangerous game every ten or twenty yards. Bending down was a fearful exertion. . . .

Then I sat down on the snow again, with my head in my hands, resting and panting. My ankles ached from being flexed so much and I found the going fearfully exhausting, but I eventually reached the rocks below the Diamir Gap, where I dived under a huge snow mushroom for shade. The way the time went was fantastic; it was noon already. I was racked by a terrible thirst, but had nothing left to drink. The sun burned viciously down, but there was no water anywhere, though the rocks were plastered with ice; not a drop trickled from them.

Now I had to face the rise to the subsidiary summit which had worried me on my way up. I wanted to recover a bit before tackling it and sat down in the snow again. My reasoning processes were suddenly blotted out, though it was quite a pleasant feeling.

I opened my eyes and looked about me. I must have fallen asleep, for another hour had gone by. Where was I, anyway? I saw tracks and cairns everywhere. Was I on a skiing trip? Gradually consciousness returned; I was nearly 26,000 feet up on Nanga Parbat, and all alone. The ski tracks were nothing but wind channels, and the cairns over there, rock towers. Up among the rocks of the subsidiary summit I heard voices, or was it only the wind? Perhaps my friends were waiting for me up there. I staggered to my feet again with a great effort and circumvented a steep crag, from which a debris chute went up. I worked my way up it from stone to stone, hanging on to my ski sticks for support. After every step my weary body sank down on the debris, and this time I really thought my strength had given out for good. How often have I said it? But I had to go on, for I knew there was no other way of getting back to living people; so I had to get up that slope. It took me an hour to cover a hundred feet, and as I felt then, the long ascent I had made yesterday seemed more and more improbable. Some flat snow patches followed, apparently without end, but I had reached the Diamir Gap at the lowest point between the subsidiary and north summits.

Before me there now lay once again that enormous wavy snow plateau, scored and furrowed, far away behind it the Silver Saddle. My eyes sought the horizon, working inward over the sill of the Silver Saddle, across and along the plateau's snow up toward where I stood. I hoped to see someone coming up to meet me, but could distinguish nobody. If only I had a drop of tea — one single drop — that might see me safely across the next few hours. I could think of nothing but drinkable liquid; my thirst had become a torture of hell, driving me literally mad. I had swallowed my last drop yesterday, and now there was this murderous heat, this positive dehydration. My gums were like straw, my blood must be thick and viscous. . . .

As I went slowly on I kept my eyes fixed on the saddle. At last I saw some dots, or were my eyes deceiving me? No, those must be my friends. I wanted to shout and cheer, but could not produce a sound. Anyway, they were coming. Should I wait for them? No, it was too far for them to come; I would go on and meet them. I went on, step by step, mechanically, stumbling, weary. Next time I looked across the waves of the plateau the dots had vanished. The disappointment was shattering, till I caught sight of them again; then — no — the vast expanse of snow was empty! I was definitely alone in the endless, hopeless waste of ice.

Hunger became as unbearable as thirst. I knew there was a packet of Ovosport in my rucksack, somewhere over there. Somewhere . . . where? I crossed slopes without end, going a long way off the direct line, just to get a bite of something, in the hope of renewing my strength. All the time I had to take great care not to hurt my ankles, which were giving out on me, with my crampons. A slight sprain would be enough to finish me. I looked at the saddle again; the dots were in a different place and I realized that they were rocks on some mountains thrusting up from behind it. . . .

Perhaps I could find my old tack, by climbing down and across to the right. I went on interminably, back and forth, up and down. I knew I couldn't keep it up much longer. The only thing that kept me going was the thought of having some food inside me. I had almost decided to give up the search, when I saw the clear imprint of a boot; I was back on my trail. Which way, though, to my rucksack — up or down? I went on down, but was soon racked by maddening doubts. I ought to be able to see a rucksack. . . .

I found it at last. I fell down and rummaged in it as I lay there, but couldn't locate any Ovosport; instead I found a package of Dextroenergen. When I tried to swallow a tablet it stuck like flour in my mouth, so I did the only thing left and grabbed some snow. I wasn't keen about it, as I knew it might have disastrous results, but there was no other way out. I crushed the tablets, mixed them with the snow, and ate the resulting mess. It tasted wonderful and revived me beyond expectation; I found I could swallow again, there was spittle in my mouth once more, and I tried to move on again. Very soon, however, my thirst was more searing than ever, my tongue stuck to my gums, my throat was as raw as a rasp, and I foamed at the mouth a good deal. So I took another dose of the same brew, but the relief was very short, and my thirst came back even more unendurably than before. The snow robbed me of my last vestige of strength and my progress across the plateau became a veritable torture.

I moved on at a snail's pace, finding it necessary to take twenty breaths to a single stride. Every yard or two I fell down on the snow. My ski sticks were my last succor; Samaritan-fashion they supported me and saved my life. . . .

Evening was drawing on; once again the sun was going down and long shadows moved slowly across the snow. I knew I could not survive a second night in the open and fought my way onward, using my last reserves. I stumbled on, pursued, hunted, and confused by my own shadow. I was no longer myself; I was only a shadow — a shadow behind a shadow. I cursed the wind whorls which made my way so fearfully difficult. At length I was at the plateau's lowest dip, with only a few hundred yards separating me from the broad sweep of the Silver Saddle, opening like a gateway before me. How the tempests must have raged to produce the upheavals on these flat expanses! There was no means of avoiding the snow structures, many feet high, however much I tried to skirt them. I was staggering like a drunkard, falling, crawling, standing, walking, falling again . . . then I remembered the Pervitin again. It was the only chance; its brief renewal of my strength might last long enough for me to get down to the tent. That is, if I hadn't already used the last reserve of strength left in me, for I felt absolutely finished. Blood and spittle were coming out of my mouth, which was completely gummed up, and I had to force the three tablets down as if they were wooden wedges. I began counting the yards, as the rim of snow drew nearer.

At half-past five I was on the farther rim of the Silver Saddle and at last I could see down to the Rakhiot Glacier and the camps on it once again. The whole route of the climb lay spread before me, and I could see the tents clinging half buried, to the slopes. It was an indescribably comforting sight; I felt just as if I were coming home. Yet I could see nobody moving about down there. Surely they could not have evacuated the camps? Peace unbroken reigned over everything, not a soul stirred, not a sound marred the silence. I looked across to Rakhiot Peak and again I noticed the dark spot, the little hurricane tent — and then, two smaller dots. Those were definitely people, on the Rakhiot traverse, porters perhaps. This time there could be no mistake, they really were people!

Then at last I knew I was safe. The knowledge that I was near my teammates gave me newborn confidence. My old tracks were still in good condition and I traversed slowly along them to the ridge. For the moment I felt fresher again, either because of the Pervitin or because of the blessed feeling of relief; breathing became easier, too, but I still had to use extreme care. The crampon came loose again and I took it off in a rage and threw it out over the South Face, without further ado. I made relatively rapid progress down the exposed ridge, moving forward through crust past the Whipped Cream Roll, till at 7:00 P.M. — forty-one hours after leaving the spot — I approached the tent.

Hans now came to meet me. He did not know how to hide his emotion and buried himself behind his camera. We embraced, speechless. I was so parched that I could not utter a sound. . . .

This seminal article appeared in the *American Alpine Journal* in 1963, a time when Yosemite climbing was in its comparative infancy and when the techniques originated in the Valley had not yet been applied to the great granite ranges of the world. Today, of course, with the "great problems" of mountaineering largely solved, climbers perceive the challenge as one of applying American methods to formidable rock faces all over the world. The question that rages among Yosemite climbers—and recurs throughout this volume—is one of ethics: At what point is the contest between man and mountain reduced to merely one between equipment and mountain?

# YVON CHOUINARD

# Modern Yosemite Climbing

Yosemite climbing is the least known and understood and yet one of the most important schools of rock climbing in the world today. Its philosophies, equipment, and techniques have been developed almost independently of the rest of the climbing world. In the short period of thirty years, it has achieved a standard of safety, difficulty, and technique comparable to the best European schools.

Climbers throughout the world have recently been expressing interest in Yosemite and its climbs although they know little about it. Even most American climbers are unaware of what is happening in their own country. Yosemite climbers in the past have rarely left the Valley to climb in other areas, and conversely few climbers from other regions ever come to Yosemite; also, very little has ever been published about Yosemite. Climb after climb, each as important as any done elsewhere, has gone completely unrecorded. One of the greatest rock climbs ever done, the 1961 ascent of the Salathé Wall, received four sentences in the *American Alpine Journal*.

Just why is Yosemite climbing so different? Why does it have techniques, ethics, and equipment all of its own? The basic reason lies in the nature of the rock itself. Nowhere else in the world is the rock so exfoliated, so glacier-polished, and so devoid of hand-holds. All of the climbing lines follow vertical crack systems. Every piton crack, every handhold is a vertical one. Special techniques and equipment have evolved through absolute necessity.

*Special Problems.* Since Yosemite has characteristics all of its own, it also has its special problems and difficulties. Because the Valley lies at an altitude of only 4,000 feet, the cliffs are often covered with trees and bushes, and the cracks are usually filled with dirt and grass, making it more difficult, time-consuming, and uncomfortable for the first ascent party.

Situated in the center of sunny California, the threat of stormy weather is not serious; however, when an occasional storm does hit, usually in the spring or fall, it can be serious because most climbers are not prepared mentally, physically, or materially for it. American mountaineers have tended to belittle the climbing in Yosemite because of the fact that it lacks the storms of the high mountains, but personally I have never suffered so much from the weather as I have in Yosemite.

Bad weather in California means hot weather. The usual climbing temperature is 85° to 90° during the day and 50° at night. Temperatures above 100° are common. During June and July of 1961 there were fifteen consecutive days with temperatures of over 95°! It is usually too hot to do much climbing from late July to the first of September. The heat poses a related problem, that of carrying great loads up the walls. The *minimum* water that must be taken on the big climbs is 1½ quarts per man a day. Water, food, and bivouac equipment, combined with the usual forty-five pitons and thirty-five carabiners, make a considerably heavier load than one carried on a compa-rable climb in the high mountains. On a two- or three-day climb, the second man climbs with a fairly heavy pack, while the leader hauls up another. The latter always has two ropes, one to climb with and the other to haul up extra pitons or the pack.

*Safety.* Even with the standard of extreme difficulty which has been achieved, safety has not been disregarded. There are many reasons for this, the most important, of course, being the American's love of safety and security and his innate fear of death, which have caused revolutionary innovations in belaying and equipment. Pitons are used far more numerously for protection than in Europe. Objective danger is also less in Yosemite than anywhere else in the world. There is little danger of natural rockfall, loose rock, or bad storms; as the rock is so smooth and steep and has few ledges, a fall usually only helps to build one's confidence.

*Free Climbing.* Not only is every piton crack vertical, but nearly every handhold is a vertical one. Laybacking, jamming, chimneying, pinchholds, and friction climbing are the usual techniques. Face climbing, such as one finds in the Tetons or the Rockies, is a rarity.

Most persons who have never climbed in the Valley are under the impression that the rock is similar to that in Chamonix or the Bugaboos. This is not so. They have completely different types of rock. Yosemite granite does not fracture in angular blocks as does the granite of the French Alps or even the rest of the Sierra Nevada. The Valley is actually a series of exfoliation domes that have been cut in half by a river and glaciers. This means that most of the climbing is on flakes, be they small and thin or large dihedrals. Pitons are placed almost always behind a flake or in a vertical inside corner. This vertical-crack climbing takes not only a great deal of technique but also enormous strength. Yosemite climbers develop certain characteristic muscles as a direct result of using vertical holds.

There is undoubtedly more chimney climbing in Yosemite than in any area in the world. Chimneys range from those that require one-arm and one-leg techniques to others that have chockstones bigger than a house, from perfect "Rébuffat" types to flaring, bomb-bay, horizontal "horror" chimneys, and from short slots to some that are over 1,000 feet high. Also characteristic of the Valley is friction climbing on glacier-polished slabs. There are climbs in the Valley that have hundreds of feet of this. Very difficult moves have been made on these slabs, using friction, fingernail holds, and edging on tiny flakes. These must be treated as if one were only a few feet off the ground because the second one loses confidence, even for a moment, hands sweat, legs shake, feet slip— and one is out in space.

All the techniques of free climbing were established not in Yosemite but at Tahquitz Rock in Southern California. From the 1930s to the present day, it has been the training ground for nearly every prominent Valley climber. This magnificent rock has over seventy routes on massive, exfoliated granite, similar to Yosemite's except for its lack of glacial polish and dirt in the cracks. This means that a move will go free at Tahquitz where normally in Yosemite it would require direct aid. Because of its accessibility, compactness, and sound piton cracks, Tahquitz offers ideal conditions for pushing free climbing to its limits. Most of the routes were first done with direct aid, but over a period of time nearly every one has been done free. It was the first area to have Class 5.9 climbs and continues to have the greatest concentration of Class 5.8, 5.9, and 5.10 routes in the country.

When one finds a layback or a friction pitch at Tahquitz, it is a textbook-type pitch; a layback is a pure layback requiring pure layback technique, a friction pitch requires pure friction technique. Nothing else will do. One can develop granite-climbing technique here far better than in Yosemite or anywhere else. I can not impress it enough on climbers from other areas to climb at Tahquitz *before* going to Yosemite. Every spring even the native climbers spend a week at Tahquitz getting in shape for the Valley walls.

*Artificial Climbing.* Because most piton cracks are vertical and there are few ceilings, the double-rope technique, standard throughout the rest of the world, is never used in

Yosemite. Nor is tension used except on overhanging rock. Instead, only one rope is run through all of the pitons and large numbers of runners are used to eliminate rope drag. The use of one rope has greatly increased the efficiency, simplicity, and speed of artificial climbing.

Stirrups (slings) made of one-inch-wide nylon webbing have taken the place of step stirrups. There are many reasons for this: (1) the slings grip the sides and cleats of the climbers' heelless *Kletterschuhe* and give a much greater feeling of security and comfort, especially when belaying in slings for a long period of time. (2) The slings can be used for runners around large blocks, bushes, or trees. (3) In an emergency they can be cut up and used for rappel slings. (4) They can be carried more neatly on the person or pack. (5) They can be used for prusiking more efficiently. The only additional things needed are three small loops of ¼-inch or ⁵⁄₁₆-inch cord. (6) They make no noise, so that the belayer can hear the little familiar sounds that help him to understand, without looking up, what the leader is doing and to anticipate the belay signals. (7) They allow one to "sit" in one's slings, thus saving a great deal of energy. (8) There is less chance of dropping them either when a piton pulls out or through carelessness. As far as I can tell, they have no disadvantages over step stirrups. Possibly the reason why they have not been adopted by Europeans is that they are unable to obtain the flat nylon webbing needed for their construction.

Each climber carries three 3-step slings. The leader never leaves them in place but moves them up from piton to piton. A carabiner is kept on each sling and is never removed. On low-angle rock, only one sling is used; on steeper rock, two are used to clip into the next piton. When cleaning out a pitch, two or even three slings are often clipped together to reach pitons that are far apart.

The actual technique is done thus: a piton is placed, a carabiner is clipped in, the rope is inserted, and finally the slings are clipped onto this carabiner. On doubtful pitons, the slings are clipped in *before* the rope is inserted; the climber steps up and tests the piton and *then* inserts the rope. This leaves less slack in the rope if the piton should pull out. Of course, a carabiner must be used whose gate can still be opened while the carabiner supports body weight.

*Equipment.* The first pitons were developed for use in the Dolomites in limestone, where a piton is expected to flow into a very irregular crack or hole and fill all the tiny internal pits and irregularities and have such great holding power that it can never be taken out. It was generally considered that only a piton of very malleable steel or iron had the qualities to fulfill these requirements. All European pitons today are still being made thus whether they are going to be used in limestone or not.

John Salathé was the first to realize the need of a piton for climbing on granite. During his attempts on the Lost Arrow, he saw that he needed a stiffer, tougher piton that could be driven into solid veins of rotten granite without buckling, that was lighter than an iron piton, that had greater holding power, and that yet could be taken out faster and more easily and be used over and over again. Out of old Model A Ford axles, he forged some beautiful horizontals, which to this day are almost revered by those lucky enough to own them.

The alloy-steel piton is based on a theory radically different from that of the iron piton. It is expected not to follow cracks but rather to act like a spring, pressing against the sides. It has been proven to have greater holding power in granite and similar rock because it can be driven harder and deeper without buckling into the typical smooth cracks, so that it is actually tighter. The entire length of the piton is stiff, so that the head does not bend when removed, thus making it possible to do a several-day, 300-piton climb without leaving a single piton in place. The invention of the alloy-steel piton is as important to rock climbing as is the new ice screw to ice climbing.

In the early 1950s a new piton was invented by another famous Yosemite climber, Charles Wilts, which helped as much as anything to set such a high standard of artificial climbing. This piton, with a blade the size of a postage stamp, was appropriately called the "knife blade." It was the first piton to be made of chrome-molybdenum aircraft steel and could be used in very thin cracks where no other piton could possibly enter. Although they were originally made for artificial climbing, it was soon found that these pins often had even greater holding power than angle pitons. Gerry Gallwas in 1957 forged some regular horizontals out of chrome-molybdenum steel (SAE 4130) for the 1957 ascent of Half Dome; some of these have been used over a hundred times and are still in use.

Yosemite, like any granitic area, has many wide piton cracks. Wooden wedges were never much used because these large cracks are usually filled with dirt. Several persons made large angle pitons, some up to four inches wide, of various materials. Some, made by William Feuerer for the 1958 ascent of El Capitan, were fashioned from aluminum channel, angle iron, and cut-off stove legs.

All of these pitons were made by individuals in home workshops and available only to personal friends. Salathé sold a few, but most climbers thought his price of fifty-five cents too expensive! In 1958 the author started to make this newer type of equipment on a commercial basis. He developed a new aluminum carabiner, stronger than existing steel models, which had a gate that could still be opened under a climber's weight and shaped to be used in combination with the Bedayn carabiner in the Yosemite method of artificial climbing. Ringless alloy-steel angle pitons were invented that were superior in every way to existing models. The larger angle pitons were made of heat-treated alloy aluminum to save weight. A full line of horizontals of alloy-steel was developed, ranging from a knife blade to a wedge.

Abortive attempts on Kat Pinnacle's west face showed the need for a piton which would go into tiny bottoming cracks* which even knife blades failed to enter. From the need came the "RURP." This "Realized Ultimate Reality Piton" helped to usher in the A5 climbing and was instrumental in allowing tens of existing bolts to be passed

---

*A crack where the piton hits bottom before being fully inserted.

up and chopped out. These diminutive pins are far from being just novelties but have become an absolute necessity on nearly all of the newer climbs.

The importance of this new equipment can best be emphasized by saying that since 1958 every major rock climb in North America has used my equipment. The future of rock-climbing equipment lies in the use of the lighter steel and aluminum alloys. Weight is now the major problem to be overcome.

*Ethics and Philosophies.* The most obvious split between European and Yosemite rock-climbing philosophies is whether to leave pitons in or not. In Europe they are left in place. In Yosemite, even if a climb has been done a hundred times, the pitons are still removed. I believe that nearly everyone, whether European or American, agrees that, if practical, a route should not remain pitoned. It is entirely practical in Yosemite to take the pitons out. With the pitons removed and with no guidebook to show the way, a third or succeeding ascent of a route is as difficult as was the second. It is conceivable that a climber who is capable of doing the Bonatti Pillar on the Petit Dru with all the pitons in might not be able to climb the North Face of Half Dome, although both climbs unpitoned are of equal difficulty.

In the Alps climbing is not called artificial until a stirrup is used. Free climbing in California means that artificial aid of *any* sort is not used, whether it be a sling around a knob of rock, a piton for a handhold, foothold, or to rest on. After a piton is placed for safety, it may not be used for aid in climbing without changing the classification of the climb.

Especially on short climbs, free climbing is forced to its limits. Guidebooks list not only the first ascents of a route but also the first free ascent. Some climbers feel that it is more of an honor to do the first *free* ascent than the actual first.

Nowhere else, except on the sandstone climbs of the Southwest, is the need for expansion bolts more pronounced than in the Valley. However, this does not mean that they have been indiscriminately used. Climbers have gone to extremes to avoid placing one of them, except for an anchor, where the ethics are less stringent. The usual attitude toward bolts is that they should be carried only by the better climbers because only they know when a bolt *must* be placed. If a bolt is put in and a later party feels it unnecessary, then it is chopped out. Lack of equipment, foul weather, or a less-than-expert leader is never an excuse for a bolt.

It has become popular in other parts of North America, especially in the Northwest, to lay fixed ropes up a climb to avoid having to bivouac or take a chance with the weather. These ropes create an umbilical cord from man to where he truly belongs and to where he can quickly retreat if things get tough. This manifests American love of security and shows that the climber should not be there in the first place. The only routes now being done with fixed ropes in Yosemite are those that take so long on the first ascent that they could not be done in any other way; such are the multiday routes on El Capitan.

Perhaps I have given the reader the impression that I feel that Yosemite is the only place to climb and that its philosophies and ethics are the last word. Personally, I would rather climb in the high mountains. I have always abhorred the tremendous heat, the dirt-filled cracks, the ant-covered foul-smelling trees and bushes which cover the cliffs, the filth and noise of Camp 4 (the climbers' campground), and worst of all, the multitudes of tourists which abound during the weekends and summer months. Out of the nearly three hundred routes in the Valley, there are less than fifty which I should care to do or repeat. The climbing as a whole is not very aesthetic or enjoyable; it is merely difficult. During the last couple of years there has been in the air an aura of unfriendliness and competition between climbers leaving a bitter taste in the mouth. Like every disease, it was initially spread by a few, and now it has reached a point where practically no one is blameless.

The native climbers are a proud bunch of individuals; they are proud of their Valley and its climbs and standards. An outsider is not welcomed and accepted until he proves that he is equal to the better climbs and climbers. He is constantly on trial to prove himself. When he is climbing, he is closely watched to see that he does a free pitch free, that he does not place more than the required number of pitons in an artificial pitch, and that he does the climb speedily. Climbers have left the Valley saying that they will never return because of the way they were treated by the native climbers. These problems will, in time, resolve themselves as the Yosemite climbers move afield and see that there is no room or need for competition or enmity in the mountains.

There have been times when I have felt ashamed to be a Yosemite climber, and there are times when I feel as if I truly hate the place; but then there are times when I should rather be there than anywhere else in the world. If at times I hate the place, it is probably because I love it so. It is a strange, passionate love that I feel for this Valley. More than just a climbing area, it is a way of life.

*The Future of Yosemite Climbing.* Nearly all of the great classical lines in Yosemite have been ascended. All of the faces have been climbed by at least one route. This does not mean that there are no new routes left, because there are countless new lines on the cliffs which lie between the great formations. Some will be as difficult as any yet done, but that is all they will be. They will offer very little aesthetic pleasure. The rock is often poor, the cliffs covered with bushes, and the cracks filled with dirt and moss; blank areas will require bolts. As a line becomes less logical and direct, the aesthetic beauty of the climbing also diminshes.

To do a winter climb for the sake of making the first winter ascent is senseless. Winter conditions can be better than in the summer. To do a route under actual winter conditions means climbing immediately after a storm, which is nearly impossible and suicidal. Because the rock is so smooth, ice will not adhere to it except during and directly after a storm. To climb then means having to clear off all the verglas on the holds because the ice is too thin and badly anchored to climb on directly. To clean off all the verglas is a slow process. At Yosemite's low altitude, the hot California sun early in the morning loosens great sheets of ice and sends them crashing down.

Solo climbing will not be practical until the routes are pitoned. Otherwise, because of the great amounts of direct aid, a two-man party can climb faster and more efficiently on the big climbs. I doubt that the big walls will be pitoned for a long time to come. Besides, at present solo climbing is against the law.

Climbing for speed records will probably become more popular, a mania which has just begun. Climbers climb not just to see how fast and efficiently they can do it, but far worse, to see how much faster and more efficient they are than a party which did the same climb a few days before. The climb becomes secondary, no more important than a racetrack. Man is pitted against man.

The future of Yosemite climbing lies not in Yosemite, but in using the new techniques in the great granite ranges of the world. A certain number of great ascents have already been done in other areas as a direct result of Yosemite climbers and techniques, notably the North Face of Mount Conness in the Sierra Nevada, the West Face of the South Tower of Howser Spires in the Bugaboos, the two routes on the Diamond on Longs Peak in Colorado, the Totem Pole and Spider Rock in Arizona, the North Face of East Temple in the Wind Rivers, the northwest corner of the Petit Dru *(voie Américaine)*, and the first American ascent of the Walker Spur of the Grandes Jorasses in the French Alps. Although these ascents are as fine and as difficult as any in their respective areas, they are merely the beginning of a totally new school of American climbing, that is to say, technical climbing under Alpine conditions. The opportunities here are limitless. I have personally seen in the Wind River Range and Bugaboos untouched walls that are as difficult and as beautiful as any ever done in the history of Alpinism. There are in the Wind Rivers alone opportunities for fifty Grade VI climbs. The western faces of the Howser Spires in the Bugaboos are from 3,000 to 5,000 feet high. The Coast Ranges, the Logan Mountains, the innumerable ranges of Alaska, the Andes, the Baltoro Himalaya all have walls which defy the imagination.

Who will make the first ascents of these breathtaking rock faces? From the Americas the climbers can come only from Yosemite. The way it now is, no one can climb enough in the high mountains to get in shape to do a Grade VI climb, either in the mountains or in Yosemite. These extraordinary climbs will be done by dedicated climbers who are in superb mental and physical condition from climbing year round; who are used to climbing on granite, doing much artificial climbing, and putting in and taking out their own pitons; who are familiar with the problems of living for a long time on these walls, hauling up great loads, standing in slings, sleeping in hammocks for days at a time; and who have the desire and perseverance needed to withstand the intense suffering, which is a prerequisite for the creation of any great work of art. Yosemite Valley will, in the near future, be the training ground for a new generation of super-Alpinists who will venture forth to the high mountains of the world to do the most aesthetic and difficult walls on the face of the earth.

History is a lie agreed upon, and the history of the first ascent of Mont Blanc in 1786, as it was understood by nineteenth-century readers, was surely a case in point. For years the climb was credited to Jacques Balmat, a Chamonix guide whose aim had been to claim a prize offered in 1760 by Horace-Bénédict de Saussure—or, by some books, to de Saussure himself. The scientist who allegedly was dragged to the summit by Balmat, Dr. Michel-Gabriel Paccard, was denied his rightful place in the annals of mountaineering until 1909. The passage below is excerpted from *Men, Myths and Mountains*.

# RONALD W. CLARK

# Mont Blanc and the Scientists

The Alps, of which Mont Blanc is the highest peak, run in a 600-mile crescent from the Mediterranean in the southwest to the outliers of the Carpathians to the northeast, dropping on the south to the flat Italian plain and sinking more slowly on the north into France, the central Swiss plain, or the hills of southern Germany. The international frontier roughly follows the watershed, with Italy to the south, and, on the west, north, and east, the succession of France, Switzerland, Germany, Austria, and Yugoslavia. Nearly 1,200 glaciers are fed from the snowfields which extend above a permanent snow line varying in height between 8,000 and 9,500 feet, according to aspect. Traversed by the trade routes linking Europe's northern plains to Italy and the south, the Alps offer almost every variety of mountain scenery, from the snowy splendors of the Mont Blanc massif and the Bernese Oberland to the stark colors and sheer rock walls of the eastern Alps in general and the Dolomites in particular.

Looking south from the city of Geneva on a clear day, it is often possible to see a huge white dome hanging in the air above the intervening forests and hills. Like Hilaire Belloc's view of the Alps from the Weissenstein—"a sight in the sky that made me stop breathing, just as great danger at sea, or great surprise in love or a great deliverance will make a man stop breathing"—this sight of Mont Blanc is uplifting, a spectacle which even today challenges many men and women who see it to go nearer, look closer, maybe even to reach its summit.

Yet although the Swiss painter Konrad Witz used the dome of Mont Blanc as a background to his *Miraculous Draft of Fishes* in the fifteenth century, another three hundred years passed before this highest summit of the Alps was even given a name.

Lack of interest in mountains for their own sake was not the only reason Mont Blanc was ignored until little more than two hundred years ago. Monte Viso, away to the west in the Cottian Alps, rises within sight of a minor pass which since Hannibal's day has offered a shortcut from the lower Rhone Valley to the plains of Italy. The Matterhorn soars up above the Théodule, now an easy glacier pass but in earlier times an even simpler route from northern Italy to the Upper Rhine. The Mont Cenis, the St. Gotthard, the Simplon, and the Brenner are other passes which have for long been trade routes between Italy and Northern Europe. Their passage by a constant stream of travelers led to at least some knowledge of the nearby peaks.

Mont Blanc had no such "trade route" until, in 1965, the road tunnel was opened between Chamonix and Courmayeur. To the west of the Chamonix Valley, above which the mountain rises, a circuitous route leads from St.-Gervais to Bourg St. Maurice and then, via the Little St. Bernard, to Aosta and the plains. To the east lies the Great St. Bernard, a classic route to the south even before Napoleon took the Grande Armée across it. And today the Coldes Montets and the Col de la Forclaz are part of the highway down to Martigny. Yet for centuries the vale of Chamonix itself was almost a dead end, while the summit of Mont Blanc, towering up to the south, could be seen from only a few vantage points along the narrow, constricted valley.

The mountain was, in fact, so little known that the first significant account of the area, *An Account of the Glaciers or Ice-Alps of Savoy*, written for Britain's Royal Society by William Windham, a young Englishman, and Pierre Martel, a Genevese engineer, failed even to mention it. In 1741 Windham visited Chamonix with Dr. Pococke, a famous oriental traveler. They took local guides and porters, walked up to where the Montenvers Hotel now stands, and then, greatly daring, ventured onto the glacier below. "You must imagine your Lake [the Lake of Geneva]," Windham wrote, "put in Agitation by a strong Wind, and frozen all at once; perhaps even that would not produce the same appearance." Windham's significant phrase effectively christened the Mer de Glace, the most famous glacier in the Alps.

Three years later, Windham and Martel wrote the account of the journey. It came at the right moment, for the Romantic revolution of Haller was about to get under way. The problem of the glaciers, which was to exercise physicists for more than a century, would now give scientific muscle to Haller's aesthetic delight in mountains. Of what were glaciers really made? How were they formed? What was the mechanism of their progress? These were questions to whose solution an increasing number of scientists began to devote their energies. As they studied the problems, the second horse in the scientific tandem which was to drive men up the Alps made its appearance. Could men breathe and live at the heights from which the glaciers descended? Was there any truth in the legend that even a single night spent out on the upper snows would be fatal? These questions demanded an answer from doctors and physiologists.

To serve such explorers the local men who knew the routes below the snow line were encouraged to go higher, to work out the best ways of moving through the maze of crevasses which crisscross the glaciers, and to rediscover and develop the elementary rules for safe movement above the snow line outlined by Simler three centuries previously.

The leader in this movement, which created a watershed separating the medieval era of Alpine climbing from the scientific epoch, was a Genevese, Horace-Bénédict de Saussure. A wealthy young man and brilliant scholar, de Saussure was to devote the greater part of his life to Alpine travel and to recording what he saw. But it is with Mont Blanc that he is mainly, and rightly, connected. His first visit to Chamonix was made in 1760, at the age of twenty. He was enchanted with the unspoiled valley, explored some of the surrounding heights, and offered a prize to anyone who could discover a route up Mont Blanc. He repeated the offer on his second visit, the following year. As before, there were no takers. In fact it was not until 1775 that the first serious attempt was made to climb the mountain.

Meanwhile, the mood of the times, personified by de Saussure, had encouraged two other Genevese scientists, the brothers Deluc, to climb the 10,000-foot Buet, which rises splendidly to the north of the Chamonix Valley. From the top they carried out scientific observations and, looking south, saw Mont Blanc, which, "towering above the valleys, seemed capable of supplying a river for ages to come, so loaded was it with snow from base to summit."

In 1784 two outliers of Mont Blanc, the Aiguille du Goûter and the Dôme du Goûter, were climbed by Chamonix guides. With the pace quickening, it seemed that the top of Mont Blanc itself must soon be reached.

The best viewpoint from which to study the routes followed by the early explorers of Mont Blanc is the Brévent, a mountain grandstand on the northern side of the Chamonix Valley. Looking across to the slopes of Mont Blanc, one sees a narrow wooded ridge, the Montagne de la Côte, and the rocky spur which rises to the Aiguille du Midi. Between them there streams down the Glacier des Bossons, an illustration of why the word "tongue" is applied to the lower reaches of a glacier. To the west of the Montagne de la Côte is the Glacier de Taconnaz and, above its junction with the Bossons, the narrow rock rib of the Grands Mulets. Above this again there is the huge snow reservoir of the Grand Plateau, and higher still the summit slopes.

It was on the ridge of the Montagne de la Côte that the Chamonix guides had from the first concentrated their efforts. They had been balked by lack of experience, by the problems of working a way through the crevassed slopes onto the higher reaches of the mountain, by lack of time due to fear of spending a night out on the snow, and by a dread of the unknown, nourished by superstitious fears of what might await them on the heights.

In June 1786 Jacques Balmat, a twenty-five-year-old local man who had hunted chamois, searched for crystals, and knew the lower slopes of the mountain well, made

Guide Jacques **BALMAT**

AND

*Dr. Michel-Gabriel*
**PACCARD**

MADE THE FIRST SUCCESSFUL
ASCENT OF MONT BLANC IN
1786 AND THEN SPENT THE
REST OF THEIR LIVES IN A
DISPUTE OVER WHICH ONE
DESERVED CREDIT.

**H.B. de SAUSSURE** OFFERED A
PRIZE FOR THE FIRST CLIMB AND
MADE THE SECOND ASCENT
HIMSELF.

AAHon

a solitary attempt to get to the top. In spite of failing light he pressed on and was forced to spend the night sheltering in the bottom of a small crevasse before returning to Chamonix the next day. His survival of a night out on the snows disproved one local superstition, but he had been badly burned by snow glare. His face was soon peeling, and in desperation he called on the local doctor. His visit to Dr. Michel-Gabriel Paccard, the twenty-nine-year-old son of a Chamonix lawyer, sealed the fate of Mont Blanc.

Balmat's main object was de Saussure's reward. Paccard, who had already taken part in a number of attempts, was intent on making scientific observations from the summit. Thus the ambitions of the two men differed, although their immediate aim was the same. They agreed to join forces and made plans throughout July.

On the morning of August 8, with the prospect of good weather ahead, the two men decided that the time had come. That evening they said good-bye to their wives and left Chamonix. A mile or so down the valley, by the hamlet of La Côte, they met and took the rough track leading upward along the crest of the Montagne de la Côte. At dusk they found a convenient shelter in the rocks, wrapped themselves in rugs, and settled down for the night.

"At two the white line [of the dawn] appeared and soon the sun rose without a cloud, brilliant and beautiful, the promise of a glorious day." Balmat said later. "I awoke the Doctor, and we began our day's march. At the end of a quarter of an hour we were struggling with the glacier of the Taconnay, a sea full of great crevasses whose depth could not be measured by the eye. The snow bridges gave way beneath our feet. The Doctor's first steps were halting and uncertain, but the sight of my alertness gave him confidence and we went on safe and sound."

Here is the first hint of what later became known as the Balmat controversy, the argument about whether Balmat had led a helpless doctor up the mountain or whether the better-educated doctor had been the man in charge. Paccard was, in fact, an experienced mountaineer judged by the standards of the time, and there is little doubt that the two men's different abilities complemented each other.

They crossed the glacier without incident and made for the Grands Mulets, where Balmat carved his initials on one of the rocks. Above them lay the great snow bowl of the Grand Plateau. By the time they reached it, the wind was rising, and their progress became slower and more difficult. Badly buffeted, they were at times pinned to the ground.

In front of them lay the Calotte, the huge snowy dome of Mont Blanc. To their right, westward, there were broken and hazardous ridges. To the east, however, there sloped up to the skyline two parallel lines of rocks, the Rochers Rouges. Between them lay a snow trough — the *ancien passage,* as it later came to be known.

It was already midafternoon as the two men turned up along this corridor, a comparatively easy route but one dangerously exposed to avalanches from the upper slopes. Their luck held. They reached the skyline and turned up it toward the summit, but the height was affecting them badly by this time. "As I rose higher," Balmat later recorded, "the air became much less easy to breathe, and I had to stop almost every ten steps and wheeze like one with consumption. I felt as if my lungs had gone and my chest was quite empty. I folded my handkerchief over my mouth, which made me a little more comfortable as I breathed through it. The cold got worse and worse, and to go a quarter of a league took an hour."

At one place they looked back and realized that they could be seen from Chamonix. Balmat remembered the shopkeeper from whom they had bought provisions, the only man in Chamonix . . . who had known of their project. He took out his glass, claimed that he could see the men in the marketplace watching them, and waved his hat.

Once more they plodded on, heads down, watching only the snow at their feet. Then, all at once, they were there. "I looked round, trembling for fear that there might be some further new unattainable aiguille," Balmat continued. "But no! no! I no longer had any strength to go higher; the muscles of my legs seemed only held together by my trousers. But behold I was at the end of my journey; I was on a spot where no living being had ever been before, no eagle nor even a chamois! I was the monarch of Mont Blanc! I was the statue on this unique pedestal."

Paccard was, of course, a second statue, but in Balmat's story he gets short shrift, more often on his knees than on his feet, relying always on the steady Balmat — a perversion of the facts that was not to be righted for more than a century.

It was nearly half-past six. They were 15,782 feet up, on the top of Europe. Both men were dressed as though for a valley stroll, and their only equipment was the primitive alpenstock that each man carried, a long wooden pole tipped with an iron ferrule. It was amazing that they had reached the top; it was more amazing that they should survive.

Undeterred by the hour, Paccard began to make scientific observations with the equipment he carried in his pockets. It took him half an hour. The two men enjoyed one final look around the huge panorama, "its four hundred glaciers shining in the sunlight," as Balmat recalled. Then they moved off down the ridge they had ascended. Their boots had made little impression on the hard snow, but they kept to the route by following the line of small round holes made by their alpenstocks. The shadows came up to meet them, and it was almost dark before they were off the Grand Plateau. There was still some light in the sky, but only with difficulty could they make their way across the glacier to the comparative safety of the rocks at the top of the Montagne de la Côte. Here they decided to bivouac.

They slept, or dozed, until six in the morning. Then, with hands badly frostbitten and eyes damaged by the snow glare, they made their way down to Chamonix.

Back home, Balmat inspected his face in a mirror. "Then I saw for the first time what I looked like. I was unrecognizable. My eyes were red, my face was black, my lips were blue. Whenever I laughed or yawned the blood spouted from my lips and cheek, and I could only see in a dark room."

But Mont Blanc had been climbed. Tairraz, the innkeeper, sent the news to de Saussure, who arrived in Chamonix a fortnight later. But when he attempted to repeat the climb himself, his experiences proved how lucky Paccard and Balmat had been. With a strong party, he reached the top of the Montagne de la Côte, but here the weather broke. Snow and rain obscured the upper slopes of the mountain, and it was clear that under such conditions neither Paccard nor Balmat would have survived.

Not until the following year, 1787, was de Saussure successful. Accompanied not only by his valet but by eighteen guides who carried his scientific equipment, he spent more than three hours on the summit, testing the boiling point of water at that height, the temperature of the snow, and the pulse of his guides.

De Saussure was a man who combined to a marked degree the qualities of scientist and genuine mountain lover, a dual interest which illuminates his description of the panorama. "Light mist, hanging over the lower valleys, hid their details as well as the distant sights such as the plains of France and Lombardy, but I did not worry about that. For what I really saw, and saw as never before, was the skeleton of all those great peaks whose connection and real structure I had so often wanted to comprehend. I hardly believed my eyes. It was as though I were dreaming when I saw below me the Midi, the Argentière, and the Géant, peaks whose very bases I had before found it so difficult and dangerous to reach."

The conquest of Mont Blanc, first by Paccard and Balmat, then by de Saussure, had a critical effect on mountaineering. It ushered in the age during which men climbed the Alps with almost exclusively scientific objectives and learned their mountain craft merely as a means to that end.

Unfortunately, the first ascent was to be followed by one of the most disagreeable of all mountain controversies. It began when Marc-Théodore Bourrit, a Genevese artist and mountain traveler who had made a number of unsuccessful expeditions on Mont Blanc, arrived in Chamonix a few weeks after the triumph of Paccard and Balmat. Willing to admit Balmat's success, Bourrit was less willing to admit that Paccard, a professional man like himself, had succeeded where he had failed. He interviewed Balmat and shortly afterward published in a Geneva journal an account of the climb that was to hold the field for years. In this story Balmat was the unqualified hero; Paccard, the millstone around the guide's neck. Paccard is believed to have written a reply, but this, the famous "Paccard manuscript," was not published and has never been found. Bourrit's version was accepted. It gained even greater credibility when, almost half a century later, a few years after Paccard's death, Balmat was interviewed by the irrepressible Alexandre Dumas, who reproduced the guide's account, a story remembered with advantages, in his *Impressions de Voyage*.

De Saussure, too, was not without faults and played a part in keeping alive the myth that Balmat rather than Paccard was mainly responsible for the triumph. As Graham Brown and Gavin de Beer wrote in *The First Ascent of Mount Blanc*, "One man, Professor de Saussure, could have killed the myth at its very beginning and should have done so. Perhaps he had let his jealousy of Dr. Paccard override his conscience, or political expediency frame his relations with Bourrit, but whatever may have been the factors which moved him, it is not easy to forgive the way in which he finally condoned Bourrit's attack so that he may almost be said to have supported it."

It was not until the 1900s that the work of the American H. F. Montagnier and the Swiss Dr. H. Dubi brought to light the truth about that first ascent. Suspicious of Balmat's story, Montagnier discovered Paccard's diary, and Dr. Dubi found that of a Baron von Gersdorf who had watched the ascent from Chamonix with a telescope and made detailed notes of what he saw. Since the baron had no reason for bias, his account may be considered incontrovertible: Paccard and Balmat had taken turns in leading the way up the exhausting slopes of the Calotte. On the summit, Paccard, far from being worn out and incapable, had busied himself for half an hour taking readings with thermometer and barometer. Success had, in fact, been equally shared.

The argument about who had played the leading role in the ascent of Europe's highest mountain was in some ways parochial. More far-reaching was the effect of the climb on the development of mountaineering. Its significance was in part psychological. What men had done once they could do again, and if they could do it on the highest mountain in Europe, they could do it on the lower summits. There were, moreover, no dragons on the heights. Paccard and Balmat plodding upward, de Saussure with his leisurely caravan and subsequent accounts given to the intelligentsia of Geneva, had between them revealed a new upper continent for exploration.

This excerpt from *A Tramp Abroad* (1880), Mark Twain's occasionally factual account of his travels, spoofs the "scientific" Alpine expeditions by gentlemen climbers which followed on the heels of Balmat, Paccard, and de Saussure. If the literature of mountaineering offers anything funnier, we don't know of it.

# SAMUEL L. CLEMENS

# The Ascent of the Riffelberg

After I had finished my readings, I was no longer myself; I was tranced, uplifted, intoxicated, by the almost incredible perils and adventures I had been following my authors through, and the triumphs I had been sharing with them. I sat silent some time, then turned to Harris and said, "My mind is made up."

Something in my tone struck him; and when he glanced at my eye and read what was written there, his face paled perceptibly. He hesitated a moment, then said, "Speak."

I answered, with perfect calmness, "I WILL ASCEND THE RIFFELBERG."

If I had shot my poor friend, he could not have fallen from his chair more suddenly. If I had been his father, he could not have pleaded harder to get me to give up my purpose. But I turned a deaf ear to all he said. When he perceived at last that nothing could alter my determination, he ceased to urge, and for a while the deep silence was broken only by his sobs. I sat in marble resolution, with my eyes fixed upon vacancy, for in spirit I was already wrestling with the perils of the mountains, and my friend sat gazing at me in adoring admiration through his tears. At last he threw himself upon me in a loving embrace and exclaimed in broken tones, "Your Harris will never desert you. We will die together!"

I cheered the noble fellow with praises, and soon his fears were forgotten and he was eager for the adventure. He wanted to summon the guides at once and leave at two in the morning, as he supposed the custom was; but I explained that nobody was looking at that hour; and that the start in the dark was not usually made from the village but from the first night's resting-place on the mountainside. I said we would leave the village at 3 or 4 P.M. on the morrow; meantime he could notify the guides, and also let the public know of the attempt which we proposed to make.

I went to bed, but not to sleep. No man can sleep when he is about to undertake one of these Alpine exploits. I tossed feverishly all night long, and was glad enough when I heard the clock strike half-past eleven and knew it was time to get up for dinner. I rose, jaded and rusty, and went to the noon meal, where I found myself the center of interest and curiosity; for the news was already abroad. It is not easy to eat calmly when you are a lion, but it is very pleasant, nevertheless.

As usual, at Zermatt, when a great ascent is about to be undertaken, everybody, native and foreign, laid aside his own projects and took up a good position to observe the start. The expedition consisted of 198 persons, including the mules; or 205, including the cows. As follows:

| CHIEFS OF SERVICE | SUBORDINATES |
|---|---|
| Myself | 1 Veterinary Surgeon |
| Mr. Harris | 1 Butler |
| 17 Guides | 12 Waiters |
| 4 Surgeons | 1 Footman |
| 1 Geologist | 1 Barber |
| 1 Botanist | 1 Head Cook |
| 3 Chaplains | 9 Assistants |
| 2 Draftsmen | 4 Pastry Cooks |
| 15 Barkeepers | 1 Confectionery Artist |
| 1 Latinist | |

| TRANSPORTATION, ETC. | |
|---|---|
| 27 Porters | 3 Coarse Washers and |
| 44 Mules | Ironers |
| 44 Muleteers | 1 Fine ditto |
| | 7 Cows |
| | 2 Milkers |

Total, 154 men, 51 animals. Grand Total, 205.

| RATIONS, ETC. | | APPARATUS | |
|---:|---|---:|---|
| 16 | Cases Hams | 25 | Spring Mattresses |
| 2 | Barrels Flour | 2 | Hair ditto |
| 22 | Barrels Whisky | | Bedding for same |
| 1 | Barrel Sugar | 2 | Mosquito-nets |
| 1 | Keg Lemons | 29 | Tents |
| 2,000 | Cigars | | Scientific Instruments |
| 1 | Barrel Pies | 97 | Ice Axes |
| 1 | Ton of Pemmican | 5 | Cases Dynamite |
| 143 | Pair Crutches | 7 | Cans Nitroglycerin |
| 2 | Barrels Arnica | 22 | 40-foot Ladders |
| 1 | Bale of Lint | 2 | Miles of Rope |
| 27 | Kegs Paregoric | 154 | Umbrellas |

It was full four o'clock in the afternoon before my cavalcade was entirely ready. At that hour it began to move. In point of numbers and spectacular effect, it was the most imposing expedition that had ever marched from Zermatt.

I commanded the chief guide to arrange the men and animals in single file, twelve feet apart, and lash them all together on a strong rope. He objected that the first two miles was a dead level, with plenty of room, and that the rope was never used except in very dangerous places. But I would not listen to that. My reading had taught me that many serious accidents had happened in the Alps simply from not having the people tied up soon enough; I was not going to add one to the list. The guide then obeyed my order.

When the procession stood at ease, roped together, and ready to move, I never saw a finer sight. It was 3,122 feet long — over half a mile; every man but Harris and me was on foot, and had on his green veil and his blue goggles, and his white rag around his hat, and his coil of rope over one shoulder and under the other, and his ice ax in his belt, and carried his alpenstock in his left hand, his umbrella (closed) in his right, and his crutches slung at his back. The burdens of the pack-mules and the horns of the cows were decked with the Edelweiss and the Alpine.

I and my agent were the only persons mounted. We were in the post of danger in the extreme rear, and tied securely to five guides apiece. Our armor-bearers carried our ice axes, alpenstocks, and other implements for us. We were mounted upon very small donkeys, as a measure of safety; in time of peril we could straighten our legs and stand up, and let the donkey walk from under. Still, I cannot recommend this sort of animal — at least for excursions of mere pleasure — because his ears interrupt the view. I and my agent possessed the regulation mountaineering costumes, but concluded to leave them behind. Out of respect for the great numbers of tourists of both sexes who would be assembled in front of the hotels to see us pass, and also out of respect for the many tourists whom we expected to encounter on our expedition, we decided to make the ascent in evening dress.

At fifteen minutes past four I gave the command to move, and my subordinates passed it along the line. The great crowd in front of the Monte Rosa hotel parted in twain, with a cheer, as the procession approached; and as the head of it was filing by I gave the order — "Unlimber — make ready — HOIST — and with one impulse up went my half-mile of umbrellas. It was a beautiful sight, and a total surprise to the spectators. Nothing like that had ever been seen in the Alps before. The applause it brought forth was deeply gratifying to me, and I rode by with my plug hat in my hand to testify my appreciation of it. It was the only testimony I could offer, for I was too full to speak.

We watered the caravan at the cold stream which rushes down a trough near the end of the village, and soon afterward left the haunts of civilization behind us. About half-past five o'clock we arrived at a bridge which spans the Visp, and after throwing over a detachment to see if it was safe, the caravan crossed without accident. The way now led, by a gentle ascent, carpeted with fresh green grass, to the church at Winkel-matten. Without stopping to examine this edifice, I executed a flank movement to the right and crossed the bridge over the Findelenbach, after first testing its strength. Here I deployed to the right again, and presently entered an inviting stretch of meadowland which was unoccupied save by a couple of deserted huts toward its farthest extremity. These meadows offered an excellent camping place. We pitched our tents, supped, established a proper guard, recorded the events of the day, and then went to bed.

We rose at two in the morning and dressed by candlelight. It was a dismal and chilly business. A few stars were shining, but the general heavens were overcast, and the great shaft of the Matterhorn was draped in a sable pall of clouds. The chief guide advised a delay; he said he feared it was going to rain. We waited until nine o'clock, and then got away in tolerably clear weather.

Our course led up some terrific steeps, densely wooded with larches and cedars, and traversed by paths which the rains had guttered and which were obstructed by loose stones. To add to the danger and inconvenience, we were constantly meeting returning tourists on foot or horseback, and as constantly being crowded and battered by ascending tourists who were in a hurry and wanted to get by.

Our troubles thickened. About the middle of the afternoon the seventeen guides called a halt and held a consultation. After consulting an hour they said their first suspicion remained intact — that is to say, they believed they were lost. I asked if they did not *know* it? No, they said, the *couldn't* absolutely know whether they were lost or not, because none of them had ever been in that part of the country before. They had a strong instinct that they were lost, but they had no proofs — except that they did not know where they were. They had met no tourists for some time, and they considered that a suspicious sign.

Plainly we were in an ugly fix. The guides were naturally unwilling to go alone and seek a way out of the difficulty; so we all went together. For better security we moved slow and cautiously, for the forest was very dense. We did not move up the mountain, but around it, hoping to strike across the old trail. Toward nightfall, when we were about tired out, we came up against a rock as big as a cottage. This barrier took all the remaining spirit out of the men, and a panic of fear and despair ensued. They moaned and wept, and said they should never see their homes and their dear ones again. Then they began to upbraid me for bringing them upon this fatal expedition. Some even muttered threats against me.

Clearly it was no time to show weakness. So I made a speech in which I said that other Alp-climbers had been in as perilous a position as this, and yet by courage and perseverance had escaped. I promised to stand by them, I promised to rescue them. I closed by saying we had plenty of provisions to maintain us for quite a siege—and did they suppose Zermatt would allow half a mile of men and mules to mysteriously disappear during any considerable time, right above their noses, and make no inquiries? No, Zermatt would send out searching expeditions and we should be saved.

This speech had a great effect. The men pitched the tents with some little show of cheerfulness, and we were snugly under cover when the night shut down. I now reaped the reward of my wisdom in providing one article which is not mentioned in any book of Alpine adventure but this. I refer to the paregoric. But for that beneficent drug, not one of those men would have slept a moment during that fearful night. But for the gentle persuader they must have tossed, unsoothed, the night through; for the whiskey was for me. Yes, they would have risen in the morning unfitted for their heavy task. As it was, everybody slept but my agent and me—only we two and the barkeepers. I would not permit myself to sleep at such a time. I considered myself responsible for all those lives. I meant to be on hand and ready, in case of avalanches. I am aware, now, that there were no avalanches up there, but I did not know it then.

We watched the weather all through that awful night, and kept an eye on the barometer, to be prepared for the least change. There was not the slightest change recorded by the instrument during the whole time. Words cannot describe the comfort that that friendly, hopeful, steadfast thing was to me in that season of trouble. It was a defective barometer, and had no hand but the stationary brass pointer, but I did not know that until afterward. If I should be in such a situation again, I should not wish for any barometer but that one.

All hands rose at two in the morning and took breakfast, and as soon as it was light we roped ourselves together and went at that rock. For some time we tried the hook-rope and other means of scaling it, but without success—that is, without perfect success. The hook caught once, and Harris started up it hand over hand, but the hold broke and if there had not happened to be a chaplain sitting underneath at the time, Harris would certainly have been crippled. As it was, it was the chaplain. He took to his crutches, and I ordered the hook-rope to be laid aside. It was too dangerous an implement where so many people were standing around.

We were puzzled for a while; then somebody thought of the ladders. One of these was leaned against the rock, and the men went up it tied together in couples. Another ladder was sent up for use in descending. At the end of half an hour everybody was over, and that rock was conquered. We gave our first grand shout of triumph. But the joy was short-lived, for somebody asked how we were going to get the animals over.

This was a serious difficulty; if fact, it was an impossibility. The courage of the men began to waver immediately; once more we were threatened with a panic. But when the danger was most imminent, we were saved in a mysterious way. A mule which had attracted attention from the beginning by its disposition to experiment, tried to eat a five-pound can of nitroglycerin. This happened right alongside the rock. The explosion threw us all to the ground, and covered us with dirt and debris; it frightened us extremely, too, for the crash it made was deafening, and the violence of the shock made the ground tremble. However, we were grateful, for the rock was gone. Its place was occupied by a new cellar, about thirty feet across by fifteen feet deep. The explosion was heard as far as Zermatt; and an hour and a half afterward, many citizens of that town were knocked down and quite seriously injured by descending portions of mule meat, frozen solid. This shows, better than any estimate in figures, how high the experimenter went.

We had nothing to do, now, but bridge the cellar and proceed on our way. With a cheer the men went at their work. I attended to the engineering, myself. I appointed a strong detail to cut down trees with ice axes and trim them for piers to support the bridge. This was a slow business, for ice axes are not good to cut wood with. I caused my piers to be firmly set up in ranks in the cellar, and upon them I laid six of my forty-foot ladders, side by side, and laid six more on top of them. Upon this bridge I caused a bed of boughs to be spread and on top of the boughs a bed of earth six inches deep. I stretched ropes upon either side to serve as railings, and then my bridge was complete. A train of elephants could have crossed it in safety and comfort. By nightfall the caravan was on the other side and the ladders taken up. . . .

Next morning I was considering in my mind our desperate situation and trying to think of a remedy, when Harris came to me with a Baedeker map which showed conclusively that the mountain we were on was still in Switzerland — yes, every part of it was in Switzerland. So we were not lost, after all. This was an immense relief; it lifted the weight of two such mountains from my breast. I immediately had the news disseminated and the map exhibited. The effect was wonderful. As soon as the men saw with their own eyes that they knew where they were, and that it was only the summit that was lost and not themselves, they cheered up instantly and said with one accord, let the summit take care of itself, they were not interested in its troubles.

Our distresses being at an end, I now determined to rest the men in camp and give the scientific department of the Expedition a chance. First, I made a barometric observation, to get our altitude, but I could not perceive that there was any result. I knew, by my scientific reading, that either thermometers or barometers ought to be boiled, to make them accurate; I did not know which it was, so I boiled both. There was still no result; so I examined these instruments and discovered that they possessed radical blemishes: the barometer had no hand but the brass pointer and the ball of the thermometer was stuffed with tinfoil. I might have boiled those things to rags, and never found out anything.

I hunted up another barometer; it was new and perfect. I boiled it half an hour in a pot of bean soup which the cooks were making. The result was unexpected: the instrument was not affected at all, but there was such a strong barometer taste to the soup that the head cook, who was a most conscientious person, changed its name in the bill of fare. The dish was so greatly liked by all, that I ordered the cook to have barometer soup every day. It was believed that the barometer might eventually be injured, but I did not care for that. I had demonstrated to my satisfaction that it could not tell how high a mountain was, therefore I had no real use for it. Changes of the weather I could take care of without it; I did not wish to know when the weather was going to be good, what I wanted to know was when it was going to be bad, and this I could find out from Harris's corns. Harris had had his corns tested and regulated at the government observatory in Heidelberg, and one could depend upon them with confidence. So I transferred the new barometer to the cooking department, to be used for the official mess. It was found that even a pretty fair article of soup could be made with the defective barometer; so I allowed that one to be transferred to the subordinate messes.

I next boiled the thermometer, and got a most excellent result; the mercury went up to about 200° Fahrenheit. In the opinion of the other scientists of the Expedition, this seemed to indicate that we had attained the extraordinary altitude of two hundred thousand feet above sea level. Science places the line of eternal snow at about ten thousand feet above sea level. There was no snow where we were, consequently it was proven that the eternal snow line ceases somewhere above the ten-thousand-foot level and does not begin anymore. This was an interesting fact, and one which had not been observed by any observer before. It was as valuable as interesting, too, since it would open up the deserted summits of the highest Alps to population and agriculture . . .

The success of my last experiment induced me to try an experiement with my photographic apparatus. I got it out, and boiled one of my cameras, but the thing was a failure: it made the wood swell up and burst, and I could not see that the lenses were any better than they were before.

I now concluded to boil a guide. It might improve him, it could not impair his usefulness. But I was not allowed to proceed. Guides have no feeling for science, and this one would not consent to be made uncomfortable in its interest.

In the midst of my scientific work, one of those needless accidents happened which are always occuring among the ignorant and thoughtless. A porter shot at a chamois and missed it and crippled the Latinist. This was not a serious matter to me, for a Latinist's duties are as well performed on crutches as otherwise — but the fact remained that if the Latinist had not happened to be in the way a mule would have got that load. That would have been quite another matter, for when it comes down to a question of value there is a palpable difference between a Latinist and a mule. I could not depend on having a Latinist in the right place every time; so, to make things safe, I ordered that in the future the chamois must not be hunted within limits of the camp with any other weapon than the forefinger.

My nerves had hardly grown quiet after this affair when they got another shake-up—one which utterly unmanned me for a moment: a rumor swept suddenly through the camp that one of the barkeepers had fallen over a precipice!

However, it turned out that it was only a chaplain. I had laid in an extra force of chaplains, purposely to be prepared for emergencies like this, but by some unaccountable oversight had come away rather short-handed in the matter of barkeepers.

On the following morning we moved on, well refreshed and in good spirits. I remember this day with peculiar pleasure, because it saw our road restored to us. Yes, we found our road again, and in quite an extraordinary way. We had plodded along some two hours and a half, when we came up against a solid mass of rock about twenty feet high. I did not need to be instructed by a mule this time. I was already beginning to know more than any mule in the Expedition. I at once put in a blast of dynamite, and lifted that rock out of the way. But to my surprise and mortification, I found that there had been a chalet on top of it.

I picked up such members of the family as fell in my vicinity, and subordinates of my corps collected the rest. None of these poor people were injured, happily, but they were much annoyed. I explained to the head chaleteer just how the thing happened, and that I was only searching for the road, and would certainly have given him timely notice if I had known he was up there. I said I had meant no harm, and hoped I had not lowered myself in his estimation by raising him a few rods in the air. I said many other judicious things, and finally when I offered to rebuild his chalet, and pay for the breakages, and throw in the cellar, he was mollified and satisfied. He hadn't any cellar at all, before; he would not have as good a view, now, as formerly, but what he had lost in view he had gained in cellar, by exact measurement. He said there wasn't another hole like that in the mountains—and he would have been right if the late mule had not tried to eat up the nitroglycerin.

I put a hundred and sixteen men at work, and they rebuilt the chalet from its own debris in fifteen minutes. It was a good deal more picturesque than it was before, too. The man said we were now on the Feli-Stutz, above the Schwegmatt—information which I was glad to get, since it gave us our position to a degree of particularity which we had not been accustomed to for a day or so. We also learned that we were standing at the foot of the Riffelberg proper, and that the initial chapter of our work was completed.

We had a fine view, from here, of the energetic Visp, as it makes its first plunge into the world from under a huge arch of solid ice, worn through the foot-wall of the great Gorner Glacier; and we could also see the Furgenbach, which is the outlet of the Furgen Glacier.

The mule road to the summit of the Riffelberg passed right in front of the chalet, a circumstance which we almost immediately noticed, because a procession of tourists was filing along it pretty much all the time.* The chaleteer's business consisted in furnishing refreshments to tourists. My blast had interrupted this trade for a few minutes, by breaking all the bottles on the place; but I gave the man a lot of whisky to sell for Alpine champagne, and a lot of vinegar which would answer for Rhine wine, consequently trade was soon as brisk as ever. . . . I formed the caravan in marching order, presently, and after riding down the line to see that it was properly roped together, gave the command to proceed. In a little while the road carried us to open, grassy land. We were above the troublesome forest, now, and had an uninterrupted view, straight before us, of our summit — the summit of the Riffelberg.

We followed the mule road, a zigzag course, now to the right, now to the left, but always up, and always crowded and incommoded by going and coming files of reckless tourists who were never, in a single instance, tied together. I was obliged to exert the utmost care and caution, for in many places the road was not two yards wide, and often the lower side of it sloped away in slanting precipices eight and even nine feet deep. I had to encourage the men constantly, to keep them from giving way to their unmanly fears.

We might have made the summit before night, but for a delay caused by the loss of an umbrella. I was for allowing the umbrella to remain lost, but the men murmured, and with reason, for in this exposed region we stood in peculiar need of protection against avalanches; so I went into camp and detached a strong party to go after the missing article.

The difficulties of the next morning were severe, but our courage was high, for our goal was near. At noon we conquered the last impediment — we stood at last upon the summit, and without the loss of a single man except the mule that ate the glycerin. Our great acheivement was achieved — the possibility of the impossible was demonstrated, and Harris and I walked proudly into the great dining room of the Riffelberg Hotel and stood our alpenstocks up in the corner.

Yes, I had made the grand ascent; but it was a mistake to do it in evening dress. The plug hats were battered, the swallowtails were fluttering rags, mud added no grace, the general effect was unpleasant and even disreputable.

There were about seventy-five tourists at the hotel — mainly ladies and little children — and they gave us an admiring welcome which paid us for all our privations and sufferings. The ascent had been made, and the names and dates now stand recorded on a stone monument there to prove it to all future tourists.

I boiled a thermometer and took an altitude, with a most curious result: *the summit was not as high as the point on the mountainside where I had taken the first altitude.*

---

*"Pretty much" may not be elegant English, but it is high time it was. There is no elegant word or phrase which means just what it means. — M.T.

Suspecting that I had made an important discovery, I prepared to verify it. There happened to be a still higher summit (called the Gorner Grat), above the hotel, and notwithstanding the fact that it overlooks a glacier from a dizzy height, and that the ascent is difficult and dangerous, I resolved to venture up there and boil a thermometer. So I sent a strong party, with some borrowed hoes, in charge of two chiefs of service, to dig a stairway in the soil all the way, and this I ascended, roped to the guides. This breezy height was the summit proper — so I accomplished even more than I had originally purposed to do. This foolhardy exploit is recorded on another stone monument.

I boiled my thermometer, and sure enough, this spot, which purported to be two thousand feet higher than the locality of the hotel, turned out to be nine thousand feet *lower*. Thus the fact was clearly demonstrated, that, *above a certain point, the higher a point seems to be, the lower it actually is.* Our ascent itself was a great achievement, but this contribution to science was an inconceivably greater matter.

Cavilers object that water boils at a lower and lower temperature the higher and higher you go, and hence the apparent anomaly. I answer that I do not base my theory upon what the boiling water does, but upon what a boiled thermometer says. You can't go behind the thermometer.

Funny, yes, but the thesis may not be altogether absurd. Disaster is not the object of climbing —
a revolver is handier — but its nearness is surely the appeal. This witty little piece first appeared
in *Mountain* in 1974.

# IAN McNAUGHT DAVIS

# Drop, Plop, Fly, or Die

Last year I was invited to the Annual Dinner of the London section of the Fell and
Rock Climbing Club of the English Lake District — how's about that for being in touch
with where it's at? Far from being "Harrison's on Wednesday evening, up the Ml to
Derbyshire grit or limestone for a quick Sunday, and the Lake District every other
weekend in the Ford Cortina" types, they turned out to be your original aged ramblers
planning mass walks across the "Downs" or the "Chilterns."

I was scheduled to give one of my normally high-octane boring speeches, which have
kept me fed throughout the past few winters.

Having arrived rather late, I hadn't been able to absorb either atmosphere or alcohol
and felt coldly analytical as I toyed with my prawn cocktail or whatever concoction
the catering profession was passing as sumptuous fare that week. I looked around at an
incredible cross section of the British climbing scene and reflected on what the hell I
was going to talk about as soon as I had drunk the tepid coffee served by the usual
grumpy waitresses anxious to be off to their bed-sits in Balham.

Well, I thought, they must have climbed at one time, so why weren't they climbing
now? It couldn't have been simply a matter of age — there are as many men over sixty
leading hard climbs as there are women of any age. So what was the core pleasure of
climbing that they had stopped enjoying? According to Les Holliwell, real climbers
enjoy one thing above all else, and that is seizing two good holds made of warm, sunlit

granite and pulling up on them, possibly over and over again. And of course he's absolutely right. But there is more to it than that; just as football is about kicking people, cricket about throwing or hitting balls at people, and car racing about crashing cars, so climbing is about falling off.

Taking advantage of my total recall mind, I quickly scanned the pundits on this particular issue. Blackshaw doesn't mention it, Winthrop Young ignores it; but Whymper records it, boasts about it, revels in it. And there it stood plain, the pleasure center of climbing — falling off.

In the old days, before chocks, wires, nuts, hexcentrics, and other modern protection hardware, climbers who fell off usually died. The few that survived became hero figures. As in the case of V.C. winners, tales of how they won their manhood became distorted and linked with courage and bravery, instead of stupidity and folly. It was difficult to obtain a true opinion when the results were so often so terminal.

Nowadays, of course, the true importance of falling off has been fully recognized, and hardware and techniques have been developed to prolong and intensify the pleasure, so we are in a better position to analyze its significance.

As the number of survivors has increased, it has become clear that there is a wide methodology in the art of falling off, and a whole vocabulary has been developed to describe the numerous advanced techniques. (I believe this is the first time these have been cataloged. I must, however, warn any inexperienced climbers that the following procedures should only be adopted when no other alternative is available.)

*To Bomb Off:* to make an uncontrolled free fall, usually associated with fingers or holds giving out unexpectedly.

*To Flirt Off:* to undergo slow, semicontrolled loss of contact with the rock, usually on a slab or easy snow. Can quickly be converted to a "bomb" (see above).

*To Flash Off:* to display rapid, showy, nonserious loss of control, usually on an outcrop.

*To Plop Off:* to fall into water. Alternatively, according to certain authoritative Northern (U.K.) sources, to fall while making it.

*To Crater* (U.S.): to fall and hit the ground.

*To Total* (U.S.): to bomb and subsequently crater from anything over 100 feet (not recommended).

*A Birdman:* a prolonged free fall, where advanced techniques such as shouting "I'm off" or flapping the arms can be used to prolong the experience.

*To Slip:* to make a technical error. Can develop into a birdman-crater-total sequence on the part of beginners, but intermediate and advanced students can usually limit the consequences unless tired.

*To Fall Off:* to undergo a careless, nontechnical fall. Usually done by advanced climbers on easy routes when bored or tired.

*A Lob:* a dynamic leap for a nonexistent hold. Rapidly converted by nonexperts into a bomb.

Early attempts were made by several distinguished climbers, and groups of climbers, to develop the techniques of falling. Particularly important in this respect were the following.

*Alf Bridge:* Worked on the theory that falls could be a series of controlled jumps from minute hold to minute hold. He was successful in proving this by making unbelievable controlled falls without injury. Unfortunately this line of development seems to have lost momentum with the development of better protection techniques on which most climbers rely to reduce falling distances. It is useful on slabs, but of limited use on walls and, as I can testify, no use at all on overhangs.

*Hamish Nicol:* President, Climbers' Club. Made a considerable number of high-velocity experiments and, as a founder of the Alpine Climbing Group, was one of the first people to break the stigma attached to falling off. Reputed to have over thirty falls, totalling over 4,000 feet, to his credit, with only a fractured skull and jaw to show for it.

*Lord Hunt:* Doyen of the falling fraternity, and once known as "The Tumbling Knight." His contributions to the art have been released only to a select few friends.

*Cambridge University:* Educational establishment that made considerable early contributions to the art, particularly on beginners' meets. At the height of their gravitational phase the president was reputed to keep a weekly "lob book" of his falls.

I reflected on how many fallers I had known, the unknown diver from some sea-cliff crux, the "giggling glider" who laughed his way down many a crag — they were all real contributors to the essence of our sport. Waking with a start, I looked around the room and immediately realized why the London Fell and Rockers had lost interest in climbing and were now content with tedious pastoral strolls. So my speech began:

"Ladies and Gentlemen, it appears that many of you have lost interest in climbing, and perhaps tonight you will take time to think why. The real reason is that you have forgotten that climbing is about falling off, and you have built up a resistance to enjoying this key element of your sport. I am going to bring back the thrill of the first fall, the sensation of the summer wind blowing through your hair as you do a birdman with the smell of ivy in your nostrils. . . ."

And so it went on, lyrical, revealing, and brilliant. I have never been invited again.

This rocky needle, rising above the Mer de Glace near Chamonix, thwarted Dent and his celebrated guide, Alexander Burgener, *nineteen* times before they mastered it in 1878. Dent, a young surgeon, was one of the first "modern" climbers in that he favored the technically challenging smaller peaks over the massive, snow-covered mountains that drew the pioneers of Alpine climbing.

# CLINTON DENT

# The First Ascent of the Dru

In July last year, J. Oakley Maund and I arrived at Chamonix with one fixed determination. Either we would climb the Dru, or, at the worst, would, as far as in us lay, prove its inaccessibility. By my wish our first attempts were to be made by the old route leading toward the lower peak. And here let me state, lest I forget it, that the weather was on nearly all occasions of such a description that no parliamentary expressions can possibly do justice to it. Time after time we were balked by snow, wind, or rain. Day after day we sat waiting in vain for the favorable moment, till hope deferred, and a long course of table d'hôte dinners, without exercise, combined to make the heart sick. A couple of fine days would occur, and a start be effected. Then came the rain again, and we had to return, soaked and despondent. What time we were not being rained upon on the Montanvert, we were steaming and drying over Couttet's kitchen fire. On hydropathic principles we found this state of the elements an excellent cure for the mountain fever. Enough! Let me record what we did achieve in the rare intervals of decent weather.

Our first attempt was made with Johann Jaun and Andreas Maurer as guides. A lank-visaged porter, somewhat weak in the joints, who must have echoed Hamlet's interrogation as to the necessity of bearing fardels, carried our tent up to the grass slopes by the Charpoua Glacier. Here are many and excellent camping places. Dried dwarf rhododendron bushes abound, and water is plentiful, especially on the Moiné side of the slopes. Leaving the porter at 2 A.M. still in a prostrate condition, we wended our way up the glacier, which was in first-rate order. All were in high spirits at the prospect of, at least, a good climb. Not a bit of it. The rock face over which access to the lower peak is alone possible was covered with snow in the most treacherous condition imaginable. The guides most properly refused to go on, pointing out that to descend in the afternoon, with the snow soft and loosely bound to the rocks, would be unwarrantably dangerous. Back we went, therefore, and met the sniggers and sneers of the worthy Chamoniards with an imperturbability bred on long experience.

Twice again within the next fortnight we tried, with the same guides. Result the same, except that we didn't go so far and got more wet. The excellent Jaun now left us, and Alexander Burgener came on as chief guide. Following his advice, a complete change of tactics was adopted. We decided to abandon all idea of attacking the lower peak, and made up our minds to try the higher east summit by our old '74 route.

And now let me digress for a moment and give credit where credit is due. It is due to the Messrs. Pendlebury's guides, especially, I believe, to Peter Baumann, who, in 1873, on his first inspection, marked out the true line of ascent as far as it was visible. Again, and above all, the whole of our success is due to Burgener's sagacity and great guiding qualities. I knew that any guide was immeasurably superior to an amateur in the knack of finding the way. I was aware that in quickness on rocks the two could hardly be compared. But I had always thought that the amateur excelled in one great requisite — pluck. This record will, I hope, show that in one instance at least this was an error. But for Burgener's indomitable obstinate pluck we should never have climbed the Dru.

Leaving the Montanvert about 1 A.M., we reached the rocks below the col somewhat late, for our route up the glacier was bad. There was a great deal of reconnoitering, and a considerable amount of talking. However, we had a good climb, and settled the best route up some part of the couloir leading to the ridge. There was still too much snow on the rocks. A fancied insufficiency of guiding power — a decidedly insufficient supply of rope — and a strong idea that a new route was not to be worked out at a first attempt — combined to drive us back to Chamonix the same evening.

Après cela le déluge—and for a long time all mountaineering was impossible. Desperate were our attempts to amuse ourselves. Lawn tennis, with parti-colored balls and wooden bats, in front of Couttet's was the fashion for a while. Then we went a-crayfishing, Maund driving us to Châtelard in Couttet's basket carriage, and chirruping pleasantly to an ancient spotted gray steed. Then I chirruped him back again — and next day the spotted gray was "très malade," and my right arm very stiff. Under Maund's able tuition, and following his experienced directions at the fishing ground, we caught nothing.

Then I fell a-musing and studied human nature, and wondered at the various imperfections of development the muscle, known to anatomists as the gastrocnemius, could exhibit in the legs of our countrymen, and marveled why they took such pains in their costume to display its usually unsymmetrical proportions; and wondered why Couttet's barometer kept on rising, and pondered over . . . Suffice it that at last Maund, to my infinite regret, left, from motives of fraternal duty, coupled with the rooted conviction that the rain would probably go on till the winter snows came.

And so it came to pass that with J. W. Hartley, and Alexander Burgener, and Andreas Maurer, as guides, I found myself one August day at a new and improved camping place, a good deal higher than our old bivouac. We left it at 3:45 A.M. and got early onto the rocks. A tremendous day we had. Bit by bit the best routes were worked out. Snow still lay thick everywhere. The rocks themselves were fearfully cold, and glazed within layers of slippery ice. It was a day of exploration. First the guides climbed to the col. Then Burgener and I climbed ropeless to the same spot. To those in search of excitement I recommend above everything these rocks when glazed. But for a growing conviction that the upper crags were not so bad as they looked, we should never have perservered that day. We reached at last a great knob of rock close to the col, and for a time Burgener and I sat alone, silently staring at the precipices of the upper peak. This was the turning point of our year's climbing. Up to that moment I had only felt doubts as to the inaccessibility of the mountain. Now a certain feeling of confident elation began to creep over me. The aspect of a mountain varies marvelously according to the beholder's frame of mind. These same crags had been, at one time or another, deliberately pronounced impossible by each of us severally. Good judges had ridiculed the idea of getting up them. Yet, somehow, they looked different that day. Here and there we fancied we could trace short bits of practicable rock. Gradually, uniting and communicating passages developed themselves. At last we turned and looked at each other; the same train of ideas had been independently coursing through our minds. Burgener's face flushed, and we rose almost together, exclaiming, "*Es muss möglich sein.*" The rest of the day was devoted to bringing down our ladder from the col to a point much lower and nearer the main peak. Then followed one of the nastiest descents I ever experienced. We had made our way over the great snow patches, for the stones fell too freely in the couloir to render that safe. At one time we had 150 feet of rope paid out between one position of comparative security and the one next below it. One step, and the snow would crunch up healthily and give good hold. The next, and the leg plunged in as far as it could reach. Yet another, and a layer of snow, a foot deep, would slide hissing off, and expose bare black ice beneath, or treacherous loose stones. Not till 9 P.M. did we reach Chamonix. But I had seen all I wanted, and now I would have staked my best hat on the possibility of climbing the mountain. The usual atrocious weather which kept us back after this attempt was in consequence doubly vexatious.

Perhaps the monotonous repetition of failures on our peak influences my recollection of what took place subsequently. Perhaps—as I sometimes think, even now—an intense desire to accomplish our ambition ripened into a realization of actual occurrences, which really were only efforts of imagination. Anyhow when, on September 7, we once more sat before the campfire, I could hardly persuade myself that so much had taken place since the attempt last mentioned. It seemed but a dream, whose reality could be disproved by an effort, that we had gone to Zermatt in a storm and hurried back again in a drizzle; that we had left Chamonix and tried the peak again in a tempest; that I had returned to England utterly dispirited and downcast; that I had posted back after forty-eight hours' sojourn in my native land, on receiving by telegraph the welcome intimation that the weather at last looked promising. A confused jumble and whirl of thoughts crowded the brain. I heard the parting farewell from our pleasant party as the diligence lumbered away from Chamonix; this was chased away by the slow heavy clank of the railway carriages entering the station. I rubbed my eyes and looked up. Was that the Dru clear and bright above? The outline seemed strangely familiar. Surely that was Hartley there, occupied in the congenial employment of greasing his face with the contents of a little squeeze bottle — and there was Burgener. But what was this shapeless sleeping mass? Gradually it dawned on me that I was but inverting a psychological process and trying to make a dream out of a reality. Hartley was there; Burgener was there; and the uncomely bundle was the outward form of the most incompetent guide in the Alps. Not till after did we learn that our friend had previously distinguished himself with Maund on the North Face of the Breithorn. Not till the next day did we fully realize how bad a guide might be. We kicked him and he awoke. Then he made the one true remark I heard him utter. He said he had been drunk the day before. Then relapsed; and during the remainder of the time he was with us enunciated nothing but falsehoods.

From four in the morning the next day till seven in the evening when we reached our bivouac again, we worked incessantly. Not so the Driveler — for so we christened our new guide appropriately. Hartley dragged him up the glacier. Twice we pointed out to him half-hidden crevasses, and twice he acknowledged our courtesy by disappearing into them. Finally on the rocks we unroped and let him be. For seven hours he crouched under a little rock, not daring to move up or down, or even to take his knapsack off his back.

For the first time on this occasion we climbed above the col and bore off to the left onto the real rock peak. At first it was easy, but progress was distressingly slow, with only one guide and a short rope, for the Driveler far below had most of that commodity encircling his person. Hartley must have enjoyed his day. Unfortunately for him he was by far the lightest member of the party. Accordingly, we argued, he was less likely to break the rickety old ladder than we were. He was the lightest, so he was most conveniently lowered over nasty places when they occurred.

In the good old times if you wanted your chimneys swept you summoned a master sweep. This worthy would come attended by a satellite, in the shape of a boy. The boy was of such size and shape that he fitted tolerably tightly into your chimney. He then clambered up and did the work, while the master sweep remained below to encourage, preside over, and subsequently to profit by his apprentice's exertions. On much the same principle did we climb this part of the mountain. Hartley was the boy, while

Burgener and I, however unworthily, enacted the role of the master sweep. Gallantly did our friend fulfill his duties. Whether climbing up a ladder lightly out of the perpendicular, leaning against nothing, and with overhanging places above; whether let down by a rope tied around his waist so that he dangled like the sign of the Golden Fleece outside a harberdasher's shop; or hauled up before he was ready, with his raiment in an untidy mass around his neck; in each and all of these exercises he was equally at home; and would be let down or would come up, smiling. Over one place, where Burgener and I exerted ourselves to the utmost to hold the ladder against a slightly overhanging rock face, with an ugly-looking bunch of great icicles above, we must have spent an hour. On a later occasion by a deviation of about fifteen or twenty feet we climbed to the same spot in a few minutes with perfect safety, without using any ladder.

Once more, on September 11, and for the last time, we sat on the rocks just above the camping place. Never had we been so confident of success. Instructions had been given to our friends below to look out for our appearance on the summit between 12 and 2 P.M., the next day. Hartley had brought a weakly little stick which, it was arranged, was to crown our labours, and decorate the summit, on the morrow. But the old source of disquietude harassed us. Our eyes turned anxiously to the west. There, a single huge belt of cloud hung heavily right across the sky—livid in color above, but tinged a crimson red below. Hartley was despondent at the prospect it suggested. But perhaps its very watery look hinted to my mind that it might be a Band of Hope. From below the smell of savory soup was wafted gently up, "stealing and giving odour." We took courage, then descended and took sustenance.

At 4 A.M. on September 12 we left. Kaspar Maurer, younger brother of Andreas before mentioned, now accompanied us, for our old enemy the Driveler had been sent away with a flea in his ear—an almost unnecessary adjunct, as anyone who had slept in the same tent with him could testify. Notwithstanding that Maurer was ill, we mounted rapidly, for the way was tolerably familiar, and we all meant business. Our position now was this. By our exploration of September 8 we knew that from the col it was possible to ascend to a considerable height on the main mass. Again, from telescopic observations and the slope of the rocks we were certain that the final arête was easy. Immediately above the col the only choice was to cross over rather than onto the southeast face while ascending. A projecting buttress of rock, some two or three hundred feet in height, cuts off the view onto the face from the col. We hoped by turning straight up behind this to hit off the arête just above the point where it merges into the precipitous northeast wall. The rocks behind this buttress are visible only from near the head of the Charpoua Glacier, but we had never properly examined them.

We followed the couloir running up from the head of the glacier, keeping well to the left to a little below the col. At this point it became necessary to cross the couloir, and for that purpose we employed the long ladder, which we had placed in position the day before. Right glad were we to see the rickety old structure, albeit it creaked and groaned dismally under our weight, and ran its splinters into our persons at all points of contact. Yet there was a certain companionship about this same weather-beaten ladder, and I felt as if it was almost a hardship that it could not share more in our promising success. Next we fastened a double rope, about twenty feet in length, and swung outselves down a rough cleft as if we were barrels of split peas going into a ship's hold. Up again, and the excitement waxed stronger as we neared the doubtful part. Then Alexander lay flat on his stomach, and wriggled round a projecting rock, disappearing suddenly from view. We followed, progressing like the skates down the panes of glass in an aquarium tank, and found ourselves huddled together on a little ledge. An overhanging rock above compelled us to assume the anomalous attitudes enforced on the occupant of a little-ease dungeon. What next? An eager look up, and part of the doubt was solved. There was a way—but such a way. A narrow flat couloir, its angle plastered with ice from top to bottom invited, or forbade, further progress. Above, a pendulous mass of great icicles, black and long like a bunch of elephants' trunks, crowned the gully. We tucked ourselves away on one side, and the guides performed the best feat of rock climbing I can imagine possible. Unroped they worked up, hacking out the ice, their backs and elbows against one sloping wall and their feet against the other. The masses of ice dashing down, harder and harder as they ascended, showed how they were working. Suddenly a slip above—a shout—a crash of falling ice. Then a brief pause, broken after a few minutes by a triumphant yell from above, and the end of a rope dangled down close to us. Using this latter aid considerably, we mounted and found the top of the couloir blocked up by a great overhanging boulder, dripping still where the icicles had just been broken off. "Come on," said voices from above. "Up you go," said a voice from below. I leaned as far back as I could, and felt for a handhold. There was none. Then right, then left—still none. So I smiled feebly, and said, "Wait a minute." Thereupon, of course, they pulled with a will, and struggling and kicking like a spider irritated with tobacco smoke, I topped the rock gracefully. How the first man did it is, and always will be, a mystery to me. Then we learned that a great mass of ice had broken away under Maurer's feet while in the couloir, and that he must have fallen had not Alexander pinned him to the rock with one hand. From the number of times that this excape was described to me during the next day or two I am inclined to think it was a near thing. "The worst is over," said Alexander. I was glad to hear it, but, looking upward, had my doubts. The higher we went, the bigger the rocks seemed to be. Still there was a way, and it was not so unlike what I had often pictured.

Another tough scramble, and we stood on a comparatively extensive ledge. Already we had climbed more than half of the only part of the mountain as to the nature of which we were uncertain. A few steps on, and Burgener grasped me suddenly by the arm. "Do you see the great red rock up yonder?" he whispered, hoarse with excitement; "in ten minutes we shall be there, and on the arête—and then—" I felt that nothing could stop us now; but a feverish anxiety to see what was beyond, to look onto the last slope, which we knew must be easy, impelled us on, and we worked harder than ever to overcome the last few obstacles. The ten minutes expanded into something like thirty before we really reached the rock. All of a sudden the mountain seemed to change its form. For hours we had been climbing the hard dry rocks. Now these appeared to vanish, and — blessed sight — snow lay thick, half hiding, half revealing the last slope of the arête. A glance showed that we had not misjudged. Even the cautious Maurer admitted that as far as we could see all was well; but he added, "Up above there, possibly — " And now, with the prize almost within our grasp, a strange desire to halt and hang back came on. Alexander tapped the rock with his ax, and let out his pent-up excitement in a comprehensive anathema of Chamonix guides. Already we could anticipate the half-sad feeling with which we should touch the top itself. The feeling soon gave way. "Forward," we cried, and the ax crashed through the layers of snow into hard blue ice beneath. A dozen steps, and then a bit of rock scrambling; then more steps along the south side of the ridge — some more rock, and we topped the first eminence. Better and better it looked as we went on. "See there!" cried Alexander, suddenly; "the actual top." There was no mistaking the two huge stones we had so often looked at from below. A few feet below them, and on our left, was one of those strange arches formed by a great transverse boulder, and through the hole we saw blue sky. Nothing could lie beyond, and, still better, nothing could be above. On again, while I could hardly stand still in the great steps the leader hacked out. A short troublesome bit of snow work followed, where the heaped-up cornice had fallen back from the final rock. Then Hartley courteously allowed me to unrope and pass him, and in a second I clutched at the last broken rocks, and hauled myself up onto the flat sloping summit. There for a moment I stood alone, gazing down on Chamonix. The dream of five years was accomplished. The Dru was climbed.

Our first care was to level the telescope in the direction of Couttet's hotel. There was not much excitement there, but in front of the Imperial we were pleased to think we saw somebody gazing in our direction. Accordingly with much pomp and ceremony the stick (which I may here state was borrowed without leave) was fixed up. Then to my horror Alexander produced from a concealed pocket a piece of scarlet flannel, like unto a baby's undergarment, and tied it on. I protested in vain. In a moment the objectionable rag was floating proudly in the breeze. Determined that our ascent should not be questioned by any subsequent visitors, we left the following articles: one half-pint bottle containing our names, preserved by a paper stopper from the inclemency of the weather; two wooden wedges (use unknown), two ends of string, three burnt fuses, divers chips, one stone-man, the tenpenny staff, and the infant's petticoat.

Of the view I can say but little. I remember that Chamonix looked very nice from this distance. I remember that the Aiguille Verte seemed much less above us, and the lower peak much more below us (at least eighty feet), then we had expected. Anyhow, I know that the comparative meagerness of the panorama did not affect our spirits, nor detract from the completeness of the expedition. The Dru is essentially a mountain to be climbed for its own sake. . . .

J. J. Bennen's exploits as a guide came principally alongside John Tyndall, who is represented here with "Rescue from a Crevasse." That piece might be read first, for it illuminates the flaws in Bennen's character that contributed to his death on the Haut de Cry in 1864. Three years earlier the guide had accompanied Tyndall on the first ascent of the Weisshorn, and together they had made three unsuccessful attempts on the Matterhorn, the trophy claimed by Whymper in 1865. Gossett, an engineer and a climber of little renown, wrote this story of the fatal avalanche for the *Alpine Journal*, where it was published as "A Narrative of the Accident."

# PHILIP C. GOSSETT

# The Death of Bennen

On February 28, 1864, we left Sion with Bennen to mount the Haut de Cry. We started at 2:15 A.M. in a light carriage that brought us to the village of Ardon, distant six miles. We there met three men that were to accompany us as local guides and porters — Jean Joseph Nance, Frederic Rebot, who acted as my personal guide, and Auguste Bevard. We at once began to ascend on the right bank of the Lyzerne. The night was splendid, the sky cloudless, and the moon shining brightly. For about half an hour we went up through the vineyards by a rather steep path, and then entered the valley of the Lyzerne, about 700 feet above the torrent. We here found a remarkably good path, gradually rising and leading toward the Col de Chéville. Having followed this path for about three hours, we struck off to the left, and began zigzagging up the mountainside through a pine forest. We had passed what may be called the snowline in winter a little above 2,000 feet. We had not ascended for more than a quarter of an hour in this pine forest before the snow got very deep and very soft. We had to change leader every five or six minutes, and even thus our progress was remarkably slow. We saw clearly that, should the snow be as soft above the fir region, we should have to give up the ascent. At 7 A.M. we reached a chalet, and stopped for about twenty minutes to rest and look at the sunrise on the Diablerets. On observing an aneroid, which we had brought with us, we found that we were at the height of about 7,000 feet; the temperature was −1° C.

The Haut de Cry has four arêtes, the first running toward the west, the second south-east, the third east, and the fourth northeast. We were between the two last-named arêtes. Our plan was to go up between them to the foot of the peak, and mount it by the arête running northeast. As we had expected, the snow was in much better state when once we were above the woods. For some time we advanced pretty rapidly. The peak was glistening before us, and the idea of success put us in high spirits. Our good fortune did not last long; we soon came to snow frozen on the surface, and capable of bearing for a few steps and then giving way. But this was nothing compared to the trouble of pulling up through the pinewood, so instead of making us grumble it only excited our hilarity. Bennen was in a particularly good humor, and laughed aloud at our combined efforts to get out of the holes we every now and then made in the snow. Judging from appearances, the snowfield over which we were walking covered a grad-ually rising Alp. We made a second observation with our aneroid, and found, rather to our astonishment and dismay, that we had only risen 1,000 feet in the last three hours. It was ten o'clock: we were at the height of about 8,000 feet; temperature = −1.5° C. During the last half hour we had found a little hard snow, so we had all hope of success. Thinking we might advance better on the arête, we took to it, and rose along it for some time. It soon became cut up by rocks, so we took to the snow again. It turned out to be here hard frozen, so that we reached the real foot of the peak without the slightest difficulty. It was steeper than I had expected it would be, judging from the valley of the Rhone. Bennen looked at it with decided pleasure; having completed his survey, he proposed to take the eastern arête, as in doing so we should gain at least two hours. Rebot had been over this last-named arête in summer, and was of Bennen's opin-ion. Two or three of the party did not like the idea much, so there was a discussion on the probable advantages and disadvantages of the northeast and east arêtes. We were losing time; so Bennen cut matters short by saying, *"Ich will der Erste über die arête!"* Thus saying, he made for the east arête; it looked very narrow, and, what was worse, it was considerably cut up by high rocks, the intervals between the teeth of the arête being filled up with snow. To gain this arête, we had to go up a steep snowfield, about 800 feet high, as well as I remember. It was about 150 feet broad at the top, and 400 or 500 at the bottom. It was a sort of couloir on a large scale. During the ascent we sank about one foot deep at every step. Bennen did not seem to like the look of the snow very much. He asked the local guides whether avalanches ever came down this couloir, to which they answered that our position was perfectly safe. We had mounted on the northern side of the couloir, and having arrived at 150 feet from the top, we began crossing it on a horizontal curve, so as to gain the east arête. The inflexion or dip of the couloir was slight, not above 25 feet, the inclination near thirty-five degrees. We were walking in the following order: Bevard, Nance, Bennen, myself, Boissonnet, and Rebot. Having crossed over about three-quarters of the breadth of the couloir, the two leading men suddenly sank considerably above their waists. Bennen tightened the rope. The snow was too deep to think of getting out of the hole they had made, so they advanced one or two steps, dividing the snow with their bodies. Bennen turned around and told us he was afraid of starting an avalanche; we asked whether it would not be better to return and cross the couloir higher up. To this the three Ardon men opposed themselves; they mistook the proposed precaution for fear, and the two leading men continued their work. After three or four steps gained in the aforesaid manner, the snow became hard again. Bennen had not moved — he was evidently undecided what he should do; as soon, however, as he saw hard snow again, he advanced and crossed parallel to, but above, the furrow the Ardon men had made. Strange to say, the snow supported him. While he was passing I observed that the leader, Bevard, had about 20 feet of rope coiled around his shoulder. I of course at once told him to uncoil it and get on the arête, from which he was not more than 15 feet distant. Bennen then told me to follow. I tried his steps, but sank up to my waist in the very first. So I went through the furrows, holding my elbows close to my body, so as not to touch the sides. This furrow was about 12 feet long, and, as the snow was good on the other side, we had all come to the false conclusion that the snow was accidentally softer there than elsewhere. Boissonnet then advanced; he had made but a few steps when we heard a deep, cutting sound. The snowfield split in two about 14 or 15 feet above us. The cleft was at first quite narrow, not more than an inch broad. An awful silence ensued; it lasted but a few seconds, and then it was broken by Bennen's voice: *"Wir sind alle verloren."* His words were slow and solemn, and those who knew him felt what they really meant when spoken by such a man as Bennen. They were his last words. I drove my alpenstock into the snow, and brought the weight of my body to bear on it; it went in to within three inches of the top. I then waited. It was an awful moment of suspense. I turned my head toward Bennen to see whether he had done the same thing. To my astonishment, I saw him turn around, face the valley, and stretch out both arms. The ground on which we stood began to move slowly, and I felt the utter uselessness of any alpenstock. I soon sank up to my shoulders and began descending backward. From this moment I saw nothing of what had happened to the rest of the party. With a good deal of trouble I succeeded in turning around. The speed of the avalanche increased rapidly, and before long I was covered up with snow and in utter darkness. I was suffocating, when with a jerk I suddenly came to the surface again. The rope had caught most probably on a rock, and this was evidently the moment when it broke. I was on a wave of the avalanche, and saw it before me as I was carried down. It was the most awful sight I ever witnessed. The head of the avalanche was already at the spot where we had made our last halt. The head alone was preceded by a thick cloud of snowdust; the rest of the avalanche was clear. Around me I heard the horrid hissing of the snow, and far before me the thundering of the foremost part of the avalanche. To prevent myself sinking again, I made use of my arms much in the same way as when swimming in a standing position. At last I noticed that I was moving slower; then I saw the pieces of snow in front of me stop at some yards' distance; then the snow straight before me stopped, and I heard on a large scale the same creaking sound that is produced when a heavy cart passes over hard-frozen snow in winter. I felt that I also had stopped, and instantly threw up both arms to protect my head in case I should again be covered up. I had stopped, but the snow behind me was still in motion; its pressure on my body was so strong that I thought I should be crushed to death. This tremendous pressure lasted but a short time, and ceased as suddenly as it had begun. I was then covered by snow coming from behind me. My first impulse was to try and uncover my head — but this I could not do: the avalanche had frozen by pressure the moment it stopped, and I was frozen in. While trying vainly to move my arms, I suddenly became aware that the hands as far as the wrist had the faculty of motion. The conclusion was easy, they must be above the snow. I set to work as well as I could; it was time, for I could not have held out much longer. At last I saw a faint glimmer of light. The crust above my head was getting thinner, and it let a little air pass, but I could not reach it anymore with my hands; the idea struck me that I might pierce it with my breath. After several efforts I succeeded in doing so, and felt suddenly a rush of air toward my mouth; I saw the sky again through a little round hole. A dead silence reigned around me; I was so surprised to be still alive, and so persuaded at the first moment that none of my fellow sufferers had survived, that I did not even think of shouting for them. I then made vain efforts to extricate my arms, but found it impossible; the most I could do was to join the ends of my fingers, but they could not reach the snow any longer. After a few minutes I heard a man shouting: what a relief it was to know that I was not the sole survivor! to know that perhaps he was not frozen in and could come to my assistance! I answered; the voice approached, but seemed uncertain where to go, and yet it was now quite near. A sudden exclamation of surprise! Rebot had seen my hands. He cleared my head in an instant, and was about to try and cut me out completely, when I saw a foot above the snow, and so near to me that I could touch it with my arms, although they were not quite free yet. I at once tried to move the foot; it was my poor friend's. A pang of agony shot through me as I saw that the foot did not move. Poor Boissonnet had lost sensation, and was perhaps already dead. Rebot did his best: after some time he wished me to help him, so he freed my arms a little more, so that I could make use of them. I could do but little, for Rebot had torn the ax from my shoulder as soon as he had cleared my head (I generally carry an ax separate from my alpenstock — the blade tied to the belt, and the handle attached to the left shoulder). Before coming to me Rebot had helped Nance out of the snow; he was lying nearly horizontally, and was not much covered over. Nance found Bevard, who was upright in the snow, but covered up to the head. After about twenty minutes the two last-named guides came up. I was at length taken out; the snow had to be cut with the ax down to my feet before I could be pulled out. A few minutes after 1 P.M. we came to my poor friend's face. . . . I wished the body to be taken out completely, but nothing could induce the three guides to work any longer, from the moment they saw that it was too late to save him. I acknowledge that they were nearly as incapable of doing anything as I was. When I was taken out of the snow the cord had to be cut. We tried the end going toward Bennen, but could not move it; it went nearly straight down and showed us that there was the grave of the bravest guide the Valais ever had, and ever will have. The cold had done its work on us; we could stand it no longer, and began the descent. We followed the frozen avalanche for about twenty-five minutes, that being the easiest way of progressing, and then took the track we had made in the morning; in five hours we reached Ardon. . . .

Bennen's body was found with great difficulty the third day after Boissonnet was found. The cord end had been covered up with snow. The curé d'Ardon informed me that poor Bennen was found eight feet under the snow, in a horizontal position, the head facing the valley of the Lyzerne. His watch had been wrenched from the chain, probably when the cord broke; the chain, however, remained attached to his waistcoat. Three years ago I met one of my Ardon guides; he told me that Bennen's watch had been found by a shepherd several months after the accident. This shepherd had been one of the party who went up to look for Bennen; during the following summer he had watched the melting of the avalance. When mounted, the watch obeyed.

George Herbert Leigh Mallory was a magnetic character whose force of personality as much as his climbing skill made him legendary among climbers. The mystery surrounding his death — did he and Irvine reach the summit of Everest in 1924 before succumbing, or did they not? — is the principal thing for which he is remembered today, but to his own generation it was his life as much as his death that was a source of marvel. This affectionate recollection of the great climber is taken from a book known more for its bitter account of the author's war experiences, *Good-by to All That*, published in 1929.

# ROBERT GRAVES

---

# Climbing with Mallory

George Mallory did something better than lend me books, and that was to take me climbing on Snowdon in the school vacations. I knew Snowdon very well from a distance, from my bedroom window at Harlech. In the spring its snow cap was the sentimental glory of the landscape. The first time I went with George to Snowdon we stayed at the Snowdon Ranger Hotel at Quellyn Lake. It was January and the mountain was covered with snow. We did little rock climbing, but went up some good snow slopes with rope and ice ax. I remember one climb the objective of which was the summit; we found the hotel there with its roof blown off in the blizzard of the previous night. We sat by the cairn and ate Carlsbad plums and liver-sausage sandwiches. Geoffrey Keynes, the editor of the *Nonesuch Blake*, was there; he and George, who used to go drunk with excitement at the end of his climbs, picked stones off the cairn and shied them at the chimmney stack of the hotel until they had sent it where the roof was.

George was one of the three or four best climbers in climbing history. His first season in the Alps had been spectacular; nobody had expected him to survive it. He never lost his almost foolhardy daring; yet he knew all that there was to be known about climbing technique. One always felt absolutely safe with him on the rope. George went through the war as a lieutenant in the artillery, but his nerves were apparently unaffected — on his leaves he went rock climbing.

When the war ended he was more in love with the mountains that ever. His death on Mount Everest came five years later. No one knows whether he and Irvine actually made the last five hundred yards of the climb or whether they turned back or what happened; but anyone who had climbed with George felt convinced that he did get to the summit, that he rejoiced in his accustomed way and had not sufficient reserve of strength left for the descent. I do not think that it was ever mentioned in the newspaper account of his death that George originally took to climbing when he was a scholar at Winchester as a corrective to his weak heart.

George was wasted at Charterhouse, where, in my time at least, he was generally despised by the boys because he was neither a disciplinarian nor interested in cricket or football. He tried to treat his classes in a friendly way and that puzzled and offended them. There was a tradition in the school of concealed warfare between the boys and the masters. It was considered no shame to cheat, to lie, or to deceive where a master was concerned; yet to do the same to a member of the school was immoral. George was also unpopular with the housemasters because he refused to accept this state of war and fraternized with the boys whenever he could. When two housemasters who had been unfriendly to him happened to die within a short time of each other he joked to me: "See, Robert, how mine enemies flee before my face." I always called him by his Christian name, and so did three or four more of his friends in the school. This lack of dignity in him put him beyond the pale both with the boys and the masters. Eventually the falseness of his position told on his temper; yet he always managed to find four or five boys in the school who were, like him, out of their element, and befriended them and made life tolerable for them. Before the final Everest expedition he had decided to resign and do educational work at Cambridge with, I believe, the Workers' Educational Association. He was tired of trying to teach gentlemen to be gentlemen.

I spent a season with George and a large number of climbers at the hotel at Pen-y-Pass on Snowdon in the spring of 1914. This time it was real precipice climbing, and I was lucky enough to climb with George, with H. E. L. Porter, a renowned technician of climbing, with Kitty O'Brien, and with Conor O'Brien, her brother, who afterward made a famous voyage around the world in a twenty-ton or five-ton or some even-less-ton boat. Conor climbed principally, he told us, as a corrective to bad nerves. He used to get very excited when any slight hitch occurred; his voice would rise to a scream. Kitty used to chide him: "Ach, Conor, dear, have a bit of wit," and Conor would apologize. Conor, being a sailor, used to climb in bare feet. Often in climbing one has to support the . . . weight of one's body on a couple of toes—but toes in stiff boots. Conor said that he could force his naked toes farther into crevices than a boot would go.

But the most honored climber there was Geoffrey Young. Geoffrey had been climbing for a number of years and was president of the Climbers' Club. I was told that his four closest friends had all at different times been killed climbing; this was a comment on the extraordinary care with which he always climbed. It was not merely shown in his preparations for a climb—the careful examination, foot by foot, of the Alpine rope, the attention to his boot nails, and the balanced loading of his knapsack — but also in his cautiousness in the climbing itself. Before making any move he thought it out foot by foot, as though it were a problem in chess. If the next handhold happened to be just a little out of his reach or the next foothold seemed at all unsteady he would stop and think of some way around the difficulty. George used sometimes to get impatient, but Geoffrey refused to be hurried. He was short, which put him at a disadvantage in the matter of reach. He was not as double-jointed and prehensile as Porter or as magnificent as George, but he was the perfect climber. And still remains so. This in spite of having lost a leg while serving with a Red Cross unit on the Italian front. He climbs with an artificial leg. He has recently published the only satisfactory textbook on rock climbing. I was very proud to be on a rope with Geoffrey Young. He said once, "Robert, you have the finest natural balance that I have ever seen in a climber." This compliment pleased me far more than if the Poet Laureate had told me that I had the finest sense of rhythm that he had ever met in a young poet.

It is quite true that I have a good balance; once, in Switzerland, it saved me from a broken leg or legs. My mother took us there in the Christmas holidays of 1913–14, ostensibly for winter sports, but really because she thought that she owed it to my sisters to give them a chance to meet nice young men of means. About the third day that I put on skis I went up from Champéry, where we were staying and the snow was too soft, to Morgins, a thousand feet higher, where it was like sugar. Here I found an ice run for skeleton toboggans. Without considering that skis have no purchase on ice at all, I launched myself down it. After a few yards my speed increased alarmingly and I suddenly realized what I was in for. There were several sharp turns in the run protected by high banks, and I had to trust entirely to body balance in swerving around them. I reached the terminus still upright and had my eyes damned by a frightened sports-club official for having endangered my life on his territory.

In an essay on climbing that I wrote at the time, I said it was a sport that made all others seem trivial. "New climbs or new variations of old climbs are not made in a competitive spirit, but only because it is satisfactory to stand somewhere on the earth's surface where nobody else has stood before. And it is good to be alone with a specially chosen band of people — people that one can trust completely. Rock climbing is one of the most dangerous sports possible, unless one keeps to the rules; but if one does keep to the rules it is reasonably safe. With physical fitness in every member of the climbing team, a careful watch on the weather, proper overhauling of climbing apparatus, and with no hurry, anxiety, or stunting, climbing is much safer than fox hunting. In hunting there are uncontrollable factors, such as hidden wire, holes in which a horse may stumble, caprice or vice in the horse. The climber trusts entirely to his own feet, legs, hands, shoulders, sense of balance, judgment of distance."

The first climb on which I was taken was up Crib-y-ddysgel. It was a test climb for beginners. About fifty feet up from the scree, a height that is really more frightening than five hundred, because death is almost as certain and much more immediate, there was a long sloping shelf of rock, about the length of an ordinary room, to be crossed from right to left. It was without handholds or footholds worth speaking of and too steep to stand upright or kneel on without slipping. It shelved at an angle of, I suppose, forty-five or fifty degrees. The accepted way to cross it was by rolling in an upright position and trusting to friction as a maintaining force. Once I got across this shelf without disaster I felt that the rest of the climb was easy. The climb was called the Gambit. Robert Trevelyan, the poet, was given this test in the previous season, I was told, and had been unlucky enough to fall off. He was pulled up short, of course, after a few feet by the rope of the leader, who was well belayed; but the experience disgusted him with climbing and he spent the rest of his time on the mountains just walking about.

Belaying means making fast on a projection of rock a loop of the rope which is wound around one's waist, and so disposing the weight of the body that, if the climber above or below happens to slip and fall, the belay will hold and the whole party will not go down together. Alpine rope has a breaking point of a third of its own length. Only one member of the climbing team is moving at any given time, the others are belayed. Sometimes on a precipice it is necessary to move up 50 or 60 feet before finding a secure belay as a point from which to start the next upward movement, so that if the leader falls and is unable to put on a brake in any way he must fall more than twice that length before being pulled up. On the same day I was taken on a spectacular though not unusually difficult climb on Crib Goch. At one point we traversed around a knife-edge buttress. From this knife-edge a pillar-like bit of rock, technically known as a monolith, had split away. We scrambled up the monolith, which overhung the valley with a clear 500-foot drop, and each in turn stood on the top and balanced. The next thing was to make a long, careful stride from the top of the monolith to the rock face; here there was a ledge just wide enough to take the toe of a boot, and a handhold at convenient height to give an easy pull-up to the next ledge. I remember George shouting down from above: "Be careful of that foothold, Robert. Don't chip the edge off or the climb will be impossible for anyone who wants to do it again. It's got to last another five hundred years at least."

I was only in danger once. I was climbing with Porter on an out-of-the-way part of the mountain. The climb, known as the Ribbon Track and Girdle Traverse, had not been attempted for about ten years. About halfway up we came to a chimney. A chimney is a vertical fissure in the rock wide enough to admit the body; a crack is only wide enough to admit the boot. One works up a chimney sideways with back and knees, but up a crack with one's face to the rock. Porter was leading and fifty feet above me in the chimney. In making a spring to a handhold slightly out of reach he dislodged a pile of stones that had been wedged in the chimney. They rattled down and one rather bigger than a cricket ball struck me on the head and knocked me out. Fortunately I was well belayed and Porter was already in safety. The rope held me up; I recovered my senses a few seconds later and was able to continue.

The practice of Pen-y-Pass was to have a leisurely breakfast and lie in the sun with a tankard of beer before starting for the precipice foot in the late morning. Snowdon was a perfect mountain for climbing. The rock was sound and not slippery. And once you came to the top of any of the precipices, some of which were a thousand feet high, but all just climbable one way or another, there was always an easy way to run down. In the evening when we got back to the hotel we lay and stewed in hot baths. I remember wondering at my body — the worn fingernails, the bruised knees, and the lump of climbing muscle that had begun to bunch above the arch of the foot, seeing it as beautiful in relation to this new purpose. My worst climb was on Lliwedd, the most formidable of the precipices, when at a point that needed most concentration a raven circled around the party in great sweeps. This was curiously unsettling, because one climbs only up and down, or left and right, and the raven was suggesting all the diverse possibilities of movement, tempting us to let go our hold and join him.

The author and his partner, Reinhold Messner, were making a philosophical statement when they embarked upon this epochal ascent: that climbing had become an overly technical exercise and that the confrontation of man and mountain had to be pared back to its basics. When they attained the summit of Mount Everest on May 8, 1978, they stepped over the edge of life, as we in less rarefied air understand it, and into that euphoric state frequently described by those who have been snatched back into life after "dying" on the operating table. For Habeler and Messner, no part of their arduous climb was as fraught with peril as the very moment of their success.

# PETER HABELER

# Everest Without Oxygen

Once again we set off. The tracks of our predecessors, which could still be seen in the snow, served as an excellent orientation guide. The clouds were moving over from the southwest, from the bad weather corner of the Himalayas. We had to push ourselves even more because that promised bad news. We found ourselves in the lower reaches of the jet stream, those raging winds of speeds up to 124 miles per hour upon which the enormous passenger planes are carried from continent to continent. We had traversed the troposphere and were approaching the frontier of the stratosphere. Here cosmic radiation is multiplied. Only a few minutes without our snow goggles sufficed even in the fog to diminish our powers of vision. In a very short space of time direct insolation would lead to snow blindness and painful conjunctivitis.

Reinhold and I photographed and filmed as often as we had the opportunity. To do this, we had to take off our snow goggles and we also had to remove our overgloves. Each time it became more difficult for us to put the gloves back on again. But losing them would have led to the very rapid paralysis and frostbite of our hands.

Since it was no longer possible to go on in this deep snow, we had made a detour toward the southeast ridge. Here the wall dropped 6,500 feet down to the southwest. One false step and we would have plunged down into the Valley of Silence. The exposed, very airy climb on brittle rock without any rope demanded extreme concentration. Reinhold was right behind me. I took the lead to the South Summit. Completely without warning, we suddenly found we had passed through the clouds and now stood on the summit approach of the mountain, the last stage before our goal.

At this point the storm attacked us with all its might and forced us back. However, in spite of the storm and the fatigue my fear of the mountain had dissipated with the clouds. I was quite sure of myself. Over there lay the main summit, almost near enough to touch, and at this precise moment I was sure we were going to do it; Reinhold, too, told me later, "This was the moment in which I was convinced of the definitive success of our adventure."

A sort of joyful intoxication overcame the two of us. We looked at each other — and shrank back. From Reinhold's appearance I could only conclude that my own was very similar. His face was contorted in a grimace, his mouth wide open while he gasped, panting for air. Icicles hung in his beard. His face was almost without human traits. Our physical reserves were exhausted. We were so utterly spent that we scarcely had the strength to take ten paces in one go. Again and again we had to stop, but nothing in the world could have held us back now.

We had roped ourselves together because the summit ridge, as Hillary has already described it, was overhung by great cornices. It is true, however, that in an emergency a rope would not have helped us.

We crawled forward at a snail's pace, trusting to instinct alone. The sun glistened on the snow and the sky above the summit was of such an intense blue that it seemed almost black. We were very close to the sky and it was only with our own strength alone that we had arrived up here at the seat of the gods.

Reinhold signaled to me with a movement of his hand that he wanted to go on ahead. He wanted to film me climbing up over the ridge, with the bubbling sea of clouds below.

To do this he had to take off his snow goggles in order to focus the camera better. It occurred to me that his eyes looked inflamed, but I thought nothing more of it, no more than he did. Our altitude was now 28,500 feet, and we had obviously reached a point at which normal brain functions had broken down, or at least were severely limited. Our attentiveness and concentration declined; our instinct no longer reacted as reliably as before; the capacity for clear logical thinking had also apparently been lost. I only thought in sensations and loose associations, and slowly I was overcome by the feeling that this threatening fearful mountain could, in fact, be a friend, if only I could understand him properly.

Today I am certain that it is in these positive and friendly sensations that the real danger on Everest lies. When one approaches the summit, one no longer perceives the hostile, the absolutely deadly atmosphere that has penetrated before. I have probably never been so close to death as I was during this last hour before reaching the summit, not even that time on the Wilder Kaiser mountain when I fell a hundred feet down the rope in a free fall, and miraculously survived unhurt. Then at least I was still aware of the danger of death, but now I was not. The urgent compulsion to descend again, to give in to fatigue, that had overcome me already in Camp V, and which body and soul had rebelled against, the feeling of this being a deadly and threatening adventure, had disappeared. I was now feeling the complete opposite. I had been seized by a real sense of euphoria. I felt somehow light and relaxed, and believed that nothing could happen to me. Undoubtedly many of the men who have disappeared forever in the summit region of Everest had also fallen victim to this treacherous euphoria. I can well imagine Mick Burke sitting happily smiling on the summit, and thinking to himself, "How beautiful it all is up here; I'd like to stay here." And then his life was snuffed out like the flame of a candle. It must have been exactly the same with him. At this altitude the boundaries between life and death are fluid. I wandered along this narrow ridge, and perhaps for a few seconds I had indeed gone beyond the frontier that divides life from death. By a piece of good fortune I was allowed to return. I would not risk it a second time; my reason forbids me to gamble with my life in such a way again.

After our return, Reinhold and I were hailed as victors over Everest, but this is false. Everest was neither conquered nor overcome by us — it simply tolerated us. And if we can talk about a victory at all, then it is at the most a victory over our own bodies, over fear.

It was a very personal, lonely victory in a struggle that each of us fought alone, and the victory was not achieved in the last feet that still lay before us. It had already been achieved at the moment when we took the first step out into the unknown. And it was secured and documented when we returned alive from the kingdom of the dead.

In spite of all my euphoria, I was physically completely finished. I was no longer walking of my own free will, but mechanically, like an automaton. I seemed to step outside myself, and had the illusion that another person was walking in my place. This other person arrived at the Hillary Step, that perilous 82-foot-high ridge gradient, and then climbed and pulled himself up in the footsteps of his predecessors. He had one foot in Tibet and the other in Nepal. On the left side there was a 6,500-foot descent to Nepal; on the right the wall dropped 13,000 feet down toward China. We were alone, this one other person and myself. Although he was connected to me by the short length of rope, Reinhold no longer existed.

This feeling of being outside myself was interrupted for only a few moments. A cramp in my right hand bent my fingers together, and tore me violently back to reality. I was attacked by a suffocating fear of death. "Now I've had it." This thought went through my head: "Now the lack of oxygen is beginning its deadly work."

I could see the Sherpa in front of me who, a few days ago, had been brought down to the base camp. With him, too, it had started this way, and by the time the doctors had attended to him, he was already paralyzed on one side. Presumably he would never recover again properly. Nevertheless — he was alive; he was rescued. But up here that was impossible. I massaged my right forearm, I bent my fingers back, turned my hand, and then the cramp eased.

THE HARMONIOUS PARTNERSHIP OF **PETER HABELER** AND **REINHOLD MESSNER**, WHICH LED TO THEIR SUCCESSFUL CLIMB OF MT. EVEREST IN MAY OF 1978, EXEMPLIFIES THE "NEW STYLE" OF CLIMBING. IN SMALL GROUPS AND WITH A MINIMUM OF EQUIPMENT, THESE YOUNG MEN ATTACK 8,000 METER PEAKS — AND WIN!

THE CONQUEST OF EVEREST BY **EDMUND HILLARY** AND **TENZING NORKAY** IN 1952 REPRESENTED THE ULTIMATE ACHIEVEMENT OF THE "OLD STYLE." THEIR TRIUMPH WAS THE RESULT OF A CAREFULLY PLANNED, WELL ORGANIZED, AND COMPLETELY EQUIPPED EXPEDITION UNDER THE COMMAND OF **COL. JOHN HUNT.**

From then on I prayed, "Lord God, let me go up right to the top. Give me the power to remain alive, don't let me die up here." I crawled on my elbows and knees and prayed uninterruptedly, more fervently than I ever had done in my life before. It was like a dialogue with a higher being. And again I saw myself crawling up, below me, beside me, higher and higher. I was being pushed up high, and then suddenly I was up again on my own two feet: I was standing on the summit.

It was one-fifteen in the afternoon of the eighth of May 1978.

And then suddenly Reinhold was with me too, still carrying his camera, at the three-legged Chinese surveying instrument. We had arrived. We embraced each other. We sobbed and stammered, and could not keep calm. The tears poured from under my goggles into my beard, froze on my cheeks. We embraced each other again and again. We pressed each other close. We stepped back at arm's length and again fell around each other's necks, laughing and crying at the same time. We were redeemed and liberated, freed at last from the inhuman compulsion to climb on.

After the crying and the sense of redemption came the emptiness and the sadness, the disappointment. Something had been taken from me; something that had been very important to me. Something that had suffused my whole being had evaporated, and I now felt exhausted and hollow. There was no feeling of triumph or victory. I saw the surrounding summits, the Lhotse, the Cho Oyu. The view toward Tibet was obscured by clouds. I knew that I was standing now on the highest point in the whole world. But, somehow, it was all a matter of indifference to me. I just wanted to get home now, back to that world from which I had come, and as fast as possible.

The twenty-seven-day climb of the Wall of the Early Morning Light on El Capitan has been viewed by the public at large as a great mountaineering accomplishment; by some climbers as glorified flagpole sitting; by others as the very rape of nature; and by "Batso" Harding himself, trying to maintain his sense of proportion about the whole thing, "an exercise in vertical freight handling." Royal Robbins was so incensed by the climb that, a few months afterward, he duplicated it in *six* days while chopping out forty of the 330 anchors drilled in by Harding and his partner, Dean Caldwell. Was this controversial ascent "peak bagging" at its worst, with no concern for ethics or style? Or was it a worthy first ascent, characterized by sound planning, expertise, and persistence? You be the judge.

# WARREN HARDING

# Reflections of a Broken-down Climber

*Climbing would be a great, truly wonderful thing if it weren't for all that damn climbing.*

— JOHN OHRENSCHALL

As I sit on the veranda of my quarters at T. M. Herbert's *Rock of Ages Home for Old Climbers,* enjoying my graham crackers and warm milk, I think about the past eighteen years . . . my rise and fall as a rock climber . . . what a fine person I used to be . . . where did I go wrong?

Finally I realize what's wrong with me . . . why I'm rather oblivious to many of the things around me. It's simply that I've spent too many nights and days dangling from Yosemite's granite walls. My once keen analytical mind has become so dulled by endless hours of baking in the hot sun, thrashing about in tight chimneys, pulling at impossibly heavy loads, freezing my ass off on long cold nights in various examples of the "ideal bivouac gear," that now my mental state is comparable to that of a Peruvian Indian, well stoked on coca leaves. . . .

I've been at it too long ... thought that when I'd cleverly run in front of a rapidly moving truck (September 1969) I'd be spared any further indignities (i.e., climbing). But my badly smashed right leg recovered sufficiently to allow me to pursue this ridiculous activity.

A couple of years ago I had met a rather unsavory character name of Dean "Wizard" Caldwell (Wizard?). As our acquaintance dragged on, I discovered that we had much in common. For one thing we were both rather lazy ... an important quality of the serious climber. We talked much of past glories and future plans. But for the most part didn't actually do anything. Grandiosity of our plans seemed to be directly proportional to the amount of booze we would consume at a sitting. One night in the Mountain Room, completely taken by Demon Rum, we decided we would climb El Capitan's Wall of the Early Morning Light ... the Big Motha Climb!

We knew it was quite safe to indulge in such talk since neither of us was capable of climbing anything.... Dean had some badly torn ligaments, result of stumbling over a tree stump while walking to the potty room in Camp 12. My right leg was still pretty bad ... weak knee would barely bend. Tried a new climb, east edge of Royal Arches, only got out about forty feet. We adopted the name of "March of Dimes Climbing Team."

Fall—beginning to get worried now ... physical condition has sufficiently improved; we can stall no longer. Began carrying loads up to the "base camp"; cloak of secrecy surrounding our activities ... "great hairy giants" were all around waiting to annihilate any trespassers on "their route." Fearfully Wizard and Batso skulked around the valley. Difficult to be discreet carrying things like twelve gallons of water, big sacks of food, bivvy gear, six hauling bags, and the like. Eventually got things sorted out and bagged up. Led and fixed the first two pitches.

Then, of course, the weather turned bad ... sitting it out at Dave Hanna's place, we were shocked to learn that the dreaded Royal Robbins had suddenly appeared in the valley ... what now? Would he come charging up the wall ... just plow us under? Desperately, we moved out.

Almost predictably, rain started falling as we reached the top of the first pitch where our five hauling bags were hanging.... So in midafternoon we set up our first bivouac. Bat tents with plastic tube tents over them. It soon became obvious that we had vastly underestimated the time that this venture would take us. Fortunately we had also greatly *overestimated* the amount of food and water required for a day's sustenance. We had figured twelve days stretchable to fifteen days. (Turned out to be "stretchable" to twenty-six days.)

End of second week ... things looked different—very bad! We'd been on a rock wall longer than anybody else ever had (at least in Yosemite) ... last two days in a wretched state of *soggification*. As the fifteenth day dragged on, still raining, we realized we were in a very critical position. We were only about halfway up ... at the bottom of the Dihedrals, where our hopes of finding a good crack had come to nothing.

Our mental and physical condition had somewhat deteriorated from the effects of the soaking rainstorm, the general wear and tear of bashing our way up 1,500 feet of the hardest climbing we'd ever experienced.

Dave Hanna and Pete Thompson came up to the base of the wall. . . . Bullhorn voices from below informed us that the weather forecast was not very encouraging: clearing tomorrow, but another storm on its way. . . .

We pondered the situation as the rain continued through the day and into the night. Realized it could take another ten days to go the rest of the way. Carefully inventoried the rest of our remaining food. We'd have to radically reduce our rations if we were to stretch them out to even come close to finishing the climb.

But the thought of giving up the climb seemed simply unacceptable. It wasn't at all hard for us to make up our minds to press on . . . somehow try to make it. Another factor: the thought of trying to descend the 1,500 feet of mostly overhanging wall with our gear made us retch!

Next morning we informed Dave and Pete of our decision to continue. They seemed to feel we were insane but . . .

Weather cleared . . . a day to get dried out and reorganized, then come to grips with the Dihedrals. Only took us five days to get up this delightful area . . . lots of A4 nailing, bolting, riveting up overhanging bulges. On about the twentieth day we heard unfamiliar shouts from below. The shouter identified himself as T. M. Herbert.

"Hi, T.M. — good to see ya! What're you up to?"

"We've come to rescue you!"

". . . Whaaaaat?"

About this time Dean (leading) noticed ropes being lowered over the rim about 800 feet above. A great deal of shouting ensued. Most of our — uh — "rhetoric" would be unprintable in all but the most "advanced" periodicals. We did make it quite clear that we were fine, had the situation well in hand, were not about to be rescued. Fortunately those in charge of the rescue operation elected to suspend the effort, thereby sparing everyone some rather bizarre scenes: rescuers landing on Timothy Tower to find "exhausted" climbing team enjoying a fine mini-feast of salami, cheese, bread, and an entire bottle of Cabernet Sauvignon (Christian Brothers, of course) all in a beautiful moonlit setting. Dialogue. "Good evening! What can we do for you?"

"We've come to rescue you!"

"Really? Come now, get hold of yourselves — have some wine. . . . " The action could have gone anywhere from there . . . a quiet intelligent conversation with the would-be rescue team returning in the morning via their fixed ropes. Or had the rescue team been overzealous, a wild insane piton hammer fight might have followed. For we were very determined not to be hauled off our climb. We'd put too damn much into it to give up now! The hard part was behind us.

We were still feeling quite strong in spite of being on very slim rations for the past week. Perhaps our minds were becoming a bit fuzzy, though . . . had dark, cloudy visions of the National Park Service being influenced by envious, money-hungry climbers who would like nothing better than to fill their pockets with dollars while removing two clowns from a climb they didn't deserve to be on. The wall would remain (with all the hard work done) in a virginal state, awaiting a team of super climbers who could do it in real style. . . .

So onward and upward! . . .

Finally there was Dean battling his way up what we hoped would be the last pitch. But as he came to the end of the climbing rope, still about sixty feet below the rim, the day, too, came to an end! Frustrating — disappointing to be so near and yet have to wait until the next day, but no use taking a chance of blowing it now. . . .

Next morning I was totally unprepared for what I saw as I floundered up the last overhang onto the ledge at the rim . . . a veritable army of newsmen, friends, would-be rescuers (and a beautiful girl, Beryl Knauth). As I anchored myself to the ledge, I suddenly felt an overwhelming feeling of emotional release — sort of came "unglued" for a moment. Pulling myself together, I joined the happy carnival atmosphere that prevailed at the summit: batteries of camera snouts trained on us, gorging ourselves on all the food and champagne! All sorts of friends and well-wishers, ecstatic kisses and embraces — what a marvelous little orgy! Only thing lacking was a Mexican mariachi band!

But if I could have foreseen what would happen in the next few months I might have been tempted to say, "Oh, screw it all!" and bail off the top — well not really! With all the bullshit there were a lot of good things.

But there were ominous cluckings from certain pious experts about the degenerative effect on climbing of all the publicity attendant on such a climb. It would tend to attract hordes of unworthy persons to the rock walls and mountains — got to reserve all this for us "good guys." Keep the masses out! Maintain the esoteric image of climbing, raise the standards, etc., etc. . . .

It comes to mind that climbing is rather commercialized, certainly highly publicized, in Britain. Has this resulted in total deterioration of British climbers and climbing areas? It's my impression that it has not! Apparently Britain's relatively small climbing area is quite heavily used. Is the countryside becoming one huge garbage dump? I've been told by those who have been there that it definitely is not. Why? Could it be that the people, even though they are large in numbers, have come to know and love their mountains and desire to take care of them?

Elitists will argue that it is necessary to discourage the masses from mountain areas. No doubt this would work quite well in a feudal system where a small nobility had complete control of the peasantry. But such is not the case — theoretically, at least, this country operates as a democracy. . . . All, worthy or not, have equal right to the public lands. Again, theoretically, the use and preservation of our mountain areas would seem to depend on the vote of the masses. How, then, can we expect the support of the average citizen in conservation if he is told the mountains are too good for him, that they should be reserved for a minority of self-styled "good guys"?

Perhaps the hope of the "Valley Christians" lies in some form of regimentation patterned after the meticulous system of climber control so magnificently conceived and employed by the Soviets. Apparently well-structured training programs are carried out — screw-offs quickly weeded out — examinations and ratings given, climbs assigned only to the properly qualified — everyone kept in his place!!

But this is digressing . . . back to what's important: climbing.

Why did we climb the Wall of the Early Morning Light as, how, and where we did? . . . I always felt that the route should follow the right-leaning cracks in the lower section — traverse into the Dihedrals, then roughly straight up. This was not prompted by *Comician* ideals, but rather by some undefinable aesthetic attraction this particular area held for me. As with some other routes — Leaning Tower, Half Dome South Face — I was not concerned about how many bolts it might take. It was simply that it appealed to me and I wanted very much to climb it!

With the storms — three in all — food shortage, and, most significant of all, the rescue fiasco, the whole thing, reflected by the press, captured the imagination of the public. Oddly enough, the "high adventure" magazines, *True, Argosy*, etc., showed only the mildest interest . . . maybe it was just a glorified flagpole-sitting exhibition after all.

But whatever it was (the real climbers knew!), there definitely was general interest. An exciting, fun-filled whirlwind tour of public appearances followed our return to the valley. Fame and fortune were ours! — though I did seem to be getting quite a bit more of one than the other: like my share of the proceeds — $1,500 for four months' work. It didn't exactly seem like a "get rich quick" scheme. Anyway, at least there was great professional satisfaction: I had advanced from my lowly status of unemployed construction worker to the enviable position of unemployed TV star!

The emotional and monetary aspects of something like the aftermath of the Wall of the Early Morning Light are little short of amazing! Whether they like it or not, the principals involved suddenly become a business organization (or perhaps, a disorganization!). Some personalities can change significantly, others don't. Warm friendships and camaraderie can be replaced by cold contempt and suspicion. Happy laughter can turn to nervous, polite chuckles.

But we all know each other better now . . . for whatever that's worth. I still believe that it's entirely possible to work with the various commercial aspects of climbing without destroying the flavor.

Do I really want to, though? What is this climbing trip all about, anyway? Does it really matter if a particular climb is done in any particular "style"? Is there one "true code of ethics" that is admirably suited to all climbers? There are those who profess to have the real answer. In other fields, so did Jesus Christ, Karl Marx, and Adolf Hitler!

I have often been asked why I seldom, if ever, write my views on all this ethics business. In thinking about it, I realize I really don't give a damn. If all or most other climbers feel a need for the comfort and shelter of structured thinking — if there are those who feel a need to establish and promulgate these principles and lead the masses to a better *1984*-ish life, fine with me! I still feel inclined to do my own thinking. As long as the V.C. [Valley Christians] don't get their own secret police and employ Spanish Inquisition methods, I won't worry about being imprisoned, stretched on a rack, forced to confess my sins, and then burned at the stake as a heretic. Rather, to the self-appointed gurus, I say: Bugger off, baby, bugger off!

As I observed earlier, I'm entirely fed up with all this crap about bolts, bat hooks, press releases, commercialism, etc., etc. . . . At a trade show in Chicago, Dean and I received the electrifying news (rumor?) that R.R. and Don Lauria had just completed the second ascent of the Wall of the Early Morning Light, and had chopped out all the bolts and rivets; all this in only six days!

Naturally many people at the show asked our reaction to this. At the time, the best we could come up with were weak little attempts at humor: "Oh, well — they're just faster than us. Chopping bolts? Whatever's fair, etc., etc."

But the questions still came, especially upon returning to Yosemite Valley.

"Well, Harding, how does this grab you? What do you think about the bolt-chopping thing?" Frankly, I hardly knew what to say, or think. For one thing, it didn't seem worth while to go to all the trouble of finding out what had really happened. . . .

Still, some people thought that I should be concerned about all this — shocked, offended perhaps. Fact is, I don't give a rat's ass what Royal did with the route, or what he thought he accomplished by whatever it was he did. I guess my only interest in the matter would be the possibility of some clinical insight into the rather murky channels of R.R.'s mind.

Perhaps he is confusing climbing ethics with some fine (obscure?) point of prostitution morality . . . like, perhaps, a 100-bolt climb, e.g., Tis-sa-ack (or a $100-a-night call girl) is very proper; but a 300-bolt climb (or a $300-a-night call girl) is gross, immoral, or whatever. Or maybe Royal has gone the way of Carry Nation — substituting hammer and chisel for hatchet! And then again, maybe it's got something to do with rivets — I don't know. In a way, I feel sorry for Royal (a veritable Alpine Elmer Gantry) with all these problems, bearing the responsibility of keeping rock climbing the "heavy," complex thing it must be . . . (?)

Many years ago, when I first started climbing, it really seemed like fun, I truly enjoyed busting my ass trying to somehow get up something like Lost Arrow Chimney . . . or picking out a new route . . . but always feeling good about it. But suddenly it just seems like a drag. Maybe I should have stuck with sports car driving. . . .

Perhaps this turned-off feeling will pass; the relaxed atmosphere in the foothill location of *Rock of Ages* is conducive to mending the soul. It's good to be in such fine company: Al Steck and Steve Roper sitting at a table playing checkers, mind and vision too dim to cope with the rigors of chess . . . Chuck Pratt whiling away the hours conducting some imaginary symphony orchestra. Truly beautiful to see Earth Mothers, Jan and Beryl, bustling about in their long pioneer gowns, looking after the old fellows . . .

The sun is slowly sinking. Another day is drawing to a close. All the old climbers are putting away their toys and games, soon will be drifting off to their quarters to await the cheery call to dinner. Perhaps some of the more daring will have a small glass of Red Mountain.

I remain in my chair a bit longer — I try to probe further back through the years . . . before the Wall of the Early Morning Light . . . but it all seems like "I've seen this movie before" . . . always the good guys versus bad guys. Maybe I should have played cowboys and Indians; only trouble is, I'd surely have been an Indian!

The North Face of the Eiger (in German, Nordwand) towers over the Swiss village of Grindelwald; it is also known as the Murder Wall (Mordwand), and with good reason: it has thrown back the assaults of hundreds of men and killed forty-four. When Toni Kurz and his fellows—Edi Rainer, Willy Angerer, and Anderl Hinterstoisser—made their ultimately tragic attempt in 1936, the Eiger had yet to be climbed. But even after the first ascent was achieved two years later, the Eiger remained the most perilous mountain in the Alps and perhaps the world. Two accounts of later calamities on the passage between the Spider and the Fly may be found here—one by Jack Olsen, another by Arthur Roth. This gripping story is taken from Harrer's memorable book *The White Spider*.

# HEINRICH HARRER

# The Tragedy of Toni Kurz

As is often the case with mountain folk, whose features have been carved by wind and storm so that they look older in their youth, younger in their old age, Albert von Allmen's face is ageless. He might be in his middle thirties or middle fifties.

The mountains have been von Allmen's strict teachers and loyal friends, even if his profession leads him more into than onto the peaks. For Albert is a sector guard on the Jungfrau Railway. He is responsible for everything along the line inside the Eiger, and sees to it that nothing goes wrong in that long tunneled section; but he is equally interested in everything that goes on outside. True, he doesn't quite understand the young people who are trying to climb the terrific Eiger precipice, but, even if he thinks them a little deranged, he has a soft spot for them. Von Allmen's eyes are kindly eyes. They are surrounded by many little creases which record not only cares and the hard life of the mountains, but also the joy of laughter.

At noon on July 21, 1936, Albert was standing outside the gallery entrance at Kilometer 3.8, after opening the heavy wooden door.

It was a Tuesday. Ever since Saturday the eighteenth there had been four climbers on the face: two Austrians, Edi Rainer and Willy Angerer, and two Bavarians, Anderl [*Andreas*] Hinterstoisser and Toni Kurz. Everyone had fallen for the fresh-faced, clean-limbed Toni Kurz, not only because he was himself a professional guide, but because of his laugh. When Toni laughed, it was as if life itself were laughing. All young men, these; Angerer, the eldest, was twenty-seven, Kurz and Hinterstoisser just twenty-three. They had already climbed almost as high on the face as Sedlmayer and Mehringer the year before, on their ill-fated attempt from which they did not return. But these four would come back safely; what had been seen of them during the last few days gave solid grounds for hope that this time there would be no disaster.

None of those present had seen such magnificent climbing. True, one of the climbers, apparently Angerer, seemed to have been struck by a stone. That was why the party had been moving so slowly for the last two days, and that was probably why they had decided to turn back. The descent over ice fields and rock cliffs swept by falling stones and avalanches looked ghastly enough; but the four men were moving steadily, if very slowly, downward toward the safety of the easier ground below, in obvious good heart and without a moment's hesitation. The three fit ones were continually attending to the one who had clearly been hurt. They couldn't be bad, these lads who looked after each other so well. They must be fine fellows, even if a bit crackpot.

Albert von Allmen thought of the Sunday tourists and excursionists, the blasé men and the ladies in high heels who went to the tunnel window at Eigerwand Station and uttered their "ahs" and "ohs" as they gazed at what seemed to them the terrifying gulfs and immeasurable heights of the Eiger's precipice. It was people like those, hungering for sensation, who were now crowding around the telescopes at Grindelwald and Kleine Scheidegg. And then, too, there were the pronunciamentos of the know-it-alls, busy weighing up the chances of another catastrophe or of the safe return of four living men to the valley.

They *must* get back safely, thought Albert. His sympathy lay with youth, youth generally, but particularly these four youngsters on the face. It would be a good idea to take a look at them and hear for himself how they were getting on. Allmen pushed back the bolts of the heavy wooden doors and stepped out into the open, as he had done a hundred times before. He was used to the grim aspect of the face; but that day, perhaps because there were people on it, it seemed particularly horrific. A layer of glassy ice overlaid the rock; here and there a stone came clattering down; many of those lethal bullets went humming menacingly down for thousands of feet quite clear of the face. Then, too, there was the hissing of snow avalanches as they slid down, whole cascades of snow and ice. The very thought that there were living men somewhere up in that vertical hell was oppressive. Could they still be alive?

Von Allmen shouted, listened, shouted again.

Then the answer reached him. A cheery, gay answer. The voices of four young people shouting, yodelling. Albert couldn't see them, but, judging by the sound, they couldn't be more than three or four hundred feet above him. It seemed incredible to him that anyone could climb down those icy perpendicular or even overhanging rocks, continually swept by falling stones; but these crazy kids had so often shown how possible it is to climb impossible things. And, above all, there was that cheery shout coming down from above:

"We're climbing straight down. All's well!"

All well with all of them. The sector guard's heart beat faster for joy.

"I'll brew you some hot tea," he shouted back.

Smiling with pleasure, Albert von Allmen went back through the gallery door to his shelter inside the mountain and put a huge kettle on for tea. He could already see, in his mind's eye, the arrival of the four lads, exhausted, injured perhaps by stones, maybe seriously frostbitten, but alive and happy. He would meet them with his steaming tea. There was no better drink than hot tea for frostbitten, exhausted men. He was slightly cross at the time it was taking the water to start bubbling; the lads would be here in a minute or two.

But the lads didn't come in a minute or two.

Long after the tea was ready, they hadn't come. Albert set the golden-brown drink on a low flame, just enough to keep it hot without getting stewed.

Still the lads didn't come; and the sector guard, this man whose age it was impossible to guess, had time for second thoughts. . . .

On Saturday, July 18, 1936, the two ropes Angerer-Rainer and Hinterstoisser-Kurz started up the face. At first they moved independently; at the level of the bivouac previously occupied by the two Austrians they roped up as a foursome. The rope joining them was no longer a dead length of hemp for them but, as it were, a living artery, seeming to say: "For better or for worse, we belong together." This was an uncommonly daring but in no sense featherbrained undertaking.

They climbed the exceptionally severe crack below the Rote Fluh sucessfully. Above it, Andreas Hinterstoisser was the first to achieve the traverse to the First Ice Field, climbing in textbook fashion with the help of the rope. This technique of the "rope traverse" had already been discovered and developed before World War I by that master of rock climbing Hans Dülfer, during his first ascents of the East Face of the Fleischbank and the West Wall of the Totenkirchl in the Kaisergebirge. In this way Dülfer showed how to link climbable pitches by the use of a diagonal "lift" from the rope on unclimbable ones. The current joke about the Dülfer technique ran: "You go as long as it goes, and when it doesn't go anymore, you just do a traverse and go on."

It was this kind of traverse which Hinterstoisser did on the Eiger face. He had discovered the key to the climb. When they had all completed the traverse, he retrieved the traversing rope. In doing so he threw away the key. If it came to a retreat, the door to the way back was now locked behind them . . . but who was thinking of a retreat?

Many were watching the four men through field glasses. And the spectators forgot their criticisms in admiration, even astonishment, at the speed and assurance with which the two ropes crossed the First Ice Field, climbed up beyond it, and reached the barrier between it and the Second—the greater—Ice Slope. Since the Sedlmayer-Mehringer attempt, everyone knew how difficult those rocks must be.

But what had happened? Suddenly the second pair, Rainer and Angerer, were seen to be following the leaders slowly and hesitantly. Hinterstoisser and Kurz were already moving up to the rocks above the Rote Fluh. The other two remained motionless for a long time. Then it could be seen that one was supporting the other. Had there been an accident?

It will never be known exactly what happened, but it seems almost certain that

Angerer was struck by a stone and Rainer was busy tending him. Presently Hinterstoisser and Kurz could be seen letting a rope down from their stance, which was plainly safe from bombardment by stones. Their joint efforts succeeded in bringing Angerer up to them. Then Rainer followed quickly, without making use of the emergency rope.

The tiny nest in the rocks above the Rote Fluh thus became the first bivouac place for this party of four. They had reached an incredibly high level on their first day — more than halfway up the face.

On the morning of Sunday the nineteenth there were more crowds around the telescopes. They saw the four men leave the bivouac at about seven o'clock. And how was the injured man? Obviously better, for instead of retreating, they were climbing on, across the huge slope of the Second Ice Field. All the same, they were moving more slowly than on the first day. Were they all tired, then, or was it all because of the injured man? Why didn't they turn back?

One fact stands out for certain: the four men were a united, indissoluble party. Kurz and Hinterstoisser, climbing in the lead again, never thought of leaving Rainer behind with the injured man. The Austrians didn't want to rob the other two of their chance of reaching the top. And so they all stayed together, though the leaders had frequently to wait for quite a time.

The weather was neither fine nor definitely bad. In the context of the Eiger, conditions were bearable. By the end of this Sunday the party had reached the Third Ice Field; a little below the bivouac which had proved fatal to Sedlmayer and Mehringer, the four men made ready to spend their second night in the open. It had been a good day's work, but they had not gained enough height to make sure of a successful push forward to the top on the following day. What kind of night would it be? In what condition is Angerer and how are the other three? The spectators down in the valley don't know any of the answers. They withdraw for the night, rubbernecks, reporters, guides, and mountaineers. Tomorrow will show. . . .

The next day was Monday, July 20. Once again no movement could be seen in the bivouac till seven o'clock. It was a tiny place, with hardly room to sit down. Once again Kurz and Hinterstoisser began to climb the steep ice slope leading to the "Death Bivouac." After about half an hour they stopped. The others were not following them. Nobody knows what the four men said to each other. Whatever it was, the decision taken was crucial and bitter for the leaders, a matter of life and death for the other two. It was clear that Angerer was no longer in a condition to climb any farther.

All of a sudden the Hinterstoisser party could be seen climbing down to the bivouac, where they remained for some time; then they all began the descent together. A human being was more important that the mere ascent of a mountain face. Perhaps the united strength of the whole party would succeed in bringing the injured man down?

They crossed the great slope of the Second Ice Field comparatively quickly; but the descent of the rock step, on the doubled rope, to the first took several hours to accomplish. Once again the watchers were amazed at the care and assurance with which the ropes were handled. But night fell just as the men reached the lower ice field. Close to where Sedlmayer and Mehringer's second bivouac had been, they camped for their third night on the face. There could not be a stitch of dry clothing on their bodies and this third bivouac must needs sap their strength; yet three must now have enough strength for the fourth. They had only managed to come down about 1,000 feet during the whole day; fully another 3,000 of the face still gaped below them. Still, once the traverse and the Difficult Crack were behind them, the safety of the valley would not be so far away. They knew that part of the wall from having climbed down it once already.

Yes, but that traverse . . .

It would be the crux of this new day, Tuesday, July 21. All four seem to have stood the bivouac quite well, for they came down the ice slope to the start of the traverse at a good pace; but at that point those watching could suddenly see only three men at work. Had one of them fallen off?

Mists wreathed about the face, the wind rose, the rattle of falling stones grew sharper, avalanches of powder snow swept the track of yesterday's descent. The worst danger from falling stones would be over as soon as the four men were safely across the traverse. But where had the fourth got to?

When the cloud curtain parted again, the men at the telescopes could see all four climbers again, but Angerer, apparently *hors de combat*, was taking no part in the attempts to master the traverse. One man seemed to be taking the lead in these efforts — surely it must be Hinterstoisser, the man who first dealt with this key point on the way up. But now there is no traversing rope fixed to the rock. And the rock doesn't seem to be climbable without artificial aids.

The weather was worsening; it had in fact already broken. The water which had all along been pouring down the rocks must have hardened into ice. All the experts with field glasses could sense the fearsome tragedy to come. Retreat was cut off; nobody could move over the glassy film overlaying the rock, not even an Andreas Hinterstoisser. The precious hours of the entire morning were consumed by vain, frustrating, incredibly exhausting and dangerous attempts. And then came the last desperate decision: to climb straight down the vertical rock face, some 600 or 700 feet high, which at some points bulges far out even beyond the vertical.

The only way led through the line of fire from stones and avalanches. Sedlmayer and Mehringer had taken a whole day to climb that pitch, and that in fine weather on dry rock. Now all hell had broken loose on the mountain. But it was the only chance.

They began to get the ropes ready for the descent through thin air.

It was at this moment that they heard Albert von Allmen's shouts coming up from below.

Someone shouting, so close at hand? Then things could not go wrong! A man's voice, giving strength and courage and the certainty that the bridge back to the living world was still there. And in spite of the dangers and their awareness of the seriousness of their situation, they all joined in yodelling back: "All's well!" Not a single cry for help, not even an admission of their terrifying peril.

All well. . . .

Albert von Allmen was getting cross. How long was he expected to keep their tea warm? Presently his irritation changed to apprehension. Two whole hours had gone by since he spoke to the climbers, and still no movement at the entrance to the gallery. Could they have climbed down past it? Could they have missed the ledge, which runs across to the window?

The sector guard went back to the door. The face was looking grim and ghastly now; visibility was very restricted; mists were steaming up everywhere. Stones and avalanches were singing their pitiless song. Albert shouted.

And back came an answer.

This time no cheery yodel, but a shocking answer coming now from one man, the last lone survivor, crying for help . . . Toni Kurz.

The voice of a brave, unbelievably tough young guide, cradled in Bavaria in the shadow of the Watzmann; a man who had rescued many in distress on the mountains, but who had never yet shouted for help. But now he was shouting, shouting desperately for his very life.

"Help! Help! The others are all dead. I am the only one alive. Help!"

The wind, the avalanches, and the whistling stones forbade a more exact exchange of information. In any case, Albert von Allmen by himself could bring no aid. He shouted, "We'll be coming," and hurried back into the gallery to telephone.

Eigergletscher Station, down below, answered his call.

"Allmen speaking. There's been a fearful disaster on the face. There's only one survivor. We must fetch him in. Have you any guides with you?"

Yes, there were guides down there—Hans Schlunegger, with Christian and Adolf Rubi, all from Wengen. Yes, they could come up, of their own accord, even in face of instructions. It was a case of humanity triumphing over the regulations.

For Bohren, the chief guide of Grindelwald, in his concern for the guides under him, had issued a communication to the Guides' Commission in Bern, and to the Central Committee of the Swiss Alpine Club, which had also been repeated in the *Grindelwald Echo*.

> One cannot help regarding the contemplated climbing attempts on the North Face of the Eiger with serious misgivings. They are a plain indication of the great change which has taken place in the conception of the sport of mountaineering. We must accept that the visitors who take part in such attempts are aware of the dangers they are themselves risking; but no one can expect the dispatch of guides, in unfavorable conditions, on a rescue operation, in case of any further accidents on the Eiger's North Face. . . . We should find it impossible to force our guides to take a compulsory part in the kind of acrobatics which others are undertaking voluntarily.

That was the chief guide's stated position. Nobody could have held it against the guides at Eigergletscher Station if they had refused to take a single step onto the face when they heard of the accident. But there was one man still alive. They were all determined to rescue him, to snatch him, if possible, from the clutches of that fatal wall.

The railway provided a train, which immediately took them to the gallery window at Kilometer 3.8; through it they stepped onto the face, glistening under its coat of ice. Clouds of snow dust blew into their faces as they quietly traversed diagonally upward on the slippery, treacherous ledges, till they reached a point about 300 feet below where Toni Kurz was hanging from the rope in a sling.

There was mixed despair and relief in his voice — still astonishingly strong — as he heard his rescuers and answered them.

"I'm the only one alive. Hinterstoisser came off and fell the whole way down. The rope pulled Rainer up against a snap link. He froze to death there. And Angerer's dead, too, hanging below me, strangled by the rope when he fell. . . ."

"All right, pal. We've come to help you!"

"I know," shouted Toni. "But you've got to come from above, to the right, up through the crack where we left some pitons on the way up. Then you could reach me by three descents on the doubled rope."

"That's impossible, pal. Nobody could climb it with this ice about."

"You can't rescue me from below," Kurz shouted back.

Day was drawing to its close. The guides would have to hurry if they were to get back safely to the gallery window before dark. They shouted up the wall, "Can you stick it for one more night, pal?"

"No! No! No!"

The words cut the guides to the quick. They were never to forget them. But any aid was out of the question in the dark, on this face, in this weather.

"Stick it, pal!" they shouted. "We'll be back first thing in the morning!"

They could hear Toni's shouts for a long time, as they climbed down.

The young Berchtesgaden guide must have despaired of seeing the night through. But life had a strong hold on him; in spite of the gale, the volleys of stone, the fearsome cold, he survived the night, swinging backward and forward in his rope sling. It was so cold that the water thawed by the warmth of his body froze again immediately. Icicles eight inches long formed on the points of the crampons strapped to his boots. Toni lost the mitten from his left hand; his fingers, his hand, then his arm, froze into shapeless immovable lumps. But when dawn came, life was still awake in his agonized body. His voice, too, was strong and clear, when the guides got in touch with him again.

Arnold Glatthard had by now joined Schlunegger and the Rubi brothers. The four guides together were ready to fight this merciless wall for the life of their young colleague from Bavaria. The rocks were covered with an appalling glaze of ice. It seemed almost impossible to climb at all. And there was Toni pleading again: "You can only rescue me from above. You must climb the crack. . . ."

It was impossible. Even Kurz and Hinterstoisser in their full and unimpaired strength could not have climbed the crack in such conditions. It was a pitch which even in fine weather would have seriously tested these four men, first-class guides, brought up in a great tradition, master climbers all, but little versed in the technique of modern, artificial climbing. It would have called for just that kind of "acrobatics" against which Chief Guide Bohren had taken such a strong stand.

However, the four guides succeeded in reaching a point only about 130 feet below where Toni Kurz was hanging on the rope. So far did the overhang beetle out over the abyss that they could no longer see him from there. If Kurz had another rope on which to rope himself down, he would be saved. But how to get one to him? Attempts with rockets failed. The rope went shooting past Kurz, far out from the face. There was only one thing left.

"Can you let a line down," they asked him, "so that we can attach a rope, rock pitons, and anything else you need?"

"I have no line," came the reply.

"Climb down as far as you can, then, and cut away Angerer's body. Then climb up again and cut the rope above you. Then untwist the strands of the piece of rope you have gained, join them, and let the resulting line down."

The answer was a groan: "I'll try."

A little while later they heard the strokes of an ax. It seemed incredible that Kurz could hold on with one frozen hand and swing the ax with the other. Yet he managed to cut the rope away; only, Angerer's body didn't fall, for it was frozen solid to the rock. Almost in a trance, answering the last dictates of the will to live, Kurz climbed up again, cut away the rope there. The maneuver had won him twenty-five feet of rope, frozen stiff. And then began the unbelievable work of untwisting the strands. Every climber knows how difficult that is, even on firm ground, with two sound hands. But Toni Kurz was suspended between heaven and earth, on an ice-glazed cliff, threatened by falling stones, sometimes swept by snow slides. He worked with one hand and his teeth . . . for five hours. . . .

A great avalanche fell, narrowly missing the guides. A huge block whizzed close by Schlunegger's head. And then a body came hurtling past. Toni's? No, it wasn't Toni's, but Angerer's, freed from the imprisoning ice. Those were hours of agony for Toni, fighting for his life, agonizing too for the guides, who could do nothing to help, and could only wait for the moment when Kurz might still achieve the incredible.

Presently the fabricated line came swinging down to the rescue party. They fastened a rope to it, with pitons, snap links, a hammer. Slowly those objects disappeared from the view of the guides. Toni Kurz's strength was ebbing fast; he could hardly draw up the line, but somehow he managed it. Even now the rope wasn't long enough. The guides attached a second to it. The knot where the two ropes were spliced swung visible but unreachable out there under the great overhang.

Another hour passed. Then, at last, Toni Kurz was able to start roping down, sitting in a sling attached to the rope by a snap link. Inch by inch he worked his way downward. Thirty, forty, fifty feet down ... a hundred feet, a hundred and twenty. Now his legs could be seen dangling below the overhang.

At that moment the junction knot jammed in the snap link of the sling in which Toni was sitting as he roped down. The knot was too thick and Toni could not force it through the link. They could hear him groaning.

"Try, lad, try!" the frustrated rescuers cried to encourage the exhausted man. Toni, mumbling to himself, made one more effort with all his remaining strength, but he had little left; his incredible efforts had used it almost all up. His will to live had been keyed to the extreme so long as he was active; now the downward journey in the safety of the rope sling had eased the tension. He was nearing his rescuers now; now the battle was nearly over, now there were others close at hand to help....

And now this knot ... just a single knot ... but it won't go through.... "Just one more try, pal. It'll go!"

There was a note of desperation in the guides' appeal. One last revolt against fate; one last call on the last reserves of strength against this last and only obstacle. Toni bent forward, trying to use his teeth just once more. His frozen left arm with its useless hand stuck out stiff and helpless from his body. His last reserves were gone.

Toni mumbled unintelligibly, his handsome young face dyed purple with frostbite and exhaustion, his lips just moving. Was he still trying to say something, or had his spirit already passed over to the beyond?

Then he spoke again, quite clearly. "I'm finished," he said.

His body tipped forward. The sling, almost within reaching distance of the rescuing guides, hung swinging gently far out over the gulf. The man sitting in it was dead.

This piece describes the near-fatal descent from one of the great climbs in history—the first of an 8,000-meter mountain—by four of the heroic names of the sport, Louis Lachenal ("Biscante"), Lionel Terray, Gaston Rébuffat, and Maurice Herzog. Annapurna was attained by the French expedition in 1950; within five years Everest, K2, and Kanchenjunga were climbed as well. When a Chinese team scaled Gosainthan in 1964, the last of the world's ten tallest mountains, all in the Himalayas, had fallen.

# MAURICE HERZOG

# Back from Annapurna

"We've made it. We're back from Annapurna!"

Rébuffat and Terray received the news with great excitement.

"But what about Biscante?" asked Terray anxiously.

"He won't be long. He was just in front of me! What a day—started out at six this morning—didn't stop . . . got up at last."

Words failed me. I had so much to say. The sight of familiar faces dispelled the strange feeling that I had experienced since morning, and I became, once more, just a mountaineer.

Terray, who was speechless with delight, wrung my hands. Then the smile vanished from his face: "Maurice—your hands!" There was an uneasy silence. I had forgotten that I had lost my gloves: my fingers were violet and white and hard as wood. The other two stared at them in dismay—they realized the full seriousness of the injury. But, still blissfully floating on a sea of joy remote from reality, I leaned over toward Terray and said confidentially, "You're in such splendid form, and you've done so marvelously, it's absolutely tragic you didn't come up there with us!"

"What I did was for the expedition, my dear Maurice, and anyway you've got up, and that's a victory for the whole lot of us."

I nearly burst with happiness. How could I tell him all that his answer meant to me?

The rapture I had felt on the summit, which might have seemed a purely personal, egotistical emotion, had been transformed by his words into a complete and perfect joy with no shadow upon it. His answer proved that this victory was not just one man's achievement, a matter for personal pride; no — and Terray was the first to understand this — it was a victory for us all, a victory for mankind itself.

"Hi! Help! Help!"

"Biscante!" exclaimed the others.

Still half-intoxicated and remote from reality, I had heard nothing. Terray felt a chill at his heart, and his thoughts flew to his partner on so many unforgettable climbs; together they had so often skirted death, and won so many splendid victories. Putting his head out, and seeing Lachenal clinging to the slope a hundred yards lower down, he dressed in frantic haste.

Out he went. But the slope was bare now; Lachenal had disappeared. Terray was horribly frightened, and he could only utter unintelligible cries. It was a ghastly moment for him. A violent wind sent the mist tearing by. Under the stress of emotion Terray had not realized how it falsified distances.

"Biscante! Biscante!"

He had spotted him, through a rift in the mist, lying on the slope much lower down than he had thought. Terray set his teeth, and glissaded down like a madman. How would he be able to brake without crampons, on the wind-hardened snow? But Terray was a first-class skier, and with a jump turn he stopped beside Lachenal, who was suffering from concussion after his tremendous fall. In a state of collapse, with no ice ax, balaclava, or gloves, and only one crampon, he gazed vacantly around him.

"My feet are frostbitten. Take me down . . . take me down so that Oudot can see to me."

"It can't be done," said Terray sorrowfully. "Can't you see we're in the middle of a storm? . . . It'll be dark soon."

But Lachenal was obsessed by the fear of amputation. With a gesture of despair he tore the ax out of Terray's hands and tried to force his way down; but soon saw the futility of his action and resolved to climb up to the camp. While Terray cut steps without stopping. Lachenal, ravaged and exhausted as he was, dragged himself along on all fours.

Meanwhile I had gone into Rébuffat's tent. He was appalled at the sight of my hands and, as rather incoherently I told him what we had done, he took a piece of rope and began flicking my fingers. Then he took off my boots with great difficulty, for my feet were swollen, and beat my feet and rubbed me. We soon heard Terray giving Lachenal the same treatment in the other tent.

For our comrades it was a tragic moment: Annapurna was conquered, and the first eight-thousander had been climbed. Every one of us had been ready to sacrifice everything for this. Yet, as they looked at our feet and hands, what can Terray and Rébuffat have felt?

Outside, the storm howled and the snow was still falling. The mist grew thick and darkness came. As on the previous night, we had to cling to the poles to prevent the tents being carried away by the wind. The only two air mattresses were given to Lachenal and myself, while Terray and Rébuffat both sat on ropes, rucksacks, and provisions to keep themselves off the snow. They rubbed, slapped, and beat us with a rope. Sometimes the blows fell on the living flesh, and howls arose from both tents. Rébuffat persevered; it was essential to continue, painful as it was. Gradually life returned to my feet as well as to my hands, and circulation started again. Lachenal, too, found that feeling was returning.

Now Terray summoned up the energy to prepare some hot drinks. He called to Rébuffat that he would pass him a mug, so two hands stretched out toward each other between the two tents and were instantly covered with snow. The liquid was boiling though scarcely more than 60° centigrade (140° Fahrenheit). I swallowed it greedily and felt infinitely better.

The night was absolute hell. Frightful onslaughts of wind battered us incessantly, while the never-ceasing snow piled up on the tents. . . .

"Rébuffat! Gaston! Gaston!"

I recognized Terray's voice.

"Time to be off!"

I heard the sounds without grasping their meaning. Was it light already? I was not in the least surprised that the other two had give up all thought of going to the top, and I did not at all grasp the measure of their sacrifice.

Outside, the storm redoubled in violence. The tent shook and the fabric flapped alarmingly. It had usually been fine in the mornings. Did this mean the monsoon was upon us? We knew it was not far off—could this be its first onslaught?

"Gaston! Are you ready?" Terray called again.

"One minute," answered Rébuffat. He did not have an easy job: he had to put my boots on and do everything to get me ready. I let myself be handled like a baby. In the other tent Terray finished dressing Lachenal, whose feet were still swollen and would not fit into his boots. So Terray gave him his own, which were bigger. To get Lachenal's onto his own feet, he had to make slits in them. As a precaution he put a sleeping bag and some food into his sack and shouted to us to do the same. Were his words lost in the storm? Or were we too intent on leaving this hellish place to listen to his instructions?

Lachenal and Terray were already outside.

"We're going down!" they shouted.

Then Rébuffat tied me on the rope and we went out. There were only two ice axes for the four of us, so Rébuffat and Terray took them as a matter of course. For a moment as we left the two tents of Camp V, I felt childishly ashamed at leaving all this good equipment behind.

Already the first rope seemed a long way down below us. We were blinded by the squalls of snow and we could not hear each other a yard away. We had both put on our *cagoules,* for it was very cold. The snow was apt to slide, and the rope often came in useful.

Ahead of us the other two were losing no time. Lachenal went first and, safeguarded by Terray, he forced the pace in his anxiety to get down. There were no tracks to show us the way, but it was engraved on all our minds—straight down the slope for 400 yards, then traverse to the left for 150 to 200 yards to get to Camp IV....

Our situation was not desperate, we were certainly not lost. We would have to go lower down; the traverse must begin farther on—I remembered the serac which served as a milestone. The snow stuck to our *cagoules,* and turned us into white phantoms noiselessly flitting against a background equally white. We began to sink in dreadfully, and there is nothing worse for bodies already on the edge of exhaustion.

Were we too high or too low? No one could tell. Perhaps we had better try slanting over to the left! The snow was in a dangerous condition, but we did not seem to realize it. We were forced to admit that we were not on the right route, so we retraced our steps and climbed up above the serac which overhung us. No doubt, we decided, we should be on the right level now. With Rébuffat leading, we went back over the way which had cost us such an effort. I followed him jerkily, saying nothing, and determined to go on to the end. If Rébuffat had fallen I could never have held him.

We went doggedly on from one serac to another. Each time we thought we had recognized the right route, and each time there was a fresh disappointment. If only the mist would lift, if only the snow would stop for a second! On the slope it seemed to be growing deeper every minute. Only Terray and Rébuffat were capable of breaking the trail, and they relieved each other at regular intervals, without a word and without a second's hesitation.

I admired this determination of Rébuffat's for which he is so justly famed. He did not intend to die! With the strength of desperation and at the price of superhuman effort he forged ahead. The slowness of his progress would have dismayed even the most obstinate climber, but he would not give up, and in the end the mountain yielded in face of his perseverance.

Terray, when his turn came, charged madly ahead. He was like a force of nature: at all costs he would break down these prison walls that penned us in. His physical strength was exceptional, his willpower no less remarkable. Lachenal gave him considerable trouble. Perhaps he was not quite in his right mind. He said it was no use going on; we must dig a hole in the snow and wait for fine weather. He swore at Terray and called him a madman. Nobody but Terray would have been capable of dealing with him—he just tugged sharply on the rope and Lachenal was forced to follow.

We were well and truly lost....

Camp IV was certainly on the left, on the edge of the Sickle. On that point we were all agreed. But it was very hard to find. The wall of ice that gave it such magnificent protection was now ironical, for it hid the tents from us. In mist like this we should have been right on top of them before we spotted them.

MAURICE
# HERZOG

RAISED THE FRENCH TRICOLOR IN VICTORY IN 1950 AS HE STOOD ATOP ANNAPURNA, THE FIRST 8,000 METER PEAK TO BE CONQUERED.

BUT HE AND FELLOW CLIMBER LOUIS LACHENAL NEARLY LOST THEIR LIVES WHEN THEY MET SEVERE STORMS ON THE DESCENT.

AFTERWARD, HERZOG WAS FORCED TO DICTATE HIS BEST-SELLING ACCOUNT OF THE ORDEAL —FROSTBITE HAD COST HIM HIS FINGERS.

Perhaps if we called, someone would hear us? Lachenal gave the signal, but snow absorbs sound and his shout seemed to carry only a few yards. All four of us called out together: "One . . . two . . . three . . . help!"

We got the impression that our united shout carried a long way, so we began again: "One . . . two . . . three . . . help!" Not a sound in reply!

Now and again Terray took off his boots and rubbed his feet; the sight of our frost-bitten limbs had made him aware of the danger and he had the strength of mind to do something about it. Like Lachenal, he was haunted by the idea of amputation. For me, it was too late: my feet and hands, already affected from yesterday, were beginning to freeze up again. . . .

Night had suddenly fallen and it was essential to come to a decision without wasting another minute; if we remained on the slope, we should be dead before morning. We would have to bivouac. What the conditions would be like, we could guess, for we all knew what it meant to bivouac above 23,000 feet.

With his ax Terray began to dig a hole. Lachenal went over to a snow-filled crevasse a few yards farther on, then suddenly let out a yell and disappeared before our eyes. We stood helpless: Would we, or rather would Terray and Rébuffat, have enough strength for all the maneuvers with the rope that would be needed to get him out? The crevasse was completely blocked up save for the one little hole which Lachenal had fallen through.

"Lachenal!" called Terray.

A voice, muffled by many thicknesses of ice and snow, came up to us. It was impossible to make out what it was saying.

"Lachenal!"

"I'm here!"

"Anything broken?"

"No! It'll do for the night! Come along."

This shelter was heaven-sent. None of us would have had the strength to dig a hole big enough to protect the lot of us from the wind. Without hesitation Terray let himself drop into the crevasse, and a loud "Come on!" told us he had arrived safely. In my turn I let myself go: it was a regular toboggan slide. I shot down a sort of twisting tunnel, very steep, and about thirty feet long. I came out at great speed into the opening beyond and was literally hurled to the bottom of the crevasse. We let Rébuffat know he could come by giving a tug on the rope.

The intense cold of this minute grotto shriveled us up, the enclosing walls of ice were damp and the floor a carpet of fresh snow; by huddling together there was just room for the four of us. Icicles hung from the ceiling and we broke some of them off to make more headroom and kept little bits to suck — it was a long time since we had had anything to drink.

That was our shelter for the night. At least we should be protected from the wind, and the temperature would remain fairly even, though the damp was extremely unpleasant. We settled ourselves in the dark as best we could. As always in a bivouac, we took off our boots; without this precaution the constriction would cause immediate frostbite. Terray unrolled the sleeping bag which he had had the foresight to bring, and settled himself in relative comfort. We put on everything warm that we had, and to avoid contact with the snow I sat on the movie camera. We huddled close up to each other, in our search for a hypothetical position in which the warmth of our bodies could be combined without loss, but we couldn't keep still for a second. . . .

Terray generously tried to give me part of his sleeping bag. He had understood the seriousness of my condition, and knew why it was that I said nothing and remained quite passive; he realized that I had abandoned all hope for myself. He massaged me for nearly two hours; his feet, too, might have frozen, but he didn't appear to give the matter a thought. I found new courage simply in contemplating his unselfishness; he was doing so much to help me that it would have been ungrateful of me not to go on struggling to live. Though my heart was like a lump of ice itself, I was astonished to feel no pain. Everything material about me seemed to have dropped away. I seemed to be quite clear in my thoughts and yet I floated in a kind of peaceful happiness. There was still a breath of life in me, but it dwindled steadily as the hours went by. Terray's massage no longer had any effect upon me. It was all over, I thought. Wasn't this cavern the most beautiful grave I could hope for? Death caused me no grief, no regret—I smiled at the thought.

After hours of torpor a voice mumbled, "Daylight!"

This made some impression on the others. I only felt surprised—I had not thought that daylight would penetrate so far down.

"Too early to start," said Rébuffat.

A ghastly light spread through our grotto and we could just vaguely make out the shapes of each other's heads. A queer noise from a long way off came down to us—a sort of prolonged hiss. The noise increased. Suddenly I was buried, blinded, smothered beneath an avalanche of new snow. The icy snow spread over the cavern, finding its way through every gap in our clothing. I ducked my head between my knees and covered myself with both arms. The snow flowed on and on. There was a terrible silence. We were not completely buried, but there was snow everywhere. We got up, taking care not to bang our heads against the ceiling of ice, and tried to shake ourselves. We were all in our stockinged feet in the snow. The first thing to do was to find our boots.

Rébuffat and Terray began to search, and realized at once that they were blind. Yesterday they had taken off their glasses to lead us down and now they were paying for it. Lachenal was the first to lay hands upon a pair of boots. He tried to put them on, but they were Rébuffat's. Rébuffat attempted to climb up the chute down which we had come yesterday and which the avalanche had followed in its turn.

"Hi, Gaston! What's the weather like?" called up Terray.

"Can't see a thing. It's blowing hard."

We were still groping for our things. Terray found his boots and put them on awkwardly, unable to see what he was doing. . . .

At the bottom of the crevasse there were still two of us looking for our boots. Lachenal poked fiercely with an ice ax. I was calmer and tried to proceed more rationally. We extracted crampons and an ax in turn from the snow, but still no boots.

Well—so this cavern was to be our last resting place! There was very little room—we were bent double and got in each other's way. Lachenal decided to go out without his boots. He called frantically, hauled himself up on the rope, trying to get a hold or to wiggle his way up, digging his toes into the snow walls. Terray from outside pulled as hard as he could. I watched him go; he gathered speed and disappeared.

When he emerged from the opening he saw the sky was clear and blue, and he began to run like a madman, shrieking, "It's fine, it's fine!"

I set to work again to search the cave. The boots *had* to be found, or Lachenal and I were done for. On all fours, with nothing on my hands or feet, I raked the snow, stirring it around this way and that, hoping every second to come upon something hard. I was no longer capable of thinking—I reacted like an animal fighting for its life.

I found one boot! The other was tied to it—a pair! Having ransacked the whole cave, I at last found the other pair. But in spite of all my efforts I could not find the movie camera, and gave up in despair. There was no question of putting my boots on—my hands were like lumps of wood and I could hold nothing in my fingers; my feet were very swollen—I should never be able to get boots on them. I twisted the rope around the boots as well as I could and called up the chute, "Lionel . . . boots!"

There was no answer, but he must have heard, for with a jerk the precious boots shot up. Soon after, the rope came down again. My turn. . . . I pulled myself out by clutching Terray's legs; he was just about all in and I was in the last stages of exhaustion. Terray was close to me and I whispered, "Lionel . . . I'm dying!"

He supported me and helped me away from the crevasse. Lachenal and Rébuffat were sitting in the snow a few yards away. The instant Lionel let go of me I sank down and dragged myself along on all fours.

The weather was perfect. Quantities of snow had fallen the day before and the mountains were resplendent. Never had I seen them look so beautiful—our last day would be magnificent. . . .

I knew the end was near, but it was the end that all mountaineers wish for—an end in keeping with their ruling passion. I was consciously grateful to the mountains for being so beautiful for me that day, and as awed by their silence as if I had been in church. I was in no pain, and had no worry. My utter calmness was alarming. Terray came staggering toward me, and I told him, "It's all over for me. Go on . . . you have a chance . . . you must take it . . . over to the left . . . that's the way."

I felt better after telling him that. But Terray would have none of it: "We'll help you. If we get away, so will you."

At this moment Lachenal shouted, "Help! Help!"

Obviously he didn't know what he was doing . . . or did he? He was the only one of the four of us who could see Camp II down below. Perhaps his calls would be heard. They were shrieks of despair, reminding me tragically of some climbers lost in the

Mont Blanc massif whom I had endeavored to save. Now it was our turn. The impression was vivid: we were lost.

I joined in with the others: "One . . . two . . . three . . . *help!* One . . . two . . . three . . . *help!*" We tried to shout together, but without much success; our voices could not have carried more than ten feet. The noise I made was more of a whisper than a shout. Terray insisted that I should put my boots on, but my hands were dead. Neither Rébuffat nor Terray, who were unable to see, could help much, so I said to Lachenal, "Come and help me to put my boots on."

"Don't be silly, we must go down!"

And off he went once again in the wrong direction, straight down. I was not in the least angry with him; he had been sorely tried by the altitude and by everything he had gone through.

Terray resolutely got out his knife, and with fumbling hands slit the uppers of my boots back and front. Split in two like this, I could get them on, but it was not easy and I had to make several attempts. Soon I lost heart—what was the use of it all, anyway, since I was going to stay where I was? But Terray pulled violently and finally he succeeded. He laced up my now gigantic boots, missing half the hooks. I was ready now. But how was I going to walk with my stiff joints?

"To the left, Lionel!"

"You're crazy, Maurice," said Lachenal, "it's to the right, straight down."

Terray did not know what to think of these conflicting views. He had not given up like me, he was going to fight; but what, at the moment, could he do? The three of them discussed which way to go.

I remained sitting in the snow. Gradually my mind lost grip—why should I struggle? I would just let myself drift. I saw pictures of shady slopes, peaceful paths, there was a scent of resin. It was pleasant—I was going to die in my own mountains. My body had no feeling—everything was frozen.

"Aah . . . aah!"

Was it a groan or a call? I gathered my strength for one cry: "They're coming!" The others heard me and shouted for joy. What a miraculous apparition! "Schatz . . . it's Schatz!"

Barely two hundred yards away Marcel Schatz, waist-deep in snow, was coming slowly toward us like a boat on the surface of the slope. I found this vision of a strong and invincible deliverer inexpressibly moving. I expected everything of him. The shock was violent, and quite shattered me. Death clutched at me and I gave myself up.

When I came to again, the wish to live returned and I experienced a violent revulsion of feeling. All was not lost! As Schatz came nearer, my eyes never left him for a second—twenty yards—ten yards—he came straight toward me. Why? Without a word he leaned over me, held me close, hugged me and his warm breath revived me.

I could not make the slightest movement—I was like marble. My heart was overwhelmed by such tremendous feelings and yet my eyes remained dry.

"It is wonderful—what you have done!"

The 1953 expedition that resulted in Hillary and Tenzing Norkay's reaching the top of the world had been two years in the making and represented a triumph for everyone involved, from leader John Hunt on down. No climb, with the possible exception of Edward Whymper's ascent of the Matterhorn in 1865, has been more copiously described in print, with generally lackluster effect. The major exception to the rule is Hillary's *High Adventure*, published in 1955. The passage below commences at Camp IX, where Hillary and Tenzing part company with their support party of George Lowe, Alf Gregory, and Sherpa porter Ang Nyima.

# EDMUND HILLARY

# The Final Assault

I watched our support party disappear down the ridge and then turned to examine our campsite more closely. It wasn't really much of a place. Above us was a rock cliff— black and craggy, but at least devoid of loose stones to fall on us. From the foot of the cliff a little snow slope ran at an easy angle for eight or nine feet to the top of the steep and exposed South Face of the mountain. This little slope was to be our campsite. It was certainly far from flat and it was going to need a lot of work on it before we could possibly pitch a tent. We carefully moved all the gear to one side and then set to work with our ice axes to remove the surface snow off a reasonably large area. Ten inches down, we struck rock, and after half an hour's hard work we had cleared an area about eight feet long and six feet wide. The slope underneath was made up of stones and rubble all firmly glued together with ice. This was much harder going. With the picks on our ice axes we chopped away at the slope, prizing out the separate stones and scraping away the rubble. But our progress was very slow. We weren't using any oxygen at all, but we found we could work very hard indeed for periods of ten minutes or so. Then we'd have to stop and have a short rest. With the debris we chopped out of the slope we tried to build up the platform on the downhill side, but almost invariably saw it collapse and go roaring down over the bluffs below. At times we were buffeted by wind and snow, yet we worked doggedly on, knowing that our tent was our only chance of survival against the rigors of the night.

At 6:30 A.M. we crawled slowly out of the tent and stood on our little ledge. Already the upper part of the mountain was bathed in sunlight. It looked warm and inviting, but our ledge was dark and cold. We lifted our oxygen onto our backs and slowly connected up the tubes to our face masks. My thirty-pound load seem to crush me downward and stifled all enthusiasm, but when I turned on the oxygen and breathed it deeply, the burden seemed to lighten and the old urge to get to grips with the mountain came back. We strapped on our crampons and tied on our nylon rope, grasped our ice axes, and were ready to go.

I looked at the way ahead. From our tent very steep slopes covered with deep powder snow led up to a prominent snow shoulder on the southeast ridge about a hundred feet above our heads. The slopes were in the shade and breaking trail was going to be cold work. Still a little worried about my boots, I asked Tenzing to lead off. Always willing to do his share, and more than his share if necessary, Tenzing scrambled past me and tackled the slope. With powerful thrusts of his legs he forced his way up in knee-deep snow. I gathered in the rope and followed along behind him.

We were climbing out over the tremendous South Face of the mountain and below us snow chutes and rock ribs plummeted thousands of feet down to the Western Cwm. Starting in the morning straight on to exposed climbing is always trying on the nerves and this was no exception. In imagination I could feel my heavy load dragging me backward down the great slopes below; I seemed clumsy and unstable and my breath was hurried and uneven. But Tenzing was pursuing an irresistible course up the slope and I didn't have time to think too much. My muscles soon warmed up to their work, my nerves relaxed, and I dropped into the old climbing rhythm and followed steadily up his tracks. As we gained a little height we moved into the rays of the sun, and although we could feel no appreciable warmth, we were greatly encouraged by its presence. Taking no rests, Tenzing plowed his way up through the deep snow and led out onto the snow shoulder. We were now at a height of 28,000 feet. Towering directly above our heads was the South Summit — steep and formidable. And to the right were the enormous cornices of the summit ridge. We still had a long way to go.

Ahead of us the ridge was sharp and narrow but rose at an easy angle. I felt warm and strong now, so took over the lead. First I investigated the ridge with my ice ax. On the sharp crest of the ridge and on the right-hand side loose powder snow was lying dangerously over hard ice. Any attempt to climb on this would only produce an unpleasant slide down toward the Kangshung Glacier. But the left-hand slope was better — it was still rather steep, but it had a firm surface of wind-blown powder snow into which our crampons would bite readily.

Taking every care, I moved along onto the left-hand side of the ridge. Everything seemed perfectly safe. With increased confidence I took another step. Next moment I was almost thrown off balance as the wind crust suddenly gave way and I sank through it up to my knee. It took me a little while to regain my breath. Then I gradually pulled my leg out of the hole. I was almost upright again when the wind crust under the other foot gave way and I sank back with both legs enveloped in soft loose snow to the knees.

It was the mountaineer's curse — breakable crust. I forced my way along. Sometimes for a few careful steps I was on the surface, but usually the crust would break at the critical moment and I'd be up to my knees again. Though it was tiring and exasperating work, I felt I had plenty of strength in reserve. For half an hour I continued on in this uncomfortable fashion, with the violent balancing movements I was having to make completely destroying rhythm and breath. It was a great relief when the snow condition improved and I was able to stay on the surface. I still kept down on the steep slopes on the left of the ridge, but plunged ahead and climbed steadily upward. I came over a small crest and saw in front of me a tiny hollow on the ridge. And in this hollow lay two oxygen bottles almost completely covered with snow. It was Evans and Bourdillon's dump.

I rushed forward into the hollow and knelt beside them. Wrenching one of the bottles out of its frozen bed, I wiped the snow off its dial — it showed a thousand pounds pressure — it was nearly a third full of oxygen. I checked the other — it was the same. This was great news. It meant that the oxygen we were carrying on our backs only had to get us back to these bottles instead of right down to the South Col. It gave us more than another hour of endurance. I explained this to Tenzing through my oxygen mask. I don't think he understood, but he realized I was pleased about something and nodded enthusiastically.

I led off again. I knew there was plenty of hard work ahead and Tenzing could save his energies for that. The ridge climbed on upward rather more steeply now and then broadened out and shot up at a sharp angle to the foot of the enormous slope running up to the South Summit. I crossed over onto the right-hand side of the ridge and found the snow was firm there. I started chipping a long line of steps up to the foot of the great slope. Here we stamped out a platform for ourselves and I checked our oxygen. Everything seemed to be going well. I had a little more oxygen left than Tenzing, which meant I was obtaining a slightly lower flow rate from my set, but it wasn't enough to matter and there was nothing I could do about it anyway.

Ahead of us was a really formidable problem and I stood in my steps and looked at it. Rising from our feet was an enormous slope slanting steeply down onto the precipitous East Face of Everest and climbing up with appalling steepness to the South Summit of the mountain 400 feet above us. The left-hand side of the slope was a most unsavory mixture of steep loose rock and snow, which my New Zealand training immediately regarded with grave suspicion, but which in actual fact the rock-climbing Britons, Evans and Bourdillon, had ascended in much trepidation when on the first assault. The only other route was up the snow itself, and still fairly discernible here and there were traces of the track made by the first assault party, who had come down it in preference to their line of ascent up the rocks. The snow route it was for us! There looked to be some tough work ahead, and as Tenzing had been taking it easy for a while I hardheartedly waved him through. With his first six steps I realized that the work was going to be much harder than I had thought. His first two steps were on top of the snow, the third was up to his ankles, and by the sixth he was up to his hips. But almost lying against the steep slope, he drove himself onward, plowing a track directly upward. Even following in his steps was hard work, for the loose snow refused to pack into safe steps. After a long and valiant spell he was plainly in need of a rest, so I took over.

Immediately I realized that we were on dangerous ground. On this very steep slope the snow was soft and deep with little coherence. My ice ax shaft sank into it without any support and we had no form of a belay. The only factor that made it at all possible to progress was a thin crust of frozen snow which tied the whole slope together. But this crust was a poor support. I was forcing my way upward, plunging deep steps through it, when suddenly with a dull breaking noise an area of crust all around me about six feet in diameter broke off into large sections and slid with me back through three or four steps. And then I stopped; but the crust, gathering speed, slithered on out of sight. It was a nasty shock. My whole training told me that the slope was exceedingly dangerous, but at the same time I was saying to myself, "Ed, my boy, this is Everest — you've got to push it a bit harder!" My solar plexus was tight with fear as I plowed on. Halfway up I stopped, exhausted. I could look down 10,000 feet between my legs and I have never felt more insecure. Anxiously I waved Tenzing up to me.

"What do you think of it, Tenzing?" And the immediate response: "Very bad, very dangerous!" "Do you think we should go on?" and there came the familiar reply that never helped you much but never let you down: "Just as you wish!" I waved him on to take a turn at leading. Changing the lead much more frequently now, we made our unhappy way upward, sometimes sliding back and wiping out half a dozen steps and never feeling confident that at any moment the whole slope might not avalanche. In the hope of some sort of a belay we traversed a little toward the rocks but found no help in their smooth holdless surface. We plunged on upward. And then I noticed that, a little above us, the left-hand rock ridge turned into snow and the snow looked firm and safe. Laboriously and carefully we climbed across some steep rock and I sank my ice ax shaft into the snow of the ridge. It went firm and hard. The pleasure of this safe belay after all the uncertainty below was like a reprieve to a condemned man. Strength flowed into my limbs and I could feel my tense nerves and muscles relaxing. I swung my ice ax at the slope and started chipping a line of steps upward — it was very steep but seemed so gloriously safe. Tenzing, an inexpert but enthusiastic step cutter, took a turn and chopped a haphazard line of steps up another pitch. We were making fast time now and the slope was starting to ease off. Tenzing gallantly waved me through and with a growing feeling of excitement I cramponed up some firm slopes to the rounded top of the South Summit. It was only 9 A.M.

With intense interest I looked at the vital ridge leading to the summit — the ridge about which Evans and Bourdillon had made such gloomy forecasts. At first glance it was an exceedingly impressive and indeed a frightening sight. In the narrow crest of this ridge, the basic rock of the mountain had a thin capping of snow and ice — ice that reached out over the East Face in enormous cornices, overhanging and treacherous, and only waiting for the careless foot of the mountaineer to break off and crash 10,000 feet to the Kangshung Glacier. And from the cornices the snow dropped steeply to the left to merge with the enormous rock bluffs which towered 8,000 feet above the Western Cwm. It was impressive all right! But as I looked, my fears started to lift a little. Surely I could see a route there? For this snow slope on the left, although very steep and exposed, was practically continuous for the first half of the ridge, although in places the great cornices reached hungrily across. If we could make a route along that snow slope we could go quite a distance at least.

With a feeling almost of relief I set to work with my ice ax and cut a platform for myself just down off the top of the South Summit. Tenzing did the same, and then we removed our oxygen sets and sat down. The day was still remarkably fine and we felt no discomfort through our thick layers of clothing from either wind or cold. We had a drink out of Tenzing's water bottle and then I checked our oxygen supplies. Tenzing's bottle was practically exhausted, but mine still had a little in it. As well as this we each had a full bottle. I decided that the difficulties ahead would demand as light a weight on our backs as possible, so determined to use only the full bottles. I removed Tenzing's empty bottle and my nearly empty one and laid them in the snow. With particular care I connected up our last bottles and tested to see that they were working efficiently. The needles on the dials were steady on 3,300 pounds per square inch pressure — they were very full bottles, holding just over 800 liters of oxygen each. At 3 liters a minute we consumed 180 liters an hour, and this meant a total endurance of nearly 4½ hours. This didn't seem much for the problems ahead, but I was determined if necessary to cut down to 2 liters a minute for the homeward trip.

I was greatly encouraged to find how, even at 28,700 feet and with no oxygen, I could work out slowly but clearly the problems of mental arithmetic that the oxygen supply demanded. A correct answer was imperative — any mistake could well mean a trip with no return. But we had no time to waste. I stood up and took a series of photographs in every direction, then thrust my camera back to its warm home inside my clothing. I heaved my now pleasantly light oxygen load onto my back and connected up my tubes. I did the same for Tenzing and we were ready to go. I asked Tenzing to belay me and then with a growing air of excitement I cut a broad and safe line of steps down to the snow saddle below the South Summit. I wanted an easy route when we came back up here weak and tired. Tenzing came down the steps and joined me and then belayed once again.

I moved along onto the steep snow slope on the left side of the ridge. With the first blow of my ice ax my excitement increased. The snow — to my astonishment — was crystalline and hard. A couple of rhythmical blows of the ice ax produced a step that was big enough even for our oversize high-altitude boots. But best of all, the steps were strong and safe. A little conscious of the great drops beneath me, I chipped a line of steps for the full length of the rope — forty feet — and then forced the shaft of my ice ax firmly into the snow. It made a fine belay and I looped the rope around it. I waved to Tenzing to join me, and as he moved slowly and carefully along the steps I took in the rope as I went on cutting steps. It was exhilarating work—the summit ridge of Everest, the crisp snow, and the smooth, easy blows of the ice ax all combined to make me feel a greater sense of power than I had ever felt at great altitudes before. I went on cutting for rope length after rope length.

We were now approaching a point where one of the great cornices was encroaching onto our slope. We'd have to go down to the rocks to avoid it. I cut a line of steps steeply down the slope to a small ledge on top of the rocks. There wasn't much room, but it made a reasonably safe stance. I waved to Tenzing to join me. As he came down to me I realized there was something wrong with him. I had been so absorbed in the technical problems of the ridge that I hadn't thought much about Tenzing except for a vague feeling that he seemed to move along the steps with unnecessary slowness. But now it was quite obvious that he not only was moving extremely slowly but was breathing quickly and with difficulty and was in considerable distress. I immediately suspected his oxygen set and helped him down onto the ledge so that I could examine it. The first thing I noticed was that from the outlet of his face mask there were hanging some long icicles. I looked at it more closely and found that the outlet tube—about two inches in diameter—was almost completely blocked up with ice. This was preventing Tenzing from exhaling freely and must have made it extremely unpleasant for him. Fortunately the outlet tube was made of rubber, and by manipulating this with my hand I was able to release all of the ice and let it fall out. The valves started operating and Tenzing was given immediate relief. Just as a check I examined my own set and found that it, too, had partly frozen up in the outlet tube, but not sufficiently to have affected me a great deal. I removed the ice out of it without a great deal of trouble. Automatically I looked at our pressure gauges—just over 2,900 pounds (2,900 pounds was just over 700 liters; 180 into 700 was about 4)—we had nearly four hours' endurance left. That meant we weren't going badly.

I looked at the route ahead. This next piece wasn't going to be easy. Our rock ledge was perched right on top of the enormous bluff running down into the Western Cwm. In fact, almost under my feet, I could see the dirty patch on the floor of the cwm which I knew was Camp IV. In a sudden urge to escape our isolation I waved and shouted, then as suddenly stopped as I realized my foolishness. Against the vast expanse of Everest, 8,000 feet above them, we'd be quite invisible to the best binoculars. I turned back to the problem ahead. The rock was far too steep to attempt to drop down and go around this pitch. The only thing to do was to try and shuffle along the ledge and cut handholds in the bulging ice that was trying to push me off it. Held on a tight rope by Tenzing, I cut a few handholds and then thrust my ice ax as hard as I could into the solid snow and ice. Using this to take my weight, I moved quickly along the ledge. It proved easier than I had anticipated. A few more handholds, another quick swing across them, and I was able to cut a line of steps up onto a safe slope and chop out a roomy terrace from which to belay Tenzing as he climbed up to me.

We were now fast approaching the most formidable obstacle on the ridge—a great rock step. This step had always been visible in aerial photographs and in 1951 on the Everest Reconnaissance we had seen it quite clearly with glasses from Thyangboche. We had always thought of it as the obstacle on the ridge which could well spell defeat. I cut a line of steps across the last snow slope and then commenced traversing over a steep rock slab that led to the foot of the great step. The holds were small and hard to see and I brushed my snow glasses away from my eyes. Immediately I was blinded by a bitter wind sweeping across the ridge and laden with particles of ice. I hastily replaced my glasses and blinked away the ice and tears until I could see again. But it made me realize how efficient was our clothing in protecting us from the rigors of even a fine day at 29,000 feet. Still half-blinded, I climbed across the slab and then dropped down into a tiny snow hollow at the foot of the step. And here Tenzing slowly joined me.

I looked anxiously up at the rocks. Planted squarely across the ridge in a vertical bluff, they looked extremely difficult, and I knew that our strength and ability to climb steep rock at this altitude would be severely limited. I examined the route out to the left. By dropping fifty or a hundred feet over steep slabs, we might be able to get around the bottom of the bluff, but there was no indication that we'd be able to climb back onto the ridge again. And to lose any height now might be fatal. Search as I could, I was unable to see an easy route up to the step or in fact any route at all. Finally, in desperation, I examined the right-hand end of the bluff. Attached to this and over-hanging the precipitous East Face was a large cornice. This cornice, in preparation for its inevitable crash down the mountainside, had started to lose its grip on the rock and a long narrow vertical crack had been formed between the rock and the ice. The crack was large enough to take the human frame, and though it offered little security it was at least a route. I quickly made up my mind—Tenzing had an excellent belay and we must be near the top—it was worth a try.

Before attempting the pitch I produced my camera once again. I had no confidence that I would be able to climb this crack and with a surge of competitive pride which unfortunately afflicts even mountaineers I determined to have proof that at least we had reached a good deal higher than the South Summit. I took a few photographs and then made another rapid check of the oxygen—2,550 pounds pressure (2,550 from 3,300 leaves 750; 750 is about ¾; ¾ off 800 liters leaves about 600 liters; 600 divided by 180 is nearly 3½). Three and a half hours to go. I examined Tenzing's belay to make sure it was a good one and then slowly crawled inside the crack.

In front of me was the rock wall, vertical but with a few promising holds. Behind me was the ice wall of the cornice, glittering and hard but cracked and there. I took a hold on the rock in front and then jammed one of my crampons hard into the ice behind. Leaning back with my oxygen set on the ice, I slowly levered myself upward. Searching feverishly with my spare boot, I found a tiny ledge on the rock and took some of the weight off my other leg. Leaning back on the cornice, I fought to regain my breath. Constantly at the back of my mind was the fear that the cornice might break off, and my nerves were taut with suspense. But slowly I forced my way up—

wriggling and jamming and using every little hold. In one place I managed to force my ice ax into a crack in the ice, and this gave me the necessary purchase to get over a holdless stretch. And then I found a solid foothold in a hollow in the ice and next moment I was reaching over the top of the rock and pulling myself to safety. The rope came tight—its forty feet had been barely enough.

I lay on the little rock ledge panting furiously. Gradually it dawned on me that I was up the step and I felt a glow of pride and determination that completely subdued my temporary feeling of weakness. For the first time on the whole expedition I really knew I was going to get to the top. "It will have to be pretty tough to stop us now" was my thought. But I couldn't entirely ignore the feeling of astonishment and wonder that I'd been able to get up such a difficulty at 29,000 feet even with oxygen.

When I was breathing more evenly I stood and, leaning over the edge, waved to Tenzing to come up. He moved into the crack and I gathered in the rope and took some of his weight. Then he, in turn, commenced to struggle and jam and force his way up until I was able to pull him to safety—gasping for breath. We rested for a moment. Above us the ridge continued on as before—enormous overhanging cornices on the right and steep snow slopes on the left running down to the rock bluffs. But the angle of the snow slopes was easing off. I went on chipping a line of steps, but thought it safe enough for us to move together in order to save time. The ridge rose up in a great series of snakelike undulations which bore away to the right, each one concealing the next. I had no idea where the top was. I'd cut a line of steps around the side of one undulation and another would come into view. We were getting desperately tired now and Tenzing was going very slowly. I'd been cutting steps for almost two hours and my back and arms were starting to tire. I tried cramponing along the slope without cutting steps, but my feet slipped uncomfortably down the slope. I went on cutting. We seemed to have been going for a very long time and my confidence was fast evaporating. Bump followed bump with maddening regularity. A patch of shingle barred our way and I climbed dully up it and started cutting steps around another bump. And then I realized that this was the last bump, for ahead of me the ridge dropped steeply away in a great corniced curve, and out in the distance I could see the pastel shades and fleecy clouds of the highlands of Tibet.

To my right a slender snow ridge climbed up to a snowy dome about forty feet above our heads. But all the way along the ridge the thought had haunted me that the summit might be the crest of a cornice. It was too late to take risks now. I asked Tenzing to belay me strongly and I started cutting a cautious line of steps up the ridge. Peering from side to side and thrusting with my ice ax, I tried to discover a possible cornice, but everything seemed solid and firm. I waved Tenzing up to me. A few more whacks of the ice ax, a few very weary steps, and we were on the summit of Everest.

It was 11:30 A.M. My first sensation was one of relief—relief that the long grind was over; that the summit had been reached before our oxygen supplies had dropped to a critical level; and relief that in the end the mountain had been kind to us in having a pleasantly rounded cone for its summit instead of a fearsome and unapproachable cornice. But mixed with the relief was a vague sense of astonishment that I should have been the lucky one to attain the ambition of so many brave and determined climbers. It seemed difficult at first to grasp that we'd got there. I was too tired and too conscious of the long way down to safety really to feel any great elation. But as the fact of our success thrust itself more clearly into my mind I felt a quiet glow of satisfaction spread through my body — a satisfaction less vociferous but more powerful than I had ever felt on a mountaintop before. I turned and looked at Tenzing. Even beneath his oxygen mask and the icicles hanging from his hair I could see his infectious grin of sheer delight.

What are mountains for? To the brutish climber, wrote John Ruskin, "the Alps themselves . . . you look upon as soaped poles in a bear garden, which you set yourselves to climb and slide down again, with shrieks of delight . . . and you rush home, red with cutaneous eruption of conceit, and voluble with convulsive hiccough of satisfaction." Irving, the Winchester schoolmaster who introduced George Leigh Mallory to the mountains, encountered few such climbers in his long years as a climber and instructor. Rather, he knew that what the mountains were for, if they could be said to be "for" anything at all, was the apprehension of beauty. This admirable essay concludes *The Romance of Mountaineering*, a splendid book published in 1938.

# R. L. G. IRVING

# Solvitur in Excelsis

In the opening chapter of this book the personal note was prominent. In the other chapters it has not done more than help to bring some unity of design into the succession of varied and widely separated incidents that make the story. My views of the relative importance of events, and of the developments in the character and the aims of mountaineering, have affected my selection of the pictures put before you. Put this, at least, to my credit, that I have added nothing to the description of such climbs as are not already chronicled in Alpine history which can rob you of the pleasure of finding your own way upon a mountain. I hope there is not a single climb mentioned in this book which you will find easier or less attractive for my having done it. In this I have tried to act up to my views of what constitutes the joy of climbing.

My endeavor has been to return thanks for the glorious feast of good things which men have enjoyed upon mountains; and in spite of the omission of what you may think important, and in spite of shortcomings inevitable to one who takes a great subject for the first book he writes, I still hope that I have given the impression that ours is the greatest of all sports, and that it is something more than a sport.

And now, in these concluding words, the personal note will sound again. Perhaps there never has been a book of mountaineering experiences in which no boast was found. And this is my boast: that no one ever had his devotion to mountains rewarded with a greater measure of pure enjoyment. The use of the past tense does not mean that the sources of enjoyment have dried up and become a memory only. Mountaineering has shown me, as no other sport has, what a delusion is the belief that pleasure is the companion of youth and not of age. In youth we seldom realize our pleasures; we are too apt to look for results, and to judge by the misleading standards of quantity, so that the full rapture of the moment escapes us. Men talk of the perfect happiness of schooldays. What nonsense! They were good, but we had not the knowledge to make the most of them. A boy who has hardly tasted wine does not enjoy a famous vintage as does your old connoisseur. He may be able to drink more without suffering for it, just as he can climb more peaks and in less time; that is all. The years bring better understanding and fuller knowledge of what matters most; of what use is life, if they do not? At the age of fifty, on a modest peak of 9,000 feet, we can capture things that we missed upon the Matterhorn twenty-five years earlier. The surprise and passionate exultation of those first big climbs of our youth, our coming-of-age as a mountaineer, will not recur. But is it not as good to watch these emotions come, as you stand by the side of those who are making their entrée into the new world above the snow line?

In an age in which men's beliefs are shaken, when the ultimate end of life announced by mathematical philosophy is complete annihilation, the question why we climb is likely to be answered, and impatiently answered: "Because we like it." There is something beyond that, however, which is worth considering, if there is any good in the pursuit of knowledge. If it is worth while to assign true values to influences and events, then it is not altogether a vain thing for men to weigh their mountaineering experiences, and see what showing they make in the balance sheet of life. Let us take a very few examples from the men who have attempted in words to justify their faith.

These are the benefits which Mummery claims for the man who wrestles with gaunt bare slabs and icy gullies. "Equally, whether he succeeds or fails, he delights in the fun and jollity of the struggle. . . . I do not pretend to be able to analyze this feeling, still less to be able to make it clear to unbelievers. It must be felt to be understood, but it is potent to happiness and sends the blood tingling through the veins, destroying every trace of cynicism and striking at the very roots of pessimistic philosophy." Nor is he insensitive to the contemplative side. "I should still wander among the upper snows, lured by the silent mists and the red blaze of the setting sun, even though physical or other infirmities, even though, in after aeons, the sprouting of wings and other angelic appendages may have sunk all thought of climbing and cragsmanship in the whelming past." You can see the man's real fierce love of mountains as things adorable in themselves behind the mask of humor.

This is Mr. Bourdillon's most conclusive reason for climbing mountains:

One reason is never give openly, rather is disguised and hidden and never even allowed in suggestion, and I venture to think it is because it is really the inmost moving impulse in all true mountain lovers, a feeling so deep and so pure and so personal as to be almost sacred — too intimate for ordinary mention. That is, the ideal joy that only mountains give — the unreasoned, uncovetous, unworldly love of them, we know not why, we care not why, only because they are what they are; because they move us in some way which nothing else does; so that some moment in a smoke-grimed railway carriage, when in the pure morning air the far-off cloud of Mont Blanc suddenly hung above the mists as we rounded the curves beyond Vallorbe, or, still fairer, from the slopes near Neuchâtel, the whole Bernese range slept dreamlike in the lake at our feet, lives in our memories above a hundred more selfish, more poignant joys; and we feel that a world that can give such rapture must be a good world, a life capable of such feeling must be worth the living.

Yes, that is it: the assurance that what we see is good, and that life is good if we can realize it. There are no moments that stand out in our long hours of glorious experience like those in which we came to some high point, and, as we looked out over what was before us, we knew certainty, and doubt was impossible. Those moments are as great rocks to which the frail tabernacle of our mind is held fast, when the mists of doubt and the winds of fear come about it. We cannot help being shaken or having our vision darkened, but we know that we have had moments of clearer vision, and that in them we had certainty. A certainty of what? It is hard to put it into words. It was a certainty that beauty and truth and generosity were real things, that there was something embracing all of these that gave direction to life, and an assurance that their reality need not be doubted when we saw them as we generally do, as in a glass, darkly.

Regarding the beauty of mountains, the view of Ruskin has prevailed and still prevails over that of Dr. Johnson. Indeed Alpine literature has suffered so much from overproduction and standardization in the matters of sunrises and sunsets and summit views that only the brave or the unsophisticated will dare to add their personal contribution. That does not mean that dawn and evening and wide horizons on the upper snows are less beautiful; it means that their beauty has been reproduced too often to the best of men's ability, and that the readers of Alpine literature already carry in their minds pictures which show them how futile is the attempt to crush the infinite beauty of reality within the bounds of language.

There are two qualities in beauty more clearly revealed to me on high mountains than in any other place. One is harmony: the harmony of the infinitely small with the infinitely great, where perfection of beauty in detail is found at every stage of the building of the whole. The tiny six-pointed star that drifts down onto your coat has beauties that multiply with every increase in the power of the microscope. And yet these beauties are all eclipsed for our limited vision when we see them built up into the leaves and flowers of frost that grow under the winds of winter on the upper rocks of British hills, the consolation nature awards to the smooth, hard slabs that can offer no lodging places to the flowers of summer. Crevasses open to let us see translucent canopies, so delicate that a touch of the sun will shatter them, so beautiful that we forgive the inconvenience they cause thereby to our material progress. Yet we almost forget they exist as we look at the glistening draperies that fall for thousands of feet over the form of a great peak like Monte Rosa or Siniolchum. In the light that beats upon you on a snow crest, out of the deep, palpitating blue of the dome of sky, and leaps up from the tiny facets of the ice crystals around you, the countless waves of energy seem to be moving with one purpose, a purpose in which you must have your part.

The second quality is quiet strength. There is something in the serene loveliness of a scene in the High Alps more truly spiritual and undying than in the beauty of things whose life, like our own, may be measured in hours, in seasons, or in years. The following words of Théodore Camus may help to show you what I mean. Camus was one of the many young men of Lyons who have lost their hearts to the Alps by looking at their distant snows from the hills that rise above the Saône. Not long before his death, when he knew that the illness which had attacked him must be fatal, he was talking to his sister, a nun, of his increasing detachment from things that belonged to earth, and he added: "There is just one thing to which I hold as close as ever, which for me shines with a wonderful brilliance that remains undimmed though it belongs to the things of earth; I mean the High Alps at heights of three or four thousand meters. This is the loveliest thing on earth, and how few there are who know it! When I die, it is to them that I shall send one of my last good-byes, and every day I thank God, not for having created them, but for having made me know them. It is as if, in doing that, He had allowed me to have a glimpse of the infinite, through a window open only to a few privileged beings, of that infinite which cannot be described, for all descriptions are so far below the truth."

This is the beauty in mountaineering which, when we have made it ours, we can keep always with us.

There is also a beauty only seen in action, in the midst of vigorous play, when our heart is beating fast to supply our calls upon it, and our face is close up against the mountain's as we pause for breath. We struggle through the hours of a long day to make our will prevail and win the game, and all the time the mountain maintains its calm as though it knew it was its beauty that had conquered us. Nor can our idea of beauty be complete without the struggle. The Greeks are the people who have been most eager in the pursuit of beauty as an ideal, and it was in their games that it most often found expression. Nor is it only through the eye, but also through the sense of touch and other senses that beauty is gathered into our experience and helps to fashion our soul. It is no exaggeration of the fancy to claim that the climber knows the beauty of rock, its firmness, its variety of color, form, and texture better than a mere walker. Many of the loveliest formations of ice and snow are only approachable by him, and only he knows the full fragrance of the cool air on the ridge that has cost him hours of toil on burning slopes to win.

And besides all the intimate charm that mountains reveal only to those who are not content to sit at their feet and watch, but are determined to win them, there is the beauty of artistry that is called into existence by all great sports. There is beauty in any action performed as perfectly as means permit — we may even concede that the action of a motor engine is in this sense beautiful at times. There was more than mere efficency in the way Mallory or Franz Lochmatter would climb a slab, or in the action of a good step cutter, where every blow is struck exactly in the right place and every ounce of effort tells in the result, while the poise of the body in the slippery steps responds to every movement of the swinging ax.

On high mountains there are never fifty thousand spectators as at a cup tie or a test match, from whom the cry of "Beautiful! beautiful!" is drawn by a clever dribble or a glance to leg. There is only the breathless silence of two or three companions, strung out upon some narrow footholds, as they watch the series of well coordinated movements that carry a leader past a protruding boss. Nevertheless it is a spontaneous tribute to this beauty of action.

Guido Rey aptly compares the man who claims to know the charm of mountains without ever risking his life upon them to a man who would claim to be a navigator without ever having left the shore, or to have known what the love of a woman can be from having sung serenades beneath her window.

Only when men become as gods will they have full knowledge of the nature of beauty, and meanwhile they may follow all sorts of paths in their pursuit of it. It is the pleasantest of all life's quests, and the climber, as he pursues his pilgrimage, is reminded at every stage of it that he is in the right way. From start to finish he has the pageant of the sky enacted daily and nightly, and he is in the best place of all to see. He knows the clouds from within and from above as well as from beneath; he can watch the magic of their birth upon the crest, and of their reabsorption into the invisible. He can feel beauty in the morning air and in the soft grass, as well as in the rocks and snow. The meadows are dressed for him with a profusion of color that any gardener would envy, not only in the valley levels but where the mountain form beneath the dress sets off their beauty; and high among the rocks he will find a gentian or a tuft of *Eritrichium* that will seem beside the wealth of the meadows like the widow's mite after the offerings of the rich — more than them all.

As he rises, the dome of sky grows vaster, and the clouds and colors that come and go within it show variations that are never seen at levels where intensity of tone is lost in a softer air. No sky in any part of the world has the depth of blue that frames a foreground of snow upon a great peak. There are men who seem to think the Alps in sunshine are not beautiful because they are unpaintable; one might as well refuse to see beauty in a symphony of Beethoven because it cannot be played on one octave of the piano.

When the summit is reached, it may happen that the details of the view, beautiful as they are, are lost in the impression of some all-pervading quality in beauty, that remains recognizable wherever nature is unspoiled. I never really saw the beauty of our Hampshire county till years after I was grown up. It was just after I came back from the Alps. It was not, of course, the contrast, but the realization of this same essential quality; I had been studying a *magnum opus,* and I now saw the same workmanship in the quieter tones of a different subject on a smaller canvas.

And now, if I want to travel on a magic carpet to the summit of an Alpine peak, I go to a certain place, high upon the downs, when the northwest wind is blowing (I cannot think how Charles Kingsley can have preferred the color-destroying northeast), and I look between two beech trunks that might be the framing of a deep-cut col, and across the shadows moving on the lower ground, to a great range of distant peaks built up into the sky. They have not the calm fixity of mountains, but they give a sense of truer reality than any picture I could hang upon my walls. Mountains may help us to see beauty in a work of art; they insist upon our looking for the nature of beauty at its source.

There is another instinct which has led men to climb: the desire to know, to get nearer to the truth of things. Fully alive as Saussure was to the beauty of Mont Blanc, he would not have made its ascent but for his desire to know what it could tell him. Looking from the summit over the array of peaks and valleys at last spread open before him, he says: "I realized their relations to each other, their connecting links and their structure, and one look removed doubts which years of work had not been able to clear up."

The scientific value of climbing has diminished; we have other ways of measuring heights and of solving topographical problems; the desire to get nearer to truth is still a motive. It may be nothing but a wish to test our skill by matching it against the resistance of the mountain or against the performances of others; it may be a wish to know whether the human body can do its work at 28,000 feet — this is one of the reasons given by promoters of the Everest expedition; it may prove to still-greater satisfaction that muscular effort successfully directed to a good end is one of the great sources of contentment; it may be to get above an atmosphere of doubt as to the direction of life; and it may be nearly all these things at once.

And from the mountain we shall get nothing but the truth. It lays bare our weaknesses, while opening to us a source of strength. We learn from it the limit of our capabilities, and while it rewards us for success and for unsuccessful effort more truly than we know, we must never expect it to pass over a mistake. Deceits and subterfuges and vanities, on which a man may raise himself higher than he deserves in civilized life, slip away from under him in the field of sport, and most completely of all upon a mountain. Even those arch-imposters of Tarascon, Tartarin and Bompard, are exposed to one another among the stern solitudes of Mont Blanc. It is pleasant to have such a perfect testimonial to the truth-compelling nature of our effort from a great novelist who was not a mountaineer. "Écoutez-moi, ami, d'abord, je n'ai jamais tué de lion." That from Tartarin! And when Tartarin says after a temporary reinflation of spirit, "Du courage, Gonzague, du courage!" Bompard replies, "C'est justement de ça que je manque!"*

You may remember the cricketer among A. A. Milne's "Rabbits" who maintained a certain reputation on an MCC [*Marylebone Cricket Club*] tie and a faculty for getting run out. In an Alpine hotel it is possible to find men whose club badges, and continued bad luck in the matter of weather, lead you to form an estimate of their value on a mountain which is a good deal higher than that of the guides or amateurs who climb with them. I am sure such cases are rare; the certainty that a climb will disclose a man's true value discourages pretense. And a climber who can be trusted to say when he feels the slightest doubt as to his safety is a far better companion on the rope than one who may be too proud to ask for help, too self-confident or too ignorant to see the need for special care.

A big climb is done under ideally loyal conditions, when each member of the party gives ungrudgingly of his best, and each shares almost equally in the success. It is one of the drawbacks of a great game like cricket that the unlucky man who has made naught and missed a catch or two has a very different share in the victory from the man who has made a hundred or taken half the wickets. The weakest member of a climbing rope, unless he is a mere passenger, hoisted up a climb far beyond his powers, has made a big contribution to success.

It is only when a spirit of rivalry intrudes itself, when the tale of achievement is told, in fact when men get away from the influence of the mountain itself, that we find climbers claiming special credit for their own exploits and belittling those of others. Balmat and Paccard climb Mont Blanc with a single aim and in loyal cooperation. It is the jealousy of Bourrit, the personal ambition of Balmat, and the desire to adorn a tale on the part of Dumas, that obscure the truth for over a hundred years.

We see the bare rock of the character of those who share our fortunes on a mountain. That is why the friendships—even that word may fail to convey the closeness of the bond—made by climbing mountains are unlikely to be upset by misunderstandings. Those who climb and continue to climb mountains for the love of them acquire a kind of mountain view of life; though the path pursued in common may occasionally divide, yet, provided the goal is kept in sight, they are bound to draw nearer to each other again.

It is not only our friends whose true nature is revealed by mountains, it is the character of the mountains themselves. They are always correcting or adding to our knowledge of them, if we climb to learn, and not to excel or anticipate a rival. My own possibilities of doing the latter are gone, and any young man who reads this chapter may well think that it is the attempt of an old man to console himself with the philosophic view. Let me, therefore, quote from a paper that I read to the Alpine Club

---

*"Listen, my friend: first, I've never killed a lion." "Courage, Gonzague, courage!" "That's exactly what I lack!"

twenty-five years ago, in the early years of my climbing with Gibson and Mallory, Bullock and Tyndale, which called forth a protest signed by numerous distinguished climbers against the temerity of my proceedings.

Each season as it passes leaves us some fresh indications of how to make a wise selection from our many sources of delight. And I have settled to my own satisfaction that mere novelty possesses but faded charms in the Alps. I cannot deceive myself into thinking I am an explorer because I am the first to scale a few hundred feet of rock which have been known to climbers before I was born. . . . And so far is novelty from being necessary to me in my Swiss expeditions, that whenever I have been wise enough to make a second ascent of a peak, I have enjoyed it no less and sometimes more than the first, and likewise with a third and even a fourth. Nevertheless, until we have followed one fairly difficult route upon a mountain we do not properly know it. One aspect of them we may see when walking over their snowfields on a fine day, but before we have come to grips with them we are mere acquaintances. There is an overpowering sense of personality about a peak when we feel his broad snowy chest almost touching our own, when his great rocky shoulder rubs against ours, and our hands clutch at his hard rough skin to get a hold. Some sort of struggle is an excellent beginning to a lasting friendship.

We soon learn to value mountains by other standards than that of fighting power. And it often rests with us to decide whether they shall restore or exhaust our energies, whether they shall develop or test our powers of endurance, whether they shall deepen or disturb the current of our lives. Occasions constantly arise when we underestimate the difficulties, or the weather plays us false. And then we can enjoy what is better than any self-imposed struggle; for the satisfaction of accomplishing a climb of cataloged severity is nothing to the joy of fighting a way out of difficulties and dangers that come unforeseen. The heroes of mountaineering are not those who have fallen in an attempt on some almost inaccessible pinnacle, but those who perished like Carrel on the Grand Staircase.

I would not alter anything I wrote then in the full enjoyment of youth.

We all helped to keep a record of those early years, and the paper from which I have just quoted ends thus:

When I read through the simple story of our climbs — it has reached its fourth volume — there is nothing that gives me more satisfaction than to find that we can still appreciate as of old the simple snow climb. We do a few audacious things, we should not be young if we did not; but we have tried to live up to our belief that there is an influence more purifying than danger in the beauty of the snows; and that among the countless ridges and recesses of the Alps we shall find an outlet for the energies of youth without having constantly before our eyes the immediate prospect of dissolution.

During the war, in Flanders, Mallory wrote an account of the last big climb he did with me. I will quote a few words from it. It refers to the moments when the difficulties were over, and the excitement of the struggle ended in the certainty of success up to the final easy ridge of Mont Blanc.

> The end was too certain. He began to fear an anticlimax, a disappointment in things attained. Wasn't it like a slice of bread and jam, the last unjammed portion? Wasn't the adventure ended, and this merely a depressing fatigue? But in the mere act of firmly planting the feet he found an answer to that last doubt; at each step upward and steeper there throbbed a dim faith refuting the heresy. The spirit didn't come so far to slip all down to nothing, all parts of such experience were significant; the dream stretched to the very end.

And on the summit of Mont Blanc, reached not long before sunset:

> In this the summit, crowning the day? How cool and quiet! We're not exultant; but delighted, joyful; soberly astonished. Have we vanquished an enemy? None but ourselves. Have we gained success? That word means nothing here. To struggle and to understand — never this last without the other, and such is the law.

After his very first visit to the Alps this habit of searching after truth, this desire to assign to things their true values, became characteristic of Mallory. That visit, I am sure, gave to a mathematical scholar, regarded as below rather than above the average ability of the scholars of his years, a philosophic outlook which made him an untiring learner. There was a Mallory termed highbrow by his companions on Everest in 1922 and 1924, the man chaffed by Longstaff: "Mallory, you know the one good thing the Bolsheviks have done in Russia? They've obliterated the intelligentsia." But it was not a different Mallory from Mallory the mountaineer, it was an essential part of the latter. To see the correct value of a thing, especially of mountaineering itself, was a purpose in his life. I have never been so proud of having introduced Mallory to mountains as when I found him saying after the great climb in 1922 to 27,000 feet, when there was a question of a third attempt: "Though I was prepared to take risks with my fingers, I was prepared to take none with my heart, even had General Bruce allowed me." It showed that Mallory put a true value on mountaineering, far higher than that of any mere achievement, even the conquest of Everest.

The great *truth* that climbing teaches us is that the physical struggle and the contemplative aim are parts of one indivisible whole. Every effort of the muscles that lifts us a little higher is giving us an assurance, absorbed unconsciously into our being, that in the right use of matter to a spiritual end we can fulfill our destiny.

What is snow? It is at once solid, liquid, and gas; it is soft, and it is hard; it is beautiful and serene and yet threatening. And when the crystalline bonds of an inclined mass of snow erode and break, the resulting avalanche becomes one of nature's most destructive forces, as swift, as awesome, as randomly violent as a tornado. You may think that all you want to know about avalanches is that you would rather not be caught in one, but there is more to be learned, in this passage from *On Mountains: Thinking About Terrain.*

# JOHN JEROME

# Avalanches

*Like the weather, forest fires, and the inner city, avalanches are a powerful stronghold against empirical analysis, not because they yield no measurable information, but because they yield so overwhelmingly much.*
— GEORGE SIBLEY, "Part of a Winter," *Mountain Gazette*

At one time in my squandered youth I taught school in the rimrock country of West Texas. For off-hours sport another teacher and I used to go out regularly to the farther reaches of that desolate landscape, climb up to the top of the cap rock, and roll boulders down the canyon sides.

We would hike along the upper ledge in search of the largest rocks we could dislodge. When we found one we would grunt and strain to pry it loose, dodging the scorpions and centipedes disturbed by our labors, and tip it over the edge. It would . . . roll. Gaining speed slowly, it would tumble and lurch and finally pick up enough momentum to take an occasional ponderous leap. It would knock down a small mesquite tree here and there, but mostly it would only mash cactus and knock splinters off other rocks en route. Often as not it would catch a flat spot — on itself or on the canyon wall — and simply slide to a disappointing stop, sometimes within ten feet or so of its launch site.

But that would be counterbalanced by the next one, which might roll all the way to the bottom, leap the dry creek bed there, and work its way a few shuddering yards up the opposite slope — eliciting, I suppose, a weak cheer from the two of us as we watched: that, somehow, was the object of the silly game.

For a few months this became our obsessive pastime, which tells you as much about the availability of recreation as it does of the mental state of West Texas schoolteachers. We would walk for miles in search of just the right boulder and began carrying along a six-foot steel pinch bar — twenty or thirty sweaty pounds' worth — just to help us pry loose the really big ones. Inevitably we found our ultimate rock, a monster nearly as tall as we were, poised so delicately on the rim that we could actually make it teeter slightly where we found it. Still, it took most of a Saturday morning of hard physical labor to break it free. I seem to recall that we actually considered walking the three or four miles back to the car and driving home for pick and shovel to make the job easier. But we succeeded without the extra tools.

There is no real punch line to this story. We tipped it over the edge and were instantly frightened by the enormity of what we had accomplished. We both sat down as if stunned before it had rolled twenty feet. It went all the way, thundering and thrashing and shaking the very earth, setting off a minor rock avalanche in the scree slope beneath the rimrock. It took out at least one good-sized mesquite and leaped completely over another one, with however many thousand pounds of accumulated momentum; it cleared the creek bottom, rolled up the other side for a bit, poised uncertainly for a moment, and rolled back down again to come to rest in the creek bed, where it undoubtedly still lies twenty years later. But it was truly scary while it rolled, and without talking about it my friend and I simply turned — once it had finally shuddered to a stop — and headed back for the car. We never went rock rolling again.

It was mindless, small-boy vandalism, and it bothers me now that we did it, and did it with such glee — although even now, in a new age of sensitivity to natural processes, I can't see that we were doing much more than speeding up erosion. The memory reminds me of Thoreau enthusiastically arching firebrands into Walden Pond at night and exulting in the beauty of the sight. Or Wallace Stegner, not too many years before my West Texas adventures, rhapsodizing about tossing burning tire carcasses into the Grand Canyon. All our heads have been changed since then. That doesn't excuse or ameliorate the earlier insensitivity.

The only point in bringing up such a senseless activity in a chapter about avalanches is to recognize that there is a certain fascination — in all of us, I think — with massive physical occurrences. Whether it is small-boy vandalism or not is moot: I could no more talk about mountains and snow and then ignore avalanches than I could speak of volcanoes without mentioning Krakatoa's spectacular fireworks. Avalanches are amazing. In one sense they are a metaphor for what is always going on in the mountains anyway at a much slower pace: a kind of erosional equivalent of time-lapse photography, compressing eons' worth of erosion into instants of real time, seeming to pull down the mountains at a frightening rate. Yet in most cases, where slide paths are comfortably established and no man-made structures intrude, the great snowfields can slide away to their hearts' content all winter long, and the next summer's visitors may find no more evidence of avalanching than an occasional twisted sapling. Does the avalanche that slides in the hidden mountain vastness make a roar?

The avalanches we know about, however, do affect man. Avalanches are amazing because their destructive power is so much greater than their physical dimensions would seem to warrant. One researcher, working before the improved communications of the twentieth century, recorded nearly 17,500 avalanches in the Swiss Alps in one year alone. The snow avalanche is an utterly common occurrence. Yet like tornadoes — with which in fact they have a lot in common — each avalanche is a freak of nature. A major avalanche, swooping down on a hapless village, will mow down a line of houses, then inexplicably hop over a single house, only to smash the next to matchsticks. Fatalities have resulted from avalanches twenty yards wide and a hundred yards long, the bodies dug from a pile of snow at the end only two or three feet deep. And of course human beings have been swept up in an avalanche, carried a mile or so downslope over vertical distances in the thousands of feet, and — you guessed it — spit out uninjured. Stories of tornadolike whimsicality have been thoroughly documented: the avalanche smashes house and barn, wipes out family and livestock, leaves not a stick standing — and three hundred yards up the opposite slope someone finds an intact china closet where it was swept from the house, not a single dish chipped.

That whimsicality has led to a great deal of superstition and hysteria surrounding avalanches, much of it among not so primitive people. What seems like sheer capriciousness in the behavior of an avalanche usually turns out to be only the working of physical laws and properties that are on the second or third order of observability. Avalanche research aimed at sifting out those laws and properties, in hopes of predicting avalanche action and preventing or reducing the destruction therefrom, has been going on since the 1930s, primarily in research operations above Davos, Switzerland, and around Alta, Utah, the latter under the supervision of the United States Forest Service. The research is always underfunded and working against incredible obstacles; if the Swiss are ahead of the United States in it, that is because they had the object lesson of World War I as a stimulus. Out of approximately 80,000 Austrian and Italian troops serving in the Tirol, almost half were lost to avalanches. "The mountains in winter," said skiing pioneer Matthias Zdarsky, who had been put to work teaching mountaineering to the Austrian troops, "were more dangerous than the Italians."

(Zdarsky, incidentally, was caught in an avalanche himself in 1916, during rescue work aimed at uncovering soldiers buried by a previous slide. He suffered no fewer than eighty separate fractures and dislocations during the few minutes of the experience — during all of which he was fully conscious — before finding himself lying uncovered on the surface of the snow. Rehabilitation took eleven years, but Zdarsky lived to ski again.)

Avalanche research has made considerable headway in understanding the mechanisms at work in forming and releasing the great gouts of snow that wreak so much destruction. In the process, in science's methodical way, various classifications and categories of avalanche phenomena have been proposed. The classifications are somewhat inexact, and every large avalanche has aspects of several different types. But it is only through such classification that a beginning has been made in understanding the avalanche's terrible destructiveness.

Local mountain folk have long divided avalanches into two basic categories: the airborne, blowing-snow avalanche — *Staublawine* in Switzerland — and the ground avalanche, or *Grundlawine*. The former are the most explosively destructive, perhaps largely as a result of their tremendous speed. The Great Glärnisch slide in 1898 happened to be timed from start to finish. A large cornice gave way near the summit of Vorder-Glärnisch at 11:20 A.M. and poured over the village of Glarus — four and a third miles away and 5,750 feet lower — in a little over one minute. (The billowing cloud of snow that accompanied it didn't settle for another six minutes.) The avalanche thus reached a speed of somewhere between 225 and 250 miles per hour. It can perhaps be assumed that witnesses in 1898 did not have stopwatches in hand, but modern measurements with deliberately started avalanches have shown that speeds of over 220 miles per hour are not out of the question for a large airborne avalanche, and 180- to 190-mile-per-hour winds are common.

The forces generated by winds of that velocity alone are sufficient to accomplish much of the freak damage that airborne powder avalanches regularly cause. Skiers have been sucked into them from *above* the slide's starting point. Trees that manage to remain standing have their limbs stripped off — but more frequently the trees themselves are snapped off at ground level before the body of the avalanche reaches them, from the force of the snow-free air blast running ahead of the slide itself.

The physical process that creates such forces has been likened to that which governs gas flowing through a pipe — and there's even a curious resemblance to the behavior of glaciers. When particles in suspension are flowing through the atmosphere, they drag air along with them by friction. The air is almost a passive stream being dragged along by particles under the force of gravity; thus the energy of the particles is spread to a much larger mass. As with gas in a pipe (and glaciers), friction along the edges slows down the outer layers of this "tube" of air flowing down the slope, and pressure then causes the inner, central mass to accelerate. Hence the resemblance to such curious behavior as fire storms: once the mass is set in motion, it is self-accelerating.

New particles are constantly being sucked in from the sides, and extreme turbulence is set up in the outer layers of moving air. The greater the speed, the greater the turbulence; irregularities in the path — cliffs, trees, gulleys — also increase the turbulence. These swirling turbulences generate speeds perhaps twice as fast as those of the slide itself, creating rapid, intermittent blasts — lasting about a tenth of a second each — at sharp angles to the main thrust of the avalanche. There are vertical swirls as well as horizontal ones, of course, which helps explain some of the freak effects of airborne avalanches.

The extremely turbulent air seems to do more damage than either the main blast of air or the snow load. A house struck by these short, sharp blasts will simply disintegrate as if it had been shelled by artillery. Fragments and debris are frequently left in a circular pattern, giving rise to earlier theories that it is pressure differential — as in tornado destruction — that causes the damage. The oblique blasts, however, are a more consistent explanation. One researcher describes a twelve-inch concrete wall attacked by such gusts: the concrete was simply blasted away from between the metal reinforcing rods, leaving only twisted steel where the wall had stood.

Any ramplike structure — a cliff, rocks in the path, even a building "securely" tucked into the slope — will launch a ground avalanche into the air. But once a critical speed is reached — estimated to be about 50 miles per hour — no ramp is necessary; turbulence along the ground will shove the slide into the air all by itself. It is not necessary for an airborne avalanche to achieve massive size to become destructive, incidentally. In Austria in 1952 a slide only 20 feet wide plucked a bus from a line of vehicles on a small bridge and tumbled it over the side. Eleven out of 35 aboard were killed; another bus in front and a car behind were left untouched.

Ground avalanches, particularly those containing wet, loose snow, can cause the same degree of damage, but it is different in kind, generated by the tremendous power of great weights of snow driven inexorably into valley structures. Ground avalanches move much more slowly — often at 20 miles an hour or less — but they set up like concrete when they stop. Using averages from avalanches measured in the past — a 6,500-foot descent at 22 miles per hour for a million tons of snow and rock — avalanche scientists estimate that a destructive force on the order of 20 million horsepower is not unusual for such slides. The final deposit from that kind of avalanche can be a hundred feet thick, can wipe out roads and railroad tracks, and can dam rivers, causing flooding. When roads and railroads are thus blocked, they are often simply tunneled out under the debris until spring melts the accumulated ice. Rivers will eventually tunnel their own way to release. An avalanche in the French Alps in 1862 dammed the river Isère; the river cut a tunnel beneath the ice, and the ice itself was used as a bridge for seventeen months — through the heat of two summers.

Mountaineers are by definition individualists, but even among individualists there are, well, *individualists*—hippies, if you will. In the 1960s the seat of the climbing counterculture was the Yosemite Valley, and Chris Jones tells its story in this chapter from *Climbing in North America*. In truth, this piece is about more than the odd characters who came, saw, in some cases conquered, and went; it is about the whole Yosemite scene in that decade when the climbing world began to recognize that the principles of modern rock climbing—the techniques that would render no wall impossible—were being carved out here.

# CHRIS JONES

# The Granite Crucible

During the early 1960s Yosemite Valley was an unknown quantity. The locals quietly, almost furtively, advanced the standards of American climbing, but the climbing world remained blissfully ignorant. Outsiders read about [Warren] Harding's ascent of El Capitan in the 1959 *American Alpine Journal*, but over the next three years the *Journal* was curiously silent about Yosemite. The lack of information and the long, drawn-out ascent of the Nose made it a hard place to fathom. However, a few outsiders came to see for themselves. And not only see. They started to climb the walls.

None of the earliest visitors was ready for the mental and technical demands of El Capitan, but in the spring of 1962 Ed Cooper and Canadian Jim Baldwin came for the express purpose of making a new route on El Cap. The year before, they had established the Grand Wall (V) on Squamish Chief, a gaunt, 2,000-foot cliff near Vancouver, British Columbia. On the Grand Wall, in the Cascades, and in the Bugaboos, Cooper demonstrated he had the mind for big walls.

To the climbers in [Royal] Robbins's circle the bizarre events surrounding the Grand Wall meant that the outsiders already had two strikes against them when they arrived in Yosemite. First, Cooper and Baldwin took about a month to fix ropes on the Grand Wall. In some places, they bolted up alongside perfectly usable cracks. Suitable pitons were unavailable locally, and Cooper maintained that it was simpler to bolt than to manufacture pitons. Second, because of Squamish Chief's location above a highway, the lengthy ascent attracted wide interest. One weekend a reputed 12,000 cars crowded into the area. The climbers were celebrities in nearby Squamish, which enjoyed a tourist boom. They were furnished with free food and lodging, which delayed the climb even more. They went up on the wall, placed a few pitons, fiddled around with the ropes, and then hurried down to dinner and the bar. They had never had it so good!

The publicity appalled the Yosemite regulars, for whom the sport was a personal affair above sensationalizing. It appeared to them that Cooper was another Harding in his striving for publicity. Indeed, much of the antagonism toward Harding was over the publicity issue. (When Harding and Robbins hiked toward Half Dome in 1955, they met a group of tourists. While Robbins hid behind a boulder, Harding enthusiastically described their plans.)

Robbins's attitude toward Cooper was hostile from the start. He sent underlings to convey messages and made a point of not speaking to him. What galled Robbins was the way the outsiders immediately started to fix ropes on El Cap. He felt they should climb lesser routes to establish their right to preempt such a prize. The locals were upset that outsiders were climbing what they themselves were reluctant to do until they could carry it off in the correct style. At least, these were the reasons espoused by Robbins. The more likely cause of the annoyance was the idea that outsiders might launch out on a new route on Yosemite's finest wall without flinching at the magnitude of the task.

Cooper and Baldwin chose a daunting route. Their Dihedral Wall would follow an unrelentingly steep and direct line up a series of leaning corners. After the first lead there were no more stances for 1,000 feet. They whittled away at the climb through the spring. Up and down they went, sometimes not even reaching the previous high point. The climbing was difficult and the exposure sensational. Baldwin confessed, "Going up there day after day eats your mind. I'll get a little smashed the night before and convince myself that it'll be raining in the morning."

They climbed 900 feet before Baldwin had a heart-stopping accident. His Prusik knots slipped, and he slid 100 feet before he stopped where the rope was anchored to the wall. His hands were burned from clutching the rope, and his Prusik knots were nearly worn through.

Because of the summer climbing ban on El Cap, they could not get back on the route until the fall, and during the summer it was rumored that Robbins might go up on it when he returned from the Alps. Pushed into action, Cooper and Baldwin were back on the wall in September. Their party was materially strengthened by the addition of Californian Glen Denny. They advanced their fixed ropes to the 2,000-foot level and then returned late in November to complete the route in a six-and-a-half-day push.

The locals were a proud bunch. They had definite ideas about what was good style and what was not. Several people took exception to the Dihedral Wall. They liked neither the fixed ropes nor the long siege. However, the exemplary Salathé Wall had

EL CAPITAN

ROYAL ROBBINS

WARREN HARDING

YVON CHOUINARD

IN THE MID-1800'S, THE ALPS WERE CALLED "THE PLAYGROUND OF EUROPE."

BUT IN THE LAST 30 YEARS, YOSEMITE HAS BEEN THE PROVING GROUND FOR REVOLUTIONARY TECHNIQUES.

itself been fixed over the lower third. It was not so much that Cooper fixed ropes that was open to criticism, but that he established them so far up the route and took so long to do it. The locals' concern over climbing ethics can be looked upon as an attempt to keep climbing adventurous, to prevent the rocks from being overwhelmed with rope. It can also be looked upon as a competition where the elite cry foul on the less experienced.

The Yosemite experts were rattled by the Dihedral Wall; it was an unpleasant crack in the Yosemite façade. The façade had already been weakened by Layton Kor, who had stormed up several difficult routes. In 1963 he planned a trip to the Alps, but the lure of Yosemite proved too great.

The early-season weather was dreadful. While most of the climbers hung around the coffee shop, Kor headed up toward the Steck-Salathé on Sentinel. It was caked with snow and ice. No one had attempted a big-wall Yosemite climb in winter, but Kor was nothing if not an innovator. He half-seriously commented, "I want to see if I'm afraid to die." Apparently he was. After a couple of desperate leads he and his partner came down.

Kor teamed with several fast-rising newcomers. One was Berkeley math student Eric Beck. As soon as Beck got his scholarship grant, he went to Yosemite, where he fell under the influence of climbing guru Steve Roper. Roper was in with the big shots and had a fund of outrageous stories. The wide-eyed newcomers received a steady stream of comment and ribald advice.

Like most of the Yosemite regulars who climbed for six months a year, Beck was perpetually poor. One way to solve the money dilemma was to "scarf" discarded food in the cafeteria. One day at breakfast Beck reached for an abandoned cereal bowl. At the same moment the owner returned. "Hey, that's ours," he complained. When he got a better look at Beck he had second thoughts and added, "Here, you can have it anyway." Not long after this episode the head busboy saw some climbers eyeing the leftover sausage. He grabbed the sausage and brought it over. The climbers warmed to their new ally, and he found them a congenial lot and told his underlings to give them any leftover grub. Life was pretty soft until the busboy became a climbing bum.

The bad weather continued into the spring of 1963, but Kor was impatient. He had to have his own route on El Capitan. He and Beck established ropes over the lower third of their intended route, the West Buttress. Beck was new to big-wall climbing and was awed by the exposure and the scale. One time when he arrived at a belay stance and it was his turn to lead, Kor said, "The next pitch looks really scary"; and in a keen, expectant voice, "Bet I can lead it pretty fast if you want to take the next one."

With the bad weather and the continual nervous strain, Beck was not overanxious to go up on the wall. Suffering from a "mind inversion," he backed off the climb, and Roper joined Kor to finish it. They fixed ropes to mid-height and then completed the route in a three-day effort.

Kor and Roper made a well-matched pair. Both were lively personalities with a love of black humor, and both were fast aid climbers. They and Denny next prepared to attempt the third ascent of the Nose. Robbins and his friends had made the second ascent in seven days. Kor and company were out to cut the time to shreds. (Robbins scoffed when he heard their ambitions.) They reached the foot of the wall in the dark. At the first hint of daylight Roper pounded in a piton. Three and a half days later they were on top.

Roper was an avid speed climber. In an ostensibly uncompetitive sport the time taken to complete a route was a simple method of comparison. The Steck-Salathé on Sentinel Rock was at this time a standard test piece among the better climbers. Robbins had done the route five times and eliminated all but forty feet of the aid. On his last trip he cut the time to ten hours. On their first trip up the Steck-Salathé, Roper and Frank Sacherer shaved two hours off Robbins's time.

When the jubilant pair arrived back in camp, a subdued Robbins offered his congratulations and magnanimously opened a bottle of champagne. The chronically shy Sacherer had never tasted champagne before and remarked that it tasted like Coke.

Two days later, Robbins and Frost ate an early breakfast in the Yosemite cafeteria and let it be known that they hoped to be back in time for lunch. They made it back just too late for lunch. After breakfast they had hiked up to Sentinel Rock, climbed the Steck-Salathé in "three hours and fourteen minutes," and returned. Robbins had made his point.

Ed Cooper was back in Yosemite in 1963. He had interested *The Saturday Evening Post* in a story on a projected new climb on Half Dome. Although they were unaware of the pending contract, the Yosemite regulars knew Cooper's penchant for publicity. That very spring he had informed the media of another projected Yosemite climb, and they had not forgotten the Grand Wall ballyhoo. Cooper and Berkeley hot-rod enthusiast Galen Rowell spent a few days fixing ropes on the lower pitches and then descended in poor weather. They expected to return and finish the job when Rowell's exams were over.

No one had been more put out by Cooper's Dihedral Wall climb than Robbins. When he saw what was happening on Half Dome, he recognized an opportunity to even the score. As Cooper and Rowell descended to the valley, Robbins and Dick McCracken went up to the base of Half Dome. They set out in doubtful weather, and after four days of difficult climbing they were on top of the Direct Northwest Face.

Certainly Robbins had done the climb in a finer style than was Cooper's intent, but opinion was sharply divided as to whether his action was admirable. It was the last straw for Cooper. Without bothering to collect his equipment from the base of the climb, he left for New York and a new life as a stockbroker.

Nineteen sixty-three was a productive year for Robbins. One week after the Half Dome climb, he and McCracken were on another Grade VI, the East Side of Upper Yosemite Fall. Perhaps his finest effort was during four stormy days in May, when he made the second ascent of Harding's Leaning Tower route (VI) alone. It was the first solo ascent of a major Yosemite wall.

## THE VALLEY SCENE

In the early sixties there were typically ten to twenty climbers in residence in Yosemite. Of this number only two or three were from outside California. By the mid-sixties the number of climbers doubled, and outsiders were beginning to outnumber the locals. Two events helped to bring about these changes: the demystifying of the routes that followed the 1964 publication of Roper's *Climber's Guide* and the belated recognition of Yosemite climbing in moutaineering publications. The *American Alpine Journal* barely mentioned Yosemite during the early sixties. The magnificent Salathé Wall was covered in a four-sentence note tucked away at the back. Rock climbing was vaguely considered not quite "on."

In 1963 the *Journal* made amends. The first four articles were devoted to Yosemite. Most influential was Chouinard's "Modern Yosemite Climbing," which began: "Yosemite climbing is the least known and understood and yet one of the most important schools of rock climbing in the world today." The article opened the eyes of climbers throughout the country to the revolution that was sweeping through the valley. Written with conviction and passion, it was full of advice for the out-of-state climber, who learned that he would not be accepted "until he proves that he is equal to the better climbs and climbers. He is constantly on trial to prove himself."

Chouinard ended with a stirring call to arms: "Yosemite Valley will, in the near future, be the training ground for a new generation of super-Alpinists who will venture forth to the high mountains of the world to do the most aesthetic and difficult walls on the face of the earth." This prophecy had the right ring to it. Whether it was accurate will be for a later generation to judge.

Back in the nitty-gritty of Yosemite, Chouinard noted "an aura of unfriendliness and competition between climbers, leaving a bitter taste in the mouth." Of course, competition and sport are closely linked. The climbers acted out Western man's precepts in the framework of Yosemite: get ahead; make something of yourself. Robbins was firmly on top of the pecking order. A remote, hard-to-fathom figure who took himself seriously and liked to appear well read, he constantly put himself on trial to maintain his position.

One afternoon at the Climber's Camp in the Tetons, Robbins was hanging around with the Vulgarians when someone suggested a push-up contest. Within moments people were straining and sweating on the ground, but not Robbins. He disdained to join in. Not long afterward, so the story goes, one of the Vulgarians was walking outside the campground when he saw a naked torso rhythmically heaving up and down. He gingerly crept forward, eagerly expecting to see a couple making love. To his surprise the torso belonged to Robbins—practicing push-ups.

Sometime later Robbins was again enjoying a bull session with the Vulgarians. During a lull in the conversation he seized his chance: "Hey, you guys, do you want to have a push-up contest?"

Competition was part of a greater whole. The beauty and meaning of the Yosemite experience were more important. By late fall of 1963 only Baldwin, Beck, and Berkeley climber Chris Fredericks remained in Camp IV, trying to hold on to a year of precious memories and shared experiences. They spent their last money on coffee in the cafeteria, a scheme which allowed them to stay dry and consume unlimited amounts of sugar and cream. Finally, they went to the rangers and inquired if departing tourists had left any food. They had: a motley assortment of half-used catsup, cookies, mustard, and other leftovers. The climbers eagerly took their spoils back to Camp IV to the men's room, the only place with a heater. There they assigned points to each item according to its survival potential; cookies rated higher than mayonnaise. Beck summed the points and divided by three. The bargaining commenced, and each man eventually left with an armful of odds and ends. They held out one more week.

The young Berkeley group were back the next year. The rapidly emerging technical force among them was graduate physics student Frank Sacherer, an intense, tight individual whose concentration on climbing and physics was fanatical. He climbed like a man possessed and deliberately forced himself to use minimal protection. On one occasion he was way above Beck's belay stance without a single intermediate piton. Beck anxiously called up to him to put in a piton. Sacherer spat back "Shut up, you chicken shit."

Sacherer directed his energies toward eliminating aid and was scrupulous in his demands that his partners not "cheat." After leading the first free ascent of the ominous Crack of Despair (5.10), Sacherer belayed his second from deep inside the crack. Tom Gerughty was in his first month as a climber. As he struggled up the crack, he took a quick rest on a bolt. Sacherer heard his panting slow down, sensed what had happened, and mercilessly yelled, "Get your foot off the bolt, Gerughty!"

In short succession he led Gerughty up the fingertip crack on the Dihedral and up the overhanging jam crack on the right side of the Hourglass. Sacherer cursed when their rappel rope hung up on the descent from the latter climb. In a burst of fury, he climbed back up the rope hand over hand.

Pratt and Robbins had been the star free climbers in the early 1960s, but Sacherer surpassed them. They had a deliberate, controlled style; his was to get mad at the rock, and he often appeared on the verge of falling. If Pratt initiated 5.10 in Yosemite, it was Sacherer who brought it to fruition. When Pratt and Fredericks repeated his Hidden Chimney on Bridalveil Fall, East Side, they had to struggle hard to get up. Perhaps the best free-climbing achievement of 1964 was Pratt and Sacherer's one-day ascent of the 1,200-foot Lost Arrow Chimney (V, 5.10). Sacherer later said, "The day you do that Arrow Chimney is the day you do more work than any other day of your life."

The next year Sacherer had to spend more time at his physics books. To stay in shape, he and Beck undertook a vigorous course of training. When they got back to Yosemite, it was with telling effect. They eliminated eighty aid pitons on Middle Cathedral Rock's Direct North Buttress (V, 5.10) and created a stir when they did the west face of Sentinel in a day, the first one-day ascent of a Yosemite Grade VI.

By 1966 Sacherer was through. He realized that if he kept up this pace, he would probably be killed. His nerves were frayed, and there was an offer of a good job in Europe. His companions carried on the free-climbing boom: Pratt and Fredericks on the poorly protected Twilight Zone, and Fredericks on English Breakfast Crack. In a different vein Beck soloed the northwest face of Half Dome. The next years saw a consolidation of Sacherer's achievements, but it was to be some time before free-climbing standards were raised once more.

## TAHQUITZ ROCK

While the Berkeley group pushed the standards of free climbing in Yosemite, Bob Kamps and Tom Higgins made a similar advance at Tahquitz Rock. First, however, they had to equal Robbins's landmark achievements. One of their first breaks was free-climbing the Blankety-Blank (5.10). Robbins heard about the feat and came back to duplicate it. Much to the delight of the locals, he slipped a couple of times, and his peaked white cap, almost a Robbins "trademark," came floating to the ground. Yet when Higgins and Kamps repeated several of Robbins's climbs, their respect only grew. Higgins took a long fall from the top of a nasty pitch on Robbins's El Camino Real.

In 1964 Higgins established Jonah (5.10), a climb that takes a blank, unpromising line, but rather than setting the stage for another advance, this climb seemed to Higgins to be the culmination of his Tahquitz explorations. The best natural lines had been climbed, and Jonah and his later Sham shared stances with already established routes. Though technically dazzling, the newer routes lacked the character of the classic climbs and had a contrived air about them.

Tahquitz remained the number one climbing area in Southern California, yet it curiously lacked the characters and legends that have enlivened other important rock climbing centers. In keeping with the Southern California mania for driving, Tahquitz was a commuters' rock. Unlike its New York counterpart, the Shawangunks, it never developed a strong social scene.

## BACK ON THE WALLS

The year 1964 was not only notable for free-climbing advances; it was a heavy year on the big walls in Yosemite. Early in the season Pratt and Robbins made the second ascent of the West Buttress of El Capitan. In June Robbins was joined by Frost in the five-day second ascent of the Dihedral Wall. On the Dihedral Wall Robbins adapted the Jumar, a cam-action device developed for crevasse rescue, to big wall climbing. As in prusiking, the second followed a pitch by "Jumaring" up the anchored climbing rope; however, Jumars are far quicker to use than Prusik knots. Jumars were also used to move loads up the wall. The haul rope passed through a pulley, and a Jumar was used to brake the load. A sling was attached to the haul rope with a second Jumar, and the climber stood down heavily on the sling to move the load. Before this innovation two methods were in general use. One was to haul the bags, typically weighing thirty to forty pounds, hand over hand; in the other, a climber prusiked up a fixed rope with a haul bag suspended from his waist. These and other refinements in technique, such as the reinforced nylon "belay seat" and the nylon bivouac hammock, which provided some semblance of comfort in the middle of a featureless wall, helped the climbers in several ways. They speeded up the climbing, made it less arduous, and gave the climbers the confidence to attack ever more demanding routes.

In the summer of 1964 Warren Harding returned to Yosemite, intent on climbing one of the few remaining virgin walls, the South Face of Mount Watkins. He interested Pratt in the project, and they set out to recruit a third. However, the experienced were not interested, and the interested lacked the necessary experience. They had resigned themselves to a two-man effort when Chouinard, fresh out of the army, arrived in camp. He immediately signed on.

It was mid-July, and the temperature in the shade was in the mid-nineties. On the South Face of Mount Watkins there was no shade, and the white granite bowl of the face acted like a giant reflector. They entered an inferno.

At the end of the third day the situation was critical. They were exhausted from the heat. They had barely enough water for another day of climbing, and the summit was two days away. The following morning the brilliant white globe of the sun returned, and by midafternoon a blank headwall blocked progress. They were approaching the end of their endurance, and for the first time they considered retreat. But even retreat meant another day in the oven. They doggedly carried on. Each in turn went up and laboriously worked on bolt placements until he was exhausted. Pratt and Chouinard were less experienced at bolting. Chouinard broke two drill bits, and between them they managed only to equal the three bolts Harding inserted alone. When Harding got back in the lead, he felt he must complete the job. Without placing another bolt he lassoed a stunted tree twenty feet above and prusiked up; the way to the top was open.

## THE NORTH AMERICA WALL

By the mid-1960s Robbins had established himself as the preeminent Yosemite climber. He had made the first and second ascents of El Capitan's Salathé Wall, as well as the second ascents of the other three routes on El Cap. Although his partners on these climbs included either Frost or Pratt or both, it is fair to say that Robbins was the motivating force.

To be on top was fine, but to stay on top demanded a continual extension of the possible. Robbins needed a climb that would crown his achievements. El Capitan was the obvious cliff. The unclimbed southeast face was a wall markedly less promising than the previous El Cap climbs. Instead of clean granite broken by cracks and dihedrals, there is a massive intrusion of friable black diorite, which resembles a crude map of the North American continent, the North America Wall. Partnered by Glen Denny, Robbins made several probes in the fall of 1963. The following spring, together with Frost, they climbed the lower half of the wall. By now they felt sufficiently confident to dispense with fixed ropes on a new El Cap route, and they left no ropes after their reconnaissance.

The upper section of the North America Wall looked so questionable that Robbins and Frost wanted the strongest possible four-man team. Pratt was an obvious choice. When Denny appeared unlikely to make it, Chouinard was clearly the strongest contender, but he was as individualistic as Robbins. The two had seldom seen eye to eye. However, for the North America Wall personal quirks were buried.

With the short October days and the 200 pounds of gear with which they started, they took most of three days to reach the previous high point. Their progress was the number one topic among valley climbers, and every day a small group gathered to watch. One day a sprightly man in his sixties hiked to the foot of the wall and gazed intently upward. He refused the binoculars that were offered, saying he could see quite clearly. At this stage they were entering a critical section where the route was in doubt; the various crack systems might not join up. However, John Salathé pointed out to the onlookers where he thought the climbers would have to go. He was exactly right.

Early on the afternoon of the ninth day the four climbers coiled their ropes on top. They had accomplished the hardest big wall climb in North America (VI, 5.8, A5).


## THE BOLTING ISSUE

On the North America Wall and elsewhere the leading Yosemite climbers made a major effort to avoid placing bolts. They would go into extreme A5 nailing and hang sky hooks from tiny flakes rather than drill a hole. They saw bolts as radically different from pitons. With bolts, climbers were free of the natural configuration of the rock and could go anywhere at will, provided, of course, they had the time and equipment. The unrestrained use of bolts opened up areas of rock where there were no natural lines and made success inevitable. These were the major objections to Harding's Leaning Tower route. However, the point at issue during the early 1960s was the use of bolts to avoid difficult nailing or to protect a free climb where better climbers would do without. Unskilled climbers were using bolts to overcome routes that were beyond them when using "traditional" means. The issue was hotly debated around campfires and in the pages of *Summit*, from Chouinard's "Are Bolts Being Placed by Too Many Unqualified Climbers?" through a whole spectrum of attack and counterattack. The purists wanted to keep climbing difficult. They despised the success-at-any-cost attitude of the bolting enthusiasts. How Frank Smythe would have smiled to hear his arguments brought up to date!

In this debate the purists were partially successful. There have been outbreaks of bolting on established routes, but there is now nothing like the proliferation of earlier days. However, the issue of whether bolts should be used to connect up blank areas of rock, to create direct routes or "diretissimas," or even used at all was not then addressed. It has not been resolved to this day.

Due to his army service Chouinard had missed an attempt on El Cap's West Buttress, on which he had his eye. He was determined to make his own contribution on El Cap. After the four-man first ascent of the North America Wall the next step was obvious: a two-man push. His partner for the project was T. M. Herbert.

A then essential item of a climber's equipment was a swami belt, a continuous length of nylon webbing wrapped several times around the waist, to which the climbing rope is attached. Herbert once mail-ordered a quantity of webbing. When it arrived, he cut off a suitable piece for a swami belt. As he did, he saw that the supplier had apparently marked the fifty-foot length with adhesive tape. Leading the crux pitch of the Mechanics Route at Tahquitz, he notices that his swami belt was loose. When he reached the belay, he anxiously checked the webbing. The adhesive tape covered a makeshift join!

Chouinard and Herbert reconnoitered their projected route, but while penduluming, they dropped the bolt kit and had to descend from about the level of Heart Ledge. On the fourth day of their all-out try, the rain began in earnest. That night sheets of water ran down the wall, and they huddled together to stay warm. By the sixth day they had placed all but nine of their thirty-one bolts. They were low on food and still had 1,000 feet to go. They considered retreat, but they were not sure how to do it. They had taken a diagonal line, and below them was 2,000 feet of unknown ground. Could they risk the descent with just nine bolts?

They carried on totally immersed in the vertical rock that was their whole existence. Days flowed together, and the pitches became indistinct in their minds. At nightfall on the ninth day they wearily pulled themselves on top of the Muir Wall.

The Muir Wall and the North Face of Edith Cavell were perhaps Chouinard's finest achievements. Both epitomized much about his approach: a search for the ultimate experience. After the North America Wall he wrote that they could have carried on for another nine days. Two men had hauled while two had led; things were under control. On the Muir things were not under control. They had made the bold stroke, and they had pulled it off. Writing of the Muir Wall in 1968, Robbins characterized it as the "most adventurous ascent on rock ever accomplished by Americans."

The years that followed the ascent of the Muir Wall were a period of consolidation in Yosemite. The big guns of the early 1960s had made their mark and moved on. Their successors struggled in the hot California sun. The young Bay Area group spearheaded by Sacherer made remarkable advances on the shorter routes. They were obvious candidates for Grade VI. However, they were so much the inheritors of the Yosemite mantle, so overwhelmed by the big-wall aura, that few of them could get themselves up for El Capitan. Indeed, when the Nose began to be repeated, the majority of the climbers were not Yosemite residents. Their lack of familiarity with Yosemite conditions was compensated by their freedom from the psychological millstone.

In 1966 a French rope and two home teams climbed the Nose, equaling the total number of ascents during the preceding eight years. The next year the trend continued. There were five ascents of the Nose and the third and fourth ascents, respectively, of the Dihedral and Salathé walls. Yet for every success there were several failures. Whatever reasons the unsuccessful parties gave, and they ranged from equipment failure to vitamin overdoses, the crux of the matter was that people were still scared of big walls. Nonetheless, the aura that surrounded the fabled Yosemite walls was receding. The super-climbs were within the reach of the newcomers.


## THE YOSEMITE INFLUENCE

In 1957 El Capitan lay untouched, and Yosemite was unknown. By 1967 a hard core of dedicated individuals, totally committed to climbing, had pushed away the barriers and reached a new frontier.

Yosemite techniques and attitudes began to spread around the world. In the Chamonix Alps, Americans made a direct start to the famed West Face of the Dru and solved the long-standing problem of the South Face of the Fou. When John Harlin and Robbins made the direct West Face of the Dru, it became apparent that *Les Américains* were ahead of the Europeans on granite walls. The locals were in awe of the technological wizardry, and American chrome-moly pitons commanded a high price in Chamonix. Before long Europeans adopted many of the Yosemite big-wall innovations.

The Yosemite influence was not only one of pure technique. Ambitious Americans drew inspiration and confidence from the heady achievements in the valley. They felt that they were ahead of the world on big walls and adopted the Yosemite ideal of climbing without siege tactics. Successes on the Hummingbird Ridge of Mount Logan and South America's Chacraraju and FitzRoy owed much to Yosemite.

And here's how to do it, from a teacher of rock climbing who has practiced the art since the early 1950s. From bouldering to buildering (the latter an art pioneered at Cambridge by restless undergraduates), Loughman offers sound advice, with a constant eye to developing a climbing style, which he sees as the desired culmination of a life's ascent.

# MICHAEL LOUGHMAN

# The Varieties of Climbing

The extraordinary richness of rock climbing, as it has evolved over the past thirty years, has made the sport accessible to people of all ages and nearly every physical condition, of varying personal goals and degrees of motivation, in every part of the country. Some will be satisfied climbing on a small boulder in a city park. Others will respond to the challenge of a multi-day climb on Yosemite's El Capitan. For others rock climbing is only a facet of a months-long expedition to Patagonia or the Karakoram.

Apart from geographical setting and inherent ease or difficulty, there are also very different methods of doing a climb. One climber will anchor his rope to the rock at six-foot intervals on a smooth wall, all the while scrupulously avoiding holding on to the anchors or rope to rest or help him up. They are intended only to catch a fall, but he is not likely to fall because he is as little willing to do that as to hang on the rope. His performance demands strength, technical mastery, and knowledge of himself. For another climber the same wall is at the limit of his ability. He places the same anchors at six-foot intervals, falls repeatedly, and rests on the rope. His performance demands less skill, but he is pushing his limits. He may ulitmately push on to harder climbs than the first climber.

A third climber will aspire to do the same wall solo and without a rope. Probably he has climbed it already with a rope. Setting the anchors and rope in place takes strength and technical skill, so in one sense climbing without a rope is easier. However, the solo climber must have reserves of strength, exact self-knowledge, and unshakable self-discipline. A mistake or lapse of discipline could be fatal. He may wait months or years, carefully developing and assessing his skills, before he tries the climb. He may forgo this climb in favor of something easier.

The different approaches and goals of climbers have been called the games that climbers play. The most important variables in these games are *style* and *risk*. Let's look at these important concepts and then go on to the varieties of rock climbing.

## STYLE AND RISK

One of the constants in the history of climbing — perhaps the most conspicuous — is the pursuit of ever greater challenges. Once a summit has been reached, climbers look for a more difficult summit, then for a more difficult route to it. Once a route has been done, they try more exacting or "elegant" methods of doing it, usually involving self-imposed restrictions on equipment or techniques. For example, once Mount Everest was climbed with the help of oxygen, it became desirable or more elegant to climb it without oxygen. It is these self-imposed restrictions which constitute the *style* of a climb and which maintain the challenge in the face of advancing technology. The most elegant or stylish ascent is the one done without equipment (even, for some extremists, to the point of going nude and barefoot!). The climber should go alone, should go quickly and make the most extraordinary difficulties appear easy, and, ideally, should have no prior knowledge of the route.

The concern for style has played a major role in the evolution and advance of climbing. The sharp distinction between free climbing and aid climbing, for example, is a matter of style. It has not been made by all climbers in all places. Historically, many climbers have been ready to hold on to the rope whenever it proved convenient. El Capitan was first climbed in 1958 with extensive aid, and until recently it would have been unthinkable without aid. Other climbers have eschewed aid even to the point of failing repeatedly on a hard climb. It is the ready and willing aid climbers who have pioneered the more impressive rock walls, such as El Capitan. However, the people who insist on the sharp distinction between free ascents and aided ascents have often become the better climbers. Today several El Cap routes have been climbed free or nearly free.

A climb need not be difficult in order to be done stylishly. At least a few climbers would rather do an elegant job on an easy route than simply get up a hard one.

Another constant in the history of climbing is risk, especially the risk of falling. The first and third climbers in the example at the beginning of this excerpt have both climbed in what is today judged good style; however, the solo climber has exposed himself to the possibility of a serious fall. Though climbers have sought out risk, for obvious reasons they have tried to control it. Historically, they have not placed great faith in the rope. The risk of falling has been controlled chiefly by adopting a particular stance on the slope, always keeping three points of contact with it, and proceeding in a slow and deliberate manner. The climber pauses at some resting point, studies the terrain, plans the next moves, perhaps moves forward just enough to test them, rests again, and then executes the moves to the next rest.

But climbers are tackling ever smoother and steeper terrain. Rests may be few and far between. On an exceedingly smooth slope the climber may rely on momentum. He may leap for a hold. On steep or overhanging terrain he may rely on speed, hoping to get to a distant resting point before his strength fails. In any case, strength and speed are to some extent interchangeable. It is a matter of elementary physics. Force (or strength) is necessary to set a body in motion, but bodies in motion tend to stay in motion. Often the trick in a very difficult move is to make it quickly. Climbing is becoming more dynamic. Climbing has always been a kind of dance, but it is becoming allegro instead of adagio.

The requirement of speed suggests a new kind of training (see "Talus Running"). The climber must learn to see terrain and respond to it quickly, with a minimum of thought between the seeing and the doing. He must climb more automatically, more by conditioning than by deliberation.

## PEAK BAGGING

For many people the object of climbing is the summit. It can be an easy summit by the easiest route. "Peak baggers" often have little knowledge of climbing techniques and scarcely think of themselves as climbers. The summit offers a view and a fixed point for turning around. Beyond the view, the exercise, and the companionship of the ascent, peak baggers may ask no more. Some do like to go quickly and "collect" as many summits as possible.

Among climbers the term "peak bagger" can be a pejorative, perhaps because the activity requires no unusual skills, and the elements of challenge and risk are less conspicuous. However, for the beginner peak bagging can be both instructive and stylish. And it is readily accessible. Beyond the usual requirements of high-elevation backpacking no special equipment or technical knowledge is needed to reach most mountain summits in the United States. The beginner need only go to a high elevation in nearby mountains, look around for an easy summit, and go to it. The chief hazards are knocking rocks loose, slipping on steep snow, and bad weather; nothing more than ordinary prudence is necessary to avoid these hazards. Of course, the inexperienced mountaineer may well go with a companion or two.

Peak bagging is an excellent way to strengthen your legs and build overall stamina and body condition. Backpacking will do the same, but I would rather climb a peak than carry a pack. Much high-mountain terrain consists of talus slopes, and these provide the opportunity for a valuable exercise described in the next section — talus running. As for style, the peak bagger needs no special gear. You can go quickly. You can go alone. You can make light of the difficulties, which are likely to be modest. You need not follow a map or guidebook, nor even reach the summit. You can simply concentrate on fluid and beautiful movement.

## TALUS RUNNING

So far talus running has relatively few adherents. However, it has been recognized as extraordinary training for rock climbing, especially for the new more dynamic mode of climbing.

The best talus for the beginner is nearly level and consists of blocks about three feet across. Just walking on talus takes some getting used to. You must learn how well your feet will stick on the ever changing angles of surfaces, how to move your body smoothly from one balance point to the next, how to cope with the occasional shifting of blocks under you. As you gain confidence, you can increase your speed. Because for the beginner talus running takes intense concentration, your nervous system may fatigue quickly, and you will need frequent rests. It is exactly this concentration which practice reduces to a minimum. After a while the countless little responses come easily. Body and mind are finely tuned.

When you are ready, you can move on to steeper slopes and larger blocks. On the largest blocks the hands come into play, but the talus runner continues to lope along more like a monkey than the traditional slow-paced image of a mountain climber. Like a dancer, the talus runner has endless opportunities for creative or stylish movement: graceful leaps, delicate balances, and intricate series of leaps and balances. Yet in some ways the art is more interesting than dance. The terrain is an ever changing stage, and the next demands of it are not completely known. The talus runner has a theme but must improvise upon it quickly.

Falls on talus can be serious. If you start to fall, keep your feet out of the holes between blocks. Cushion your body with your hands, but relax your body. I have collapsed in a heap many times on talus and have as yet escaped injury. Be alert also to the fact that some kinds of rock have especially sharp edges. Granite is relatively safe, but falls on fine-textured metamorphic or volcanic rocks easily produce nasty cuts.

Neither heavy mountain boots nor rock-climbing shoes are well suited to talus running. Stiff-soled boots provide poor friction and impede the springing action of the feet. Shoes properly fitted for rock climbing are too tight for talus running. Jogging or cross-country shoes are best. These should have thick but flexible soles that will protect the feet from bruises. Other than that, bruises are avoided by stepping lightly. Remember the monkey, the dancer, and the cat. They are your models.

## BOULDERING

Bouldering is rock climbing close to ground level, where an unchecked fall is not necessarily serious. The boulderer uses no rope or specialized gear except climbing shoes and gymnastic chalk (used to keep the hands dry) and needs no companions. Imagination and a tiny bit of cliff are all that is required. If the cliff is close to home or work, a few minutes a day are sufficient for this exercise.

Bouldering has played a major role in the advance of climbing standards. Often the boulderer operates only a few feet or even a few inches above gentle ground, and if a fall is inconsequential, he may push himself to the limit of his ability and make repeated efforts until he finally masters an extremely difficult and complex problem. Often several boulderers will work together on a problem, combining their inventive powers and indulging in a friendly competition until the problem is solved.

A very small cliff may appear to offer limited scope for climbing, but if the routes are too easy or routine, the inventive boulderer may put certain holds "off route" or restrict himself to a prescribed set of holds. He may do the problems with only one hand, with no hands or with no feet, or with one hand and one foot. Perhaps he will simply concentrate on a fluid and beautiful style. If the cliff is too low for sustained climbs upward, he can climb sideways.

All of these exercises are valuable training for longer climbs, but bouldering is more than preparation for other climbing; it is a recreation and art complete in itself. It is here that the climber is freest to be creative and to invent moves that are not required by the terrain.

## TOP ROPING

When bouldering, you may venture high enough above a safe landing that a fall would be serious. At some point, because of the difficulty or the length of a fall, you will want the protection of a climbing rope.

Any method that will check a falling climber by means of a rope is called a "belay." . . . The simplest involves a companion, the belayer, who assumes a braced or anchored stance above the climber, holds the rope that is tied to the climber, and takes in the slack rope. Alternatively, the belayer may be stationed at the base of the route. The rope then runs up to a pulleylike anchor point and back down to the climber. If the belay stance or anchor is directly above the climber, any fall will be short. Thus, the climber many proceed with perfect security and, as in bouldering, he may push himself to the limit.

If the top of the cliff is reached and the belay set up by means of an easy, alternate route which does not require the protection of the rope, then the climbing is called "top roping." It provides a quick and secure way for the climber to develop technique and stamina on longer, more sustained pitches of rock. However, the danger of top roping is that the climber may become dependent on the security of a top rope.

## FIFTH-CLASS CLIMBING

Often there is no easy way around to a belay stance or anchor above the climber. Some-one must climb up first. If the leader climbs without the protection of a rope, he is climbing "third class.". . . If the rope simply trails down behind the leader to a belayer stationed below, he is climbing "fourth class." Obviously, as the leader climbs higher above the belayer, there is less and less practical difference between fourth class and third class. At some point, perhaps only five or ten feet above the belayer, a fall will become very serious. In fourth-class climbing the rope serves mainly to protect the second climber, who has, in effect, a top rope.

As the leader proceeds, he may shorten the length of a possible fall by anchoring his rope to the rock at points along the way. The rope slides freely through a "carabiner" (a metal link with a gate for admitting the rope) attached to the anchor. Then if he falls ten feet above his last anchor or protection, he will drop twenty feet before the rope begins to check him. This mode of climbing, with intermediate protection points between the leader and the belayer, is called "fifth class."

On steep rock with modern equipment and methods, falls of twenty and even forty feet do not usually cause serious injury. The steeper and smoother the rock, the less likely the falling climber is to scrape or bounce against it before the rope checks him. Thus difficult terrain is often inherently safer than easy terrain. While the layman associates the greatest hazard with vertical or overhanging rock, climbers know that a fall through space to a soft landing against the end of the resilient climbing rope is relatively safe.

In twenty-seven years of rock climbing I have taken four falls longer than twenty-five feet. These falls resulted in one scraped elbow and one sprained ankle. I believe my experience is testimony to the efficiency of modern equipment and methods. Of course, the climber must know when it is reasonable to proceed to the point of a fall.

The varieties of climbing described so far are all free climbing; that is, the climber moves over the rock using only the holds the rock itself provides. He does not hold on to a rope or other gear except to place it in position to check a possible fall. He does not even lean against the rope or an anchor to rest. The rope and gear are a safety net. They serve only as protection against the worst consequences of a fall.

## AID CLIMBING

Where the rock does not offer adequate holds, the climber may attach a variety of devices to the rock for aid points. The climbing is then "aid climbing" (formerly called "sixth class."

Aid many be employed to make a route easier than it would be as a free climb, or to extend the possible worlds the climber can explore. It may require a high level of mechanical imagination and skill in addition to the same physical skills and mental control involved in free climbing. A mixture of aided moves and free moves can be especially demanding.

Although some routes are inconceivable without aid, there is a very impressive tradition of aid climbs eventually "going free." The two varieties of climbing offer different experiences, but the prevalent feeling among climbers is that free climbing is the more elegant mode. Thus the first free ascent of an aid route generally attracts recognition and approval from the climbing community, while an aided ascent of a route which has gone free does not. . . .

## BIG-WALL CLIMBING

Routes of such length and sustained difficulty that climbers usually spend several days on them are "big walls." The most famous big-wall routes are those on El Capitan in Yosemite Valley. The climbing ordinarily involves hauling heavy loads of gear, much aid climbing, and much mounting of fixed ropes by means of mechanical ascenders ("jumaring"). On big walls style is usually subordinated to the objective of getting to the top.

Big walls offer grand adventure and make great demands on the climbers' skill and tenacity, but I must here admit to certain prejudices. I have an especial dislike for hauling and jumaring. They are too much like work, and jumaring is really scary. And I don't care for aid climbing. So I am not a wall climber. I do have a couple of comments to offer as something of an outside observer.

First, I am always amazed to see eager, inexpert climbers tackle big walls. They surround themselves with piles of sophisticated gear, spend hours poring over it, then inch slowly up the wall. All too often they think that in a few days on El Cap they have reached the pinnacle of climbing accomplishment, never realizing how much they have relied on equipment. Over the years since the first big-wall climbs, improvements in equipment have made pitches which were once near the limit of the possible into relatively straightforward mechanical operations. Of course, expert climbers have maintained the challenge of big walls by free-climbing many former aid pitches or by moving on to new and more difficult aid problems. All too often, however, beginners who are drawn to big walls focus on the application of sophisticated gear rather than on the development of climbing skills.

Second, a well-developed sense of style seems to me especially important to the preservation of wall-climbing values. . . .

## FREE SOLOING

One September day in 1976, at the Shawangunks in New York State, I was leading 150 feet above the ground, clipping my rope into the fixed protection, when an elderly gentleman climbed past me a few feet to one side. He was doing an easier route, but like all Shawangunks routes, it was practically vertical. He climbed alone with no rope or gear except a few runners and carabiners slung over his shoulder. We traded greetings, and I watched him struggle with a strenuous move. It was not difficult to guess that I was watching Fritz Wiessner. He was one of the leading climbers in Europe in the 1920s; fifty years later he was free-soloing Three Pines at the "Gunks." Three Pines is a "beginner's climb," but I thought, there is something to which I aspire: a certain longevity and a purity of style which imply much.

*Free soloing* is not for beginners, as it demands exacting study. The free soloer who expects to live very long will approach the rock rather more cautiously and carefully than his colleague with a belay. He will not push his limits. He will not attempt some routes, such as face climbs on especially tiny holds, because they are less forgiving of misjudgments. He will move more slowly and deliberately, relying on great physical and mental reserves. And he will have made a thorough study of the art of climbing down.

Most expert climbers go alone and unroped on difficult terrain at least occasionally. Free soloing seems either the craziest thing a climber can do or else the ultimate accomplishment. If climbing is viewed as the exploration of one's inner resources, rather than as the conquest of a wall, then certainly free soloing is the ultimate step. I have noticed this about it: rarely has an expert climber been killed free soloing a difficult route. And never have I met a free soloer who seemed anything but humbled by the experience.

## BUILDERING

It should be no surprise that climbers are sometimes unable to resist the opportunities afforded by a building. Or that frustrated climbers turn to buildings when rock is not handy. On university campuses especially, climbers have employed ropes and the full range of climbing techniques to scale buildings. This is usually done at night and commonly gets the climbers into trouble. Once I was minding my own business on a second-story window ledge when a policeman accosted me with, "What are you doing up there?"

I responded impulsively, "I'm a burglar." He did not have the grace to laugh.

Much trouble can be saved by restricting oneself to daytime or evening "buildering" — what is, in effect, low-level bouldering on artificial structures. It is best to go without gear and to have a story ready, such as: "I tossed my cap in the air, and it landed up there."

The San Francisco Bay Area rock outcrops close to my home do not afford many opportunities for crack climbing, which employs a set of techniques distinct from those used to climb smooth or steep faces. However, good cracks are common on buildings, especially where two buildings come close together without quite touching. A fifteen-minute walk from my home through downtown Berkeley takes me past four excellent cracks and several other interesting problems.

Buildering is both practice for rock climbing and an art in itself. Problems are less obvious than those on rock, and the techniques required to solve them may be bizarre.

It is to be hoped that one day authorities will recognize that buildings are a vast and legitimate resource for recreation, especially in the inner cities. However, that recognition will require a profound social revolution.

Of course, it wasn't. Two years later, despite a permanently lame right leg as a result of this stone avalanche in Wales, Lunn resumed climbing, *alone,* and went on to become a distinguished mountaineer and author, particularly in the Alpine field. He made the first ski ascent of several peaks and wrote memorably on the craft of ski running. Below is a selection from his early work, *The Mountains of Youth* (1925).

# ARNOLD LUNN

# My Last Climb

Two days after I first arrived at Tal-y-Llyn in 1909, I wandered up to Llyn Cae, surely the loveliest of all the Welsh tarns. A magnificent gully seamed the face of the dark cliffs beyond the lake. I did not then know that this was the Great Gully of Craig y Cae, Owen Glynne Jones's favorite Welsh climb. Had I known this I should not have started the ascent at 5 P.M.

Since then a miniature landslide has converted the famous cave pitch into an easy scramble, which is a pity. But when I first climbed the gully I could have dispensed with unnecessary difficulties, for I began the climb far too late in the day. Like most men who have learned to climb in the Alps, I tended to underestimate the necessary allowance of time for a great Welsh gully, and before long I realized that if the last pitches should prove severe, I should not reach the top that night. Luckily, the last stages were interesting but straightforward, and as the light failed I scrambled out of the narrow exit of the final crack. I enjoyed the climb, and I have seen few more impressive sights than the black waters of the tarn far below, framed between the dark smooth cliffs which confine the recesses of the gully.

On the following day I met two friends, a little distance above Tall-y-Llyn. One of them was carrying a fisherman's rod, but the other was wearing well-nailed boots. This looked more hopeful, so I asked whether they would like to join me someday on a climb. Mr. Syme, the owner of the boots, had climbed before. His friend, Mr. Warren, was quite prepared to sample a Welsh gully, and they both agreed to meet me next day.

That night C. Scott Lindsay arrived, and next morning the four of us—Lindsay, my new friends, and I—set out to climb the Great Gully. A casual remark of Mr. Syme's revealed the fact that Mr. Warren was a rising surgeon on the staff of the London Hospital. Another casual remark disclosed the name of the small village where Warren and Syme were staying. I should at this moment be wearing an artificial leg but for this lucky series of accidents, beginning with the nailed boots which Syme was wearing and which had effected our introduction.

On the following day Lindsay felt like a rest, so I set off alone and climbed the east ridge of Cyfrwy, off which I fell two days later. It is an interesting climb, not very difficult judged by modern standards, but quite amusing. A steep face . . . looks sensational but is really quite easy. The best thing on the ridge is a miniature Mummery crack which calls for skill if one wishes to climb it without disproportionate effort.

On August 28 I started for my last climb. Lindsay was not feeling fit, and he left me near the top of Cader Idris. I decided to descend the east and to climb the north ridge of Cyfrwy. I was carrying a short rope which I had brought along on the chance that Lindsay might join me.

The day was perfect. The burnished silver of the sea melted into a golden haze. Light shadows cast by scudding clouds drifted across the blue and distant hills. The sun flooded down on the rocks. I slid down the crack and reached the top of the steep face of rock above "The Table." The usual route dodges the top fifteen feet of this face, and by an easy traverse reaches a lower ledge. But on that glorious afternoon I longed to spin out the joys of Cyfrwy, and I found a direct route from the top to the bottom of this wall, a steep but not very severe variation.

It was one of those days when to be alive is "very heaven." The feel of the warm, dry rocks and the easy rhythm of the descending motion gave me an almost sensuous pleasure. One toyed with the thought of danger, so complete was the confidence inspired by the firm touch of the wrinkled rocks. . . .

I was glad to be alone. I reveled in the freedom from the restraints of the rope, and from the need to synchronize my movements with the movements of companions.

I have never enjoyed rock climbing more. I have never enjoyed rock climbing since. But, at least, the hills gave me of their best, full measure and overflowing, in those last few golden moments before I fell.

A few minutes later, Lindsay, who was admiring the view from Cader, was startled by the thunder of a stone avalanche. He turned to a stray tourist, urging him to follow, and dashed off in the direction of Cyfrwy.

And this is what had happened. I had just lowered myself off the edge of "The Table." . . . There was no suggestion of danger. Suddenly the mountain seemed to sway, and a quiver ran through the rocks. I clung for one brief moment of agony to the face of the cliff. And then suddenly a vast block, which must have been about ten feet high and several feet thick, separated itself from the face, heeled over on top of me, and carried me with it into space. I turned a somersault, struck the cliff some distance below, bounded off once again, and, after crashing against the ridge two or three more times, landed on a sloping ledge about 7 feet broad. The thunder of the rocks falling through the 150 feet below my resting point showed how narrow had been my escape.

I had fallen a distance which Lindsay estimated at 100 feet. It was not a sliding fall, for except when I struck and rebounded I was not in contact with the ridge. The fall was long enough for me to retain a very vivid memory of the thoughts which chased each other through my brain during those few crowded seconds. I can still feel the clammy horror of the moment when the solid mountain face trembled below me, but the fall, once I was fairly off, blunted the edge of fear. My emotions were subdued, as if I had been partially anesthetized. I remember vividly seeing the mountains upside down after my first somersault. I remember the disappointment as I realized that I had not stopped and that I was still falling. I remember making despairing movements with my hands in a futile attempt to check my downward progress.

The chief impression was a queer feeling that the stable order of nature had been overturned. The tranquil and immobile hills had been startled into a mood of furious and malignant activity, like a dangerous dog roused from a peaceful nap by some inattentive passerby who has trodden on him unawares. And every time I struck the cliff only to be hurled downward once again, I felt like a small boy who is being knocked about by a persistent bully — "Will he never stop? . . . surely he can't hit me again . . . surly he's hurt me enough."

When at last I landed, I tried to sit up, but fell back hurriedly on seeing my leg. The lower part was bent almost at right angles. It was not merely broken, it was shattered and crushed.

I shouted and shouted and heard no reply. Had Lindsay returned home? Would I have to wait for hours before help came?

Solitude had lost its charm. I no longer rejoiced in my freedom from intrusion. On the contrary, I raised my voice and called upon society to come to my assistance. I set immense store on my membership in the Human Club, and very urgently did I summon my fellow members to my assistance.

And then suddenly I heard an answering cry, and my shouts died away in a sob of heartfelt relief.

And while I waited for help, I looked up at the scar on the cliff where the crag had broken away, and I realized all that I was in danger of losing. Had I climbed my last mountain?

During the war the cheery dogmatism of some second lieutenant home from the front was extremely consoling, for the human mind is illogical and the will to believe very potent. And so when Lindsay arrived and replied with a hearty affirmative when I asked him whether I should ever climb again, I was greatly comforted, even though Lindsay knew less of broken legs than the average subaltern of the chances of peace.

Lindsay was preceded by an ancient man who keeps the hut on Cader. He examined my leg with a critical eye and informed me that it was broken. He then remarked that I had been very ill advised to stray off the path on the "rough places" where even the natives did not venture. He grasped my leg, and moved it a little higher onto the ledge. This hurt. He then uncoiled my rope and secured me to a buttress which overhung my narrow perch.

Then Lindsay staggered onto the ledge, gave one glance at my leg, turned a curious color, and sat down hurriedly. He suggested breaking off a gate and carrying me down on it. The ancient man of Cader hazarded a tentative suggestion in favour of sacks. I demurred, for a sack may be appropriate to a corpse but is not conducive to the comfort of a wounded man.

Lindsay, by a lucky accident, remembered Warren's address, and so I sent him off to find him. He left me in charge of the tourist who had followed him, and departed with the man of Cader.

Lindsay's chance companion was useful while he stayed, for I was lying on a sloping ledge, and was glad of his shoulder as a pillow. Ten minutes passed, and my companion remarked that he thought he ought to be going. I protested, but could not move him. His wife, he said, would be getting anxious. I hinted that his wife's anxiety might be ignored. "Ah, but you don't know my wife," he replied, and, so saying, left me.

He consented to leave his cap behind as a pillow. A month later he wrote and asked my why I had not returned it. This struck me as unreasonable, but—as he justly observed—I did not know his wife.

I fell at 4 P.M. About 7:30 P.M. it became colder, and shivering made the pain worse. About 7:45 P.M. the old man of Cader returned with some warm tea which he had brewed for me, and for which I was more than grateful. Half an hour later the local policeman arrived with a search party and a stretcher.

Luckily the ledge ran across onto easy ground, but it was not until midnight—eight hours after my fall—that I reached the Angel Hotel

My leg was broken, crushed, and comminuted. Twice the preparations were made for amputation. Twice my temperature fell in the nick of time. At the end of a week I was taken home, and lay on my back for four months, much consoled by a Christian Scientist who assured me that my leg was intact. But it was not to Mrs. Eddy but to the faint hope of the hills that I turned for comfort in the long nights when pain had banished sleep.

Or *malgré lui*, as Molière would have it. This is an odd tale of inadvertence set in the wilderness of the Brooks Range of Alaska. A casual hike up the lower slope of a mountain became something else entirely when, too late, McGinniss realized that "the last fifty feet were not a scree slope at all, but that they were, in fact, the side of a cliff." This is an excerpt from his 1980 book, *Going to Extremes*.

# JOE McGINNISS

# The Mountaineer Despite Himself

The morning was foggy and still. A solid low overcast blocked all view of anything more than fifty feet above the ground. We stayed in our tents much later than usual. There seemed nothing to get up for. Nothing to see; nothing to do. And we suffered from the extreme frustration of knowing that we had such a limited amount of time remaining to us. We could spend one more night here; possibly two. Then we would have to move on, farther up the Itkillik Valley. Or down the valley. Up the map, anyway. Farther north. Because there were other areas which John Kauffmann wanted to reach on this trip.

So it seemed possible that, having come all this distance, we would never even see Cockedhat Mountain. Not that the trip would then have been deemed a failure. We had moved, not only beyond tree line, but beyond the standard definitions of concepts such as failure and success. Here, there would be a failure only if someone fell off a mountain or got mauled by a bear. Otherwise, just being here was a success. Still, to spend the remainder of the trip wandering along creek beds in heavy mist would have been, at the least, a disappointment.

I lay in the tent, reading the one book I had brought with me, the Viking portable edition of Faulkner. I had never enjoyed Faulkner very much, but I thought that now, possibly, I would find myself in the mood for his novella *The Bear*.

Ray Bane lay next to me, filling page after page in a notebook. "I don't think a wilderness experience is complete," he said, "until it's been written about."

I wandered outside for a while and tossed a willow branch or two in the fire. I was getting into a mood as gloomy as the day. What a shame that we had, apparently, used up our quota of good weather on what had been, in terms of scenery and terrain, the least dramatic portion of the trip. And what an amazing contrast between one side of Oolah Pass and the other. That bright hot sun the first three days. And now three days of Arctic mist. Here we were, more than halfway up a valley which, quite possibly, no one in modern times had viewed before, except by air. And now we weren't able to see it either. Well, only the bottom fifty feet. Even without John Kauffmann to tell us how dramatic Cockedhat Mountain looked, we could have guessed, just from studying the topographical maps, that something splendid and unusual lay at the valley's upper end. Just from the way all the little brown contour lines wriggled around. We had reached a point, however, where maps did not satisfy. We were hungry for the real thing. But we had absolutely no control over whether or not we would ever be able to see it, and absolutely no way of predicting what direction the weather pattern might take. Sometimes, Ray Bane said, weather like this blew off in a couple of days. Sometimes it settled in for weeks. The general rule, however, was that as August progressed, weather in the Arctic turned damp, as well as colder. We were right at the midline. Two weeks earlier, Ray said, he could have predicted with confidence that the sun would be shining within a couple of days. Two weeks later, he would have advised us to pack our things and move on. Right now, he could not guess. So we sat around the fire and tried to convince ourselves that the overcast was rising, or brightening, just a bit. But then new drizzle started, and we all returned to our tents.

"Okay," Ray said. "I've had enough. Drastic measures are called for." He put down his notebook and unzipped the netting at the front of our tent. He stepped outside into the mist. I laid down my Faulkner and followed.

He began shouting, in an angry, guttural voice, at the sky. He was shouting something in Eskimo, repeating the same phrases several times.

"There," he said, "that ought to do it."

"What did you say?"

"I'm not sure I really ought to translate," he said. "It's pretty vulgar." But by then everyone else had come out of their tents, too, hearing the noise, and Ray had no choice. It was, he said, an old Eskimo chant, used to anger the sun; to provoke it into coming out from its hiding place behind the clouds. In translation it was: "Sun, Sun, your vagina smells horrible." Sometimes, Ray said, crude methods prove to be the most effective.

The weather did not improve, but by midday restlessness overcame our depression.

We decided to split up and take day hikes in different directions. John Kauffmann and Boyd would go up the ravine in which we were camped. Ray said he would venture farther up the main valley so that, if the weather did improve the next day, he would have an idea of the best route to Cockedhat. Ogden said his feet were bothering him and that he really rather welcomed a day off. He would spend the afternoon in camp.

I looked at the mountain just above us. Its lower slope began across the tributary stream, just on the other side of the ravine. The slope was composed mostly of scree and talus: loose rock debris. The upper, craggy rocky section disappeared into the mist. On the map, the summit, which would be almost directly above our camp, across the ravine, seemed to be about 5,500 feet. I decided I would hike up the lower slope, until it became too difficult to go higher.

It was 1 P.M. when I began. I crossed the tributary and hiked up the east side of the ravine for about a mile. Then I began to cut diagonally up the slope, back in the direction from which I'd come. The higher I went, the steeper the side of the slope became, and when I looked down, after about forty-five minutes, I was surprised both by how far up I had come and by how sharply the slope dropped off beneath my feet. I was also surprised at the looseness of the scree. Every time I stopped, for even a moment, I could feel the slope begin to give way beneath my boots, and start to slide. Therefore, I had to keep moving.

There was a rock ledge above me. I couldn't be sure how far, maybe another two hundred feet. I started toward it, thinking that, once there, I would at least be able to sit and rest. I began scrambling diagonally, on all fours, across the scree, which got looser the higher I went, and seemed ever more prone to start sliding. I was already so high by this time, and the mountainside below me so steep, that I decided I'd be better off continuing up. From that ledge above me, I could probably find an easier and safer route down. Now, if I could only reach the ledge before the whole damn mountain started to slide. . . .

The scree was turning to powder now, and more and more was giving way beneath me with every step. I would start to slide downward, then claw my way back, always trying to move diagonally upward toward the ledge. Once a real slide started, it might not stop, and with nothing solid to cling to below the ledge, I might become part of the slide.

I was badly out of breath now, and getting worried, but I continued to scuttle, as best I could, gradually higher. The ledge appeared to be only fifty feet above me, but those fifty feet suddenly took on a new and more alarming degree of steepness. There was now almost a sheer wall of scree, and I scrambled up frantically, grabbing at any rock that looked larger than my hand. I could find nothing—neither handhold nor foothold—that would support me for more than seconds, until I reached the base of the ledge.

I wedged a boot into a crevice between two loose rocks, tested it with weight, and it held. I grabbed quickly at rocks that jutted out overhead, and found a couple of cracks into which I was able to squeeze my fingers. I clung to the side of the ledge, panting for breath. Then I made the mistake of looking down.

From below, it had seemed I could just continue to scramble up the scree all the way. I had not realized until too late that the last fifty feet were not a scree slope at all, but that they were, in fact, the side of a cliff.

I was stuck. I was hanging on to the cliff now, precariously, and there was no orderly, safe way to climb down. All I could have done was let go, which, I realized, would have meant an unbroken fall of at least thirty feet to looser rocks below, and then probably an uncontrollable slide down the scree. A process which seemed quite certain to result in, if not loss of life, then loss of consciousness and, more than likely, broken bones. Not a cheery prospect deep in the Brooks Range.

Up was the only way to go. And I had to move fast, because this temporary hold I had was giving way. This was most definitely rock climbing now; not by any stretch of definition was it hiking. What was worse, it was climbing on extremely unsuitable rock, alone, with no equipment, no training, and absolutely no aptitude for the techniques.

I moved quickly. From both fatigue and fear. My legs, when I would find a jutting rock on which to support them, were trembling so hard I was afraid that that motion alone would dislodge the rock. My calf and thigh muscles had not been expecting this; nor had the muscles of my arms. I wasn't even wearing gloves, in fact — this was supposed to have been just a little walk on the lower slope — and my fingers were now scraped and bleeding.

I paused once more, looking up. I still could not see how far I had to go to reach the ledge. What if it had not really been a ledge? What if I had judged it incorrectly from below? I was going higher and higher now, up the crumbling rock face of a mountain, and with every new frantic scramble, the consequences, were I to fall, grew more severe.

Once more I reached above me for something to cling to as I tried to push myself upward with my legs. I could feel rocks all around me giving way. This was an old decayed mountain. The whole face seemed about to collapse. Another handhold, and then another, and then — thank God! — I hoisted myself up over the ledge, onto a small plateau that was covered by a thin layer of tundra. I lay there panting, in my no longer brand-new Camp Seven wind parka. I kissed the tundra. How magnificent it felt; how splendid it looked; how fine it was to feel living earth again.

The ledge was the size of about three or four double beds pushed together. Once my breath and composure had returned, I began to look around, trying to decide what to do next. I felt like a cat up a tree, but I was a long way from the nearest fire department.

Descending the way I had come up was out of the question. But in what other direction could I go? I had approached this ledge from the southwest, originally, cutting back toward the main valley after my hike of a mile or so up the ravine. The ledge was on the western, or ravine, side of the mountain. Just east of it, there was a long, sharp drop, and then the main mountain wall rose even higher. Looking up in that direction, I could see an old, dirty glacier about a hundred yards away. It was just a rim of ice, really; flanked by moraine. There was a ridge leading out from the rock wall to the left of this glacier, a long ridge which leveled out quickly and then proceeded in a northerly direction, rising, as it did, toward what I considered the front of the mountain — the aspect which overlooked the valley. It seemed that if I started out along the ridge that led north from the ledge I was on, I might at some point be able to cut across the scree side of a basin between the ridges and reach the second, longer ridge. From there, I might proceed to the northern face of the mountain, and, I hoped, find a way back down to the valley floor.

I was reluctant to leave the hard-won security of my little ledge, but a cold mist was now swirling around me, and a steady drizzle was starting to fall. It was already 4 P.M., and if I were not back in camp by dinnertime the others would worry, and eventually come looking for me. To cause them that inconvenience would have been a serious breach of hiking etiquette. Besides, my instinct for self-preservation had made me extremely eager to get back to the valley floor.

Amazing, how relative it all was: a week earlier, a campsite halfway up a nameless side valley that led from the Itkillik River to Cockedhat Mountain in the central Brooks Range, north of the Arctic Divide, would have seemed the ultimate in wildness and remoteness. It was still not exactly an urban ambience, but from 2,000 feet higher — from a tundra-covered perch two-thirds of the way up a nameless and unstable mountain — the camp seemed the essence of security and comfort.

Within a quarter mile, the ridge that my ledge opened onto began a steep climb to a rock wall of which I wanted no part. I dropped down from the ridge and tried to work my way around the scree rim of the basin, to the ridge that led down from the glacier. It was the same syndrome as before: scurrying along on all fours with the slope sliding away beneath my feet. By now, though, I was familiar enough with the sensation to be merely worried, and not panic-stricken, and I already was sufficiently experienced in the technique to know enough not to stop.

I made it to the new ridge, which was longer, wider, and more substantial than the one I had left. I was able to walk along it comfortably, heading north, toward what would be the front of the mountain. This ridge, too, sloped upward, at first gradually, then sharply, but here, instead of a sheer, unclimbable rock wall, there was a sharp slope of loose talus and patches of tundra, up which I was able to pick my way. I was once again on hands and knees — climbing, not hiking — and the larger rocks and boulders of the talus seemed scarcely more stable than the scree, but there were little veins of tundra threaded among them, and, by choosing my route carefully, I was able to work my way to the top without mishap.

I climbed over a final row of boulders, onto a ledge, looked around, and only then realized that I had, quite by accident, ascended to the summit of the mountain. To the front summit, at least. Whether or not it was the true summit depended on where one considered that one mountain ended and another began, for a mile or so farther back, above the glacier, this ridge, and the rock wall it led to, climbed to an even higher point. But where I was now standing was what had appeared as the summit of this mountain from below, from our camp, and without having had the slightest intention of doing so, I had reached it.

Across the ravine, there was a 6,800-foot peak about a mile and half back to the southwest. It was a craggy, barren mountain, as was the one I was on, and its summit was enshrouded by fog. My own altitude seemed to be about 5,500 feet.

Looking due west, I could see to the upper end of the valley, to where the front walls of the Cockedhat Mountain mass began to rise. They appeared made of dark gray, almost slate-colored stone, but it was hard to tell much about them because even the lower slopes were quickly hidden by drifting mist.

To the east, I could look all the way down the valley, to the Itkillik Valley and, where clouds permitted, to the Oolah Mountain sector that lay beyond.

But it was the view directly across the side valley, the view of the weird, unearthly, jumbled, tilted, platelike, scaly, multilayered valley wall, that held my eye.

We had experienced some sense of it yesterday, from the head of the valley, but from here, looking straight across, from this higher altitude, the scene was much more astonishing.

I had no idea what sort of geologic activity had formed these mountains, or why they were — in angle, shape, and texture — so unlike any other mountains I'd ever seen, but looking at them through the mist, from my hard-won mini-summit, was like being given a unique glimpse into prehistoric times.

It was as if a giant had been sleeping in this valley and had rolled to one side, pressing back the northern valley wall. Then another image came to mind: the angle at which those mountain walls sloped back from the valley floor seemed the same as that angle at which human figures in certain Renaissance paintings recoiled from the image of the newly risen Christ.

I stepped forward to the front of the ledge and looked down, through the mist, to the bottom of the valley. A rainbow arched toward the lower end. Looking just below me, and slightly to the left, across the ravine, I could also see, very faintly, through my monocular, and through the mist, the specks of bright color that were our tents.

Foolishly, and in a hurry, I decided to work my way straight down the front of the ledge, instead of descending to the east, on a more gradual slope that led back down the valley, away from the camp. I had to come down chimney fashion, my back wedged against one side of a little rock chute, my feet against the other with rocks and boulders, loosened by my passage, beginning to tumble down behind me. I clung to the sides, fighting for handholds and footholds, just as I had done coming up, but there, with the rocks evern bigger, though just as loose, the situation was, in a way, even more precarious. Several times the rolling rocks, and the smaller stones and loose scree that fell behind them, almost carried me away, and at this angle it would not have been a slide that resulted in only cuts and bruises; it would have meant, once again, a fall, of undetermined distance, the consequences of which I much preferred not to imagine.

Tired and trembling, both from exhaustion and from the aftermath of fear, I slid back into camp at 6 P.M. The others were already there, Ogden, in fact, had spotted me, through binoculars, about halfway down, and had followed my progress the rest of the way.

"Jolly good show," he remarked. "Thought you might have been in for a bit of a tumble."

Freeze-dried stew and freeze-dried rice in the damp and chilly fog, and it was the best meal of the trip. I kept looking up at where I had been; not really sure I had done it, and wondering whether I had intended to all along. It was, actually, an ordinary-looking mountain, and the front summit, I determined from the map, was not much more than 1,500 feet above our camp. But I knew how deceiving appearances were. I had been up there. And it was very different from down here.

Mailer was only twenty-five when *The Naked and the Dead*, from which the passage below is taken, was published in 1948. Reviewers and librarians made much of the novel's realism — by which many meant solely its liberal use of the soldier's four-letter patois — and realism is what this excerpt provides: climbing a mountain is not sport when you don't want to and don't know how.

# NORMAN MAILER

# The Ledge

On the same afternoon that Major Dalleson was mounting his attack, the platoon continued to climb Mount Anaka. In the awful heat of the middle slopes they bogged down. Each time they passed through a draw or hollow the air seemed to be refracted from the blazing rocks, and after a time their cheek muscles ached from the continual squinting. It was a minor pain and should have been lost in the muscle cramps of their thighs, the sullen vicious aching of their backs, but it became the greatest torment of the march. The bright light lanced like splinters into the tender flesh of their eyeballs, danced about the base of their brains in reddened choleric circles. They lost all account of the distance they had covered; everything beneath them had blurred, and the individual torments of each kind of terrain were forgotten. They no longer cared if the next hundred yards was a barren rock slope or a patch of brush and forest. Each had its own painful disadvantages. They wavered like a file of drunks, plodded along with their heads bent down, their arms slapping spasmodically at their sides. All their equipment had become leaden, and a variety of sores had farrowed on every bony knob of their bodies. Their shoulders were blistered from the pack bands, their waists were bruised from the jouncing of their cartridge belts, and their rifles clanked abrasively against their sides, raising blisters on their hips. Their shirts had long washed lines of white where perspiration had dried.

They moved numbly, straggling upward from rock to rock, panting and sobbing with exhaustion. Against his will Croft was forced to give them a break every few minutes; they rested now for as long a period as they marched, lying dumbly on their backs, their arms and legs spread-eagled. Like the litter-bearers, they had forgotten everything; they did not think of themselves as individual men any longer. They were merely envelopes of suffering. They had forgotten about the patrol, about the war, their past, they had even forgotten the earth they had just climbed. The men around them were merely vague irritating obstacles into which they blundered. The hot glaring sky and the burning rock were far more intimate. Their minds scurried about inside their bodies like rodents in a maze, concentrating fruitlessly first on the quivering of the overworked limb and then on the smarting of a sore, became buried for many minutes in the agony of drawing another breath.

Only two things ever intruded on this. They were afraid of Croft and this fear had become greater as they grew more exhausted; by now they waited for his voice, plunged themselves forward a few additional yards each time he flicked them with a command. A numb and stricken apprehension had settled over them, an unvoiced and almost bottomless terror of him.

And in opposition to that, they wanted to quit; they wanted that more than anything they had ever hungered for. Each step they advanced, each tremor of their muscles, each pang in their chests generated that desire. They moved forward with a dumb blistering hatred for the man who led them.

Croft was almost as exhausted; by now he appreciated the breaks as much as they did, was almost as willing to allow each halt to drag out to double its intended length. He had forgotten the peak of the mountain, he wanted to quit too, and each time a break ended he fought a quick battle with himself, exposed himself to all the temptations of rest, and then continued. He moved on because somewhere at the base of his mind was the directive that climbing this mountain was necessary. His decision had been made in the valley, and it lay as an iron warp in his mind. He could have turned back no more easily than he could have killed himself.

All through the afternoon they straggled forward, toiling up the gentler slopes, proceeding from rock to rock when the walls of the mountain became sheerer. They traveled from one ridge to another, stumbled painfully along the slanting inclines of minor knolls, slipped and fell many times when they passed over swatches of moist clay. The mountain seemed eternally to rear above them. They glimpsed its upper slopes through the fog of their effort, followed one another up the unending serpentines, and plodded along gratefully whenever their route was level for a time.

Minetta and Wyman and Roth were the most wretched. For several hours they had been at the tail of the column, keeping up to the men ahead with the greatest difficulty, and there was a bond between the three of them. Minetta and Wyman felt sorry for Roth, liked him because he was even more helpless than they. And Roth looked to them for support, knew in the knowledge of fatigue that they would not scorn him because they were only a little less prostrated than he.

He was making the most intense effort of his life. All the weeks and months Roth had been in the platoon he had absorbed each insult, each reproof with more and more pain. Instead of becoming indifferent or erecting a protective shell, he had become more sensitive. The patrol had keyed him to the point where he could not bear any more abuse, and he drove himself onward now with the knowledge that if he halted for too long the wrath and ridicule of the platoon would come down upon him.

But, even with this, he was breaking. There came a point where his legs would no longer function. Even when he stood still they were close to buckling under him. Toward the end of the afternoon he began to collapse. It was a slow process, dragging out through a series of pratfalls, a progression of stumbling and sliding and finally of dropping prostrate. He began to tumble every few hundred feet and the men in the platoon waited gratefully while he forced himself slowly to his feet, and staggered on again. But each fall came a little more quickly than the one that had preceded it. Roth moved forward almost unconsciously, his legs buckling at every misstep. After a half hour he could no longer get up without assistance, and each step he took was doubtful, uncertain, like an infant walking alone across a room. He even fell like an infant, his feet folding under him while he sat blankly on his thighs, a little bewildered that he was not still walking.

In time he began to irritate the platoon. Croft would not let them sit down and the enforced wait until Roth was able to walk again annoyed them. They began to wait for Roth to fall and the inevitable recurrence of it rasped their senses. Their anger began to shift from Croft to Roth.

The mountain was becoming more treacherous. For ten minutes Croft had been leading them along a rock ledge up the side of a sheer bluff of stone, and the path in places was only a few feet wide. At their right, never more than a yard or two away, was a drop of several hundred feet, and despite themselves they would pitch at times close to the edge. It roused another fear in them, and Roth's halts made them impatient. They were anxious to get past the ledge.

In the middle of this ascent Roth fell down, started to get up, and then sprawled out again when no one helped him. The rock surface of the ledge was hot but he felt comfortable lying against it. The afternoon rain had just begun and he felt it driving into his flesh, cooling the stone. He wasn't going to get up. Somewhere through his numbness another resentment had taken hold. What was the point of going on?

Someone was tugging at his shoulder, and he flung him off. "I can't go on," he gasped, "I can't go on, I can't." He slapped his fist weakly against the stone.

It was Gallagher trying to lift him. "Get up, you sonofabitch," Gallagher shouted. His body ached with the effort of holding Roth.

"I can't. Go 'way!"

Roth heard himself sobbing. He was dimly aware that most of the platoon had gathered around, were looking at him. But this had no effect; it gave him an odd bitter pleasure to have the others see him, an exaltation compounded of shame and fatigue.

Nothing more could happen after this. Let them see him weeping, let them know for one more time that he was the poorest man in the platoon. It was the only way he could find recognition. After so much anonymity, so much ridicule, this was almost better.

Gallagher was tugging at his shoulder again. "Go 'way, I can't get up," Roth bawled.

Gallagher shook him, feeling a compound of disgust and pity. More than that. He was afraid. Every muscle fiber demanded that he lie down beside Roth. Each time he drew a breath the agony and nausea in his chest made him feel like weeping too. If Roth didn't get up, he knew he also would collapse.

"Get up, Roth!"

"I can't."

Gallagher grasped him under the armpits and tried to lift him. The dead resisting weight was enraging. He dropped Roth and clouted him across the back of his head. "Get up, you Jew bastard!"

The blow, the word itself, stirred him like an electric charge. Roth felt himself getting to his feet, stumbling forward. It was the first time anyone had ever sworn at him that way, and it opened new vistas of failure and defeat. It wasn't bad enough that they judged him for his own faults, his own incapacities; now they included him in all the faults of a religion he didn't believe in, a race which didn't exist. "Hitlerism, race theories," he muttered. He was staggering forward dumbly, trying to absorb the shock. Why did they call him that, why didn't they see it wasn't his fault?

And there was something else working. All the protective devices, the sustaining façades of his life had been eroding slowly in the caustic air of the platoon; his exhaustion had pulled out the props, and Gallagher's blow had toppled the rest of the edifice. He was naked another way now. He rebelled against it, was frustrated that he could not speak to them and explain it away. It's ridiculous, thought Roth in the core of his brain, it's not a race, it's not a nation. If you don't believe in the religion, then why are you one? This was the prop that had collapsed, and even through his exhaustion he understood something Goldstein had always known. His own actions would be expanded from now on. People would not only dislike him, but they would make the ink a little darker on the label.

Well, let them. A saving anger, a magnificent anger came to his aid. For the first time in his life he was genuinely furious, and the anger excited his body, drove him on for a hundred yards, and then another hundred yards, and still another. His head smarted where Gallagher had struck him, his body tottered, but if they had not been marching he might have flung himself at the men. Fought them until he was unconscious. Nothing he could do was right, nothing would please them. He seethed, but with more than self-pity now. He understood. He was the butt because there always had to be a butt. A Jew was a punching bag because they could not do without one.

His body was so small. The rage was pathetic, but its pitifulness was unfair. If he had been stronger, he could have done something. And even so, as he churned along the trail behind the men there was something different in him, something more impressive. For these few minutes he was not afraid of the men. His body wavering, his head lolling on his shoulders, he fought clear of his exhaustion, straggled along oblivious of his body, alone in the new rage of his person.

Croft, at the point, was worried. He had not taken part when Roth had collapsed. For once he had been irresolute. The labor of leading the platoon for so many months, the tensions of the three days with Hearn, had been having their effect. He was tired, his senses rasped by everything that went wrong; all the sullenness of the men, their fatigue, their reluctance to go on had been causing attrition. The decision he had made after Martinez's reconnaissance had drained him. When Roth fell down the last time Croft had turned to go back to him and then had paused. At that moment he had been too weary to do anything. If Gallagher had not struck him, Croft might have interfered, but for once he was content to wait. All his lapses and minor failures seemed important to him. He was remembering with disgust his paralysis on the river when the Japanese had called to him; he was thinking of the combat since then, all the minor blank spots that had occurred before he could act. For once he was uncertain. The mountain still taunted him, still drew him forward, but it was with an automatic leaden response of his legs. He knew he had miscalculated the strength of the platoon, his own energy. There was only an hour or two until dark and they would never reach the peak before then.

The ledge they were on was becoming narrower. A hundred feet above him he could see the top of the ridge, rocky and jagged, almost impossible to traverse. Farther ahead the ledge rose upward and crossed the ridge and beyond should be the mountain peak. It could not be more than a thousand feet above them. He wanted to have the summit in view before they halted for the night.

But the ledge was becoming dangerous. The rain clouds had settled over them like bloated balloons, and they traveled forward in what was almost a fog. The rain was colder here. It chilled them and their feet slid upon the damp rock. After a few more minutes the rain obscured the ridge above them, and they inched along the ledge cautiously, their faces to the rock wall.

The ledge was no more than a foot wide now. The platoon worked along it very slowly, taking a purchase on the weeds and small bushes that grew out of the vertical cracks in the wall. Each step was painful, frightening, but the farther they inched out along the ledge the more terrifying became the idea of turning back. They hoped that at any moment the ledge would widen again, for they could not conceive of returning over a few of the places they had already crossed. This passage was dangerous enough to rouse them temporarily from their fatigue, and they moved alertly, strung out over forty yards. Once or twice they would look down, but it was too frightening. Even in the fog they could see a sheer drop of at least a hundred feet and it roused another kind of faintness. They would become conscious of the walls, which were of a soft gray slimy rock that seemed to breathe like the skin of a seal. It had an odious fleshlike sensation which roused panic, made them want to hasten.

The ledge narrowed to nine inches. Croft kept peering ahead in the mist, trying to determine if it would become wider. This was the first place on the mountain that demanded some skill. Until now it had been essentially a very high hill, but here he wished for a rope or a mountain pick. He continued along it, his arms and legs spread-eagled, hugging the rock, his fingers searching for crevices to latch upon.

He came to a gap in the ledge about four feet wide. There was nothing between, no bushes, no roots to which they could cling. The platform disappeared and then continued on the other side. In the gap there was only the sheer drop of the ridge wall. It would have been a simple jump, merely a long step on level ground, but there it meant leaping sideways, taking off from the left foot and landing with the right, having to gain his balance while he teetered on the ledge.

He slipped off his pack carefully, handed it to Martinez behind him, and hesitated for a moment, his right leg dangling over the gap. Then he leaped sideways, wavering for a moment on the other side before steadying himself.

"Jesus, who the fug can cross that?" he heard one of them mutter.

"Just wait there," Croft said, "I'm gonna see if the ledge widens out." He traveled along it for fifty feet, and discovered it was becoming broader again. This gave him a deep sense of relief, for otherwise it would have meant turning back to find another route. And he no longer knew if he could rouse the platoon to go up again.

He leaned over the gap and took his pack from Martinez. The distance was short enough for their hands to touch. Then he took Martinez's pack and moved a few yards farther away. "Okay, men," he called, "let's start coming over. The air's a helluva sight better on this side."

There was a nervous snicker. "Listen, Croft," he heard Red say, "is that fuggin ledge any wider?"

"Yeah, more than a bit." But Croft was annoyed at himself for answering. He should have told Red to shut up.

Roth, at the tail of the column, listened with dread. He would probably miss if he had to jump, and despite himself his body generated some anxiety. His anger was still present, but it had altered into a quieter resolve. He was very tired.

As he watched them pass their packs across and leap over, his fear increased. It was the kind of thing he had never been able to do, and a trace of an old panic he had known in gym classes when he waited for his turn on the high bar rose up to torment him.

Inevitably, his turn was approaching. Minetta, the last man ahead of him, hesitated on the edge and then skipped across, laughing weakly. "Jesus, a fuggin acrobat." Roth cleared his throat. "Make room, I'm coming," he said quietly. He handed over his pack.

Minetta was talking to him as though he were an animal. "Now, just take it easy, boy. There's nothing to it. Just take it easy, and you'll make it okay."

He resented that. "I'm all right," he said.

But when he stepped to the edge and looked over, his legs were dead. The other ledge was very far away. The rock bluffs dropped beneath him gauntly, emptily.

"I'm coming," he mumbled again, but he did not move. As he had been about to jump he had lost courage.

I'll count three to myself, he thought.

One.

Two.

Three.

But he could not move. The critical second elongated, and then was lost. His body had betrayed him. He wanted to jump and his body knew he could not make it.

Across the ledge he could hear Gallagher. "Get up close, Minetta, and catch that useless bastard." Gallagher crawled toward him through Minetta's feet, and extended his arm, glowered at him, "C'mon, all you got to do is catch my hand. You can fall that far."

They looked weird. Gallagher was crouched at Minetta's feet, his face and arm projecting through Minetta's legs. Roth stared at them, and was filled with contempt. He understood this Gallagher now. A bully, a frightened bully. There was something he could tell them. If he refused to jump, Croft would have to come back. The patrol would be over. And Roth knew himself at this instant, knew suddenly that he could face Croft.

But the platoon wouldn't understand. They would jeer him, take relief from their own weakness in abusing him. His heart was filled with bitterness. "I'm coming," he shouted suddenly. This was the way they wanted it.

He felt his left leg pushing him out, and he lurched forward awkwardly, his exhausted body propelling him too feebly. For an instant he saw Gallagher's face staring in surprise at him, and then he slipped past Gallagher's hand, scrabbled at the rock, and then at nothing.

In his fall Roth heard himself bellow with anger, and was amazed that he could make so great a noise. Through his numbness, through his disbelief, he had a thought before he crashed into the rocks far below. He wanted to live. A little man, tumbling through space.

Mallory wrote far less than he was written about, but something of the romantic hold this man had on the climbing fraternity may be understood from the essay excerpted below. Written for *The Climbers' Club Journal* in 1914, it expresses with grace and force his belief that, in climbing, man confronts the sublime as in no other sport. That pursuit of the sublime — sensed most profoundly at the interface between life and death — led Mallory to mount three expeditions to the highest point on Earth. The last of these, in 1924, may have culminated in an ascent of Everest, but the outcome remains the great mystery of mountaineering, for neither Mallory nor his comrade, Irvine, was ever seen again.

# GEORGE LEIGH MALLORY

# The Mountaineer as Artist

I seem to distinguish two sorts of climber, those who take a high line about climbing and those who take no particular line at all. It is depressing to think how little I understand either, and I can hardly believe that the second sort are such fools as I imagine. Perhaps the distinction has no reality; it may be that it is only a question of attitude. Still, even as an attitude, the position of the first sort of climber strikes a less violent shock of discord with mere reason. Climbing for them means something more than a common amusement, and more than other forms of athletic pursuit mean to other men; it has a recognized importance in life. If you could deprive them of it they would be conscious of a definite degradation, a loss of virtue. For those who take the high line about it climbing may be one of the modern ways of salvation along with slumming, statistics, and other forms of culture, and more complete than any of these. They have an arrogance with regard to this hobby never equaled even by a little king among grouse killers. It never, for instance, presents itself to them as comparable with field sports. They assume an unmeasured superiority. And yet — they give no explanation.

I am myself one of the arrogant sort, and may serve well for example, because I happen also to be a sportsman. It is not intended that any inference as to my habits should follow from this premise. You may easily be a sportsman though you have never walked with a gun under your arm, nor bestrid a tall horse in your pink. I am a sportsman simply because men say that I am; it would be impossible to convince them of the contrary, and it's no use complaining; and, once I have humbly accepted my fate and settled down in this way of life, I am proud to show, if I can, how I deserve the title. Though a sportsman may be guiltless of sporting deeds, one who has acquired the sporting reputation will show cause in kind if he may. Now, it is abundantly clear that any expedition on the high Alps is of a sporting nature; it is almost aggressively sporting. And yet it would never occur to me to prove my title by any reference to mountaineering in the Alps, nor would it occur to any other climber of the arrogant sort who may also be a sportsman. We set climbing on a pedestal above the common recreations of men. We hold it apart and label it as something that has a special value.

This, though it passes with all too little comment, is a plain act of rebellion. It is a serious deviation from the normal standard of rightness and wrongness, and if we were to succeed in establishing our value for mountaineering we should upset the whole order of society, just as completely as it would be upset if a sufficient number of people who claimed to be enlightened were to eat eggs with knives and regard with disdain the poor folk who ate them with spoons.

But there is a propriety of behaviour for rebels as for others. Society can at least expect of rebels that they explain themselves. . . .

Climbers who, like myself, take the high line have much to explain, and it is time they set about it. Notoriously they endanger their lives. With what object? If only for some physical pleasure, to enjoy certain movements of the body and to experience the zest of emulation, then it is not worth while. Climbers are only a particularly foolish set of desperadoes; they are on the same plane with hunters, and many degrees less reasonable. The only defense for mountaineering puts it on a higher plane than mere physical sensation. It is asserted that the climber experiences higher emotions; he gets some good for his soul. His opponent may well feel skeptical about this argument. He, too, may claim to consider his soul's good when he can take a holiday. Probably it is true of anyone who spends a well-earned fortnight in healthy enjoyment at the seaside that he comes back a better, that is to say, a more virtuous man than he went. How are the climber's joys worth more than the seaside? What are these higher emotions to which he refers so elusively? And if they really are so valuable, is there no safer way of reaching them? Do mountaineers consider these questions and answer them again and again from fresh experience, or are they content with some magic certainty born of comparative ignorance long ago?

It would be a wholesome tonic, perhaps, more often to meet an adversary who argued on these lines. In practice I find that few men ever want to discuss mountaineering seriously. I suppose they imagine that a discussion with me would be unprofitable; and I must confess that if anyone does open the question my impulse is to put him off. I can assume a vague disdain for civilization, and I can make phrases about beautiful surroundings, and puff them out, as one who has a secret and does not care to reveal it because no one would understand — phrases which refer to the divine riot of Nature in her ecstasy of making mountains.

Thus I appeal to the effect of mountain scenery upon my aesthetic sensibility. But, even if I can communicate by words a true feeling, I have explained nothing. Aesthetic delight is vitally connected with our performance, but it neither explains nor excuses it. No one for a moment dreams that our apparently willful proceedings are determined merely by our desire to see what is beautiful. The mountain railway could cater for such desires. By providing viewpoints at a number of stations, and by concealing all signs of its own mechanism, it might be so completely organized that all the aesthetic joys of the mountaineer should be offered to its intrepid ticket holders. It would achieve this object with a comparatively small expenditure of time, and would even have, one might suppose, a decisive advantage by affording to all lovers of the mountains the opportunity of sharing their emotions with a large and varied multitude of their fellow-men. And yet the idea of associating this mechanism with a snow mountain is the abomination of every species of mountaineer. To him it appears as a kind of rape. The fact that he so regards it indicates the emphasis with which he rejects the crude aesthetic reasons as his central defense.

I suppose that, in the opinion of many people who have opportunities of judging, mountaineers have no ground for claiming for their pursuit a superiority as regards the natural beauties that attend it. And certainly many huntsmen would resent their making any such claim. We cannot, therefore, remove mountaineering from the plane of hunting by a composite representation of its merits — by asserting that physical and aesthetic joys are blent for us and not for others. . . .

It must be admitted at the outset that our periodic literature gives little indication that our performance is concerned no less with the spiritual side of us than with the physical. This is, in part, because we require certain practical information of anyone who describes an expedition. Our journals, with one exception, do not pretend to be elevated literature, but aim only at providing useful knowledge for climbers. With this purpose we try to show exactly where upon a mountain our course lay, in what manner the conditions of snow and ice and rocks and weather were or were not favorable to our enterprise, and what were the actual difficulties we had to overcome and the dangers we had to meet. Naturally, if we accept these circumstances, the impulse for literary expression vanishes; not so much because the matter is not suitable as because, for literary expression, it is too difficult to handle. A big expedition in the Alps, say, a traverse of Mont Blanc, would be a superb theme for an epic poem. But we are not all even poets, still less Homers or Miltons. We do, indeed, possess lyric poetry that is concerned with mountains, and value it highly for the expression of much that we feel about them. But little of it can be said to suggest that mountaineering in the technical sense offers an emotional experience which cannot otherwise be reached. A few essays and a few descriptions do give some indication that the spiritual part of man is concerned. Most of those who describe expeditions do not even treat them as adventure, still less as being connected with any emotional experience peculiar to mountaineering.

MALLORY AND IRVINE WERE LAST SEEN LESS THAN A THOUSAND FEET FROM THE SUMMIT OF EVEREST.

# George Leigh MALLORY

SUCCINCTLY EXPLAINED WHY A MAN CLIMBS A MOUNTAIN: "BECAUSE IT'S THERE!"

EVEREST BECAME HIS PASSION. AFTER A RECONNAISSANCE IN 1921, HE MADE AN UNSUCCESSFUL ATTEMPT IN 1922.

IN 1924, HE TRIED AGAIN — A CLIMB FROM WHICH HE NEVER RETURNED.

ANDREW IRVINE WHO ACCOMPANIED MALLORY ON HIS FINAL ASCENT.

Some writers, after the regular careful references to matters of plain fact, insert a paragraph dealing summarily with an aesthetic experience; the greater part make a bare allusion to such feelings or neglect them altogether, and perhaps these are the wisest sort.

And yet it is not so very difficult to write about aesthetic impressions in some way so as to give pleasure. If we do not ask too much, many writers are able to please us in this respect. We may be pleased, without being stirred to the depths, by anyone who can make us believe that he has experienced aesthetically; we may not be able to feel with him what he has felt, but if he talks about it simply, we may be quite delighted to perceive that he has felt as we too are capable of feeling. Mountaineers who write do not, as a rule, succeed even in this small degree. If they are so bold as to attempt a sunset or sunrise, we too often feel uncertain as we read that they have felt anything — and this even though we may know quite well that they are accustomed to feel as we feel ourselves.

These observations about our mountain literature are not made by way of censure or in disappointment; they are put forward as phenomena, which have to be explained, not so much by the nature of mountaineers, but rather by the nature of their performance. The explanation which commends itself to me is derived very simply from the conception of mountaineering, which, expressed or unexpressed, is common, I imagine, to all us of the arrogant sort. We do not think that our aesthetic experiences of sunrises and sunsets and clouds and thunder are supremely important facts in mountaineering, but rather that they cannot thus be separated and cataloged and described individually as experiences at all. They are not incidental in mountaineering but a vital and inseparable part of it; they are not ornamental but structural; they are not various items causing emotion but parts of an emotional whole; they are the crystal pools perhaps, but they owe their life to a continuous stream.

It is this unity that makes so many attempts to describe aesthetic detail seem futile. Somehow they miss the point and fail to touch us. It is because they are only fragments. If we take one moment and present its emotional quality apart form the whole, it has lost the very essence that gave it a value. If we write about an expedition from the emotional point of view in any part of it, we ought so to write about the whole adventure from beginning to end. . . .

But once again. What is the value of our emotional experience among mountains? We may show by comparison the kind of feeling we have, but might not that comparison be applied with a similar result in other spheres?

How it would disturb the cool contempt of the arrogant mountaineer to whisper in his ear, "Why not drop it and take up, say, Association football?" Not, of course, if a footballer made the remark, because the mountaineer would merely humor him as he would humor a child. That, at least, is the line I should take myself, and I can't imagine that, for instance, a proper president of the Alpine Club, if approached in this way by the corresponding functionary of the AFA, could adopt any other. But supposing a member of the club were to make the suggestion—with the emendation, lest this should be ridiculous, of golf instead of football—imagine the righteousness of his wrath and the majesty of his anger! And yet it is as well to consider whether the footballers, golfers, etc., of this world have not some experience akin to ours. The exteriors of sportsmen are so arranged as to suggest that they have not; but if we are to pursue the truth in a whole-hearted fashion we must, at all costs, go further and see what lies beyond the faces and clothes of sporting men. Happily, as a sportsman myself, I know what the real feelings of sportsmen are; it is clear enough to me that the great majority of them have the same sort of experience as mountaineers.

It is abundantly clear to me, and even too abundantly. The fact that sportsmen are, with regard to their sport, highly emotional beings is at once so strange and so true that a lifetime might well be spent in the testing of it. Very pleasant it would be to linger among the curious jargons, the outlandish manners—barbaric heartiness, medieval chivalry, "side" and "swank," if these can be distinguished, in their various appearances—and the mere facial expressions of the different species in the genus; and to see how all alike have one main object, to disguise the depth of their real sentiment. But these matters are to be enjoyed and digested in the plenty of leisure hours, and I must put them by for now. The plain facts are sufficient for this occasion. The elation of sportsmen in success, their depression in failure, their long-spun vivacity in anecdote— these are the great tests, and by their quality may be seen the elemental play of emotions among all kinds of sportsmen. The footballers, the cricketers, the golfers, the batters and ballers—to be short, of all the one hundred and thirty-one varieties, all dream by day and by night as the climber dreams. Spheroidic prodigies are immortal each in its locality. The place comes back to the hero with the culminating event—the moment when a round, inanimate object was struck supremely well; and all the great race of hunters, in more lands than one, the men who hunt fishes and fowls and beasts after their kind, from perch to spotted sea serpent, fat pheasant to dainty lark or thrush, tame deer to jungle-bred monster, all hunters dream of killing animals, whether they be small or great, and whether they be gentle or ferocious. Sport is for sportsmen a part of their emotional experience, as mountaineering is for mountaineers.

How, then, shall we distinguish emotionally between the mountaineer and the sportsman?

The great majority of men are in a sense artists; some are active and creative, and some participate passively. No doubt those who create differ in some way fundamentally from those who do not create; but they hold this artistic impulse in common: all alike desire expression for the emotional side of their nature. The behavior of those who are devoted to the higher forms of Art shows this clearly enough. It is clearest of all, perhaps, in the drama, in dancing, and in music. Not only those who perform are artists, but also those who are moved by the performance. Artists, in this sense, are not distinguished by the power of expressing emotion, but the power of feeling that emoitonal experience out of which Art is made. We recognize this when we speak of individuals as artistic, though they have no pretension to create Art. Arrogant mountaineers are all artistic, independently of any other consideration, because they cultivate emotional experience for its own sake; and so for the same reason are sportsmen. It is not paradoxical to assert that all sportsmen — real sportsmen, I mean — are artistic; it is merely to apply that term logically, as it ought to be applied. A large part of the human race is covered in this way by an epithet usually vague and specialized, and so it ought to be. No difference in kind divides the individual who is commonly said to be artistic from the sportsman who is supposed not so to be. On the contrary, the sportsman is a recognizable kind of artist. So soon as pleasure is being pursued, not simply for its face value — as it is being pursued at this moment by the cook below, who is chatting with the fishmonger when I know she ought to be basting the joint — not in the simplest way, but for some more remote and emotional object, it partakes of the nature of Art. This distinction may easily be perceived in the world of sport. It points the difference between one who is content to paddle a boat by himself because he likes the exercise, or likes the sensation of occupying a boat upon the water, or wants to use the water to get to some desirable spot, and one who trains for a race; the difference between kicking a football and playing in a game of football; the difference between riding individually for the liver's sake and riding to hounds. Certainly neither the sportsman nor the mountaineer can be accused of taking his pleasure simply. Both are artists; and the fact that he has in view an emotional experience does not remove the mountaineer even from the devotee of Association football.

But there is Art and ART. We may distinguish among artists. Without an exact classification or order of merit we do so distinguish habitually. The "Fine Arts" are called "fine" presumably because we consider that all Arts are not fine. The epithet artistic is commonly limited to those who are seen to have the artistic sense developed in a peculiar degree.

It is precisely in making these distinctions that we may estimate what we set out to determine — the value of mountaineering in the whole order of our emotional experience. To what part of the artistic sense of man does mountaineering belong? To the part that causes him to be moved by music or painting, or to the part that makes him enjoy the game?

By putting the question in this form we perceive at once the gulf that divides the arrogant mountaineer from the sportsman. It seems perfectly natural to compare a day in the Alps with a symphony. For mountaineers of my sort mountaineering is rightfully so comparable; but no sportsman could or would make the same claim for cricket or hunting, or whatever his particular sport might be. He recognizes the existence of the sublime in great Art, and knows, even if he cannot feel, that its manner of stirring the heart is altogether different and vaster. But mountaineers do not admit this difference in the emotional plane of mountaineering and Art. They claim that something sublime is the essence of mountaineering. They can compare the call of the hills to the melody of wonderful music, and the comparison is not ridiculous.

Matthiessen and field biologist George Schaller set out on a journey from northwest Nepal to the Crystal Mountain on the Tibetan plateau, seeking to observe the rut of the bharal, or Himalayan blue sheep. They also knew that where bharal were most numerous they had their best chance to glimpse that rarest of the great cats, the beautiful snow leopard. A student of Zen Buddhism, Matthiessen set out on an inner journey as well, one in which his commitment to life itself was put to the test. This passage is from his 1978 book, *The Snow Leopard*.

# PETER MATTHIESSEN

# A Fine Chance to Let Go

A cold wind out of the north. I wash my head. To reduce the drain on our food supplies, Tukten and Gyaltsen leave today for Jumla, where they will obtain some rice and sugar and perhaps mail; if all goes well, they will join us at Shey about November 10.

Yesterday I wrote letters to send off with Tukten, and the writing depressed me, stirring up longings, and worries about the children, and bringing me down from the mountain high. The effort to find ordinary words for what I have seen in this extraordinary time seems to have dissipated a kind of power, and the loss of intensity is accompanied by loss of confidence and inner balance; my legs feel stiff and heavy, and I dread the narrow ledge around the west walls of Phoksumdo that we must follow for two miles or more tomorrow. This ledge is visible from Ring-mo, and even GS [George Schaller] was taken aback by the first sight of it. "*That's* not something you'd want to do every day," he said. I also dread the snow in the high passes that might trap us in the treeless waste beyond. These fears just worsen matters, but there's no sense pretending they are not there. It is one thing to climb remote mountains if one has done it all one's life; it is quite another to begin in middle age. Not that forty-six is too old to start, but I doubt that I shall ever welcome ice faces and narrow ledges, treacherous log bridges across torrents, the threat of wind and blizzard; in high mountains, there is small room for mistake.

Why is death so much on my mind when I do not feel I am afraid of it? — the dying, yes, especially in cold (hence the oppression brought by this north wind down off the glaciers, and by the cold chop on the cold lake), but not the state itself. And yet I cling — to what? What am I to make of these waves of timidity, this hope of continuity, when at other moments I feel free as the bharal on those heights, ready for wolf and snow leopard alike? I must be careful, that is true, for I have young children with no mother, and much work to finish; but these aren't honest reasons, past a point. Between clinging and letting go, I feel a terrific struggle. This is a fine chance to let go, to "win my life by losing it," which means not recklessness but acceptance, not passivity but nonattachment.

If given the chance to turn back, I would not take it. Therefore the decision to go ahead is my own responsibility, to be accepted with a whole heart. Or so I write here, in faint hope that the words may give me courage.

I walk down around the ridge to where the torrent falls into the Suli. Beneath ever-greens and silver birch, ripples flow along the pale gray rocks, and a wren and a brown dipper come and go where water is pouring into water. The dipper is kin to the North American water ouzel, and the tiny wren is the winter wren of home — the only species of that New World family that has made its way across into Eurasia.

Drowned boulders knock beneath the torrent, and a rock thuds at my back. Trans-fixed by the bright gaze of a lizard, I become calm. This stone on which the lizard lies was under the sea when lizards first came into being, and now the flood is wearing it away, to return it once again into the oceans.

**OCTOBER 25**

We must leave Ring-mo before word comes from Dunahi that we must not. But still these B'on-pos yell and shout about their loads until Jang-bu takes cord thongs from their boots, mixes them up, and lays one on every basket, giving each man the load on which his cord is laid. The B'on-pos accept this way of dispensing justice with much grumbling.

Gloomy and restless, I set out ahead, and am some little way along the lake ledge when the rest catch up. Parts of the ledge have fallen away, and the gaps are bridged by flimsy scaffoldings of saplings. Certain sections are so narrow and precarious that more than once my legs refuse to move, and my heart beats so that I feel sick. One horrid stretch, lacking the smallest handhold in the wall, rounds a windy point of cliff that is one hundred feet or more above the rocks at lake edge, and this I navigate on hands and knees, arriving a lifetime later — but still in my old life, alas — at one of the few points in that whole first mile where one can lean far enough into the cliff to let another man squeeze by. Gasping for breath, I let the expedition pass.

For some time now, the chattering, laughing voices of the B'on-pos have been coming up behind. At that dangerous point of cliff, an extraordinary thing happens. Not yet in view, the nine fall silent in the sudden way that birds are stilled by a shadow of a hawk, or tree frogs cease their shrilling, leaving a ringing silence in the silence. Then, one by one, the nine figures round the point of rock in silhouette, unreal beneath big bulky loads that threaten each second to bump the cliff and nudge them over the precipice. On they come, staring straight ahead as steadily and certainly as ants, yet seeming to glide with an easy, ethereal lightness, as if some sort of inner concentration was lifting them just off the surface of the ground. Bent far forward against the tumplines around their foreheads, fingers wide spread by way of balance, they touch the cliff face lightly to the left side, stroke the north wind to the right. Light fingertips touch my upper leg, one, two, three, four, five, six, seven, eight, nine hands, but the intensity is such that they seem not to distinguish between cold rock face and warm blue jeans. Mute, unknowing, dull eyes glazed, the figures brush past one by one in their wool boots and sashed tunics, leaving behind in the clear air the smell of grease and fires. When the bad stretch is past, the hooting instantly resumes, perhaps at the point where they left off, as if all had awakened from a trance.

The Sherpas come, and Phu-Tsering smiles gold-toothed encouragement from under his red cap. GS appears, moving as steadily as the rest; I am glad that the cliff corner hid my ignominious advance on hands and knees. Squeezing by, GS remarks, "This is the first *really* interesting stretch of trail we've had so far." How easy it would be to push him over.

The second mile of the ledge path is pleasant, and I am able to enjoy the mythic view. Below lies the turquoise lake that has never known paddle or sail, and above, all around the sky, rise the snow mountains. A ravine that falls from a small glacier splits the rock face, opening out on a small beach of smooth pebbles. From here the trail climbs once again toward the ramparts at the northwest corner of Phoksumdo.

High above the lake, GS turns to wait; he points at something on the trail. Coming up, I stare at the droppings and mute prints for a long time. All around are rocky ledges, a thin cover of stunted juniper and rose. "It might be close by, watching us," murmurs GS, "and we'd never see it." He collects the leopard scat, and we go on. On the mountain corner, in hard gusts of wind, GS's altimeter reads 13,300 feet.

The path descends through snow and ice to silver birch woods by the shore. At its north end Phoksumdo has two arms, not visible from Ring-mo, each leading to a hidden river valley. The eastern arm, across the lake, is very beautiful and strange, rising steeply into the shadows of the mountains. This northwestern arm is the valley of the Phoksumdo River, and its delta of boggy tundra streams, of gravel bars and willow, is so like Alaska that both of us exclaim at the resemblance. A cold wind drives waves onto the dead gray beach, and when the sun sinks behind the Kanjiroba Massif at the head of the valley, it is still very early in the afternoon. Shey is two thousand feet higher than our present camp, and therefore considerably colder; with precious little fuel for lamps and no way to heat the tents, we can only hope that the western mountains there are low, and sunset later.

At dusk, the northern sky is lavender. The cold lake nags at the gray pebbles, and there is no sign of a bird.

The same point of which Matthiessen wrote in the previous piece is here addressed by one of the great names in the annals of mountaineering. Where Matthiessen saw the opportunity to "win [his] life by losing it," Messner sees mere human frailty. Exhaustion and despair strike most of those who tackle the world's formidable peaks, and some have succumbed to the temptation of a walk over the edge. Messner recognizes that the difference between those who, at the critical moment, affirm life and those who renounce it is slim indeed: one can discover, too late, that one has crossed over into the other camp.

# REINHOLD MESSNER

# The Will to Survive

Experience shows that of the most successful mountaineers of any generation, only half die from "natural causes." The others plunge to, freeze to, or otherwise meet, their deaths in the mountains. Alpine history confirms this situation as a brutal reality; it used to make me think of giving up big mountaineering. Is it, then, pure chance who doesn't come back and who survives? Or is there some connection between survival and the practical experience and circumspection of a climber? Today I am convinced that one of the most decisive factors for enduring in a life-or-death situation is the will to survive. I believe that this can even have some influence over objective dangers. I am not saying that a man's will can stop rocks breaking away or hinder the passage of avalanches — only that a man who is in contact with himself and his surroundings is unlikely to find himself in their path. I would stick my neck out and suggest that the mentally well-adjusted climber won't perish on a mountain — or, put another way, every mountain accident has a human ingredient. And if I survived on Nanga Parbat, it was only because at the time I had an overwhelming desire to survive. For all that, I nevertheless did "die" in a sense, and today I feel that to actually die would be easier after the experience. I am no longer afraid of the prospect of death, nor yet afraid of life. But the survival instinct I am talking about has little to do with all that; it depends upon a person's enthusiasm for life and his peace of mind.

The Nanga Parbat expedition, with all that followed after — frostbitten feet, the loss of a brother who was at the same time my best climbing partner, the countless lawsuits — threw me mentally off balance for a time. But soon, with the help of new activities and new friendships, inner calm and strength were reborn in me.

In recent years, I have become more and more preoccupied with the figure of Hermann Buhl, the first person to climb Nanga Parbat, but who, after his great climbing achievement in 1953, was strongly criticized. And yet Buhl did not give up climbing. On the contrary, he went on to scale the most difficult big walls of his day in the western Alps and took on new expedition goals. In 1957 he set off for Broad Peak, his second eight-thousander. At that time, Buhl was without question the most successful mountaineer in the world, yet he was a controversial figure among top climbers. Even former rope partners were hostile to him. Was this because he had achieved fame outside of mountaineering circles, or something about himself? He quite obviously suffered as a result of this attitude and gradually his whole personality changed.

I am always asking myself whether Buhl's will to survive suffered in some way, whether the Hermann Buhl who walked off the cornice in thick mist in 1957 was indeed the same Hermann Buhl who struggled back alone from the summit of Nanga Parbat in 1953, completely exhausted but determined to live. How much Buhl must have suffered under the constant personal attacks, most of which came from his erstwhile closest circle of friends. Each new achievement brought him more recognition, but at the same time more controversy. He could not avoid it. Did he then perhaps toy with the idea of surrender?

Be that as it may, finding myself in the crossfire of the critics some two decades later, I have often wished that I was buried along with Günther on the Diamir Flank. When we stood on the summit of Nanga on June 27, 1970, our will to survive was so great that we were able to find our way down the unknown Diamir side of the mountain. This was only possible because I searched out a passable route, step by step, retracing at least 1,000 meters of height. I climbed back once because a serac blocked the way, again when a rock step seemed too risky for Günther, and a third time when crevasses barred all further progress. I doubt whether today I would still have the same psychological strength to get myself out of a similarly lethal situation, but I would like to win back that strength. These days I see the biggest threat to inner harmony — which I consider to be the prerequisite for all forays into "borderline" territory — coming less from criticism and persecution than from depression, changing personal relationships, and disillusionment.

I don't know whether it would be a good thing for a person if he didn't care what happened from one day to the next, I don't know if that would herald for him a period of happiness or one of stress. I only know that he would then have to give up extreme climbing if he wanted to survive; he would be a potential suicide on a big wall.

And I am convinced that psychological erosion presents a serious threat to the extreme climber, the constant wear and tear that is caused by sustained personal attack, disillusionment, and, more than anything, a shattered emotional life. Without noticing it, a man loses, drip by drip, his will to live, and he needs this will to face life-or-death situations. Without it, he could no longer instinctively do, or want, the right thing. Walter Bonatti resigned himself to this fact and withdrew from hard mountaineering when the many grudgers began to gnaw away at his psyche. Or was it the unconscious reaction of so experienced a man, to rescue his "eroded" survival instinct? I don't know.

I feel I must be particularly wary on this point. There are still a few big mountains I am anxious to climb, and they are bound to present, sooner or later, some potentially dangerous situation. Because of this, I am searching for a new balance within myself, training myself in the art of patient acceptance. It can serve no purpose to try to outwit the many jealous and critical people, to seek to punish their triviality with arrogance. My main desire is not to let them affect me at all; they must be all the same to me, just as to the Buddhist the desires of the world are all the same. That is the only way I can ensure that one day I, too, don't walk over the edge.

This is a section of the concluding chapter of *My Climbs in the Alps and the Caucasus*, published in the year of Mummery's death on Nanga Parbat (1895). His was the first expedition to the mountain, and the last for more than thirty-five years; then two German expeditions were wiped out as mercilessly as Mummery's had been. The fearsome peak was not climbed until 1953, when Hermann Buhl reached it in dramatic fashion (see his entry). Of Mummery it may be said that he knew the pleasures of mountaineering in the Alps and the Caucasus, and its penalties in the Himalayas.

# ALBERT F. MUMMERY

# The Pleasures and Penalties of Mountaineering

Well-known climbers, whose opinions necessarily carry the greatest weight, have recently declared their belief that the dangers of mountaineering no longer exist. Skill, knowledge, and textbooks have hurled them to the limbo of exploded bogeys. I would fain agree with this optimistic conclusion, but I cannot forget that the first guide to whom I was ever roped, and one who possessed — may I say it? — more knowledge of mountains than is to be found even in the Badminton library, was none the less killed on the Brouillard Mont Blanc, and his son, more recently, on Koshtan Tau. The memory of two rollicking parties, comprising seven men, who one day in 1879 were climbing on the West Face of the Matterhorn, passes with ghostlike admonition before my mind and bids me remember that of these seven, Mr. Penhall was killed on the Wetterhorn, Ferdinand Imseng on the Macugnaga Monte Rosa, and Johann Petrus on the Fresnay Mont Blanc. To say that any single one of these men was less careful and comptetent, or had less knowledge of all that pertains to the climber's craft, than we who yet survive is obviously and patently absurd. Our best efforts must sometimes be seconded by the great goddess of Luck; to her should the Alpine Club offer its vows and thanksgivings.

Indeed, if we consider for a moment the essence of the sport of mountaineering, it is obvious that it consists, and consists exclusively, in pitting the climber's skill against the difficulties opposed by the mountain. Any increase in skill involves, *pari passu*, an increase in the difficulties grappled with. From the Breuil ridge of the Matterhorn we pass on to the Dru, and from the Dru to the Aiguille de Grépon: or to take a yet wider range, from the Chamonix Mont Blanc to the same mountain by way of the Brenva glacier and the Aiguille Blanche de Peutéret. It can scarcely be argued that Bennen and Walters were less fit to grapple with the cliff above the "Linceul" than we moderns to climb the Grépon "crack"; or that Jacques Balmat was less able to lead up the "Ancien passage" than Émile Rey to storm the ghastly precipices of the Brenva Peutéret. But if it be admitted that the skill of the climber has not increased relatively to the difficulties grapped with, it would appear to necessarily follow that climbing is neither more nor less dangerous than formerly.

It is true that extraordinary progress has been made in the art of rock climbing, and that consequently any given rock climb is much easier now than thirty years since, but the essence of the sport lies, not in ascending a peak, but in struggling with and overcoming difficulties. The happy climber, like the aged Ulysses, is one who has "drunk delight of battle with his peers," and this delight is only attainable by assaulting cliffs which tax to their utmost limits the powers of the mountaineers engaged. This struggle involves the same risk, whether early climbers attacked what we now call easy rock, or whether we moderns attack formidable rock, or whether the ideal climber of the future assaults cliffs which we now regard as hopelessly inaccessible. Doubtless my difference with the great authorities referred to above is, in the main, due to a totally different view of the raison d'être of mountaineering. Regarded as a sport, some danger is, and always must be, inherent in it; regarded as a means of exercise among noble scenery, for quasi-scientific pursuits, as the raw material for interesting papers, or for the purposes of brag and bounce, it has become as safe as the ascent of the Rigi or Pilatus was to the climbers of thirty years since. But these pursuits are not mountaineering in the sense in which the founders of the Alpine Club used the term, and they are not mountaineering in the sense in which the elect — a small, perchance even a dwindling body — use it now. To set one's utmost faculties, physical and mental, to fight some grim precipice, or force some gaunt, ice-clad gully, is work worthy of men; to toil up long slopes of screes behind a guide who can "lie in bed and picture every step of the way up, with all the places for hand and foot," is work worthy of the fiberless contents of fashionable clothes, dumped with all their scents and ointments, starched linen and shiny boots, at Zermatt by the railway.

The true mountaineer is a wanderer, and by a wanderer I do not mean a man who expends his whole time in traveling to and fro in the mountains on the exact tracks of his predecessors — much as a bicyclist rushes along the turnpike roads of England — but I mean a man who loves to be where no human being has been before, who delights in gripping rocks that have previously never felt the touch of human fingers, or in hewing his way up ice-filled gullies whose grim shadows have been sacred to the mists and avalanches since "Earth rose out of chaos." In other words, the true mountaineer is the man who attempts new ascents. Equally, whether he succeeds or fails, he delights in the fun and jollity of the struggle. The gaunt, bare slabs, the square, precipitous steps in the ridge, and the black, bulging ice of the gully are the very breath of life to his being. I do not pretend to be able to analyze this feeling, still less to be able to make it clear to unbelievers. It must be felt to be understood, but it is potent to happiness and sends the blood tingling through the veins, destroying every trace of cynicism and striking at the very roots of pessimistic philosophy.

Our critics, curiously enough, repeat in substance Mr. Ruskin's original taunt, that we regard the mountains as greased poles. I must confess that a natural and incurable denseness of understanding does not enable me to feel the sting of this taunt. Putting aside the question of grease, which is offensive and too horrible for contemplation in its effects on knickerbockers — worse even than the structure-destroying edges and splinters of the Grépon ridge — I do not perceive the enormity or sin of climbing poles. At one time, I will confess, I took great delight in the art, and, so far as my experience extends, the taste is still widespread among English youth. It is possible, nay even probable, that much of the pleasure of mountaineering is derived from the actual physical effort and from the perfect state of health to which this effort brings its votaries, and, to this extent, may plausibly be alleged to be the mere sequence and development of the pole and tree climbing of our youth. The sting of the taunt is presumably meant to lurk in the implication that the climber is incapable of enjoying noble scenery; that, in the jargon of certain modern writers, he is a "*mere* gymnast." But why should a man be assumed incapable of enjoying aesthetic pleasures because he is also capable of the physical and nonaesthetic pleasures of rock climbing?

A well-known mountaineer asserts that the fathers of the craft did not regard "the overcoming of physical obstacles by means of muscular exertion and skill" as "the chief pleasure of mountaineering." But is this so? Can anyone read the great classic of mountaineering literature, "The Playground of Europe," without feeling that the overcoming of these obstacles was a main factor of its author's joy? Can anyone read "Peaks, Passes, and Glaciers" and the earlier numbers of The Alpine Journal without feeling that the various writers gloried in the technique of their craft? Of course the skillful interpolation of "chief" gives an opening for much effective dialectic, but after all, what does it mean? How can a pleasure which is seated in health and jollity and the "spin of the blood" be measured and compared with a purely aesthetic feeling? It would appear difficult to argue that as a man cultivates and acquires muscular skill and knowledge of the mountains, he correspondingly dwarfs and impairs the aesthetic side of his nature. If so, we magnify the weak-kneed and the impotent, the lame, the halt, and the blind, and brand as false the Greek ideal of the perfect man. Doubtless a tendency in this direction may be detected in some modern thought, but, like much else similarly enshrined, it has no ring of true metal. Those who are so completely masters of their environment that they can laugh and rollick on the ridges, free from all constraint of ropes or fear of danger, are far more able to appreciate the glories of the "eternal hills" than those who can only move in constant terror of their lives, amid the endless chatter and rank tobacco smoke of unwashed guides.

The fact that a man enjoys scrambling up a steep rock in no way makes him insensible of all that is beautiful in nature. The two sets of feelings are indeed wholly unconnected. A man may love climbing and care naught for mountain scenery; he may love the scenery and hate climbing; or he may be equally devoted to both. The presumption obviously is that those who are most attracted by the mountains and most constantly return to their fastnesses are those who to the fullest extent possess both these sources of enjoyment — those who can combine the fun and frolic of a splendid sport with that indefinable delight which is induced by the lovely form, tone, and coloring of the great ranges.

I am free to confess that I myself should still climb, even though there were no scenery to look at, even if the only climbing attainable were the dark and gruesome potholes of the Yorkshire dales. On the other hand, I should still wander among the upper snows, lured by the silent mists and the red blaze of the setting sun, even though physical or other infirmity, even though in after eons the sprouting of wings and other angelic appendages may have sunk all thought of climbing and cragsmanship in the whelming past.

It is frequently assumed, even by those who ought to know better, that if mountaineering involves danger of any sort, it should never be indulged in — at all events by such precious individuals as the members of the English Alpine Club. Before considering this most pernicious doctrine, it is well to remember, that though the perils of mountaineering may not have been wholly dissipated into space by the lightning-like flashes of the Badminton and All England series; yet, nevertheless, these perils are not very great. With a single exception, the foregoing pages [of *My Climbs in the Alps and the Caucasus*] contain an account of every difficulty I have experienced which has seemed to render disaster a possible contingency. As my devotion to the sport began in 1871, and has continued with unabated vigor ever since, it will be evident that the climber's perils — insofar as a modest individual may regard himself as typical of the class — are extremely few and very rarely encountered. Such, however, as they have been, I would on no account have missed them. There is an educative and purifying power in danger that is to be found in no other school, and it is worth much for a man to know that he is not "clean gone to flesh pots and effeminacy." It may be admitted that the mountains occasionally push things a trifle too far, and bring before their votaries a vision of the imminence of dissolution that the hangman himself, with all his paraphernalia of scaffold, gallows, and drop, could hardly hope to excel. But grim and hopeless as the cliffs may sometimes look when ebbing twilight is chased by shrieking wind and snow and the furies are in mad hunt along the ridges, there is ever the feeling that brave companions and a constant spirit will cut the gathering web of peril, *"forsan et haec olim meminisse iuvabit."*

The sense of independence and self-confidence induced by the great precipices and vast silent fields of snow is something wholly delightful. Every step is health, fun, and frolic. The troubles and cares of life, together with the essential vulgarity of a pluto-cratic society, are left far below — foul miasmas that cling to the lowest bottoms of reek-ing valleys. Above, in the clear air and searching sunlight, we are afoot with the quiet gods, and men can know each other and themselves for what they are. No feeling can be more glorious than advancing to attack some gaunt precipitous wall with "comrades staunch as the founders of our race." Nothing is more exhilarating than to know that the fingers of one hand can still be trusted with the lives of a party, and that the lower limbs are free from all trace of "knee-dissolving fear," even though the friction of one hobnail on an outward shelving ledge alone checks the hurtling of the body through thin air, and of the soul (let us hope) to the realms above.

I am of course aware that it is an age which cares little for the more manly virtues, and which looks askance at any form of sport that can, by any stretch of extremest imagination, be regarded as dangerous: yet since we cannot all, for most obvious reasons, take our delight "wallowing in slimy spawn of lucre," something may surely be urged in favor of a sport that teaches, as no other teaches, endurance and mutual trust, and forces men occasionally to look death in its grimmest aspect frankly and squarely in the face. For though mountaineering is not, perhaps, more dangerous than other sports, it undoubtedly brings home to the mind a more stimulating sense of peril; a sense, indeed, that is out of all proportion to the actual risk. It is, for instance, quite impossible to look down the tremendous precipices of the Little Dru without feeling in each indi-vidual nerve the utter disintegration of everything human which a fall must involve; and the contingency of such a fall is frequently brought before the mind — indeeed, throughout the ascent, constant and strenuous efforts are needed to avoid it. The love of wager, our religious teachers notwithstanding, is still inherent in the race, and one cannot find a higher stake — at all events in these materialistic days, when Old Nick will no longer lay sterling coin against the gamester's soul — than the continuity of the cervical vertebrae; and this is the stake that the mountaineer habitually and constantly wagers. It is true the odds are all on his side, but the off chance excites to honesty of thought and tests how far decay has penetrated the inner fiber. That mountaineering has a high educational value few who have the requisite knowledge to form a fair judgment would deny. That it has its evil side I frankly admit. None can look down its gloomy death roll without feeling that our sport demands a fearful price.

Using a trail pioneered by John Salathé, the rock engineer whose ingenious equipment has been an integral part of the development of aid climbing, Ax Nelson climbed the "impossible" Lost Arrow Spire in 1947. However, Nelson's methods—which included the use of ropes slung over from the rim of the valley wall behind Lost Arrow's summit—came in for much abuse. To mute his critics, in the next year Nelson joined with Salathé to climb the Spire again, this time with no help from above. The story of their climb is one of the classics of modern mountaineering.

# ANTON NELSON

# Five Days and Nights on the Lost Arrow

What is required to climb Yosemite's Lost Arrow? For years many determined men had tried to find out just that. In trying they succeeded only in showing how terribly close to unclimbable the Arrow really is. Then, on September 3, 1947, John Salathé and I completed a successful assault which we had begun 103 hours earlier at the base of the spire.

True, men had stood atop its summit one year before when a trip from the rim was ingeniously engineered by four Sierra Club climbers. Spectacular and effective though it was, this maneuver required very little real climbing; it was in effect an admission of the Arrow's unclimbability. The problem the Arrow poses for the climber is to ascend from the base up through the ramparts of the great chimney that cuts the spire away from the cliff, and past the three intermediate ledges, called Errors, until he reaches the summit, facetiously called the Fourth or Last Error.

A full story, although it ought to be exciting, would take too much space for present purposes. In its stead, a brief description of the preparations for the ascent is presented for prospective Arrow climbers.

The equipment included a 120-foot nylon belaying rope, a 300-foot rappel rope; a 150-foot reserve rope for hauling up the thirty-pound pack and other purposes; three foot slings per climber; eighteen pitons used and reused in hundreds of places; about the same number of expansion bolts; twelve carabiners; and a "sky hook" invented by Salathé and used on the final summit pitch.

Weight and bulk of equipment were limiting factors in personal needs, also. Water was the heaviest material, so the supply was limited to three quarts per person and was carried in a plastic bag. This will last up to five days if one does not sweat too much and can discipline the growing temptation to drink. It must be admitted that friends relieved our self-denial on the fourth day with liquid lowered from the rim to Third Error. A number 2 can of fruit juice was held in reserve for a victory toast at the top. Because of the exertions of the day we wet our mouths a little at dawn, took a sip or two at midday, and drank most of our liquid at night. Charles Wilts and Spencer Austin, who had reached the previous high point on this route, warned that too much liquid is a major drawback. The dozen or more cans of fruit juice they jettisoned made one wonder how they ever had the strength to haul it all up or how they ever got in through some of the narrow places.

What small amounts of food we ate were rationed in the same way as the water. We believe that the ideal food is raisins, dates, walnuts or peanuts, and fruit-flavored gelatin candies, and that heavier foods, such as starches or meat, would hardly be digestible under the strains of Arrow climbing. We needed no more than four or five pounds per man for five days. That we should lose a great deal of weight on the climb was assured.

Our basic idea was that we would climb safely or not at all. We understood that rescue from an accident in the Great Chimney was not to be expected. Bombproof belays were in order and unprotected leads of more than ten or fifteen feet were out of order. When the leader had to take a long chance he did so only when pitons (or bolts) that were sound enough for the anticipated fall were near by and the belayer was on special alert. Then the most that could happen (and not infrequently did happen) was that the leader would take a controlled fall and go right back to work.

For climbing on the Arrow, great strength is far less important than patience and endurance. On the first ascent each of us had been on the Arrow four times before, and twice we had set out together for at least three days' work. On Memorial Day 1947 the route became the bed of a waterfall and ended in a precarious rappel. On Fourth of July weekend, much was learned during two days and a night on the rock, in which Second Error was attained for the first time. Better equipment was needed. We had thought ourselves in the pink of condition, but after only two days the state of nervous and physical exhaustion dictated retreat and far more rigorous preparation for the next attempt.

Several bivouacs on cliff walls, with or without warm clothes, taught us not to expect much rest on a climb. I took a hike the length of the John Muir Trail, practicing making long marches with little or no water. Doing that for four days in one's own home is good enough practice for mastering thirst — for learning, that is, how much thirst is to be safely endured. If one lacks time for long periods in the mountains, running steadily for an hour or so is a good way to build up the heart, lungs, nerves, and muscles for the long endurance at higher altitudes needed by any kind of mountaineering activity. To prevent the onset of cramps one needs brisk calisthenics to train climbing muscles far beyond their normal capacities. On the Arrow, failure to hold oneself to comparable preparations may be sufficient to scuttle a team's most carefully laid plans, and it has done so more than once.

For prospective Arrow climbers, it is important to have or acquire experience and competence with things mechanical; a manual acquaintance with forces, materials, and their relaitonships is a must.

This brings one to the matter of practical philosophy. One cannot climb at all unless one has sufficient urge to do so. Danger must be met — indeed, it must be *used* — to an extent beyond that incurred in normal life. That is one reason men climb; for only in response to challenge does a man become his best. Yet any do-or-die endeavors are to be condemned. Life is more precious than victory. In the safest possible climbing on the Arrow there is more than enough stimulus from probable and present danger. To know one's limitations and to keep within them is the essence of good sense. A comparatively weak party, sensitive to its weak points and keeping within their limits, will outlive and outclimb the strongest team which proceeds indiscreetly.

One thing is *not* an adequate motive for climbing: that is egotism or pride. Yes, most of us who climb usually play to the crowd, as such an article as this may demonstrate. However, mere self-assertion alone has a low breaking point. To keep going day after day under heart-sickening strenuousness requires a bigger, more powerful faith than in oneself or in any concept of superiority.

Conversely, I feel that a man who, through emotional temperament or habit, is used to the false stimulus of alcohol has two strikes against him before he undertakes a long climb. The psychological impact of continually new and increasing difficulties while one's physical resources seem to be running down is enough without being fettered by an undisciplined imagination or by emotional crutches. Human limitations are indeed more serious than the natural ones to be faced.

A brief description of the first ascent may illustrate some of the foregoing points. In 1937 the 350 feet to First Error took 6 hours; 35 pitons were used for protection. In the 1947 ascent of the Arrow, we passed that point, hauling our 30-pound pack between us, in just 3 hours, using no more than a dozen pitons. Time was a major limiting factor and all possible haste was made when there was a chance. Nearly half the distance, 650 feet, was beat out the first day in the 13 hours before darkness fell.

One the second day increasing problems really began slowing us down. We rope-traversed from the detour going out to Second Error back into the narrowest portion of the chimney where it slashes nearly 100 feet into the heart of the cliff. At midday we arrived at the vertical headwall of the chimney where Wilts and Austin had turned back on their second attempt after two and a half days. From then on the Class 6 climbing began in earnest; 350 feet were made the second day, 200 each on the next two, and the last 50 feet on the morning of the fifth day. The first pitch of the sort, 150 feet long, was mostly rotten granite. Salathé led for 8 hours without relief, save for the interruption of darkness. Two pitches above this point, massive, overhanging blocks had to be climbed by the exceedingly wide cracks between them. Often there seemed no evident route at all.

After the second day our muscles no longer cramped and we put thirst in its place. Bivouacking on the chockstones with our feet dangling, our backs aching where they were being nudged by granite knobs, and our shoulders tugging at their anchors, we got little sleep. Cold winds barely permitted us to keep warm enough for the rest essential to the digestion of food. The hours until dawn that should permit the greater comfort of climbing were passed largely in talk. Food, sleep, and water can be dispensed with to a degree not appreciated until one is in a position where little can be had.

Frank Kittredge, then superintendent of Yosemite, asked if the 1947 Labor Day ascent of the Lost Arrow were not "the longest and most difficult high climb on record, presumably on sound rock. . . ." It is merely pointed out that Lost Arrow granite can often be far from sound. The Lost Arrow *can* be climbed again, perhaps in only four days. At any rate its superb challenge is there. To those who made the first vertical traverse of its Four Errors it stands as a symbol of high and unforgettable adventure.

Mount McKinley, the highest mountain in North America, has two peaks, the South, at 20,320 feet, and the North, at 19,470. Interestingly, the lesser climb represented the greater achievement, attained as it was by a band of Alaskan sourdoughs who had never climbed before. Moreover, their feat was accomplished amid a swirl of controversy and charges of fakery that had begun in 1906, when Dr. Frederick A. Cook claimed — fraudulently, it turned out — that he reached the summit. This piece forms a chapter of Newby's *Great Ascents* (1977), perhaps the best general history of mountaineering.

# ERIC NEWBY

# Mount McKinley

In 1897, after a number of attempts which began eleven years previously, an Italian expedition, led by the Duke of Abruzzi, finally succeeded in climbing Mount St. Elias (18,008 feet) in the mountains of that name in southeast Alaska — a fifty-seven-day combined operation which involved landing on a surf-swept shore, and the crossing of a series of extremely difficult glaciers, as well as being almost eaten alive by mosquitoes.

If Mount St. Elias was difficult, Mount McKinley (20,320 feet) in central Alaska, the highest mountain in North America, proved to be even more so.

The people on the east side of the mountain called it Traleika, those who hunted caribou up to the northwestern foot of it called it Denali — both Indian names mean the "Great One" — and it was not until 1896 that it got its more mundane appellation.

In that year gold was discovered in the Yukon, and William McKinley successfully ran for President of the United States. The mountain was named after him by William A. Dickey, a Princeton graduate who had become a gold prospector. Dickey made a shrewd guess at its height, which he put at 23,000 feet. He chose the name because the President was a supporter of the gold standard.

The massif, of which the South Peak of Mount McKinley is the crown, forms the central part of the Alaska Range, extending for a distance of 150 miles from Rainy Pass at its southwestern end to the valley of the Nenana River in the northeast, through which the railway runs from Anchorage, on the Pacific Coast, to Fairbanks, 356 miles away in the interior.

There are twenty-one peaks in the McKinley Massif, all of more than 10,000 feet. Of these two exceed 13,000, one 14,000, one 17,000, and two 19,000 feet. The North Peak of Mount McKinley is 19,470 feet and the great South Peak 850 feet higher. The massif also contains within it some of the world's largest glaciers — three more than 30 miles, and two more than 40 miles long; the longest is the 46-mile Kahiltna Glacier below the southwest face of the South Peak. On almost every count Mount McKinley poses great problems to mountaineers, some of them unique.

To this day it is still extremely remote. The nearest road (until the Denali Highway was built) was 29 miles to the north, while the nearest railway is 45 miles south, both as the crow flies. Because it is in the Mount McKinley National Park, aircraft, unless working in conjunction with scientific or government-sponsored bodies, are not allowed to land near it. Even air drops of supplies are strictly controlled. It has, too, the greatest base-to-summit rise of any mountain on earth — 17,000 feet above the plateau on which it stands. Everest rises only 13,000 feet above the monastery at the Rongbuk Glacier.

"The shortest possible route to the top of Mount McKinley requires no less than 36 miles of walking, one way, not taking into account relaying of zigzagging, in addition to 18,500 feet of vertical climbing." So wrote Bradford Washburn, the great American climber. He himself climbed the mountain three times — what was the third ascent of it, in 1942, again in 1947 with his wife, and a third time, in 1951, by way of the West Buttress. Another of Washburn's great achievements was the conquest of Mount Lucania (17,150 feet), Canada's second-highest mountain, in the Yukon section of the Mount St. Elias Mountains.

Thirty-five degrees and 2,400 miles farther north than Everest — only 3½ degrees south of the Arctic Circle — the climate of Mount McKinley is sub-Arctic. It has the world's greatest rise above the tree line and, with a snow line at 4,000 feet, one of the greatest extents of vertical snow cover.

And it is cold. In May and June temperatures can fall to 30° F, or more, below zero and winds in the same months often attain velocities of a hundred or more miles an hour. In winter the temperatures on the summit drop to fifty and sixty degrees below zero. The mountain also lies in an extremely active earthquake zone.

The obstacles surrounding the mountain were well summed up by the mysterious and elusive Dr. Frederick A. Cook, who made two attempts at it, in 1903 and 1906. In the June 1904 *Bulletin* of the American Geographical Society he wrote:

> The area of this mountain is far inland, in the heart of a most difficult and trackless country, making the transportation of men and supplies a very arduous task. The thick underbrush, the endless marshes, and the myriads of vicious mosquitos bring to the traveller the troubles of the tropics; the necessity of fording and swimming icy streams, the almost perpetual cold

rains, the camps in high altitudes on glaciers, in snows and violent storms, bring to the traveller all the discomforts of the arctic explorer; the very difficult slopes, combined with higher altitude effects, add the troubles of the worst Alpine climbs. The prospective conquerer of American's culminating peak will be amply rewarded, but he must be prepared to withstand the tortures of the torrids, the discomforts of the North Pole seeker, combined with the hardships of the Matterhorn ascent multiplied many times.

The first attempt to climb it was made by a five-man party under the leadership of Judge James Wickersham in June 1903. They set out from Fairbanks, a boom town since the discovery of gold only twelve miles to the north of it in 1902. They used packhorses to carry their equipment and made their approach by way of the Peters and Jeffery glaciers to the foot of the Wickersham Wall (8,000 feet), a tremendous ice face on the north side. Not surprisingly, they turned back here, the judge convinced that the thing was unclimbable (none of the party had any climbing experience).

That same year a second expedition, led by Dr. Cook, made an attempt on the mountain following a route by way of the Peters Glacier, pioneered in 1903 by two surveyors, Brooks and Reaburn. Cook was an experienced explorer. He had been with Robert E. Peary on his expedition to Baffin Bay in 1891, and in 1899 he had been a member of Lieutenant A. de Gerlache's Belgian expedition to the Antarctic; however, this expedition also failed to make much impression, reaching a height of about 11,000 feet on the West Buttress of the North Peak.

The next expedition, in 1906, was organized by Cook and Professor Herschel C. Parker, with funds provided by Parker and a wealthy sportsman from the eastern seaboard who was unable to join the party. Other members were Belmore Browne, a naturalist and artist who wrote an account of this and subsequent expeditions in which he took part *(The Conquest of Mount McKinley)*. Altogether the party numbered seven, including two porters, a photographer, and a topographer.

From Tyonek, a village on Cook Inlet, which they reached by steamer and a smaller vessel, the party traveled by launch and horseback northwestward to the upper waters of the Yentna River and then northeastward across several tributaries of the Yentna on the flanks of the range to reach, eventually, the head of the Tokositna River, the "river that comes from the land where there are no trees." They were now on the southeast side of the mountain, and from a high point above the Tokositna Glacier they could see the South and West faces, both of which appeared hopelessly difficult.

When the party returned to Tyonek, Dr. Cook announced that he was going to take Ed Barrill, one of the porters, and another, newly hired, man up the Susitna River, which runs due north for some distance from the head of Cook Inlet in the general direction of the mountain. Before leaving he sent a telegram to a New York businessman which read: "Am preparing for a last, desperate attack on Mount McKinley."

When Cook finally reappeared at Seldovia, at the south end of Cook Inlet, where

IN ONE OF CLIMBING'S MOST COLORFUL FEATS, FOUR FAIRBANKS SOURDOUGHS WITH NO REAL MOUNTAINEERING EXPERIENCE, BECAME THE FIRST TO SCALE THE NORTH SUMMIT OF MT. McKINLEY IN 1910.

THE SOURDOUGHS

CHARLIE McGONAGALL, PETE ANDERSON, BILLY TAYLOR, (SEATED) TOM LLOYD.

Browne was waiting for him, he immediately claimed that he had reached the top from the south. Browne realized that this was impossible in the time Cook had been away — less than a month — and when he asked Barrill what he knew about Mount McKinley, he answered, "I can tell you all about the big peaks just south of the mountain, but if you want to know about Mount McKinley, go and ask Cook."

"I now found myself in an embarrassing position," Browne wrote. "I knew that Dr. Cook had not climbed Mount McKinley. Barrill had told me so, and in addition I knew it in the same way that any New Yorker would know that no man could walk from the Brooklyn Bridge to Grant's Tomb in ten minutes." On his return to civilization Cook set about publishing his account of his conquest of the mountain, *To the Top of the Continent*. It included a photograph supposed to show Barrill on the summit holding the Stars and Stripes, which was later proved to have been taken on another, far inferior summit, a day's detour up a side glacier, which Browne himself photographed on the next expedition in 1910, while reaching 10,300 feet on the southeast flank.

It was not possible to make a formal accusation against Cook until his book was published and by that time he had set off for the Arctic, where he claimed to have reached the North Pole from Axel Heiberg Island on April 21, 1908, in company with two unknown Eskimos, a year before Peary reached it on April 5, 1909. Although he may not have actually reached the Pole, Cook's Arctic journey was, nevertheless, a remarkable one.

The news of Cook's alleged climb was received with equal skepticism by the Sourdoughs (prospectors and trappers) of Fairbanks, and in the winter of 1909 Billie McPhee, a local saloonkeeper, offered to finance, to the extent of $500, an attempt on the summit by two local men. He also laid a $5,000 bet that they would reach the summit before July 4, 1910. The result was one of the most heroic amateur exploits in the history of mountaineering.

The protagonists were Tom Lloyd, who was nearer sixty than fifty, and Billy Taylor, and with them went two equally tough trappers, Peter Anderson, a Swede, and Charley McGonagall, and two others. They took two dogsleds, some rope, camping gear, and what they hoped would be enough provisions to see them through. McPhee's $500 was the extent of their capital. They left on December 20, in the depths of the winter of 1909, and, by the time they reached the base of the mountain it seems that two unnamed members of the party had already quarreled with the others and dropped out.

The attack was made by way of what was named the McGonagall Pass to the Muldrow Glacier, a route which the Sourdoughs had chosen, with great acumen, as the most likely way to the summit, and which they reached using dog teams. As high-altitude rations they carried bacon, beans, and doughnuts.

Toward the end of March 1910, eleven weeks later, much of the time battered by blizzards, they reached a height of 11,000 feet on the glacier and here set up their base camp. The only casualty was Peter Anderson, who had one toe frostbitten, but treated it lightly, with the words "a little bit sore, as a fellow would say." Then, so the story goes, after waiting some days for the weather to improve, and still using their dog teams, they reached a point below the edge of the Karstens Ridge, which separates the Muldrow Glacier from the Traleika Glacier to the east. There they set up their final camp in a hole excavated in the ice and, the following day, set off on their final attack on the summit.

At 15,000 feet they discovered that there were, in fact, two summits, the North Peak (19,470 feet) and the South Peak (20,330 feet), about 3¼ miles apart and separated from one another by the width of the Harper Glacier.

Unfortunately, they decided to climb the lower North Peak, possibly because, seeing it from certain directions, it is difficult to realize that it is 850 feet lower than the South Peak, or possibly because the North Peak was the one from which they hoped their flagpole would be visible by telescope from Fairbanks when they finally planted it there.

Finally, in early April 1910, wearing homemade crampons and using pole and double-bitted lumber axes, they succeeded in cutting a staircase up the Karstens Ridge, by way of which Anderson and Taylor, carrying a 14-foot dry spruce flagpole which they had lugged all the way up from the plain below, reached the North Peak, where they set it up with the Stars and Stripes streaming from it.

The descent was accomplished relatively quickly; but, once at Fairbanks, Taylor, who kept a log of the climb, and was the first to return (the others had gone on to work their mining claims), for some reason maintained that the party had climbed both summits—perhaps he was afraid that McPhee might lose his $5,000 wager, which was contingent on the *summit* being reached. In fact, outside Alaska, it was widely disbelieved that either summit had been climbed by the Sourdoughs, and it was not until three years later that proof that they had reached the lesser peak was forthcoming.

In 1912 Herschel Parker and Belmore Browne, together with Merl la Voy, who had also been on the 1910 expedition, and Arthur M. Aten made another attempt. Following the same route as the Sourdoughs, up the Muldrow Glacier, they set up three high camps at 15,000, 16,000, and 16,615 feet, and from this last one, where they suffered intensely from cold and an inability to eat pemmican at this altitude, they made two attacks on the summit.

> My sleeping-bag weighed seventeen pounds [Browne wrote]. It was large and made of the best blue or "black" wolf fur. When I was ready to sleep I first enclosed my feet in three pairs of the warmest, dry Scotch-wool socks. In addition I wore two suits of heavy woolen underclothing. Then came heavy woolen trousers covered with canvas "overalls" which keep the wind from penetrating, and the snow from sticking to the wool trousers. On my upper body I wore two of the heaviest woolen shirts made; they were of grey wool with a double back and large breast pockets that doubled the front thickness. Over these shirts I placed a fine woven Scotch-wool sweater and around my waist I wrapped a long "muffler" of llama wool. The collars of my shirts were brought close by a large silk scarf, while the ends of wool socks covered my wrists. Over all I wore a canvas "parka," the universal

Alaskan wind shield with a hood trimmed with wolverine fur. My head was covered with a muskrat fur cap which covered my neck and ears and tied under my chin. My hands were protected by heavy Scotch-wool gloves covered with heavy leather gloves, and my feet were enclosed, in addition to the socks, by heavy soft leather moccasins.... Despite the above elaborate precautions I can honestly say that *I did not have a single night's normal sleep above 15,000 feet on account of the cold!*

Professor Parker dressed more warmly than either La Voy or myself. He wore at night a complete suit of double llama wool besides his mountain clothing, and yet he could not sleep for the cold, although Anthony Fiala, leader of the Ziegler Polar Expedition, slept comfortably in a duplicate of Professor Parker's bag clad only in underclothes when the temperature was 70 below zero! This fact illustrates the comparative effect of cold between sea level and 15,000 feet close to the Arctic circle.

On June 29, with only 3,500 feet to climb, they left their high camp at 6 A.M. and by midmorning, climbing at an estimated rate of about 400 feet an hour, cutting steps as they went, they had reached 18,500 feet, more than the previous altitude record for North America, established by the Duke of Abruzzi on Mount St. Elias. "At a little less than 19,000 feet we passed the last rock on the ridge," Browne wrote, "and secured our first clear view of the summit. It rose as innocently as a tilted snow-covered tennis court and as we looked it over we grinned with relief—we *knew* the peak was ours."

But it was not to be. By the time the three men reached 19,300 feet a blizzard had risen; at 20,000 feet visibility was down to a few feet and with a wind of more than 50 mph the cold was so intense, around 15 degrees below zero, that they could feel it moving up their limbs from the tips of their toes and fingers. It was here, on the final dome, only about 200 yards and 150 vertical feet from the summit, with the slope no longer steep, they had to admit defeat. As Browne said, when Professor Parker gallantly suggested that they should continue and that he, too, would cut steps (Browne and La Voy had so far done this because they were practiced at the work): " ... it was not a question of chopping and La Voy pointed out our backsteps—or the place where our steps ought to be, for a foot below us everything was wiped out by the hissing snow."

Coming down from the final dome was as heartless a piece of work as any of us had ever done. Had I been blind, and I was nearly so from the trail chopping and stinging snow, I could not have progressed more slowly. Every foothold I found with my axe alone, for there was no sign of a step left. It took me nearly two hours to lead down that easy slope of one thousand feet.... We reached camp at 7:35 P.M. after as cruel and heart-breaking a day as I trust I will ever experience.

Two days later the weather improved and they were sufficiently restored to make another attempt; but again another terrible blizzard blew up and at 19,300 feet they were forced to turn back. It was cruel luck.

A few days later, by which time they had reached the base of the mountain, a severe earthquake occurred. It caused a most spectacular avalanche and also, although of course they did not know this, radically altered the physiognomy of the summit ridge by which they had attacked the mountain.

They had been beaten by the weather; but they had also had dietary problems. Their basic food was supposed to be cooked pemmican, a diet suitable for Arctic conditions but pretty indigestible stuff at high altitudes. Of living conditions at the highest camp (16,615 feet), Browne wrote; "We had now given up all thought of eating pemmican and were living, as in fact we had been living since leaving our 15,000-foot camp, on tea, sugar, hardtack (biscuits), and raisins."

Mount McKinley's South Peak was finally climbed on June 7, 1913, by a four-man team. The leader was the fifty-year-old Reverend Hudson Stuck, Episcopal Archdeacon of the Yukon, who had already done a lot of climbing in the Rockies. A "muscular Christian" if ever there was one, he had in fact emigrated from the home of muscular Christianity to North America at the age of twenty-two.

The other members of the party were Harry P. Karstens, a prospector from Fairbanks, Walter Harper, an Alaskan Indian, and Robert Tatum, a young missionary.

Stuck organized his expedition well and naturally followed what had been, before the earthquake, the well-pioneered route by way of the Muldrow Glacier. However, the saddle which led to the dome had been altered out of recognition by the earthquake and very much for the worse, and Stuck's party, too, was forced to cut an enormously long staircase up it which they used for bringing up supplies for the final attack on the peak. The first man to the top was Harper, who had led throughout the day.

On the way to it they were able to see clearly the 14-foot spruce erected as a flagpole by the Sourdough expedition three years before, and it is no denigration of the 1913 climbers, or those who preceded or followed the Sourdoughs on the mountain, to say that theirs was the greatest climb of all.

In 1957 the Italians Claudio Corti and Stefano Longhi set out on an expedition against the North Wall of the Eiger. Unknown to them, a pair of German climbers had almost whimsically decided to make the same climb; both were experienced mountaineers who should have known better than to challenge the Murder Face with so little preparation. The two teams met on the Italians' third day on the mountain and shared in the disaster. The Germans paid with their lives, as did Longhi, and Corti was saved only through what is surely the most spectacular rescue effort in Alpine history. This riveting piece is excerpted from Olsen's 1962 book *The Climb Up to Hell*.

# JACK OLSEN

# Rescue from the Eiger

It was exactly eight o'clock on Sunday morning when Alfred Hellepart began moving down the mountain into aloneness. As he walked slowly backward on the fifty-degree angle of the summit ice field, watching his friends operate the winch above him, he set about preparing himself psychologically. From long experience, he knew that one had to purge one's mind of all outside thoughts; the entire concentration had to be on the job at hand, and on the men to be rescued. One could not think at all of oneself; the slightest glimmer of fear could be deadly. Nor could he allow his thoughts to drift back to Munich, to his wife and his eleven-year-old son. From this minute on, they must be forgotten, until he had succeeded or failed in his rescue mission.

Certainly there was no need to worry about the cable. The experienced Gramminger was up at the anchorage, protecting him as he had so many times before. The men of the Mountain Guard had an almost childlike faith in their leader; they acted on his orders without question or hesitation. In practice exercises, Hellepart had carried two men on his back up the side of a mountain, and the cable had held. He would press a button in his mind and give the matter no further thought.

Now he was halfway down the summit ice field, and he tested the portable radio. The contact was excellent; he could hear Friedli loud and clear, and Friedli could hear him. When he had gone 250 feet, almost to the end of the field, he heard Friedli telling him to make himself secure on his crampons; the cable had to be disconnected from the winch and joined to the next 300-foot length by a frog coupling. Hellepart waited until the go-ahead came from the top, backed over the last few feet of the snowfield, and found himself looking down the vast sweep of the North Wall. For a moment, despite all his psychological preparations, he felt wild panic. An indescribable feeling of abandonment came over him; he could no longer see the men on the top, and instinctively he looked up at the quarter-inch cable spinning up into the mists, like a thin strand of cotton thread. Below him the North Wall fell endlessly away, down and down and down, black and menacing, broken only by a few insignificant snow ledges. Dangling from the cable, he gulped for air, and almost forgot what he had come for. Just then the voice of Gramminger broke in on the radio. "You are doing fine, Alfred," the calm voice said. "Everything is secure for you. Keep control of yourself, and remember that there are men on the wall depending on you for their lives." The soothing words brought composure back to Hellepart; he was no longer alone; he felt the strong ties to the men above, all their concentration fixed on him and his task, and he gave the order to continue letting the cable down. Off to his right, he could see a black rift coming up, one of the gaping exit cracks leading to the White Spider. He made a short traverse to the crack, and began wriggling his way obliquely downward. He did not know if this was the right route, but at the moment it was the only one. Two thousand feet below him, he could see the morning mists walking up the wall. For brief seconds, he glimpsed the village of Alpiglen, but then the mists closed together again and blanketed the valley. All around him the wind probed the holes and cracks on the mountain, and the low, hollow "whoo" gave him an uncomfortable feeling.

Now he had to find a secure stance again, to hold himself against the wall while another 300-foot roll of cable was attached above. Friedli's voice crackled down to him from above: "All is well. You will be on your way in a few minutes." The signal came, and he continued his descent. After a hundred more feet, he went on the air to tell Friedli that he was coming in sight of the Spider. Against the low howl of the wind, he talked to the summit, and during that brief conversation he heard another human voice, barely audible at first, then growing louder and coming from the east. He traversed toward the voice and came to a shattered pillar bulging out across the face. He stepped onto the pillar and sent rocks and rubble clattering down the face with his crampons. Still he went on, only partially supported by the cable, which now had assumed a sort of J shape as it followed him on the level course across the pillar. About sixty feet away, he spotted a man in a half-sitting, half-lying position on a narrow ledge pitched with a small red tent. Nervously he pushed the transmitting button and signaled the summit: "I have found a man."

Across the litter-covered pillar, Hellepart shouted, "Who are you? Are you Mayer, or Nothdurft?" The voice came back: *"Italiano."*

Slowly, still sending tons of rubble down the mountain, Hellepart continued the difficult traverse. Now he was within six or seven feet of the Italian, and he could hear the man calling, "*Mangiare!* Something to eat!" Hellepart fumbled in his pocket, found a frozen half-bar of black, hard Cailler chocolate, and tossed it across the edge to the hungry man. The Italian did not even pause to remove the wrapper. He rammed the chocolate into his mouth and began to chew. His mouth full of paper and chocolate, the man called to Hellepart: "*Sigaretta?*" But Hellepart had none. He paused for a moment and considered the situation. He could traverse the remaining few feet of the pillar, but only at increasing risk to himself, since he no longer dangled straight down from the cable. And if he reached the Italian in this manner, he would be unable to make the rescue. The two men, no matter what their condition, could not have effected the traverse back across the rubble without undue danger. Hellepart decided to retreat to the exit crack and ask the summit to pull him up to another position. From there he would try to make a straight perpendicular descent to the Italian. "Take me up," Hellepart called to the summit. "I am going to look for another route." A hard jerk on the cable yanked him off the pillar and out into space. Spinning in midair, he fought to turn himself toward the wall so that he could take up the shock of the return impact with his legs. He had barely succeeded in twisting around when he crashed into the wall feet first. "All right," said Hellepart to the summit, "haul me straight up. I will tell you when to stop."

Up he went, inches at a time, for 150 feet, and then set himself into a slow swing until he was able to grab a jutting rock straight above the Italian. "Now let me down," he instructed. As he descended a sheer gully, stones began to shake loose again, and he shouted to the Italian to take cover. Finally he dropped the last few feet and onto the ledge. While the marooned man mumbled, "*Grazie! Grazie!*" and put his arms around Hellepart, the German called triumphantly to the summit, "I am with the Italian!" It was nine-fifteen, and he had been on the wall for more than an hour. The Italian gave his name, and Hellepart reported it to the summit. Friedli asked where the others were. Hellepart said to Corti, "Where is Longhi? Where is Mayer? Where is Nothdurft?"

Corti pointed down the mountain. The two men leaned over the edge and called, but there was no response. Hellepart asked Corti in German, "Your condition?" Corti understood — the phrase is similar in both languages — and answered, "*Buona.*" But Hellepart, seeing that the man's knees were trembling, ordered him to sit down, and gave him coffee from a thermos which had been provided by the Poles. Corti was talking in Italian, and Hellepart got the impression from the torrent of words in the peculiar dialect that Nothdurft and Mayer had tried to force through to the top and that Corti had not seen them for several days. He looked at Corti's scarred hand and his bloodied head and decided that the Italian's condition was too poor to permit him to attempt a climb up to the top on a separate cable. Hellepart would have to make the carry on his back. He radioed to the summit for an Italian-speaking man to take the radio and explain the situation to Corti. Cassin's voice came on, and Hellepart handed the speaking mechanism to Corti, who seemed befuddled by it and nervously pushed the wrong buttons. Finally the contact was established, and Cassin could talk to his friend from the Ragni.

"*Rispondi*, Claudio," Cassin's voice said. "This is Cassin. Now listen to me: you have not the strength to go up by yourself. Watch how he shows you how to get up on his shoulders! Try everything to make it easy for your rescuer! Drink something when he gives you to drink. Remember, you are safe. Do not lose your spirit!" Hellepart took back the radio as the last words of Cassin crackled through the earphones: "*Coraggio*, Claudio, *coraggio!*"

Hellepart took a final look at Corti's tiny resting place. It was totally cleared of ice and snow, gobbled up by Corti in his terrible hunger and thirst. Some of his teeth were broken and splintered, shattered against the hard, cold ice for a last few useless "meals." Hellepart packed the rucksack, strapped it on the sitting Corti's back, and began lacing him into the webbing of a Gramminger-Sitz. He sat down with his back to Corti's front and pulled the harnesses of the human backpack around his own chest and up over his shoulders. This left no place for the radio; using snap links to lengthen the girth, he fixed the apparatus so that it dangled across his chest. Bearing the uncomfortable weight, he struggled to his feet and snapped the cable in place. All these preparations had taken nearly an hour. "We are ready," he said to the summit. It was ten o'clock.

Back came Friedli's voice: "We have been rearranging the equipment. It will take us a few minutes more."

Hellepart sat down with his heavy load and waited for the signal. Finally it came. "We bring you up now," Friedli called. "Prepare yourself!"

Hellepart wrenched himself into a standing position, but still the cable hung slack above him. "What is the matter?" he called to the summit.

"We are having a little trouble," Friedli answered. Long minutes went by, and then the cable began to tense. Hellepart pressed his feet against the wall and pushed outward with all his strength so that he would keep the cable from rubbing against the wall and prevent it from fouling. Now the wind began to hum across the tightening thread of steel. It sounded to Hellepart like a giant violin string, starting on a low note and gradually whining higher as it tensed, until it had reached a screaming, piercing pitch. And still they did not move up from the ledge. He looked above him at the delicate strand and wondered, for the first time, if it would hold.

On top, Friedli's fears about the winch had only increased as it had become necessary to haul Hellepart back up 150 feet to find a better route down to the Italian. By now there were 800 feet of cable reaching down the mountain. Where it made contact with the rock, it had abraded fissures of its own, increasing the friction and multiplying the force required for the upward pull. The men cranking the winch had barely been able to lift Hellepart up to his new stance, and after lowering him back down to the ledge, Friedli discussed the situation with Gramminger. "I do not think we can use the winch to pull the weight of two men," Friedli said. Gramminger agreed. While Hellepart went about his tedious task of readying Corti for the ascent, the crew on top discarded the winch and prepared to shift over to raw manpower. It was a quick improvisation, made possible only by Friedli's foresight in ordering the pulling path dug into the south ridge.

Now the cable would go up to the ridge and through a direction-changing roller placed on top of the rotten cornice. The roller would steer the cable back along the path, where thirty men were scrambling into position. At intervals of 20 feet, pulling ropes were attached to the cable by clamps which could be loosened and moved along to a new position.

Now teams of five were in place at each pulling rope, waiting for the signal from Friedli to begin the haul. A last-minute check was made of the three security brakes on the cable; they were so constructed that the cable could be pulled upward through them, but at the slightest accidental downward movement they would clamp tightly shut. As a final security, Gramminger remained at the big block of ice on the far end of the pulling path to anchor each new length of slack cable to the block as it was hauled in. Now they were ready.

With the voice of a Swiss drill sergeant, Friedli shouted to the men to haul away. They strained backward against the pulling ropes. But nothing moved. More hands were added to the ropes, and the order was repeated. Still the cable did not budge. Fearful that the combined strength of all the rescuers would snap the tensing lifeline to the two men below, Friedli frantically waved the operation to a halt. He did not think it possible that the cable had become wedged into the rock below; the soft limestone on the upper part of the Eiger might increase the friction, but it would not have been solid enough to imprison the cable against all this pressure. He decided that the mechanical equipment must have jammed. If his diagnosis was incorrect, if indeed the cable *was* fouled tightly on the mountain, they would have to abandon Corti and try to find some way to bring Hellepart back up. Nervously, Friedli went from device to device and finally came to one which had fouled. He cleared the jam and ordered the crews to begin pulling again. The cable tensed and whined in the wind; after a few long seconds, the men could feel it begin to move.

Now, at last, the long violin string had hit a pitch and held it, and Hellepart was coming up the mountain, his human cargo heavy on his back, the radio dangling clumsily in front of him. At first the ascent was not on a true perpendicular line. They swayed from side to side as the cable whipped them about; Hellepart shoved his crampons into the icy patina on the wall, seeking to steady himself, and sent slabs of ice and rock crashing down the wall. Every fifty feet he had to cling to the wall, leaning as far forward as he could, while the men on the summit secured the cable and moved up to new pulling positions. These were agonizing delays to the strong man of Munich; sometimes he would have to kneel against a tiny ledge, gripping an outcropping of rock with his knees the way a jockey grips a horse, the harsh metal edges of the radio digging into his chest. Sometimes he had to stand upright on scallops of snow, with all the weight of Corti on his shoulders. Once he said aloud, in a slightly annoyed, slightly quizzical voice, "Well, he's quite heavy, this fellow." But Corti seemed not to have heard. He was mumbling, *"Fame! Fame!"* and whenever Hellepart kneeled against the wall, Corti would push his own face into the snow and bite off big mouthfuls.

"Don't gobble so much snow!" Hellepart hollered. "It is bad for the stomach." But the famished Corti took his cold snacks anyway.

After about forty minutes of the torturous rise, the cable rasped over the last foot of the exit cracks and swung the two men onto the summit ice field. Out of the shadow of the overhang, they now could feel the rays of the sun, and Corti reacted peculiarly. "*Que bello e il sole,*" he said in a strangely loud voice. "How beautiful the sun is." Then he slumped forward into a coma. Hellepart recognized this as a shock reaction, and he knew that men in a seriously weakened condition could die from it. He would have to force the final 250 feet of the field. Up he came, staggering like a drunk under his heavy load, while Friedli shouted encouragement from the top. Now Hellepart was taking almost all of Corti's weight, receiving little assistance from the cable, which no longer hung straight down to hold them in firm suspension. The men on top knew he was forcing, and increased their own pace, once pulling too far too fast and nearly wrenching Hellepart and Corti face forward into the wet snow of the ice field. Hellepart merely regained his balance, kicked up through the sticky snow, and finally, fifty-nine minutes after the ascent had begun, stumbled with his cargo across the ridge. "Help me out of this!" he shouted to Friedli and pitched forward into the snow. Gasping for breath, while the others wrenched at the harnesses holding Corti and the radio to him, Hellepart felt a slap on the shoulder and heard an unfamiliar voice say, "Good! You have done well!" Relieved of his load, he was lifted to his feet and congratulated all around. "A cigarette!" he said. "I would like a cigarette!" Weak, and afraid he would slip off the summit, he wobbled to the safety of a bivouac hole for a smoke and a rest.

Their plane had crashed in the Andean vastness, and their location was unknown to the outside world. But these Chilean soccer players were *Alive*, as the title of Read's celebrated book affirmed, and they were determined to survive. With their supplies nearly exhausted and death looming imminent, desperation drove them to grim measures. For food they were forced to use the bodies of their dead fellow passengers. For rescue they were driven to embark upon an improbable expedition due west to Chile, and the hope that a small team could struggle to civilization and send back help.

# PIERS PAUL READ

# Stranded in the Andes

At five o'clock the next morning, Canessa, Parrado, and Vizintín prepared to go. First they dressed themselves in the clothes they had picked from the baggage of the forty-five passengers and crew. Next to his skin Parrado wore a Lacoste T-shirt and a pair of long woolen woman's slacks. On top of these he wore three pairs of jeans, and on top of the T-shirt six sweaters. Next he put a woolen balaclava over his head, then the hood and shoulders that he had cut from Susana's fur coat, and finally a jacket. Under his rugby boots he wore four pairs of socks which he covered with plastic supermarket bags to keep out the wet. For his hands he had gloves; for his eyes a pair of sunglasses; and to help him climb he held an aluminum pole which he strapped to his wrist.

Vizintín also had a balaclava. He wore as many sweaters and pairs of jeans but covered them with a raincoat, and on his feet he wore a pair of Spanish boots. As before he also carried the heaviest load, including a third of the meat, packed in either a plastic bag or a rugby sock. With it there were pieces of fat, to provide energy, and liver, to give them vitamins. The whole supply was designed to last the three of them ten days.

Canessa carried the sleeping bag. To cover his body and keep it warm he had looked for woolen clothes, feeling that elemental conditions called for elemental materials. He also liked to think that each garment had something precious about it. One of the sweaters he wore had been given to him by a dear friend of his mother, another by his mother herself, and a third had been knitted for him by his *novia*, Laura Surraco. One of the pairs of trousers he wore had belonged to his closest friend, Daniel Maspons, and his belt had been given to him by Parrado with the words, "This was a present from Panchito, who was my best friend. Now you're my best friend, so you take it." Canessa accepted this gift; he also wore Abal's skiing gloves and the skiing boots which belonged to Javier Methol.

The cousins gave the expeditionaries some breakfast before they sent them on their way. The others watched in silence. No words could express what they felt at this awesome moment; they all knew that this was their last chance of survival. Then Parrado separated once again the pair of tiny red shoes that he had bought in Mendoza for his nephew. He put one in his pocket and hung the other from the hat rack in the plane. "I'll be back to get it," he said. "Don't worry."

"All right," they all said, their spirits raised high by his optimism. "And don't forget to book us rooms in the hotel in Santiago." Then they embraced, and amid cries of ¡Hasta luego! the three expeditionaries set off up the mountain.

After they had gone about five hundred yards, Pancho Delgado came hobbling out of the plane. "Wait," he shouted, waving a small statue in his hand, "you've forgotten the Virgin of Luján!"

Canessa stopped and turned back. "Don't worry!" he shouted back. "If she wants to stay, let her stay. We'll go with God in our hearts."

They climbed up the valley, but they knew that this course took them slightly northwest and at some moment they would have to turn due west and climb directly up the mountain. The difficulty was that the slopes which encircled them looked uniformly steep and high. Canessa and Parrado began to argue about when, and how soon, they should start to climb. Vizintín, as usual, had no opinion on the subject. Eventually the two agreed. They took a reading on the plane's spherical compass and started to climb due west up the side of the valley. It was very heavy going. Not only were they faced with the steep slope, but the snow had already started to melt, and even in their improvised snowshoes they sank up to their knees. The wet snow also made the cushions sodden and therefore exceptionally heavy to drag bowlegged up the mountain. But they persevered, pausing every few yards for a short rest, and by the time they stopped by an outcrop of rocks for lunch at midday they were already very high. Beneath them they could still see the Fairchild, with some of the boys sitting on the seats in the sun watching their progress.

After their meal of meat and fat, they took another short rest and then continued on their way. Their plan was to reach the top before dark, for it would be almost impossible to sleep on the steep slopes of the mountain. As they climbed, their minds were on the view they hoped to have on the other side—a view of small hills and green valleys, perhaps with a shepherd's hut or a farmhouse already in sight.

As they had already found out, however, distances in the snow were deceptive, and by the time the sun went behind the mountain they were still nowhere near the top. Realizing that somehow they would have to sleep on the mountainside, they started to look for a level surface. To their growing dismay, it seemed that there was none. The mountain was almost vertical. Vizintín climbed an outcrop of rock (to avoid going around it in the snow) and got stuck. He very nearly toppled off because of the weight of his knapsack, and only saved himself by untying it and throwing it down onto the snow. The experience unnerved him and he started to moan that he could not go on. He was totally exhausted; to move his legs he had to lift them with his hands.

It was growing dark, and a feeling of panic was coming over them all. They came to another outcrop of rock. Parrado thought that there might be a level surface on the top and started to climb it, while Canessa waited beneath with his knapsack. Suddenly Canessa heard a shout of "Look out!" and a large rock, dislodged by Parrado's rugby boots, came hurtling past him, narrowly missing his head. "For God's sake," Canessa shouted up. "Are you trying to kill me?" Then he started to weep. He felt utterly depressed and in despair.

There was nowhere for them to sleep at the top of the outcrop, but a little farther on they came to an immense boulder, beside which the wind had blown a trench in the snow. The floor of the trench was not horizontal, but the wall of snow would prevent them from slipping down the mountainside; they therefore pitched camp and climbed into the sleeping bag.

It was a perfectly clear night and the temperature had sunk to many degrees below freezing, but the sleeping bag succeeded in keeping them warm. They also ate some more meat and drank a mouthful each of the rum they had brought with them. The view from where they lay was magnificent. There spread before them a huge landscape of snow-covered mountains lit by the pale light of the moon and stars. They felt strange lying there — Canessa in the middle — half possessed by terror and despair, yet half marveling at the magnificence of this icy beauty before them.

At last they slept or slipped fitfully into semiconsciousness. The night was too cold and the ground too hard for the three to sleep well, and the first light of the morning found them all awake. It was still cold and they remained in the sleeping bag, waiting for the sun to appear over the mountains and thaw out their boots, which had frozen solid on the rock where they had left them. While they waited they drank water from the bottle, ate some meat, and took another mouthful each of the rum.

They all watched the changing landscape as it grew lighter, but Canessa's eyes, which were the best of the three, came to concentrate on a line along the valley to the east, far beyond the Fairchild and the tail. Since the whole area was still in shadow it was hard to tell, but it seemed to him that the ground there was not covered by snow and that the line which crossed it might be a road. He said nothing about it to the others, because the idea was absurd; Chile was to the west.

When the sun came up from behind the mountains opposite them they started to climb once again — Parrado first, followed by Canessa and then Vizintín. All three were still tired and their limbs were stiff from the exertion of the day before, but they found a kind of path in the rock which seemed to lead toward the summit.

The mountain had become so steep that Vizintín did not dare look down. He simply followed Canessa at a cautious distance, as Canessa followed Parrado. What frustrated them all was that each summit they saw above them turned out to be a false one, a ridge of snow or an outcrop of rocks. They stopped by one of these rocks to eat in the middle of the day, took a short rest, and then climbed on. By the middle of the afternoon they still had not reached the top of the mountain — and though they felt themselves to be near, they were afraid of making the same mistake as the night before. They therefore looked for and found a similar trench carved by the wind beside the same kind of rock and decided to stop there.

Unlike Vizintín, Canessa had not been afraid to look down as they climbed the mountain, and each time he did so he saw that line in the far distance grow more distinct and more like a road. As they ... waited for the sunset, he pointed it out to the others. "Do you see that line over there?" he said. "I think it's a road."

"I can't see anything," said Nando, who was nearsighted. "But whatever it is, it can't be a road because we're facing due east and Chile's to the west."

"I know Chile's to the west," said Canessa, "but I still say that it's a road. And there's no snow down there. Look, Tintín, you can see it, can't you?"

Vizintín's eyesight was not much better than Parrado's. He gazed into the distance with his small eyes. "I can just see a line, yes," he said, "but I couldn't say if it was a road or not."

"It can't be a road," said Parrado.

"There might be a mine," said Canessa. "There are copper mines right in the middle of the cordillera."

"How do you know?" asked Parrado.

"I read about it somewhere."

"It's more likely a geological fault."

There was a pause. Then Canessa said, "I think we should go back."

"Go back?" Parrado repeated.

"Yes," said Canessa. "Go back. This mountain's much too high. We'll never reach the top. With every step we take we risk our lives. . . . It's madness to go on."

"And what do we do if we go back?" asked Parrado.

"Go to that road."

"And what if the road isn't a road?"

"Look," said Canessa, "my eyesight is better than yours, and I say it's a road."

"It might be a road," said Parrado, "and it might not; but there's one thing we know for certain. To the west is Chile. If we keep going to the west, we're sure to come to Chile."

"If we keep going to the west, we're sure to break our necks."

Parrado sighed.

"Well, I'm going back anyway," said Canessa.

"And I'm going on," said Parrado. "If you walk to that road and find it isn't a road, then it'll be too late to try this way again. They're already short of food down there. There won't be enough for another expedition like this, so we'll all be losers; we'll all stay up here in the cordillera."

They slept that night with their differences unresolved. At one point Vizintín was waked by lightning in the distance and he woke Canessa, fearing that a storm was about to break over them. But the night was still clear, there was no wind, and the two boys went back to sleep again.

The night did not weaken Parrado's determination; as soon as it was light he prepared himself to continue the climb. Canessa, however, seemed less sure that he was going to return to the Fairchild, so he made the suggestion that Parrado and Vizintín leave their knapsacks with him and climb a little farther up the mountain to see if they came to the top. Parrado accepted this idea and set off at once, with Vizintín behind him, but in his impatience to reach the summit Parrado climbed quickly and Vizintín was soon left behind.

The ascent had become exceptionally difficult. The wall of snow was almost vertical and Parrado could only proceed by digging steps for his hands and feet, which Vizintín used as he followed him. If he had slipped he would have fallen for many hundreds of feet, but this did not dismay him; the surface of the snow was so steep, and the sky above it so blue, that he knew he was approaching the summit. He was driven on by all the excitement of a mountaineer whose triumph is at hand and by his intense anxiety to see what was on the other side. As he climbed he told himself, "I'm going to see a valley, I'm going to see a river, I'm going to see green grass and trees —" and then suddenly the sheer face was no longer so steep. It fell sharply to a slight incline and then flattened out onto a level surface of some twelve feet wide before falling away on the other side. He was at the top of the mountain.

Parrado's joy at having made it lasted for only the few seconds it took him to scramble to his feet; the view before him was not of green valleys running down toward the Pacific Ocean but an endless expanse of snow-covered mountains. From where he stood, nothing blocked his view of vast cordillera, and for the first time Parrado felt that they were finished. He sank to his knees and wanted to curse and cry to heaven at the injustice, but no sound came from his mouth and as he looked up again, panting from his recent exertion in the thin air of the mountain, his momentary despair was replaced once again by a certain elation at what he had done. It was true that the view before him was of mountains, their peaks standing in ranks to the far horizon, but the very fact that he was above them showed that he had climbed one of the highest mountains in the Andes. I've climbed this mountain, he thought to himself, and I shall call it Mount Seler after my father.

He had with him the lipstick he used for his chapped lips and an extra plastic bag; he wrote the name "Seler" on the plastic bag with the lipstick and placed it under a stone on the summit. He then sat back to admire the view.

As he studied the mountains spread out before him he came to notice that due west, to the far left of the panorama, there were two mountains whose peaks were not covered with snow. "The cordillera must end somewhere," he said to himself, "so perhaps those two are in Chile." The truth was, of course, that he knew nothing about the cordillera, but this idea renewed his optimism, and when he heard Vizintín calling him from below, he shouted down to him in a buoyant tone of voice, "Go back and fetch Muscles. Tell him it's all going to be all right. Tell him to come up and see for himself!" And seeing that Vizintín had heard him and was climbing down again, Parrado returned to admiring the view from the top of Mount Seler.

When the two others set off for the summit, Canessa had sat back with the knapsacks and watched his road as it changed color in the changing light. The more he stared at it the more convinced he became that it was a road, but then in two hours Vizintín returned with the news that Parrado had reached the top and wanted Canessa to join him.

"Are you sure he's at the top?"

"Yes, quite sure."

"Did you get there?"

"No, but Nando says it's marvelous. He says everything's going to be all right."

Reluctantly Canessa got to his feet and clambered up the side of the mountain. He had left his knapsack with Vizintín, but still it took him an hour longer than it had taken Parrado. He followed the steps they had cut into the snow, and as he approached the summit he called out for his friend. He heard Parrado shout back and followed his directions until he too stood on the top of the mountain.

The effect of what he saw was the same on Canessa as it had been on Parrado. He looked aghast at the endless mountains stretching away to the west. "But we've had it," he said. "We've absolutely had it. There isn't a chance in hell of getting through all that."

"But look," said Parrado. "Look there to the west. Don't you see? To the left? Two mountains without any snow?"

"Do you mean those tits?"

"The tits. Yes."

"But they're miles away. It'll take us fifty days to get to them."

"Fifty days? Do you think so? But look there." Parrado pointed into the middle distance. "If we go down this mountain and along that valley it leads to that sort of Y. Now, one branch of the Y must lead to the tits."

Canessa followed the line of Parrado's arm, saw the valley, and saw the Y. "Maybe," he said. "But it'd still take us fifty days, and we've only enough food for ten."

"I know," said Parrado. "But I've thought of something. Why don't we send Tintín back?"

"I'm not sure he'd want to go."

"He'll go if we tell him to. Then we can keep his food. If we ration it out carefully, it should last us for twenty days."

"And after that?"

"After that we'll find some."

"I don't know," said Canessa. "I think I'd rather go back and look for that road."

"Then go back," said Parrado sharply. "Go back and find your road. But I'm going on to Chile."

They retraced their steps down the mountain, reaching Vizintín and the knapsacks around five in the afternoon. While they were away Vizintín had melted some snow, so they were able to quench their thirst before eating some more meat. As they were eating, Canessa turned to Vizintín and said, in the most casual tone of voice he could master, "Hey, Tintin, Nando thinks it might be best if you went back to the plane. You see, it would give us more food."

"Go back?" said Vizintín, his face lighting up. "Sure. If you think so." And before either of the other two could say anything he had picked up his knapsack and was about to strap it to his back.

"Not tonight," said Canessa. "Tomorrow morning will do."

"Tomorrow morning?" said Vizintín. "Okay. Fine."

"You don't mind?"

"Mind? No. Anything you say."

"And when you get back," said Canessa, "tell the others that we've gone west. And if the plane spots you and you get rescued, please don't forget about us."

Canessa lay awake that night, by no means sure in his own mind that he would be going on with Parrado rather than returning with Vizintín. He continued to discuss the matter with Parrado under the stars, and Vizintín went to sleep to the sound of their arguing voices. But next morning, when they awoke, Canessa had made up his mind. He would go on with Parrado. They therefore took the meat from Vizintín and anything else that might be useful to them (though not the revolver, which they had always considered a dead weight) and prepared to send him on his way.

"Tell me, Muscles," said Vizintín, "is there anything . . . I mean, any part of the bodies that one *shouldn't* eat?"

"Nothing," said Canessa. "Everything has got some nutritional value."

"Even the lungs?"

"Even the lungs."

Vizintín nodded. Then he looked at Canessa again. "Look," he said. "Since you're going on and I'm going back, is there anything of mine you think you might need? Don't hesitate to say, because all our lives depend on your getting through."

"Well," said Canessa, looking Vizintín up and down and eyeing his equipment. "I wouldn't mind that balaclava."

"This?" said Vizintín, handling the white wool balaclava which he had on his head. "Do you mean this?"

"Yes. That."

"I . . . er . . . do you think you really need it?"

"Tintin, would I ask for it if I thought I didn't need it?"

Reluctantly Vizintín stripped off and handed over his prized balaclava. "Well, good luck," he said.

"Same to you," said Parrado. "Take care going down."

"I certainly will."

"Don't forget," said Canessa. "Tell Fito we've gone west. And if they rescue you, make them come and look for us."

"Don't worry," said Vizintín. He embraced his two companions and set off down the mountain.

Is mountaineering more than sport? Does it touch upon the realms of art and perhaps religion? If so, then the climber proceeds somehow from the necessarily intense awareness of his physical being to a spiritual consciousness as well, moving from the seen to the unseen. Colette Richard, blind since the age of two, experiences the mountains in reverse, moving from the unseen to the seen—and yet back again, back to the mystical lure of these landmarks of a world larger than life.

# COLETTE RICHARD

# Climbing Blind

I was born at Versailles in a humble dwelling very near the palace. When I was two, my eyesight failed almost completely, leaving me with only a faint perception of light, able to distinguish between sunshine and darkness like a normal person with their eyes tightly closed.

My parents taught me a love of nature, and as a little girl I played with other children either in the Great Park of Versailles, which was like my private domain, or on the land adjoining it, where my father had a vegetable garden near the pond known as the Pièce d'Eau des Suisses.

At school I became passionately interested in geology and geography; I dreamed of volcanoes and mountains. My holidays were spent in a village in the Gatinais, where my younger brother and I played together in an old quarry. It was there, amid the fields and woods, that my longing for adventure was born. My love of mountains grew with the years, with the books that were read to me and those that I read to myself in Braille. But I have always had an intense longing for space and great expeditions. . . .

I do not go to the mountains for the same reasons as other climbers, and that is all that can be said. We approach them in a different way. And so people are often surprised by my evocation of the mountains, and my love of them. But sight is only one of our senses. There are all the things one perceives by other means, things one knows

216

by intuition, things one can hear and touch and smell and taste. In the foothills there are waterfalls, flowers, cattle bells, and raspberries.

What one experiences at higher altitudes is to my mind more precious and rare because it is difficult of access: the wind in the peaks, the footsteps of the rope party in the snow, the steady crunch of the icy ax sinking into it, the falling stones which whistle as they fall, the sounds coming from the glacier's depth. . . . And there is also, which is wonderful to me, the reflection of brilliant sunshine on untrodden snow, the warmth, the quiver, the extraordinary light that is to be found nowhere else.

There is the keen, cold air that stings the cheeks, the delicate, almost imperceptible scent of snow which has in it something of pine, of grass and of flowers. There is the use we who are sightless must make of our hands, the feeling of rock and snow. . . .

The car stopped presently in the park of Le Fayet, the thermal station. Brilliant sunshine, but not many people on the crags, and so much the better! I was roped to Monsieur Piraly; he started the ascent while I awaited my turn. I was a little frightened, naturally. I had done no rock climbing, or very little. I was afraid that it would be too much for me.

I thought of the advice I had been given — "Be perfectly relaxed, perfectly calm, convince yourself that you're in first-rate condition. There's no reason why you shouldn't make it. Blind people have no difficulty in finding footholds." Very nice in theory! My friends were wonderful. All the same, I needed to take a grip of myself if I was not to start inventing reasons for giving up the attempt.

I should have taken myself in hand a little earlier. The process did not seem to be working very well. But then I said to myself, "Well, anyway, I'm going to have a shot!" and after that I awaited Piraly's order with a kind of exhilaration that was new to me.

"Come along. But go gently. Be careful of your hand- and footholds, and take your time."

A little way off I could hear Yvonne and Pierrette talking. They had said, "We're coming to see how you get on." It seemed that I was bound to try, if only not to disappoint them. So I started.

I had a queer sense of having no strength in my arms, which was perhaps not very surprising as I was tired and not in training; and in any case, all beginners probably feel the same. But it caused me a moment of panic. I thought of what my parents would say if they could see me. I was suddenly terrified. I fumbled my holds, desperately longing to go down again, while I muttered something and Raymond and Piraly shouted encouragement from above. I had to keep on, or what would Pierrette and Yvonne think, seeing me hanging on the rope? Finally I hoisted myself painfully onto the flat top of the rock.

"Well, since you're so keen on going down again, you can do it now!"

So now I was to make a rope descent, my first. How wonderful! I trembled a little, but that would pass.

"You pass the rope around your right thigh and over your left shoulder. Spread your legs and go backward, lying more or less horizontal as you pay the rope out. Don't be afraid. You're quite safe."

Faithfully obeying orders, I made my first descent, not very cleverly. But I managed it, and the initiation gave me confidence. I stopped trembling and was ready to climb again.

This time it was Raymond who secured me with the safety rope while Piraly climbed alongside me and guided my hands and feet. One has a great sense of safety with a guide at one's side, and this is another thing that all beginners know.

"You're gripping upside down with your left hand. This is a good rock face; there are holds everywhere."

"For the hands, yes — but not for the feet."

"Why not for your feet? Try to get them to grip the surface. Your boots won't slip. The soles were made for rock climbing."

"I keep on slipping. I haven't got the knack."

"The fact is, you aren't trusting those soles. You can't get a hold with the toe or the side of your foot; it's got to be flat on the surface. There, that's better."

Raymond made jesting comments as he watched me climb. I managed somehow or other to get to him, and then started to repeat the descent.

"Spread your legs more!"

But something was going wrong. I swung to the right and did not react quickly enough to recover my balance. I hung there swinging and my body turned so that my back bumped against the rock. It all happened very quickly, and Raymond swore while with an effort he checked my fall.

"It was your own fault. You didn't do as you were told. Have you hurt yourself?"

"No."

Piraly came alongside.

"That'll do for today."

"No, I want to try again."

I knew there was nothing worse than to give up after a failure. If a horse refuses a jump you put him at it again so that he won't do the same thing twice. I was like the horse. I knew myself only too well. If I didn't do it properly now, I should never make a good rope descent, or at least I should always be afraid of them.

The next time I managed it. I got down perfectly and was delighted and enormously relieved.

"That was a very good first lesson," said Piraly. "No need to worry about what happened. It's the same with every beginner."

So after all, I was just a beginner like the rest!

Five times American teams had tried to ascend this savage mountain; five times they had failed, and five men had died in those efforts. In 1978, a team of fourteen American men and women made another attempt, and this one culminated in success for four of them—Jim Wickwire, Lou Reichardt, John Roskelly, and Rick Ridgeway, who wrote this account of the climb. The climb over, Wickwire lingered at the top, succumbing to a temptation that has been the end of many a climber, but as recorded here, somehow survived a forced bivouac just below the summit, without shelter, oxygen, or food, at 40 below zero with winds over 50 miles per hour.

# RICK RIDGEWAY

# Bivouac on K2

**SEPTEMBER 6. CAMP I, 18,400 FEET. 5:25 P.M.**

It had been an exciting day. After Rob [Schaller] shouted, "They're on their way to the summit," that morning, everyone awoke immediately, looking bleary-eyed out their tents toward the summit and, without exception, jubilant. It was a very cold morning—the thermometer in Camp I read 10 below zero Fahrenheit—but it was windless. They could see there was no wind on top, either, and it looked like a perfect summit day. Clear and crisp.

It was easy to watch the progress through the telescope. They could distinguish Lou [Reichardt] from Wick [Jim Wickwire]. They studied their slow progress, watching them make four or five steps, then lean on their axes exhausted. They knew the snow was deep; they could even see the trail as they postholed up the soft snow in the gully leading to the summit slopes. It was painfully slow, but they followed the two each step.

Spirits were very high. There was relief that all the work and toil was paying off. Each person had played a crucial role in the drama they were witnessing; every person on the team was in no small way a player integrally part of that final scene. Whatever rancor had existed, whatever disappointments and disillusionments had divided the team, dissolved with each step that placed Lou and Wick that much closer to the summit.

Concern mounted as shadows fell across the face at 3:30, and the two were still some distance below the top. Finally, about 5:15, they watched Lou and Wick crest the summit ridge. The mountain was backlit as the wind picked up, and a plume of snow blew off the ridge. The dots moved antlike the last yards to the summit. Then, at twenty feet from the top, they disappeared behind the crest. Everyone realized the true summit was out of their view, but there was no doubt. Jim Wickwire and Lou Reichardt had reached the top.

People cheered, bear-hugged, slapped backs. The moment of victory was theirs. There was still concern, however, about the late hour. Rob continued glued to the telescope. Five minutes after they had disappeared he saw a figure bound off the summit ridge. He could tell it was Lou; he had studied each of them so carefully all day, he could distinguish their idiosyncrasies. He waited. Where was Wick? Lou continued with much haste down the slope, as if panicked. Had something happened to Wick? Why was Lou almost at a run? The cheering stopped, and quiet came over them. They waited. One minute, two minutes, three minutes. Each had the same thought: he should have appeared by now. Something has gone wrong.

They quietly discussed the possibilities. Five minutes, six, seven. It was getting dark. Wick would not stay on top this late because he wouldn't be able to get back to high camp before total darkness. They watched Lou continue his rapid descent. . . .

Fifteen minutes, sixteen, seventeen. Lou was over 500 feet below the summit.

"It could have been a summit cornice," Bill [Sumner] speculated.

"Is there a cornice on this summit?"

"I don't know. I don't remember reading about one."

"It's not uncommon. Remember Bruce Carson on Trisul. He was on the summit, peeking over the edge, and didn't realize he was on a cornice. It broke off."

"There could even be a crevasse. Like the Japanese who just died on the summit over on Gasherbrum."

It was unusual to have a crevasse on a summit, but it was not unusual to have a cornice. Bill's speculation and fear were based on several case histories. . . .

Thirty-five minutes. Lou was not 1,000 feet down, nearing the place where that morning they had watched him inexplicably leave his pack. Forty minutes . . .

"There he is!"

Everyone bolted up, staring hard at the darkened face and the still back-lighted ridge crest.

"I can see him," Rob said, fixed to the telescope. "He seems to be okay."

Suddenly everyone went crazy, hugging, cheering, dancing. Wick was alive. For some reason he had stayed longer on the summit, but he was on his way down. . . .

"But it's late," someone said. "He can't make it back to Camp VI before dark."

"And there's no moon. He probably can't downclimb without moonlight."

The cheering quieted as everyone realized the implications. Above, the last light disappeared, the plume off the summit crest grew with the mountain wind. Already, in Camp I, it was much below zero. Ten thousand feet higher it had to be incomparably worse. They had made the summit, and Wick was alive — there was much relief in that — but everyone knew the real fight was just beginning. . . .

## SEPTEMBER 6. CAMP VI ABRUZZI, 25,750 FEET. 6:30 P.M.

"I apologize for being so hard to get along with these last couple of days. Must be the altitude."

"Don't worry about it," John [Roskelly] said. "I haven't been so easy to live with myself. This is our third day at 8,000 meters, and our second night without sleep. What do you expect?"

I laid my head back down on my boot — I used it each night as a pillow — and smiled.

"Yeah, I guess you're right. I'm pretty bushed. But I'll try and be a little more even-tempered."

Actually, I was completely exhausted, more than at any time on the expedition. After leaving Camp VI Direct that morning we had descended only 200 feet when we took off our packs, tied a line on them, and started dragging them, thinking it was easier to sled the heavy loads than to shoulder them. We passed Terry [Bech] on his way down and learned that Lou and Wick had gotten an early start. We reached Camp VI Abruzzi about three o'clock; the last hundred feet with those heavy loads had brought me close to my limit. . . .

By dark we had the tent pitched. I crawled into my bag but continued to shiver for some time. As soon as I got a hot brew down me, I warmed up and was able to laugh at myself and apologize to John. . . . We looked forward to a few hours' sleep before again getting up about one o'clock to prepare for our own summit bid.

We received a garbled radio call from Camp I and managed to decipher that Wick and Lou had reached the summit. The expedition was a success. Now we only hoped they made it back without bivouacking. The wind had been picking up all evening, and the sides of the tent were flapping with increasing pitch.

By eight we were worried. It was very dark. We had a policeman's whistle along for just such an emergency, and, leaning out the tent door, we blew it while flashing a headlamp beam, hoping to beacon them in. Another hour passed.

"Did you hear something?"

"Blow the whistle again."

We listened carefully. Above the wind we distinctly heard Lou's voice. We looked at each other, smiled, and grabbed the light to signal them in.

Lou had overshot our camp in the dark and was a hundred yards below the tents when he spotted our light. He had nearly given up finding camp and was hoping instead for a crevasse suitable for bivouac. When he saw the light all the strain of the last several hours gave way and the tension flowed out, as he realized he was safe. Consequently, he had an extremely difficult time climbing back to the tent. When he finally arrived he was shaking with cold, drained, on the edge of collapse. Few men would have been equal to the physical endurance of Lou that day.

We heard him arrive outside our tent, but before we could get out to help him he jammed his head through the vestibule door. I knew the hour was late, that Lou had been climbing at extreme altitude all day without stop, that he had been through a superhuman ordeal, and that all this would no doubt read in his face, but I was not prepared for the apparition that met me eye to eye.

"Good God," John said.

"Jesus," I confirmed.

His face was frozen, looking like a specter raised from a frozen underworld. Large clumps of ice were frozen in his beard—not just snow, or spindrift, but heavy pieces of blue ice. There was a large icicle hanging from his nose. His lips were puffed, red, and split from the ordeal. But his eyes still glowed with life; there was no hiding there the joy he felt to be in our tent.

We pulled him in, careful not to upset the stove, and helped him off with his crampons and boots. While John did that I mixed a brew of hot Gatorade. Lou was shaking and had difficulty speaking.

"Just a minute. You can tell us all about it in a second. First get this down you."

I held the cup to his lips, but was aghast to discover so much ice in his beard I couldn't get the rim of the cup to his lips. I set down the cup and tried to remove the ice. I pulled and yanked, and finally a big hunk broke loose and with it a clump of hair. Lou said nothing, oblivious to what I was doing, still shaking. With the larger ice hunks gone, he was able to drink the hot liquid. Wearily he leaned against John, and appeared almost to fall asleep.

"We made the summit," he said, a quiver in his voice.

"Yes, we know," we said, excitement in our voices.

"I made the summit without oxygen."

John and I looked at each other, realizing the magnitude of Lou's words. He said it simply, but with pride.

"Where's Wick?" we asked. "Is he behind you?"

"I don't know."

"What do you mean, you don't know?"

"I'm not sure where he is."

"Where did you last see him?"

"On the summit. I think he's bivouacking."

John and I looked at each other again, but this time with grave expressions. The wind was worse than ever, and it was already extremely cold.* For a moment, none of us said anything.

"Maybe he's still coming down."

*By estimates based on a thermometer reading at Camp III, where it registered 30 below zero, it was approximately 40 below that night at 8,000 meters. Accounting the chill factor for an estimated 50-knot wind, about 115 below zero Fahrenheit.

"I don't think so. It's very dark, and I think he had it in his mind to bivouac; it was something he almost anticipated."

"No headlamp?"

"It was in my pack."

"If he has his half-bag and parka, it might not be too bad."

"He doesn't. The half-bag got soaked this morning when he spilled water. He left it behind. He's got a pair of down pants he borrowed from Cherie [Bech]. Just that and his sixty/forty parka."

"Are there any crevasses up there to bivvy in?"

"I don't think so. . . . "

We turned off the stove and snuggled into our bags. In the warmth I felt safe, secure, and aware that at that moment Wick was struggling for his survival. I listened to the wind, gusting perhaps to 40 knots, and felt the cold air on my face. That survival, I thought, would be marginal.

"What time is it?"

"A little after midnight."

"We'd better get ready again about one-thirty."

"I'll let you know when it's time."

"What do you think Wick's chances are?"

"Pretty grim."

"So do I. I think in the morning we're as likely to be on rescue mission, or a body detail, as a summit attempt."

John did not answer. We both lay quiet, listening to the wind, waiting for the hour to pass until we would make preparations. I did not look forward to climbing into the cold blackness.

### SEPTEMBER 6 OR 7. SUMMIT PYRAMID, ABRUZZI FINISH. A LITTLE LESS THAN 28,000 FEET. AROUND MIDNIGHT.

*I am slipping, slowly, closer to the drop-off. Inch by inch, my bivouac sack slides down the icy slope. I dig in my boot heels, trying to jam them through the thin nylon sack that I am huddled in. I still slide. The wind is blowing hard, it is so cold. I cannot stop the slipping. . . .*

*You had better do something, Wickwire. You might be close to the edge. The edge, Wickwire. You are at the edge.*

*I must do something. I do not want to get out of this sack. I have to. I pull down the opening, and crawl out. I seem so stiff. The wind is so strong. I am out, and I start pushing the sack back up the hill. It is a long way. Ten feet, then twenty, then thirty. There I find the platform I chopped earlier. I put the sack back on it.*

*Now what is to keep me from sliding again? I have an idea. No, under these conditions, it is an inspiration. In one corner of the bivvy sack I take my ice ax and jam it through the fabric, pinning it to the snow. I do the same to the other corner, using my ice hammer. Then back inside the sack to escape the wind. But not the cold. Good thinking, Wickwire. . . .*

*Now you can concentrate on staying alive until dawn. It will not be easy. You are shaking, with no control. The first stage of hypothermia. Your toes no longer have feeling. Keep wiggling, though; keep moving them inside your boots. Maybe it will not be as bad, that way. Keep tensing, keep moving, keep circulation going. Survive, Wickwire. You know you can make it until dawn. You have done this kind of thing before. Cold nights in crevasses bivouacking on Mount Rainier.*

*But this is not Rainier. This is not 14,000 feet. This is K2, and this is 28,000 feet. . . .*

**SEPTEMBER 7. SUMMIT PYRAMID, ABRUZZI FINISH. ABOUT 26,200 FEET. 4:30 A.M.**

Hard snow, wind-tortured to small crescents like the surface of the sea frozen, and a sense of time in slow motion. The sound of crampons biting hard snow, squeaking, and the sound of quick, conscious breathing. Dark. Wind. Cold. . . .

John was ten feet away, and together we climbed, at a slow, even pace, the steepening snowfield above Camp VI, the base of the summit pyramid. It was black and moonless, but in the rarefied atmosphere starlight was sufficient to see above us the major features of the upper mountain: the enormous ice cliffs like ramparts guarding the summit fortress, and below the cliffs, the constricting couloir through the rock band. A ground blizzard blew spindrift over our boots, and studied care was necessary to place each step on the crescent sastrugi that patterned the hard snow surface. I was conscious, in the dark, of the absolute necessity for precise footwork because we had no rope.

Despite the heavy oxygen, the extreme cold, and the altitude — 8,000 meters — I felt strong. We planned to go on oxygen above the couloir, and without it I was surprised at the fast pace we kept. . . .

Our first rest came at the site of Japanese Camp VI. We sat on our parkas and picked through the refuse preserved in amber ice, and watched dawn over the Karakoram. We were at the same altitude as the summit of Broad Peak, across the valley of the Godwin Austen Glacier and the closest mountain to the Abruzzi Ridge.

"There's enough light to see," I said. "Wick might be moving by now."

"I hope so."

"God knows what kind of condition he's in. We're going to have trouble getting him down if he's in bad shape. Especially with no rope."

"If he's bad, I don't think we could get him down."

We sat still, silent, staring. The dawn filled the shadows in the lee of the great peaks. New mountains rose on the horizon, not visible from lesser altitudes. The glaciers so far below flowed inexorably in their timeless path to the sea. We hoped Wick was also witness to such grandeur.

**SEPTEMBER 7. SUMMIT PYRAMID. A LITTLE LESS THAN 28,000 FEET. FIRST DAWN.**

*You have to remember, Wickwire, to keep moving your toes. You forget to do that too often. There's no feeling left in them. Your fingers are gone, too. Maybe it won't make any difference whether you move them or not. No, you've got to try. You know it will help in the end.*

*This night has to end sometime. . . .*

*Maybe you should think about moving. That means you will have to crawl out of this magnificent bivvy sack. What a way to spend the night, huh. Covered with a piece of half-ounce rip-stop in a full gale at 28,000 feet. This is going to be one to tell stories about.*

*Probably be ice this morning. There was some yesterday; guess that means there will be some today. You should put your crampons on. Let's see, they are outside the bivvy sack here somewhere. Yeah, here they are. Now get out of the sack and put your crampons on. Okay, ol' crampon, there you go on the boot. Now lace the strap through the eye here, then it goes over the boot and crosses to this loop, then back again. Now buckle it down and make sure it is fastened. Okay. One crampon on. Sun feels good, but it is still so cold. My fingers are awfully hard. I wonder how the toes are doing inside that boot. Wait a minute, Wickwire. Look at your boot. The crampon is loose. Two steps with that rig and it would pop off and so would you. A long fall. All the way to Base Camp.*

*Ha, ha. That's funny.*

*Who needs crampons anyway. Just lie back and relax. You can go down later. Put the crampons on later. You probably don't need them anyway.*

*Feel the sun. Things seem so strange.*

*Relax.*

*What a magnificent view, huh. There are the four Gasherbrums, then Broad Peak, and farther to the right Chogolisa and Masherbrum. And the summit, just up above, an easy walk.*

*Look how ridiculously close I bivouacked to the cornice. Might have fallen through. So far down the South Face.*

*Go down later. . . .*

*Sit up, Wickwire. Focus. You're in bad shape, now straighten up. Snap out of it. Concentrate, Wickwire, concentrate. Strap the crampon tight. Put the other one on. Tighten it. Keep warming your fingers. Keep moving them. Double-check the crampons. They look better, now. That will work. . . .*

*Okay. Ready? Maybe you should go down facing in. No. You're not that bad, and it is not that steep. Not right here, but be careful at the traverse. Now start moving. Keep thinking. Concentrate. You'll loosen up in a minute. Remember, most accidents happen on descent. Be careful. . . .*

## SEPTEMBER 7. SUMMIT PYRAMID, THE NARROW COULOIR. ABOUT 27,000 FEET. 7:30 A.M.

It was about seven-thirty. I wondered, Where will we find Wickwire? Did he make it down this far before bivouacking, or was he still higher? What if he tried last night to climb down? It was black. This is very steep climbing, he would have been solo, very tired; he could have fallen. We would never learn what became of him.

Dark thoughts, fuzzy scenarios, disjointed images, dreams from a high-altitude opium den. I thought, I feel no emotion. Wick may be dead, he may be above me frozen, he may be 10,000 feet below me, crumbled on the glacier, yet I feel nothing. Last night there was alarm, there was that feeling of possible tragedy, of possible loss, that feeling of emptiness. Now I feel nothing. I recognize that Wick may be in trouble. Beyond that, no other feelings, no other thoughts except how to make the next move up this steep couloir. . . .

I have two more moves, and then I will be out of the couloir. Lift the leg, carefully place the crampon, test the handholds, pressure the leg muscles, move up. Always up, one more step higher, one more step toward the top. I am above the gully. Where to from here? There will still be some kind of traverse to turn the ice cliff above me that will lead to the snow gully and eventually to the summit snowfield. How far is John? Look up, I should see him now, he should be just around the corner. There he is, but wait. I stare at the scene before me mesmerized; I am not prepared for what I see: twisting swirls of ground spindrift. Rainbow red, blue, and violet flashes — refractions of a million crystal eyes and the fathomless indigo of rarefied sky. Brilliant white. Ice cliffs, shining with wet, sensuous smoothness. Extreme altitude and vertigo. A feeling of no time: no beginning, no end. Frozen in the scene two figures. One, below the other, blue-suited and moving slowly — John. The second, standing above, no apparent movement, legs slightly spread, arms down, a scarecrow figure yet also godlike, still not moving — frozen solid? Jim Wickwire.

I watched John climb the last few feet to Wick, who stood, not moving, in his scarecrow stance. Was Wick alive? Motionless, he stood staring down at us. Then he raised his arm — a greeting. He was alive; he had survived. I could see they were talking to each other.

I looked down to the snow and ice in front of me to concentrate on the climbing until I reached the more level stance where Wick and John were resting. As I neared, I could hear their conversation:

"I was on a small flat spot a little below the summit. Pretty cold."

"Frostbite?"

"I think so. It's hard to tell."

"Can you make it down the rest of the way by yourself?"

"Yeah. I'm doing okay. I've got the hard part behind — that traverse over here to the gully."

Wick indicated with his ice ax. I climbed up and joined the conversation. Wick looked haggard, of course, ice in his beard, eyes sunken and tired but still with a sparkle, a determination. It looked to us as if he had suffered no serious damage, but it was impossible for us, or for Wick, for that matter, to realize then the extent of his injuries. We continued to talk, joking, making light of an ordeal John and I—emotions obscured in the anesthesia of 27,000 feet—could in no way share.

"Good luck, you guys. I'll see you back in Camp VI."

"Be careful, Wick. You still have the couloir to get down. Move slow."

"Don't worry. I'll be okay."

Wick climbed past us, and John patted him affectionately on his cap. A simple gesture, and neither John nor I had any way of knowing it brought Wick close to tears. It was the first human contact in fourteen hours—fourteen hours of which he had counted each minute. It was a small gesture of affection of one human for another that Wick, for the rest of his life, would not forget. Wick climbed slowly to the top of the gully, turned inward, and began his descent.

Watching him I thought, Not now, Wick, not after what you've been through. Not after victory. Be careful, go slow, make no mistakes.

Wick's movements were mechanical and stiff, like the Tin Man of Oz with no oil. There was no way, without rope, we could assist him. We only crossed our fingers.

John called to him, "Wick, when we get back remind me to enroll you in my climbing school. You could use a few lessons."

Wick looked up and smiled that open but closed-teeth smile that meant he felt confident. I knew he could make it, and John and I turned to our next task—the summit.

A smorgasbord of climbing techniques marks this route — now popular but until 1961 impregnable — up Yosemite's fabled El Capitan. Pioneered not by John Salathé but by Royal Robbins, Chuck Pratt, and Tom Frost, the Salathé "Wall" (it is a route on the southwest face rather than the face itself) is one of "fifty classic climbs of North America" identified by Steve Roper and Allen Steck in their 1979 book of that title. Roper and Steck also founded *Ascent*, the mountaineering journal, and Steck's name is paired with that of Salathé for his first ascent of the Steck-Salathé Route on Yosemite's Sentinel Rock.

# STEVE ROPER and ALLEN STECK

# El Capitan, Salathé Wall

It has been called the finest rock climb in the world — thirty-six rope lengths of superb, varied, and unrelenting climbing on a near-vertical wall in one of nature's most masterful canyons. Is it any wonder that climbers from all over the world have come to try the Salathé Wall?

Yosemite's El Capitan is supposedly the largest mass of exposed granite on earth, but even if it ranked one hundredth, its shape alone still would be awesome to both tourists and climbers. Few protuberances interrupt the sweeping lines of the light-colored Salathé Wall, which lies to the left of the Nose, that perfectly proportioned buttress . . .

The name Salathé Wall is misleading. To begin with, the term "wall" in this instance refers, not to an entire face, but rather to a particular route. Moreover, John Salathé, who took part in two of the climbs discussed in this book, did not name or climb this route. Around 1960 Yvon Chouinard, a mountaineer, inventor, and hero worshipper, decided that the by then legendary Salathé merited a significant named feature — after all, Yosemite already had a Washington Column, a Rixon's Pinnacle, and a Harris's Hangover. Mesmerized by the great unclimbed southwest face of El Cap, Chouinard realized that somewhere on the board wall there had to be a route, and he began referring to the entire face as the Salathé Wall. When the first route on the face was done, however, the route itself came to be called Salathé Wall.

Yosemite climbers had always stared longingly at El Cap, of course, but after the revolutionary ascent of the Nose in 1958, they actively began seeking other possible routes. Many climbers of varying abilities dreamed of a second route, but the next explorers to hammer pitons into an unknown section of the monolith were Royal Robbins, Chuck Pratt, and Tom Frost. All were well-known Yosemite climbers, and all had spent many days struggling up the vertical walls of the Valley. Along with Joe Fitschen, the three men had made the second ascent of the Nose of 1960, and they were ready for a still greater challenge. What better prizer than a new route on El Cap?

No new climb the length and difficulty of El Cap's southwest face ever had been done in one push without fixed ropes, those lifelines to the ground that enable climbers high on a wall to replenish supplies at will and to retreat in a matter of hours. While taking much of the commitment out of climbing, fixed ropes seemed the only way to tackle such smooth, massive cliffs. Hoping to minimize the stringing of ropes, the three men, after much deliberation, decided they would fix the first third of the route, descend for more supplies, and then boldly set forth on the upper 2,000 feet with no fixed ropes. The loads for this upper push, which they thought might take six days, would be monstrous: sixty-five pounds of water, twenty-five pounds of food, extra ropes, sleeping gear, and a huge quantity of aluminum and steel. Never had three American climbers accomplished such a task.

On September 12, 1961, Robbins and Frost began the adventure, while Pratt, having lost the coin toss, hitchhiked to the city for additional supplies, including bolts. Roping up just a short distance to the left of the Nose, the two men planned to work farther to the left and eventually link disconnected crack systems by means of questionable traverses. By proposing this somewhat circuitous route, they hoped to avoid excessive bolting. Five hundred feet above the ground, however, they came up against a 100-foot blank section. To their relief, the angle was only fifty-five degrees, and very tenuous free moves on microflakes kept the number of bolts to thirteen. Still, it was not a propitious beginning for climbers to whom bolts were anathema.

For two days Robbins and Frost climbed tricky crack systems until establishing a high point about 600 feet above the ground. Having used up their food, as well as their entire supply of bolts, the two retreated to await Pratt's return. Several days later, all three returned to the task and succeeded in reaching and naming Mammoth Terraces, 1,000 feet above the starting point. From here they rappelled 150 feet to the base of the Heart — an enormous, indented feature of the southwest face. Caching much of their hardware at this point, the trio then rappelled 800 feet down an appallingly blank wall to the talus, leaving their ropes in place. With the first section of the route completed, the climbers relaxed and bought new supplies.

On September 19 the three men prusiked with great loads to Heart Ledge, casting their fixed ropes to the ground. The committing adventure was about to begin. Not far above Heart Ledge, the climbers tried connecting crack systems by means of a spectacular and difficult pendulum. Climbers on the ground were charting the day's progress while this "king swing" took place, and a long silence ended with cheers and yodels as the leader, after several wild attempts, finally swung his body into a narrow jam crack. A few hundred feet above this point the angle steepened to vertical, thus severely limiting the free climbing. Pitch after pitch of strenuous artificial climbing became routine for the next few days. But at least the regular appearance of ledges every 400 to 500 feet made the nights fairly comfortable.

Great orange facets and pillars constantly came into view, and the climbers weaved cleverly among them. So far the three men had followed a line picked out many weeks earlier, but on the fourth day radical and crackless overhangs forced them onto territory which had not been studied carefully from the ground. This new line brought the trio to an intimidating obstacle which afterward became known simply as the Roof. Sticking out horizontally for 15 feet, the obstacle was overcome slowly by Frost's adroit use of pitons. Perched in their aid slings, Robbins and Pratt watched fascinated as the leader's contorted body stretched sideways to make long reaches. Eventually only Frost's legs were visible, then a wildly gyrating foot, and finally just the tail of an aid sling. Above the Roof, Frost discovered he was at the base of a 200-foot, ninety-five-degree wall broken only by a curving, bottoming, and discontinuous crack. As Frost hung suspended just above the lip of the ceiling, those on the ground who had been in similar situations sighed and were silently thankful for their present location.

By late afternoon on the sixth day the three pioneers stood on a small ledge just below the rim. The final obstacle, a narrow slit which led through an overhang, was overcome with alacrity by Pratt. It proved to be one of the hardest free pitches of the route.

It was over! Five nights had been spent on the final push, and Robbins wrote later that it had been "the most rewarding climbing we had ever done." Especially gratifying was the fact that the team had not placed a single bolt on the final push; Pratt's trip to the city fortunately turned out to be a wasted one. High on the route the climbers had accomplished some very demanding aid climbing, and several times the placing of a marginal piton had taken longer than simply placing a bolt. But drilling, they reasoned, made the ascent less challenging and certainly was work fit only for drones.

Displeased with having fixed the lower part of the route, Robbins and Frost returned the next year and made the first continuous ascent in a remarkable four and a half days. Because of the forbidding appearance of the wall and the respect Valley climbers had for Robbins, Pratt, and Frost, the next ascent was not made until 1966. By 1970, however, the face had been climbed eleven times, and by the end of the 1970s the Salathé Wall was one of the most popular of the two dozen or so routes on El Cap, with one knowledgeable observer estimating the total number of Salathé ascents at 120.

Perhaps the chief reason for the route's popularity is the challenge of engaging in so much varied climbing on such a huge wall. Although no one climbs the Salathé Wall for the pleasure of a single pitch, some sections remain indelibly recorded in the climber's memory. Chimney specialists savor the Ear—a nasty, bottomless slot midway up the route—and exult over the hidden gash behind El Cap Spire, an 80-foot-high detached pinnacle. Lovers of sublime belay ledges also appreciate the latter pitch, for the top of El Cap Spire could well be Yosemite's most spectacularly situated ledge. Ten feet square and perfectly flat, the airy platform is so spacious and comfortable that some parties plan their ascent so that they are certain to spend a night on this incomparable site. For aid climbers, the section surrounding the Roof is as marvelous a setting to practice this art as anywhere on the planet. Those who prefer jam cracks can hardly wait for the summit pitch, though it is but one of many strenuous slits. Liebacks and small-hold climbing also are present for aficionados of these techniques.

As the route becomes more and more popular, it is undergoing significant changes. For example, a tremendous amount of the climb has gone free. Most of the lower-angled section on the first third of the route can be climbed by small-hold techniques; six of the ten pitches to Mammoth Terraces are rated 5.10 or higher. And, amazingly enough, the perpendicular cracks in the central section of the wall can be jammed and lie-backed. Only the area around the Roof remains mostly aid, but it is just a matter of time before some 5.12 climber alters this situation.

One deplorable change that has taken place is the proliferation of bolts along the route. The third-ascent party admirably preserved the route in its original state by excluding a bolt kit from their gear. Soon afterward, however, the leader of another party placed a bolt at a spot where he was stymied. His act set a precedent which far too many climbers have emulated. When Royal Robbins made his third ascent of the face in 1976, he found forty-two aid and anchor bolts in place, a sad commentary on the thoughtlessness of a few hurried climbers.

In recent years the Salathé Wall has attracted many foreign mountaineers, including Doug Scott, Peter Habeler, and a crack Soviet team. Articles extolling the virtues of the climb have appeared in many journals, and it seems certain to remain one of the world's most sought-after big-wall rock climbs.

In the summer of 1965, as John Harlin planned his *diretissima* assault upon the murderous Eiger, Lionel Terray died in a comparatively easy climb. With Hermann Buhl and Louis Lachenal gone as well, the mountaineering world was primed to accept a new master climber, and the Eiger Direct was to be Harlin's ticket to that title. But a German had set foot on the Eiger hours ahead of him . . .

# ARTHUR ROTH

# Wall of Death

Climbing a face like the Eiger is like playing a game of chess. You pick a route, then plan your game as many moves ahead as you can. But unlike chess, you have to play the game backward as well, to safeguard your retreat. If they had to, could they make it back down the fixed ropes from the Fly to Death Bivouac in a snowstorm? Could they make it back down in the dark, or would they have to bivouac on the Fly? Would they run out of food? How about fuel? Without fuel they couldn't melt snow for water to drink. Had they enough rope? Could they endure the cold if they couldn't find a snow hole? The questions were endlessly debated that night among the three climbers before a decision was finally reached. Caution prevailed. If the weather report showed no change in the morning, they would sit tight, wait it out, and hope that the bad weather didn't last more than another day or so.

The morning call to Kleine Scheidegg clarified nothing. The cold front, and the accompanying bad weather, had been stalled by another weather front and might not arrive until the following evening. That would give them the rest of the day and perhaps a full day on the morrow. [John] Harlin and [Dougal] Haston, remembering [Layton] Kor's report of the seeming difficulties in reaching the Fly from the Spider, now wanted a little more than thirty-six hours of good weather for the summit push. They decided to make a climb to the Spider and establish a supply cache there, then come back to Death Bivouac and check the latest weather. [Chris] Bonington now came on the radio and offered to ski in, with Mick Burke, to the foot of the fixed ropes, then climb to the first snow cave with added supplies. Perhaps Kor could make one of his lightning up-and-down climbs to pick up the stuff?

Kor, however, was somewhat disheartened. It looked as if the summit push was off for another couple of days, at least. He felt tired. The hard, concentrated climbing of the past three or four days had gotten to him. If he went down to the first snow cave, he might as well go all the way to Kleine Scheidegg and get a good night's sleep, then come back up in the morning with a rucksack of extra food. Most climbers wouldn't have considered that a rest, but Harlin and Haston knew how their friend hated to be cooped up and agreed that Kor could take off down to Kleine Scheidegg.

Later there was a report by a German observer of the climb that Kor and Harlin had had an argument over joining forces with the Germans — Kor being in favor of such a move and Harlin against it. Harlin's view is supposed to have prevailed, leading an angered Kor to take off down the face. Against this theory stands the fact that Haston mentioned nothing of such an argument in his book on the Eiger climb, and he was one of the three principals involved. Nor did Bonington say anything about such an argument in his book. According to one later written by [Jörg] Lehne and [Peter] Haag, the Germans offered several times to join forces, both when they had the advantage and when they didn't. Those offers hadn't been quite turned down; nor had they been accepted.

In the morning Harlin and Haston decided to make their supply climb to the Spider in the afternoon, and to spend the morning housekeeping and checking out their equipment, splitting it into rucksack loads. They would leave for the Spider right after the noonday call, which would give them more up-to-date information on the weather.

The noon radio call brought electrifying news. "John, there is a German climber on the Fly. Repeat, there is a German climber on the Fly!"

Harlin was thunderstruck. They were going to do it after all, beat him to the Direct! The Germans obviously ignored the bad-weather forecast, and on the strength of that gutsy decision alone, they probably deserved to reach the summit first.

"Are you sure?" Harlin asked.

There was no doubt about it, Bonington told him. In midmorning a telescope watcher had picked up one climber on the Spider, with a rope leading upward into the rock band above. Higher still, another black dot was seen, firmly anchored in the middle of the Fly snowfield, rope trailing down.

Harlin discussed the situation with Bonington on the radio. He and Haston could reach the Fly by nightfall, bivouac there, then join the German team in a push for the summit the following day. Maybe it wouldn't be a clear-cut victory for the Anglo-American team, but a mixed German-Anglo-American rope sounded good to him now. After all, he and Haston and Kor and Bonington had shared the mountain for the past month with the German climbers — why not share the summit also?

Harlin told [Peter] Gillman [a newsman and climber] to explain to Kor why they had gone on without him. Perhaps Kor could join with the second German team in its try for the summit. If there was nothing else, Harlin said, he had to get going. "Go!" Gillman said. "Go! We'll see you on the summit. Go for it!"

Harlin closed the radio link and grinned at Haston. By early afternoon they had quit Death Bivouac and were eagerly climbing up to the base of the Central Pillar. Harlin was on his way, the last leg of his greatest dream, the completion of the first Eiger Direct, the solving of the last great Alpine problem. And next there was Everest. For Haston, too, it was a happy moment. They hadn't climbed far when they overtook Siegfried Hupfauer, who was ahead of them on the candy-striped 7-millimeter Perlon rope. He was ferrying supplies up to his countrymen on the Spider and the Fly. Haston and Harlin now worked in unison with the German climber. When Hupfauer reached the head of an overhanging rope, he shouted down to Haston to start up. When Haston reached the top, he shouted down to Harlin to let him know it was safe to proceed. This method avoided the danger of inadvertently having the weight of two climbers on the rope at the same time.

Following each other, the three went across the Kor Traverse and up the Bonington Ice Gully to the head of the pillar. Just before the fixed rope reached the lower rim of the Spider, there was a hundred-foot, free-hanging drop from a flat slab of rock. That particular Prusik pitch gave Haston some problems. The heavy weight of the rucksack resulted in two bad tendencies — one was to cause the climber to spin around on the rope while jumaring, and the other was to increase the possibility of overbalancing, being pulled over backward by the heavy rucksack. But Haston finally made it to the top of the pitch without incident, grinned at Hupfauer, then yelled down to Harlin to clip in and climb.

Then Haston joined Hupfauer on the small platform to wait for the arrival of his rope mate.

Haston waited at the stance for Harlin to reach him. Normally it would take twenty minutes to jumar up that length of fixed rope. Half an hour passed, then forty-five minutes. Haston assumed that Harlin had run into some trouble with his gear. . . .

After another half hour had passed, Hupfauer told Haston he was going up to the Fly with his load of supplies. Hupfauer waved good-bye and went on ahead. Meanwhile Roland Votteler, on his way down to haul another load of supplies up the face from one of the lower snow caves, stopped to exchange greetings with Haston. Haston explained that he was waiting for Harlin, who was now an hour and a half overdue. He asked Votteler to tell him that he had decided not to wait and was going on ahead to start hacking out a cache platform on the Fly. Votteler backed off the ice stance and went rappelling down the face.

Haston clipped in his Jumar slings, yanked hard on the fixed rope to test the solidity of its placement, then started moving up the Spider. He went about a hundred feet before he turned around to look down, wondering whether Harlin might now be visi-

# THE EIGER

ALTHOUGH **CLAUDIO CORTI** (TOP LEFT) NARROWLY CHEATED DEATH IN THE ALPS' MOST SPECTACULAR RESCUE, **44** MEN HAVE DIED ON THE EIGER. **JOHN HARLIN** (BOTTOM), FLANKED BY **DOUGAL HASTON** AND **LAYTON KOR**, PERISHED ON HIS 1966 ATTEMPT AT A DIRECT ROUTE TO THE TOP. **ANDERL HECKMAIR** (RIGHT) LED THE FIRST SUCCESSFUL ASSAULT ON THE "WALL OF DEATH" IN 1938.

ble. He saw a dark figure just coming up over the lip of the small ice and rock platform at the bottom rim of the Spider. A terrific elation swept over Haston. Until that moment he hadn't quite realized how strong a sense of dread had been slowly invading his mind.

Down on the terrace of the Kleine Scheidegg hotel, Gillman was planted at the telescope, checking the progress of both teams of climbers. It was three-fifteen in the afternoon. He had been watching the German climbers pack loads up from Death Bivouac for their final assault on the summit. Gillman put the slightest of finger pressure on the eyepiece end of the scope, tilting the field of vision as he followed the line of fixed ropes up to the Spider. Suddenly a small red bundle dropped down through his circular field of vision. The red figure was turning over, "slowly, gently and with awful finality," Gillman later wrote in his account of the climb.

"Somebody's falling. A man's falling!" he shouted. He tried to follow the object, but it was nearly impossible to keep the scope on a smooth enough traverse to track an object falling swiftly through space. He saw a plume of snow puff out of a couloir near Death Bivouac, but that was all.

At Death Bivouac, Rolf Rosenzopf had just left the Crystal Room to start jumaring up the rope with another load of supplies when an avalanche of snow swept down the couloir on his left. In the middle of the snow Rolf saw a human figure go cartwheeling by. Horrified, he went back to the snow cave and abruptly sat down. His first thoughts had to be of his comrades. He had seen a red jacket and caught a glimpse of blond hair. Was it Harlin? Or could it be Votteler?

Down on the terrace at Kleine Scheidegg, Guido Tonella, the mountaineering journalist of the *Tribune de Genève*, asked Gillman whether he had seen arms and legs? Might it not have been a rucksack? Or even an anorak?

Gillman said that he had seen a figure, a human figure. It was stretched out and falling.

A correspondent for a group of English papers now looked through the telescope. Minutes earlier he had followed a figure jumaring up the fixed rope just beneath the lip of the Spider. No figure was there now. Nor could he see the fixed rope itself.

Bonington and Fritz von Almen were sent for. Soon the hotel proprietor, who had an uncanny ability to spot things on the face — climbers, chamois, even ravens — picked up a flash of red at the base of the mountain, several feet below the start of the fixed ropes. Around the red bundle were scattered pieces of brightly colored equipment, items ejected from a burst rucksack, or torn off a waist harness. Almen shook his head, then turned the telescope over to Bonington. He spotted the body right away and soon, a short distance from the red bundle, a familiar blue object that he guessed to be the climber's rucksack. Harlin had been carrying a blue rucksack. However, on-the-site confirmation was needed, so Bonington, carrying a radio, and Kor set off from Kleine Scheidegg and skied across the snow slopes at the foot of the Eiger. They came within a few hundred yards of the red bundle and at first were swept with a flush of relief.

They thought the bundle was just a piece of equipment. Layton was sure it was a bivouac sack. But then the bundle was reached and Harlin's body was clearly recognizable, despite the horribly contorted position of the limbs. Bonington came on the air to Kleine Scheidegg, saying over and over, "It's John! He's dead!" Then he and Kor sat down in the snow, weeping, overcome with grief and shock.

Up on the Spider, Haston's relief changed to concern when the figure he had taken to be Harlin he now recognized as Votteler. He swiftly climbed down, and Votteler told him that the fixed rope had broken near the top and that Harlin was nowhere to be seen. Votteler tried to console Haston. There was still the faint possibility that Harlin had survived the fall. Confirmation of disaster was swift in coming. Hupfauer came down the fixed rope from the Fly to the head of the Spider to shout down the ice field that Harlin was dead. The Germans had just received the news through their radio contact with Kleine Scheidegg. "A broken rope and gone was my greatest friend and one of Europe's best mountaineers," Haston wrote in his account of the climb, *Direttissima*, which he coauthored with Peter Gillman.

Up on the Fly the horrified German climbers were still not sure exactly who had fallen. Then a request came over the radio that they send down the unit to Haston so that he could communicate with Gilman, Kor, and Bonington. The Anglo-American radio had gone down with Harlin.

[Karl] Golikow immediately volunteered to bring down the radio, but he was in such a state of shock that he left the Fly twice without the unit, having forgotten it each time. Twice he had to return for it; finally, on his third parting, he had the radio with him. . . .

It was almost dark by now, but rather than go back to their comrades on the Fly, Golikow and Votteler decided to stay with Haston and bivouac right where they were for the night. The instinctive first reaction by members of both teams was to call off the climb. But soon the climbers were having second thoughts. There was no doubt what Harlin would have wanted them all to do. Jörg Lehne, for the German climbers, and Haston and Kor, with Bonington, now agreed to try and finish the climb on a combined rope and, should they prove successful, to name the route the John Harlin Memorial Direct, as a tribute to their fallen ropemate. Kor decided to start up the face that evening to join Haston and the German climbers for the final attack.

The next morning Golikow went down the fixed ropes to Death Bivouac and found six places where the rope was badly frayed. Because of that, it was decided that all those above Death Bivouac would take part in the final assault, while all those at Death Bivouac and below, including Kor, who had just arrived from Kleine Scheidegg, would retreat. Golikow now agreed to climb back up to the Spider and to strip all the ropes and pitons from the Spider down to the foot of the mountain on his descent.

If any two men deserved to be with the group headed for the summit, it surely had to be Layton Kor and Karl Golikow. Fate willed otherwise, and the pair were left out of the summit assault team. At Kleine Scheidegg, Burke and Bonington decided to go up to the summit via the west flank to get photographs of the climbers and to greet them when they topped out. They were able to hire a helicopter whose pilot agreed to drop them well up on the west flank. They jumped ten feet from the hovering chopper, praying their impact wouldn't start an avalanche. They checked their equipment, then headed for the summit while the helicopter slid away and back down to Kleine Scheidegg.

On the mountain itself final preparations were under way. Four German climbers were now on the upper part of the face — Lehne, [Günther] Strobel, Votteler, and Hupfauer. With them was Dougal Haston, now the only surviving member of the Anglo-American team on the face.

The rest of that day Lehne and Strobel prepared several pitches above the Fly. Meanwhile Votteler was down at the Spider bivouac, housecleaning that site and making up three haul loads of equipment and supplies to ferry up to the others. Haston and Hupfauer, with a shovel and ice hammer, were hacking out two bivouacs with enough room for four men.

Later in the afternoon it began to snow, the start of that long-heralded storm. However, when darkness fell, four of the climbers were securely bivouacked on two ledges while the fifth, Votteler, was down at the Spider bivouac site, preferring to spend the night there rather than crowd the others on their narrow ledges.

The next morning the wind rose, the temperature dropped, and the men's faces were soon covered with rime. The decision was made to have two lightly laden climbers, Lehne and Haston, out front, leading and fixing ropes, while the other three followed, hauling up supplies and bivouac equipment, taking out the fixed ropes and pitons as they advanced. There was no point in leaving the fixed ropes. They were going to reach the summit — either that, or they would die there on the wall. Retreat was not only psychologically abhorrent, but practically out of the question, because the ropes were now stripped all the way to the foot of the mountain.

The climbing for Haston and Lehne was dreadful. The visibility was sometimes down to a matter of feet, the wind was an endless series of stinging slaps of snow across the face, and, though in two pairs of gloves, the men's hands were woodenly numb with cold. Haston's Jumar clamps kept icing up and either slipping off the rope or not holding, threatening all the time to peel him clean off the face. Lehne, who was having the same problem, had to constantly pick the ice out of the teeth of his Jumars with the point of a knife that he carried in his mouth, "like a savage on the warpath," as he wrote. The ropes themselves, after exposure to the freezing snow, soon turned into rigid and obdurate cords of ice, more like steel cables than climbing ropes.

Despite the appalling conditions, they fought their way upward through hundreds of small spindrift avalanches that seemed to have an uncanny ability to filter through the slightest opening in their clothing. The rock slabs were poor and offered few places that would take a piton. By late afternoon they had managed to gain several hundred feet and were now hopeful that they were within a pitch or two of the Summit Snowfield. Lehne, not wanting to alarm his support members down at Kleine Scheidegg into any premature rescue attempts, radioed an optimistic report that they had practically reached the Summit Snowfield and were now going to bivouac for the night and finish the climb in the morning. Then his radio weakened and went dead, the batteries having failed in the intense cold.

Actually, Burke and Bonington were waiting for the climbers up on top. They had spent the preceding night in a snow hole several hundred feet down the west flank. When they reached the summit that morning and saw no sign of the climbers, they tried to hang around and wait for them to appear, but they were forced to retreat after only half an hour because of the savage winds. Down at Kleine Scheidegg, gusts of ninety miles per hour had been clocked, with the temperature registering twenty-six below zero. The wind was even fiercer and the temperature colder up on the peak. Unable to stand the summit conditions, Burke and Bonington retreated to their snow hole, prepared to wait for radio word from Kleine Scheidegg that the climbers were actually approaching the summit before going back up to meet them.

Down on the rock bands, the five men were now bivouacked for the night, enduring the whipsawing winds and below-zero cold as best they could. They were without hot food and drinks for the second night in a row. Haston was anchored to a foot-wide ledge with slings and pitons — seated, with one leg stretched along the narrow shelf and the other dangling over but supported with a sling, with the outside arm also sling-supported. He kept dozing off, only to be awakened by uncontrollable fits of shivering. Blowing spindrift snow kept working into his bivouac sack, melting on his face, then refreezing on the inside of the sack and the collar of his jacket. . . .

The next morning, down at Kleine Scheidegg, Toni Hiebeler, who was covering the event for a German publication, and three of the other members of the German direct team (the fourth was sick), now proposed to climb to the summit and wait for the appearance of the five-man final-assault team. Hiebeler radioed Bonington up on the peak, who told him that it was bloody cold up there but that he and Burke would prepare for their arrival by carving out a snow cave big enough for everyone. Kor was asked to join Hiebeler and the others but had to decline because he was going to Leysin, where Harlin was being buried later in the day.

With Lehne's radio out of commission, there was no word from the climbers on the face. However, at the first sign of dawn, the five-man team got ready to continue the climb. They had been without hot food or drink for over forty-eight hours, and the wicked cold had affected everyone's stamina. It took concentrated effort to tie or untie a simple knot. A strap on one of Haston's crampons broke, and he had to jury-rig a substitute strap from a piece of cord dug out of his rucksack. By the time he had finished this simple task, a full hour had gone by. Because of Haston's shaky crampon, Lehne and Strobel led the climb the next morning, with Haston following and the other two Stuttgart climbers bringing up the rear. . . .

And then, within shouting distance of the summit, Haston found himself facing his hardest pitch of the whole climb. Inexplicably there was a long gap in the fixed line that trailed on up the ice field. Lehne and Strobel, running out of rope, had decided to leave a stretch of ice field unprotected in case they ran into steeper ground ahead on which ropes would be imperative. However, the two climbers were soon in shouting contact with the men on the summit, and they now turned around and called down to Haston, telling him to wait where he was. They would finish the climb, then borrow a 300-foot rope from the climbers on the summit and lower the end to him. Haston shouted back what Lehne and Strobel took to be an affirmation. In fact, because of the wind, Haston hadn't heard a word of the instructions, merely some vague shouts to which he had responded.

With crampons, ice ax, and hammer, the sixty-degree slope in front of him would not normally have been difficult. However, he soon got off the line taken by the pair above, and now, not only had he no rope to follow, but he couldn't find any cut-out footholds or handholds. Furthermore, Haston had no ax or ice hammer. The two lead climbers were carrying them. All he had was a solid, dagger-pointed ice peg. Because of that substitute strap, one crampon had worked loose and was wildly skewed on his foot. His precarious position and deadened fingers wouldn't permit him to stop and fix the crampon. The other crampon was also loose. The fierce summit winds were packing drift snow into his face at such a rate as to build eaves of snow out and down over his eyebrows and partially block his already poor vision. Half-blind, he had to pat and fumble around on the snow-covered ice slope in front of him, still hoping to come across a handhold or foothold previously cut by Lehne or Strobel. To add to his miseries, he knew that if he ever came off, there was a distinct possibility that Hupfauer and Votteler below him, who were on a very poor ice belay, would be unable to hold his fall and would also be plunged to their deaths.

Stopping periodically to wipe his gloved hand across the upper part of his face and crack away the ice that blocked his vision, his thighs and calves straining because of those loose crampons, his fingers now dead to all feeling, Haston somehow kept making progress. By now he was climbing blind, stabbing for purchase with his ice peg, delicately jabbing his loose crampons into the ice. He bleakly wondered if he would have to climb all the way up the Summit Icefield without protection. Every foot of height gained, he knew, would increase the velocity of his body should he fall, subsequently decreasing the chances that Hupfauer and Votteler would hold him, or even stay on the wall themselves. But then, after the buffeting slaps of a particularly fierce wind had caused him to stop and burrow in upright against the snow wall, he saw the clouds chase away up the slope, clearing the snowfield and revealing a rope dangling down, twenty feet off to his left. At that same moment, for two or three minutes, the top part of the face was clear, and down at Kleine Scheidegg watchers picked up five tiny dots toiling their way up the Summit Snowfield. A wave of jubilation swept the hotel. Barring some last-minute complication, they were going to do it! Radio contact was established with the peak, where Bonington and Hiebeler were alerted to ready themselves to greet the climbers.

However, Haston was now faced with a desperate problem. His line had taken him up twenty feet to the right of the fixed rope. Somehow he had to traverse across that twenty feet. The rope lay down an ice gully, and a rock bulge separated him and the end of the rope. The rock prevented his climbing upward and bearing slightly left, so that his line would cross the rope. He had to traverse directly across to it, or risk losing it altogether.

He made a couple of tentative moves to his left but quickly drew back. His crampons were so loose that he dared not trust them on a traverse where he couldn't cut steps. And without an ax, or at least the spike end of an ice hammer, he had no way of cutting even a tiny foothold. The only solution he could think of was a tension traverse, but on what? He still had his ice piton. He reached as high and as far to the left as he could and with his Hiebeler clamp (a small, lightweight piece of aluminum) managed to bang the peg an inch or so into the ice. It wobbled around in its groove and would easily pull out with any upward pressure, but it might yet do. To reduce the torque, he tied off a sling around the shaft of the piton and tight up against the face. Then he clipped a carabiner into the loop of the sling, threaded his climbing rope through, and started his move.

He was acutely aware that three lives depended on a small piece of metal loosely placed in an inch-deep channel of ice. Held into the face by the tension of the rope, he managed to claw his way over the gap. Reaching the fixed rope, he clipped into it with the Hiebeler clamp, then hung there for a minute, all the tension drained from his body. He was beginning to believe that he just might possibly make it up the face after all. Minutes after he resumed climbing, he heard voices. Two vague figures gradually loomed up and took shape in the mist. Jörg and Günther, he thought, but the two leaders had already reached the summit and were now taking a break in the snow hole with their German comrades.

"It's a hard life!" Golikow shouted with a big grin. With him was Bonington, snapping away with his camera. Then the last two German climbers, Hupfauer and Votteler, were up, and Bonington, his camera frozen, was trying to take a picture of the five-man assault team on the summit — the Eiger Direct finally accomplished. . . .

Meanwhile, that same afternoon, in the village of Leysin, the same snowstorm was dropping huge snowflakes on the people gathered to watch John Harlin's body being lowered into the grave. . . . There were wreaths and messages of condolence from Harlin's climbing friends all over the world.

Simplest, and most touching, was a wreath from the members of the German Eiger Direct team. The offering bore two plain English words: "Good-bye John."

In the fall of 1968 the author and Warren Harding began their assault upon the unclimbed south face of Half Dome. Was the possibility of failure on their minds? Certainly—only a fool climbs with no thought for the worst—but to that point no climber had ever been rescued from the middle of a major Yosemite climb. Rowell and Harding, men of vast climbing experience, were unlikely objects of such aid, but the mountain has no respect for credentials.

## GALEN ROWELL

# Rescue on the South Face of Half Dome

*... the Dome ... would hardly be more "conquered" or spoiled should man be added to her list of visitors. His louder scream and heavier scrambling would not stir a line of her countenance.*

—John Muir, *The Yosemite*

I turned the page in the paperback and was deep in thought when a shout flinched me back to reality. It was Warren Harding's voice, calling for slack.

I was sitting in a belay seat as one or the other of us had been doing for almost six days now on this ledgeless wall. I reached for the Jumar, fed out four feet of slack, passed it around me, and watched it disappear upward.

We were using a new belaying system in which the rope goes through a Jumar ascender after it runs around the belayer and through an extra carabiner hooked to the anchor. We were drilling our way up a blank section. For this type of slow climbing, the system has advantages. It frees the belayer's hands and affords the leader a safer belay than total reliance on a tired climber who may be daydreaming as he sits hours at a time.

I enjoyed daydreaming. The paperback discussed man's effect on nature, and often a page would go unturned for half an hour as my thoughts wandered. I contemplated Huxley's likening of a human being on earth to a cancer cell on its host. Harmless by themselves, but endowed with the ability to reproduce until they destroy their matrix ... The analogy was certainly well taken.

I contrasted Muir's thoughts of Half Dome's permanence with Huxley's of man's destruction of his environment. Had anyone ever contemplated that the development of climbing has paralleled the population explosion? Central Europe, host to the beginnings of mountaineering, was the first part of the world to feel overpopulation, soon lessened by migrations to the New World — which has taken up mountaineering rather recently, just as population pressure has begun to be felt. I searched for connections between the two. The climber's disdain for large groups of people, regimentation, and technocracy seem to bear this out. The mountains represent the stability and austerity of nature in a world being raped by man. They are one of the few places where a man finds himself in competition with himself or his environment, not with other men.

It was this search for identity that placed us high on the 2,000-foot south face of Half Dome, little known to climbers or tourists. One's first impression is of a vast, curving slope quite devoid of features. A closer look shows an overhanging arch, leading halfway up the wall, and the realization that the wall is curved only on the edges. For the most part it is very steep (seventy-five degrees) and devoid of ledges or cracks.

We had reached the top of the arch in three days, arriving at a hauling bag hanging under a overhang from our previous attempt in 1966. Although torn and housing a swift's nest, it had contained three gallons of drinkable water and some canned food. From this point the route leads out of the arch by way of the most spectacular sixth-class lead I have seen. It nails horizontally for ten pitons and then nails the convergence of two very overhanging walls for ten more pitons. Warren called it his most strenuous lead. At the top of the arch the overhangs that we had been nailing consistently for three days ended and we climbed on a vast, open expanse of blank-appearing wall, stretching over a thousand feet to the summit.

The prospect of bolting a thousand feet of blank wall had stopped other climbers from considering the route. Studying the face through binoculars in winter and by blown-up photos, Warren and I found several disconnected crack systems. We decided that a route was possible with no more than 25 percent bolting. To make this 25 percent easier and faster, Warren developed a system of alternating bolts with rows of ground-down cliff-hangers placed in shallow drilled holes. Christened "bat hooks," they saved about half the time of regular bolts, allowing us to cover about two pitches per day on the upper headwall. Free climbing, sometimes possible on the rough and lumpy sections, accounted for possibly 20 percent of our progress.

Now we were more than 400 feet above the arch, with Warren leading. He had nailed an incipient crack for about ten pitons and then begun drilling the blank rock above. He placed eight bat hooks in a row before placing another bolt. After more bat hooks he reached the end of the rope and tied into his last two bolts. I came up, and as I started the next lead we heard a shouted signal from our support party to turn on our walkie-talkie. We made contact with Glen Denny, assuring him all was well and three more days would get us to the top. He gave us a five-day forecast for cloudy skies but no storms, and said that he would go to the top by the trail and rappel on 750 feet of rope to take pictures. Warren signed off and I continued climbing toward one of several potholes on the face.

From a distance these potholes appeared as black specks against the white granite. Through binoculars they resembled shadowy caves. We joked before the climb that these were secret entrances to a giant room in the heart of the dome in which all the gods of the ancients lived. Warren's resemblance to Satan had often been noted. We half expected to be greeted at the doorway by a two-headed Janus who would calmly say, "Come in, Warren, we have been expecting you."

Alas, the pothole did not hold such great things in store for us. It was merely a depression of dark rotten rock, perhaps five feet deep, with no level place to stand, much less sleep. Instead of a floor, it had a ramp inclined at almost fifty degrees. About fifteen feet wide, it offered protection from the winds and was a more pleasant place to bivouac than on the stark face. I anchored with several pitons, hauled up the bags and prepared for the night

Below, the clouds were putting on a grand show. Thinking of how John Muir might describe such a scene, I began to see things in a strange light. Muir was the first to recognize the importance of ice in forming Yosemite's features. Below me were two classic examples of glacier-carved mountains, Mount Broderick and Liberty Cap. Toward the Valley they present sheer façades, but toward the high country, the source of the ice, they present shiny, smooth, mottled contours like those of giant lumpy balloons. Called *roches moutonnées*, or sheep's backs, by geologists, they are caused by grinding and polishing of the glacier that overrode them.

As I watched the panorama at sunset, I seemed to be riding backward in time. From the southwest came billowing cumulus clouds moving high and fast in the sky — colored orange and red in the setting sun. From the northwest came mare's tails, a form of cirrus clouds distorted by the winds, seemingly intersecting their brothers from the southwest directly above us. But from the west came creeping, seething white clouds. They were so low that we couldn't see them until they came around the corner at the end of the Valley. The pure white veil slowly climbed the Merced River canyon and flowed between and around the sides of Mount Broderick and Liberty Cap, just as the ice must have done in the opposite direction thousands of years ago.

The sound of Vernal and Nevada falls, which lie in the canyon just below the two mountains, had always been a subtle comfort to us. Otherwise, we rarely heard sounds unless we made them. The voices of the falls had become as familiar as our own: Nevada's low rumble; Vernal's higher-pitched roar, punctuated by slapping crashes when the wind changed the point of the water's impact. Now, as the mist flowed in, they faded. As the sound deadened, the falls seemed farther and farther away. The formless cloud slowly rose, and soon Broderick and Liberty Cap were two bald islands in a sea of white mist below us. When it became dark, we closed ourselves in our special tent-hammocks. The mist gradually enclosed us in the night.

The hammocks were designed by Warren and were certainly the best yet for their purpose. They had a waterproof nylon cover that zipped shut to keep out wind and rain. The underside was heavy material with sewn straps running crosswise every few inches, converging on top in a single anchor point, instead of the two widely separated points of the usual garden-style hammock. This meant they could be hung anywhere instead of hunting for a spot where two anchors could be placed many feet apart. Even so, eight hours of continuous sleep was just not possible. Every hour or so we would wake with a pain from pressing against the rock, or with curculation cut off, or from a cold wind blowing upward against the bottom of the hammock.

Waking at midnight, I heard a new sound outside. It was the running of water and dripping of raindrops upon our hammocks. I went back to sleep, not worried because the weather forecast carried no prediction of a storm and therefore this must be a local disturbance. But several hours later, I realized my down footsack and jacket were soaking up water. The "waterproof" hammocks had been tested hanging free from a tree in the city but not leaning against a rock wall running with water. The tightly woven fabric let water soak in, but would not let it out. Pools formed at the bottom of the hammocks. We had to puncture holes to let the water out. By dawn we were both soaked to the skin. Snow covered all the mountains in the high country. The rain became sleet and then turned into snow.

We had seen a practical demonstration of the forces that form the potholes. Ours was a focal point for the drainage from the upper face. We were in a small waterfall.

There was no chance of climbing in the cold, wet conditions. Besides, we believed that the local disturbance would move on and the sun would come out to dry us before the end of the day. After a few hours we heard a distant shout and turned on our radio. Glen asked how we were and said that he would not be able to rope down from the top today but he would tomorrow when the weather was better. We said that we were all right but very wet and cold; if things continued this way we would probably give up the climb and come up the rope he strung from the top. He said that was fine and he would see us tomorrow. He never did.

The weather became worse and worse. The snow fell thicker and thicker. Incredibly, it stuck to the almost vertical face and we were soon plastered. All day we shook with cold and looked for a blue spot somewhere in the sky. It never came.

We passed a second night in the storm. A sleepless, cold, wet ordeal. Fourteen hours of November darkness.

When the light finally came, everything was white. Small powder-snow avalanches began to batter us about in our pothole. We were shaking almost uncontrollably and our fingers and toes were numb. Every article of our clothing was soaked and I was sure I could not last one more day and night. This was our eighth day and our second in the storm.

Zipped in my dripping prison, I closed my eyes and imagined myself at home with my wife, two children, and German shepherd dog. It was Sunday morning. On most Sunday mornings I stayed in bed late. Then I would loll around the heater in the hallway and reluctantly drag myself to the breakfast table for food and hot tea. What I wouldn't give for a cup of hot tea!

I realized there was no chance of Glen climbing the cables. They were surely iced and in the path of frequent avalanches from the fresh snow hanging on the steep, featureless slabs. I tried to convince Warren that we should rappel down the route. He patently refused to have anything to do with rappelling. He said it was folly and he was staying where he was. I thought it was our only hope. Warren's refusal to move put me in a dilemma. I did not want to separate, which is against most ethics of climbing, but I did not want to hang in one place and freeze to death, as I thought we might after another night in the storm. Dying without an effort to escape seemed a most unforgivable thing.

Slowly I climbed out of the hammock and began to set up a rappel alone. I would probably be forced to place several bolts, as I would not always be able to rappel to piton cracks or bolts we had placed. Warren insisted on staying. I said that I would go down to the Valley and contact the park rangers to send a helicopter to rescue him. He said okay and I started down alone.

My immediate goal was the anchor bolt at the end of Warren's last lead, eighty feet below and thirty feet to the left. I hoped to go down, swing over to the bolt, anchor in, pull down the ropes, and continue the descent. I got down the eighty feet, but because of ice on both the wall and my shoes, I could not move even two feet off the vertical track of the rope. My hands were numb, even in gloves. I realized my plan to descend was futile and decided to go back up. I clipped my Jumar ascenders on the rappel rope and put my weight on one. It slipped. I tried the other one. It slipped. The little teeth inside the gadgets were covered with ice and would not bite into the frozen rope. The two strands of the rope were both freezing to the wall and to each other. Even if I had reached the bolt, I never would have pulled down the rappel. The ascenders would not work at all. My strength was ebbing, and I was aware that I might pay dearly for my rashness.

I was infinitely cold. My mind could not conceive of being colder. In midmorning the face was letting loose much of its load from the night before. Small avalanches knocked me about as I tried to tie Prusik loops with stiff hands. The Prusik knots did hold my weight. They didn't slip down the rope. They froze in place each time I tightened one by putting weight on it. Very slowly I moved upward . . . stepping up . . . prying the frozen snow with my fingers out of gloves . . . releasing the knot and moving it up. After an hour of repetition in agonizing slow motion, I was only halfway back to Warren. My hands felt like two boards. I often felt like blacking out and I had to make conscious efforts not to faint. Warren stood in slings at the pothole helplessly; there was nothing he could do. He couldn't help pull me up in these conditions any more than I could climb the rope hand over hand. I yelled at him to find all the slings he could, clip them together, and lower them. They reached fifteen feet below him.

Life was now a line of gold rope stretching 25 feet to the bottom of the slings. My body revolted. It wanted to give up. My mind forced it to painfully and slowly move upward . . . release a knot . . . move the knot up . . . release the chest loop knot . . . move it up . . . step up . . . etc. Finally I reached the slings almost two hours after I had started. I stepped into the lowest loop and quickly worked up to the pothole. Warren took off my pack. It was half filled with snow from the avalanches which had struck me as I was getting out the Prusik handles and knots. He dug inside and got out my hammock. I quickly hung it up and got inside. I put my wooden hands between my legs and after a few minutes the agonizing pains of thawing began to shoot through me. I was now far colder and more miserable than before I had started the descent.

Just as I was warming up to the level of "very chilly" from that of "almost frozen," we heard a shout. Warren pulled a soggy-looking walkie-talkie from the bag and miraculously it worked, although it was barely intelligible. Thank God! We came across clearly at the other end! Warren said, "We cannot last another night. Get us help today. A helicopter if possible. We are very, very cold."

They received us and answered that they would see what they could do. Meanwhile the storm was weakening. The ceiling lifted and the low clouds withdrew. Snow flurries became intermittent. About an hour later we were contacted again by radio and were barely able to make out words. After several repeats we finally got the message: "Helicopter . . . will . . . land . . . summit . . . two hours. . . ."

It was now noon. The cold became more bearable. I began to smile and sing songs at the top of my lungs. We were saved. Waiting for a few hours was nothing like waiting the two days and nights we had already. Our ears were tuned for that special sound of a helicopter.

In less than two hours, Warren yelled, "Here it comes!"

I listened. . . . It was only a change in the voice of the waterfalls. Several times we thought we heard it, only to hear the falls go back to their normal voice. Finally at three o'clock we called back on the radio. I asked, "Where is the chopper?"

The reply was understood after many repeats: "Helicopter . . . coming . . . from . . . 200 . . . miles . . . here . . . before . . . five. . . ."

I asked, "How will they rescue us?"

After more tedious repeats: "Will . . . drop . . . rope . . . to . . . you . . . anchor . . . summit . . . you . . . will . . . jumar. . . ."

I asked, "How will we know when the rope is anchored?"

The answer came: "We . . . will . . . tell . . . you. . . ."

I asked, "It gets dark at five. What happens when it gets dark?"

We could not get a reply. Our unit had gone dead from waterlogging. We waited in false anticipation, listening to what would sound like a helicopter but was only the fickle voice of Vernal Fall. Thousands of questions ran through our minds, unanswered. At four-thirty we heard a noise which became louder in logarithmic progression. Around the corner of the southwest face came the helicopter.

We smiled, waved, and waited. It made lazy circles, gained altitude, flew near us, and took off out of sight. Probably just checking the situation, we thought. Ten minutes later it came back, circling again, and we saw it had a large spool dangling forty feet below it. We watched, expecting to see it drop the rope, fly toward us with the rope hanging, and land on top. Again it disappeared out of sight. We began to have grave doubts about the competence of the pilot. Twice more the chopper made passes near us. Then darkness came and the air was silent; helicopters do not fly in the mountains at night.

It certainly appeared that the pilot must not be experienced in mountain rescue work and could not figure a way to get us off. We were 700 feet below the summit, and on far too steep a face for him to fly very near.

We could think of dozens of grandiose rescue schemes. For instance, they could hover above the summit, drop a long rope to us, we would tie on, and then the helicopter would fly straight up as they do in the movies, land us on top, land itself, pick us up, and tonight we would have a steak dinner in the Valley.

Warren was the first to break illusions. He said that we might as well face up to the fact that we were going to spend another night on Half Dome whether we liked it or not. He was right. Well . . . sort of.

About an hour after dark I heard a strange noise, so I unzipped the hammock and saw a man being lowered on a rope not a hundred feet above us. Hope sent a pulsing warmth through our chilled bodies. I yelled up, "Are you one of the guys from that chopper?"

He was wearing a full down parka with a hood, carrying a walkie-talkie and a large pack, and had a headlamp strapped to his forehead. From now on, if I ever envision a guardian angel it will be in this form. I talked to the man on the rope for several minutes without recognizing him. Something about the voice, the mannerisms, and self-assuredness seemed familiar. Finally realizing who the rescuer was, I recalled an earlier scene, played on the same set, with two of the same players. Eleven years ago, the roles were transposed. Royal Robbins was coming over the top of the northwest face of Half Dome as his three-man party made the first ascent. Warren Harding was the only climber to hike to the summit to congratulate them. Now both the parts they played and the faces they climbed were reversed. Even after Royal reached us and I was talking to him, Warren didn't recognize him under all the paraphernalia. After several minutes, Warren leaned over in his slings, tried to look into Royal's face, and said, "Who are you, anyway?"

After a good laugh, Royal acted like a true guardian angel, bringing us all our wishes. Besides bringing a lifeline to the summit, the depths of his pack concealed dry down parkas, gloves, and even a thermos of hot soup. After putting on the parka and drinking my first hot liquid in eight days, I readied myself for jumaring to the top. Royal had two extra pairs of Jumar ascenders and I clipped a set on the rope and started up. Only thing was I didn't move. The ascenders slipped, just as in the morning. In descending, the rope had rubbed the face and was now wet and icy. As I was getting discouraged, Royal said that the higher I got, the dryer the rope. It was mainly wet on the bottom end from the vicinity of our pothole. I rubbed the ascenders up and down, trying to make heat from friction to melt the ice in the little teeth. I fought my way 50 feet, rubbing the gadgets briskly on the rope and pushing the cams into the rope with my thumbs. Finally the slipping stopped. Less than an hour later I reached the top, where I was greeted by seven more people, including several good friends. I was ushered into a tent pitched in the foot of summit snow and given a swig of brandy, dry clothes, and warm sleeping bag.

I realized that we had misjudged the rescue effort. Instead of checking the situation on each pass by the face, the pilot had been ferrying men and equipment from the Valley to the summit. They began immediate efforts to reach us in conjunction with our support party below the face, who also were given a Park Service walkie-talkie and helped direct Royal down to us in the moonlight on the half-mile-wide face. Since our radio was dead and we could not see the summit, we never knew what was happening.

Warren was right in a sense. We were spending another night on Half Dome, but not in the agony we expected. As he came up, Warren had more than his share of difficulties. He was wearing down-filled pants that had become waterlogged and then frozen. In order to start up the rope, he had to cut them in a few places to get sufficent movement in his legs. He had also lost considerable weight through the ordeal. Lying in the tent we heard the following message come from Royal on the walkie-talkie: "Warren seems to be having a lot of trouble. His Jumars are slipping and his pants are falling off. He's really having problems!";

We didn't know then, but by some quirk of weather and radio waves, the entire rescue was broadcast through every television set in use in Yosemite, no matter what channel was tuned in. The picture was untouched, but the sound was from the walkie-talkies — loud and clear! The next day every park employee with a television — and many tourists — knew about the rescue and the problems with Warren's pants.

By midnight everyone was on top and we spent a comfortable night on the summit. We ate canned firefighters' rations, which tasted to us like filet mignon. Early the next morning the sound of the helicopter came again. It landed on top, its blade spewing powder snow in a wide circle. Warren and I went down on the first shuttle. Are climbers scared of heights? Well, not usually, but I must admit that when the helicopter took off over the 2,000-foot face, my heart was in my stomach.

When the helicopter neared the Valley floor, our thoughts turned to hot showers, hearty meals, and walking, sleeping, and feeling like normal men again — men who owe a debt to the prompt, decisive action of the National Park Service, . . . our support party, and the climbers who selflessly performed the mechanics of the rescue. If we ever go back and finish the climb, it will surely be an anticlimax to the attempt preceding it.

"An excellent exhibition of how not to do things" — that is the author's description of the comedy of errors that marked his retreat from Everest, short of the summit. Yet he and his three fellow amateur mountaineers had registered a magnificent achievement: Without porters, without oxygen, and with the most meager of supplies and financial backing, these four had set out to climb Everest's unconquered North Face, and they were driven back only after a forty-day ascent to 24,500 feet. The passage below is excerpted from Sayre's 1964 book *Four Against Everest*.

# WOODROW WILSON SAYRE

# Anti-Belaying

So the decision stood. Today would remain our highest clutch upward. Now our eyes were only fixed downward. Even if Roger [Hart] had come up the day before, I don't think it would have made much difference. At most we might have put one more camp up another thousand feet and someone might have gotten as far as the yellow band. But in our collective condition I don't think we could have done anything more. Without the first fall it would, admittedly, have been different. I feel sure we would have gotten at least to the Great Couloir, given the good weather we had. Beyond that, without oxygen, on a difficult, as yet unclimbed route, the chances were probably over 100 to 1 against success.

Now both Norman [Hansen] and I thought only of how relatively uncomfortable it would be in the tent if Roger stayed for the night. How he would disrupt our routine! So we urged him to go back down to the col. This was a scurvy way to treat his great push. Also it was very shortsighted. We did not realize how badly we were going to need help the next day. The comfort of the moment prevailed, and we sent Roger down. We settled in for our second night at over 24,000 feet.

The next morning I had deteriorated badly. I had no strength, I was weak, I was dead on my feet. I literally fell asleep every minute that something was not going on. Norm had to bark at me to keep me conscious. He wrote that I was very slow in understanding and very slow in executing what I did understand. It was obvious that I could not carry a pack and Norm could not carry both. So he tied the two packs together on a light line and let them down the slope. They stuck again and again. Each time they did, it was my job to go down the rope and push them on down the slope. Of course, now when we wanted things to slide down, they never would. All this was very slow and tedious. I didn't notice it so much, because at every stop for a new belay I dropped off to sleep. But it was a big strain on Norm. He was getting groggy, too.

Suddenly he slipped and tobogganed down twenty-five feet, ending up in the rocks. He broke his watch. At that moment I suddenly felt that things were falling apart. We were falling all over the mountain. We were accident-prone. We were too close to the edge. "Wake up!" I said to myself. "This is going to be the fight of your life just to get off the mountain. This is for keeps!"

We called down the mountain to the others for help. We could certainly use Roger now. But they were too far away. So we continued our slow struggle downward. By twilight we made it at last to the low point of the col. HansPeter [Duttle] came down and took my pack for the short climb up to camp. It was good to be all four together again. Roger and HansPeter were having their troubles, too. Roger complained of the pain in his chest and HansPeter had an aching tooth. We all looked exhausted.

Tonight was our last night up here. Tomorrow the retreat would begin. But would I have the strength for it? Would any of us have the strength for it? For myself, I knew that I had pushed too far. Instead of going down after the first fall and night out, I had piled on myself five strenuous days of struggling upward. My strength was gone. I could just barely walk. After today's performance I felt pessimistic. It was not just the mild verbal form — of *saying* that, indeed, one or more of us might not get out of this. It was rather the sharp, unpleasant form — the inner tightening that came with *knowing* that disaster was now a very real possibility. The increasing number of falls was one sign. The growing list of our disabilities was another. What had once seemed a very reasonable trip was rapidly becoming a nightmare. The carefree romance was gone. *We must get down!*

Next morning we started the retreat. I think we all knew how serious and difficult it was going to be. We didn't just have to get down the North Col and then relax into the waiting arms of Sherpas and Base Camp personnel, who would take care of us from then on. We had ahead of us the whole long trek all the way back to Nepal, with all the various obstacles that lay between here and there. Until we got back to Nepal we could expect no help of any kind. Yet, looking at the four of us, I was most reminded of a group of sick and wounded war veterans. An observer would have been surprised if we could climb a sand dune at sea level.

And this very morning the monsoon-type clouds seemed to be closing in again. Since it was now June 6, we were lucky it had held off this long. But heavy snow could be a heartbreaking setback. Our caches were a day's journey apart over dry terrain. With heavy snow we might only make a fraction of the necessary distance, and so we would run out of food. We might lose the trail or fail to find the caches or tire ourselves too much trying to struggle through it. Could we get through in heavy snow at all? The caches had food for only five days. What if it took fifteen?

But all these were future worries. Our immediate worry was to get down the col. I was the weakest, so it was decided to send me first. Generally speaking, the first man on a rope going down has the most protected position. Going up, it is the last man. We felt it would take us too long to belay over short distances. So I was to go out a full 200 feet on an extra-long rope before I took a stance and brought the next man along. During the next hour or so we gave an excellent exhibition of how not to do things. In fact, so many mistakes were made that perhaps the whole affair is best set down as a tragicomedy on the subject of anti-belaying.

"Belaying" is defined in the mountaineering lexicon as the art of securing one's fellow against the possibility of a fall by means of a rope running from one climber to the other. The art of *ensuring* a fall of one's fellow by means of a rope running from one climber to the other has, as far as I know, no name. I can think of some apt ones, but perhaps the most neutral is "anti-belaying." A fair example of the art of anti-belaying comes rather vividly to mind.

Our hero starts on a long traverse over a steep slope of insecure snow on top of ice. His hope is to get some 500 feet of distance across this dangerous section. He starts out. The anti-belayers and he have previously agreed on a set of indispensable signals, since he will be out of sight around the swell of the slope almost as soon as he starts out. One jerk on the rope means keep tension on the rope by hauling in on it; two jerks, give some slack; three jerks, hold fast; four jerks, all okay, proceed. The anti-belayer now firmly sets his ice ax in the snow. Then, as the belayee starts off, the belayer passes the rope between himself and the belayee *around* the ice ax, thereby effectively preventing the sensing of any signals which the desperate belayee may later send.

(Rule: In belaying, the rope should run directly from the belayee to the belayer. The belayer may *independently* secure himself by ice ax, rock, or piton, but this should not be with the rope connecting the two. If it is, not only will the belayer be less sensitive to any signals from the belayee, but also he may make the effects of a fall more serious. The falling man will be jerked to a stop suddenly instead of having the extra spring furnished by the interposition of the belayer's soft, yielding body.)

So our hero proceeds, following old steps which slant down across the slope. One, two, three — everything is going fine. Then the steps turn downward a bit more and stretch a little farther apart. He takes a few quick big steps in succession. The belayer says to himself, "This rope is running out terribly quickly. I wonder if our man is falling. Better give a good tug on the rope and see."

He does so. Result: the belayee is lifted neatly out of the steps he has been following by the rearward pull of the rope, and starts slithering down the mountain.

Belayer: "Guess everything is okay. Give him slack." Having literally been pulled off his feet, the belayee is now glissading with abandon toward a vertical drop-off below.

But the backward slant of his fall gives no sense of strain on the belayer. He smiles happily.

Suddenly the strain comes, and the belayer becomes aware. "Ah, there is a fall." He heaves in. Squish. The belayee is brought to an absolute halt and is just about cut in two. But he is safe; he falleth not. However, he is being suffocated by the pull of the heavy pack in one direction and the pull of the rope in the other. Helplessly he hangs against the slope, unable to gain his footing. With a desperate effort he tries to attach the pack by one of its straps directly to the rope above, so that the strain will be eased from him. But he hasn't the strength. He calls for help. He jerks urgently on the rope for slack. No response. He is pressed so badly that his wastes are actually squeezed out of him. Finally, he eases the strain in the only way possible. He jettisons the pack and sadly watches it bounce down the slope and disappear over the brink of the cliff below, carrying with it, among other things, a $1,000 movie camera.

The anti-belayer above, feeling a little easing of the strain, nods with satisfaction. "Things must be better," he says to himself. Generously he gives out a little slack. The belayee finds a little purchase for his feet and can breathe again, which, after all, is worth the small price of a $1,000 camera.

The anti-belayer now turns his job over to an accomplice and descends the slope to assess the damage. He peers over the steep drop-off at the belayee and asks what he can do. The belayee has some ideas; but out loud, he merely pleads for some 40 feet of slack to reach a ledge beneath. The belayer disappears and relays the message to the new belayer. Thirty-five feet are given, then the big freeze. Nothing happens. Two jerks, three jerks, four jerks, twenty jerks—all are unanswered and unheeded. Standing on a steep seventy-degree slope, his legs tire. When is something going to happen? Another twenty minutes go by. Apparently never.

Craft must be employed. Carefully, he climbs three feet upward. Complete slack puzzles the brain trust upstairs. Maybe the belayee doesn't need a belay anymore. Maybe the danger is over. Tentatively, a little slack is given. The belayee gathers it in, but ever so gently. A little more, then still a little more. Maybe now he has the five extra feet he needs. He starts moving.

But he is exhausted. Who knows what slips first? A little slip increases. He starts careening downward. Now he hopes the belayer is alert after all. But the belayer has decided that this is the time to neaten and coil the excess rope. He is holding it loosely in one hand. The rope burns out of his hands, whips around and off the ice ax, and falls down the cliff. The belayee drops unchecked, catapults over the brink, falls forty feet, hits the roof of a crevasse, and falls on through. He finds himself lying on his back with his feet in the air. He stares up at the small skylight he has made thirty feet above his head. He proceeds to curse all belayers thoroughly and carefully, in order to leave nothing out.

He gets up and waits for some kind of action from above. Nothing happens. He decides no one is really interested in him anyway, so he looks around for ways to climb out of the crevasse. He tries two and fails. Then, after what can only be described as one of his most brilliant leads, he makes it out. With surprise he observes that he is only a few feet from the spot where he landed in his first fall almost a week earlier. He starts climbing up the cliff by the same route he had used before. About forty-five minutes go by, and then he hears a cheery call above him: "Hey, are you okay down there?" The answer is mercifully swallowed in the great silent snow slopes of Mount Everest—playground of the anti-belayers.

HansPeter moved grimly toward our original objective, which was the very spot to which Roger and I had returned for the extra load on the night we fell. I followed along as best I could. I had my pack back, as I had found it at the bottom of the crevasse resting beside me. But I had no rope. It was hopelessly snarled in the crevasse, so I had left it there.

If I was exhausted before, the fall had added the finishing touches. I had to rest at each step. Hours went by trying to cover those last few hundred feet. Finally I was not more than twenty paces from the flatter spot we were heading for. After that, the descent would be fairly easy. But right here was the steepest part of all, and the ice was hard under very thin snow. I just did not have the strength to move carefully enough. Suddenly I slipped a bit. My reflexes were too slow to recover. The next instant I found myself sliding downward again. It was getting monotonous. Almost mechanically, I turned over into a sitting position and went into the routine of trying to brake with my ice ax. I passed only a few feet from HansPeter. I can still remember the horrified look on his face—pinched nose, gray face, staring eyes. But by now I was practically blasé about the whole thing and I was just too tired to care. I nodded my head to him as I went by. "Here we go again," I said. "Be seein' you." And down I went. All at once I was over the edge of a big drop tumbling head over heels. I curled myself into as much of a ball as I could and clasped my hands behind my neck to save my head. There was a long fall, followed by a buffeting slide, followed by another free fall, and then a slide that finally came to a stop in deep snow.

This time, I was completely dazed by the fall. I looked up and all around, and felt I should know where I was, but I didn't. Was this McKinley? No, I knew that was wrong. But where was it? I squinted. I furrowed my brow. Somehow it seemed important. I tried to name the ridges and the peaks.

I must have sat in the snow quite a while, because suddenly I heard HansPeter behind me asking if I was all right. At that very instant everything came back to me, and I knew that this was Everest and I had just descended a third of the col in record time. I had fallen about 400 vertical feet. We were just above the big crevasse where we had spent the night on the way up.

My knee was twisted, but I could still walk on it. Otherwise, I was again unharmed. I reflected that in my four falls I had descended over 1,000 vertical feet across the face of Everest, yet I was still able to move around under my own power. This is no doubt a record of some kind, but scarcely an enviable one. Still, I was getting down the mountain.

Stephen wrote this classic essay, excerpted below, in 1867, at which time he was president of the Alpine Club and one of the most distinguished climbers in the playground of Europe. In saying good-bye to such giants as Mont Blanc, the Jungfrau, the Weisshorn, and Schreckhorn, all of which he had climbed, the thirty-five-year-old author took on the mantle of the elder statesman of mountaineering, a position he was to hold throughout his long and varied career. Regrettably known today principally as the father of Virginia Woolf, Sir Leslie made a signal contribution to English letters through his editorship of the *Dictionary of National Biography*, to which he contributed some four hundred articles.

# LESLIE STEPHEN

# The Regrets of a Mountaineer

I have often felt a sympathy, which almost rises to the pathetic, when looking on at a cricket match or boat race. Something of the emotion with which Gray regarded the "distant spires and antique towers" rises within me. It is not, indeed, that I feel very deeply for the fine ingenuous lads, who, as somebody says, are about to be degraded into tricky, selfish members of Parliament. I have seen too much of them. They are very fine animals; but they are rather too exclusively animal. The soul is apt to be in too embryonic a state within these cases of well-strung bone and muscle. It is impossible for a mere athletic machine, however finely constructed, to appeal very deeply to one's finer sentiments. I can scarcely look forward with even an affectation of sorrow for the time when, if more sophisticated, it will at least have made a nearer approach to the dignity of an intellectual being. It is not the boys who make me feel a touch of sadness; their approaching elevation to the dignity of manhood will raise them on the whole in the scale of humanity; it is the older spectators whose aspect has in it something affecting. The shaky old gentleman, who played in the days when it was decidedly less dangerous to stand up to bowling than to a cannonball, and who now hobbles about on rheumatic joints, by the help of a stick; the corpulent elder, who rowed when boats had gangways down their middle, and did not require as delicate a balance as an acrobat's at the top of a living pyramid — these are the persons whom I cannot see without an occasional sigh. They are really conscious that they have lost something which they can never regain; or, if they momentarily forget it, it is even more forcibly impressed upon the spectators. To see a respectable old gentleman of sixty, weighing some fifteen stone [210 pounds], suddenly attempt to forget a third of his weight and two thirds of his years, and attempt to caper like a boy, is indeed a startling phenomenon. To the thoughtless, it may be simply comic; but without being a Jaques, one may contrive also to suck some melancholy out of it.

Now, as I have never caught a cricket ball, and, on the contrary, have caught numerous crabs in my life, the sympathy which I feel for these declining athletes is not due to any great personal interest in the matter. But I have long anticipated that a similar day would come for me, when I should no longer be able to pursue my favorite sport of mountaineering. Someday I should find that the ascent of a zigzag was as bad as a performance on the treadmill; that I could not look over a precipice without a swimming in the head; and that I could no more jump a crevasse than the Thames at Westminster.

None of these things have come to pass. So far as I know, my physical powers are still equal to the ascent of Mont Blanc or the Jungfrau. But I am no less effectually debarred — it matters not how — from mountaineering. I wander at the foot of the gigantic Alps, and look up longingly to the summits, which are apparently so near, and yet know that they are divided from me by an impassable gulf. In some missionary work I have read that certain South Sea islanders believed in a future paradise where the good should go on eating for ever with insatiable appetites at an inexhaustible banquet. They were to continue their eternal dinner in a house with open wickerwork sides; and it was to be the punishment of the damned to crawl outside in perpetual hunger and look in through the chinks as little boys look in through the windows of a London cookshop. With similar feelings I lately watched through a telescope the small black dots, which were really men, creeping up the high flanks of Mont Blanc or Monte Rosa. The eternal snows represented for me the Elysian fields, into which entrance was sternly forbidden, and I lingered about the spot with a mixture of pleasure and pain, in the envious contemplation of my more fortunate companions.

I know there are those who will receive these assertions with civil incredulity. Some persons assume that every pleasure with which they cannot sympathize is necessarily affectation, and hold, as a particular case of that doctrine, that Alpine travelers risk their lives merely from fashion or desire for notoriety. Others are kind enough to admit that there is something genuine in the passion, but put it on a level with the passion for climbing greased poles. They think it derogatory to the due dignity of Mont Blanc that he should be used as a greased pole, and assure us that the true pleasures of the Alps are those which are within reach of the old and the invalids, who can only creep about villages and along highroads. I cannot well argue with such detractors from what I consider a noble sport.

As for the first class, it is reduced almost to a question of veracity. I say that I enjoy being on the top of a mountain, or, indeed, halfway up a mountain; that climbing is a pleasure to me, and would be so if no one else climbed and no one ever heard of my climbing. They reply that they don't believe it. No more argument is possible than if I were to say that I liked eating olives, and someone asserted that I really eat them only out of affectation. My reply would be simply to go on eating olives; and I hope the reply of mountaineers will be to go on climbing Alps. The other assault is more intelligible. Our critics admit that we have a pleasure; but assert that it is a puerile pleasure — that it leads to an irreverent view of mountain beauty, and to oversight of that which should really most impress a refined and noble mind. To this I shall only make such an indirect reply as may result from a frank confession of my own regrets at giving up the climbing business — perhaps for ever.

I am sinking, so to speak, from the butterfly to the caterpillar stage, and, if the creeping thing is really the highest of the two, it will appear that there is something in the substance of my lamentations unworthy of an intellectual being. Let me try. By way of preface, however, I admit that mountaineering, in my sense of the word, is a sport. It is a sport which, like fishing or shooting, brings one into contact with the sublimest aspects of nature; and, without setting their enjoyment before one as an ultimate end or aim, helps one indirectly to absorb and be penetrated by their influence. Still it is strictly a sport — as strictly as cricket, or rowing, or knur and spell — and I have no wish to place it on a different footing. The game is won when a mountaintop is reached in spite of difficulties; it is lost when one is forced to retreat; and, whether won or lost, it calls into play a great variety of physical and intellectual energies, and gives the pleasure which always accompanies an energetic use of our faculties. Still it suffers in some degree from this undeniable characteristic, and especially from the tinge which has consequently been communicated to narratives of mountain adventures.

There are two ways which have been appropriated to the description of all sporting exploits. One is to indulge in fine writing about them, to burst out in sentences which swell to paragraphs, and in paragraphs which spread over pages; to plunge into ecstasies about infinite abysses and overpowering splendors, to compare mountains to archangels lying down in eternal winding sheets of snow, and to convert them into allegories about man's highest destinies and aspirations. This is good when it is well done. Mr. Ruskin has covered the Matterhorn, for example, with a whole web of poetical associations, in language which, to a severe taste, is perhaps a trifle too fine, though he has done it with an eloquence which his bitterest antagonists must freely acknowledge. Yet most humble writers will feel that if they try to imitate Mr. Ruskin's eloquence they will pay the penalty of becoming ridiculous. It is not everyone who can with impunity compare Alps to archangels.

Tall talk is luckily an object of suspicion to Englishmen, and, consequently most writers, and especially those who frankly adopt the sporting view of the mountains, adopt the opposite scheme: they affect something like cynicism; they mix descriptions of scenery with allusions to fleas or to bitter beer; they shrink with the prevailing dread of Englishmen from the danger of overstepping the limits of the sublime into its proverbial opposite; and they humbly try to amuse us because they can't strike us with awe. This, too, if I may venture to say so, is good in its way and place; and it seems rather hard to these luckless writers when people assume that, because they make jokes on a mountain, they are necessarily insensible to its awful sublimities. A sense of humor is not incompatible with imaginative sensibility; and even Wordsworth might have been an equally powerful prophet of nature if he could sometimes have descended from his stilts. In short, a man may worship mountains, and yet have a quiet joke with them when he is wandering all day in their tremendous solitudes.

Joking, however, is, it must be admitted, a dangerous habit. I freely avow that, in my humble contributions to Alpine literature, I have myself made some very poor and very unseasonable witticisms. I confess my error, and only wish that I had no worse errors to confess. Still I think that the poor little jokes in which we mountaineers sometimes indulge have been made liable to rather harsh constructions. We are accused, in downright earnest, not merely of being flippant, but of an arrogant contempt for all persons whose legs are not as strong as our own. We are supposed seriously to wrap ourselves in our own conceit, and to brag intolerably of our exploits. Now I will not say that no mountaineer ever swaggers; the quality called by the vulgar "bounce" is unluckily confined to no profession. Certainly I have seen a man intolerably vain because he could raise a hundredweight with his little finger; and I daresay that the "champion billposter," whose name is advertised on the walls of this metropolis, thinks excellence in billposting the highest virtue of a citizen. So some men may be silly enough to brag in all seriousness about mountain exploits. However, most lads of twenty learn that it is silly to give themselves airs about mere muscular eminence; and especially is this true of Alpine exploits — first, because they require less physical prowess than almost any other sport, and secondly, because a good amateur still feels himself the hopeless inferior of half the Alpine peasants whom he sees. You cannot be very conceited about a game in which the first clodhopper you meet can give you ten minutes' start in an hour. Still a man writing in a humorous vein naturally adopts a certain bumptious tone, just as our friend *Punch* ostentatiously declares himself to be omniscient and infallible. Nobody takes him at his word, or supposes that the editor of *Punch* is really the most conceited man in all England.

But we poor mountaineers are occasionally fixed with our own careless talk by some outsider who is not in on the secret. We know ourselves to be a small sect, and to be often laughed at; we reply by assuming that we are the salt of the earth, and that our amusement is the first and noblest of all amusements. Our only retort to the good-humored ridicule with which we are occasionally treated is to adopt an affected strut, and to carry it off as if we were the finest fellows in the world. We make a boast of our shame, and say, if you laugh we must crow. But we don't really mean anything; if we did, the only word which the English language would afford wherewith to describe us would be the very unpleasant antithesis to wise men, and certainly I hold that we have the average amount of common sense. When, therefore, I see us taken to task for swaggering, I think it a trifle hard that this merely playful affectation of superiority should be made a serious fault. For the future I would promise to be careful, if it were worth avoiding misunderstanding of men who won't take a joke. Meanwhile, I can only state that when Alpine travelers indulge in a little swagger about their own performances and other people's incapacity, they don't mean more than an infinitesimal fraction of what they say, and that they know perfectly well that when history comes to pronounce a final judgment upon the men of the time, it won't put mountain climbing on a level with patriotism, or even with excellence in the fine arts.

The reproach of real bona fide arrogance is, so far as I know, very little true of Alpine travelers. With the exception of the necessary fringe hanging on to every set of human beings—consisting of persons whose heads are weaker than their legs—the mountaineer, so far as my experience has gone, is generally modest enough. Perhaps he sometimes flaunts his ice axes and ropes a little too much before the public eye at Chamonix, as a yachtsman occasionally flourishes his nautical costume at Cowes; but the fault may be pardoned by those not inexorable to human weaknesses. This opinion, I know, cuts at the root of the most popular theory as to our ruling passion. If we do not climb the Alps to gain notoriety, for what purpose can we possibly climb them? That same unlucky trick of joking is taken to indicate that we don't care much about the scenery; for who, with a really susceptible soul, could be facetious under the cliffs of the Jungfrau or the ghastly precipices of the Matterhorn? Hence people who kindly excuse us from the blame of notoriety hunting generally accept the "greased pole" theory. We are, it seems, overgrown schoolboys, who, like other schoolboys, enjoy being in dirt, and danger, and mischief, and have as much sensibility for natural beauty as the mountain mules. And against this, as a more serious complaint, I wish to make my feeble protest, in order that my lamentation on quitting the profession may not seem unworthy of a thinking being.

Let me try to recall some of the impressions which mountaineering has left with me, and see whether they throw any light upon the subject. As I gaze at the huge cliffs where I may no longer wander, I find innumerable recollections arise—some of them dim, as though belonging to a past existence; and some so brilliant that I can scarcely realize my exclusion from the scenes to which they belong. I am standing at the foot of what, to my mind, is the most glorious of all Alpine wonders—the huge Oberland precipice, on the slopes of the Faulhorn or the Wengern Alp. Innumerable tourists have done all that tourists can do to cocknify (if that is the right derivative from cockney) the scenery; but, like the Pyramids or a Gothic cathedral, it throws off the taint of vulgarity by its imperishable majesty. Even on turf strewn with sandwich papers and empty bottles, even in the presence of hideous peasant women singing *"Stand er auf"* for five centimes, we cannot but feel the influence of Alpine beauty. When the sunlight is dying off the snows, or the full moon lighting them up with ethereal tints, even sandwich papers and singing women may be forgotten. How does the memory of scrambles along snow arêtes, of plunges—luckily not too deep—into crevasses, of toil through long snowfields, toward a refuge that seemed to recede as we advanced — where, to quote Tennyson with due alteration, to the traveler toiling in immeasurable snow

> Sown in a wrinkle of the monstrous hill
> The chalet sparkles like a grain of salt;—

how do such memories as these harmonize with the sense of superlative sublimity?

One element of mountain beauty is, we shall all admit, their vast size and steepness. That a mountain is very big, and is faced by perpendicular walls of rock, is the first thing which strikes everybody, and is the whole essence and outcome of a vast quantity of poetical description. Hence the first condition toward a due appreciation of mountain scenery is that these qualities should be impressed upon the imagination. The mere dry statement that a mountain is so many feet in vertical height above the sea, and contains so many tons of granite, is nothing. Mont Blanc is about three miles high. What of that? Three miles is an hour's walk for a lady — an eighteen-penny cab fare — the distance from Hyde Park Corner to the Bank — an express train could do it in three minutes, or a racehorse in five. It is a measure which we have learned to despise, looking at it from a horizontal point of view; and accordingly most persons, on seeing the Alps for the first time, guess them to be higher, as measured in feet, than they really are.

What, indeed, is the use of giving measures in feet to any but the scientific mind? Who cares whether the moon is 250,000 or 2,500,000 miles distant? Mathematicians try to impress upon us that the distance of the fixed stars is only expressible by a row of figures which stretches across a page; suppose it stretched across two or across a dozen pages, should we be any the wiser, or have, in the least degree, a clearer notion of the superlative distances? We civilly say, "Dear me!" when the astronomer looks to us for the appropriate stare, but we only say it with the mouth; internally our remark is "You might as well have multiplied by a few more millions while you were about it." Even astronomers, though not a specially imaginative race, feel the impotence of figures, and try to give us some measure which the mind can grasp a little more conveniently. They tell us about the cannonball which might have been flying ever since the time of Adam, and not yet have reached the heavenly body, or about the stars which may not yet have become visible, though the light has been flying to us at a rate inconceivable by the mind for an inconceivable number of years; and they succeed in producing a bewildering and giddy sensation, although the numbers are too vast to admit of any accurate apprehension.

We feel a similar need in the case of mountains. Besides the bare statement of figures, it is necessary to have some means for grasping the meaning of the figures. The bare tens and thousands must be clothed with some concrete images. The statement that a mountain is 15,000 feet high is, by itself, little more impressive than that it is 3,000; we want something more before we can mentally compare Mont Blanc and Snowdon.

Indeed, the same people who guess of a mountain's height at a number of feet much exceeding the reality, show, when they are cross-examined, that they fail to appreciate in any tolerable degree the real meaning of the figures. An old lady one day, about 11 A.M., proposed to walk from the Eggishorn to the Jungfraujoch, and to return for luncheon — the distance being a good twelve hours' journey for trained mountaineers. Every detail of which the huge mass is composed is certain to be underestimated. A gentleman the other day pointed out to me a grand ice cliff at the end of a hanging glacier, which must have been at least one hundred feet high, and asked me whether that snow was three feet deep.

Nothing is more common than for tourists to mistake some huge pinnacle of rock, as big as a church tower, for a traveler. The rocks of the Grands Mulet, in one corner of which the chalet is hidden, are often identified with a party ascending Mont Blanc; and I have seen boulders as big as a house pointed out confidently as chamois. People who make these blunders must evidently see the mountains as mere toys, however many feet they may give them at a random guess. Huge overhanging cliffs are to them steps within the reach of human legs; yawning crevasses are ditches to be jumped; and foaming waterfalls are like streams from penny squirts. Everyone knows the avalanches on the Jungfrau, and the curiously disproportionate appearance of the little puffs of white smoke, which are said to be the cause of the thunder; but the disproportion ceases to an eye that has learned really to measure distance, and to know that these smoke puffs represent a cataract of crashing blocks of ice.

Now the first merit of mountaineering is that it enables one to have what theologians would call an experimental faith in the size of mountains — to substitute a real living belief for a dead intellectual assent. It enables one, first, to assign something like its true magnitude to a rock or a snow slope; and, secondly, to measure that magnitude in units. Suppose that we are standing upon the Wengern Alp; between the Mönch and the Eiger there stretches a round white bank with a curved outline, which we may roughly compare to the back of one of Sir E. Landseer's lions. The ordinary tourists — the old man, the woman, or the cripple, who are supposed to appreciate the real beauties of Alpine scenery — may look at it comfortably from their hotel. They may see its graceful curve, the long straight lines that are ruled in delicate shading down its sides, and the contrast of the blinding white snow with the dark blue sky above; but they will probably guess it to be a mere bank — a snowdrift, perhaps, which has been piled by the last storm. If you pointed out to them one of the great rocky teeth that projected from its summit, and said that it was a guide, they would probably remark that he looked very small, and would fancy that he could jump over the bank with an effort.

Now a mountaineer knows, to begin with, that it is a massive rocky rib, covered with snow, lying at a sharp angle, and varying perhaps from 500 to 1,000 feet in height. So far he might be accompanied by men of less soaring ambition; by an engineer who had been mapping the country, or an artist who had been carefully observing the mountains from their bases. They might learn in time to interpret correctly the real meaning of shapes at which the uninitiated guess at random. But the mountaineer can go a step further, and it is the next step which gives the real significance to those delicate curves and lines. He can translate the 500 or 1,000 feet of snow slope into a more tangible unit of measurement. To him, perhaps, they recall the memory of a toilsome ascent, the sun beating on his head for five or six hours, the snow returning the glare with still more parching effect; a stalwart guide toiling all the weary time, cutting steps in hard blue ice, the fragments hissing and spinning down the long straight grooves in the frozen snow till they lost themselves in the yawning chasm below; and step after step taken along the slippery staircase, till at length he triumphantly sprang upon the summit of the tremendous wall that no human foot had scaled before. The little black knobs that rise above the edge represent for him huge impassable rocks, sinking on one side in scarped slippery surfaces toward the snowfield, and on the other stooping in one tremendous cliff to a distorted glacier thousands of feet below.

The faint blue line across the upper névé, scarcely distinguishable to the eye, represents to one observer nothing but a trifling undulation; a second, perhaps, knows that it means a crevasse; the mountaineer remembers that it is the top of a huge chasm, thirty feet across, and perhaps ten times as deep, with perpendicular sides of glimmering blue ice, and fringed by thick rows of enormous pendent icicles. The marks that are scored in delicate lines, such as might be ruled by a diamond on glass, have been cut by innumerable streams trickling in hot weather from the everlasting snow, or plowed by succeeding avalanches that have slipped from the huge upper snowfields above. In short, there is no insignificant line or mark that has not its memory or its indication of the strange phenomena of the upper world. True, the same picture is painted upon the retina of all classes of observers; and so [Richard] Porson [the classical scholar] and a schoolboy and a peasant might receive the same physical impression from a set of black and white marks on the page of a Greek play; but to one they would be an incoherent conglomeration of unmeaning and capricious lines, to another they would represent certain sounds more or less corresponding to some English words; while to the scholar they would reveal some of the noblest poetry in the world, and all the associations of successful intellectual labor.

I do not say that the difference is quite so great in the case of the mountains; still I am certain that no one can decipher the natural writing on the face of a snow slope or a precipice who has not wandered among their recesses, and learned by slow experience what is indicated by marks which an ignorant observer would scarcely notice. True, even one who sees a mountain for the first time may know that, as a matter of fact, a scar on the face of a cliff means, for example, a recent fall of a rock; but between the bare knowledge and the acquaintance with all which that knowledge implies—the thunder of the fall, the crash of the smaller fragments, the bounding energy of the descending mass—there is almost as much difference as between hearing that a battle has been fought and being present at it yourself. We have all read descriptions of Waterloo till we are sick of the subject; but I imagine that our emotions on seeing the shattered wall of Hougoumont are very inferior to those of one of the Guard who should revisit the place where he held out for a long day against the assaults of the French Army.

Now to an old mountaineer the Oberland cliffs are full of memories; and, more than this, he has learned the language spoken by every crag and every wave of glacier. It is strange if they do not affect him rather more powerfully than the casual visitor who has never been initiated by practical experience into their difficulties. To him, the huge buttress which runs down from the Mönch is something more than an irregular pyramid, purple with white patches at the bottom and pure white at the top. He fills up the bare outline supplied by the senses with a thousand lively images. He sees tier above tier of rock, rising in a gradually ascending scale of difficulty, covered at first by long lines of the debris that have been splintered by frost from the higher wall, and afterward rising bare and black and threatening. He knows instinctively which of the ledges has a dangerous look — where such a bold mountaineer as John Lauener might slip on the polished surface, or be in danger of an avalanche from above. He sees the little shell-like swelling at the foot of the glacier crawling down the steep slope above, and knows that it means an almost inaccessible wall of ice; and the steep snowfields that rise toward the summit are suggestive of something very different from the picture which might have existed in the mind of a German student, who once asked me whether it was possible to make the ascent on a mule.

Hence, if mountains owe their influence upon the imagination in a great degree to their size and steepness, and apparent inaccessibility — as no one can doubt that they do, whatever may be the explanation of the fact that people like to look at big, steep, inaccessible objects — the advantages of the mountaineer are obvious. He can measure those qualities on a different scale from the ordinary traveler. He measures the size, not by the vague abstract term of so many thousand feet, but by the hours of labor, divided into minutes — each separately felt — of strenuous muscular exertion. The steepness is not expressed in degrees, but by the memory of the sensation produced when a snow slope seems to be rising up and smiting you in the face; when, far away from all human help, you are clinging like a fly to the slippery side of a mighty pinnacle in midair. And as for the inaccessibility, no one can measure the difficulty of climbing a hill who has not wearied his muscles and brain in struggling against the opposing obstacles. Alpine travelers, it is said, have removed the romance from the mountains by climbing them. What they have really done is to prove that there exists a narrow line by which a way may be found to the top of any given mountain; but the clue leads through innumerable inaccessibilities; true, you can follow one path, but to right and left are cliffs which no human foot will ever tread, and whose terrors can only be realized when you are in their immediate neighborhood. The cliffs of the Matterhorn do not bar the way to the top effectually, but it is only by forcing a passage through them that you can really appreciate their terrible significance.

Tasker had scaled Dunagiri, his first big Himalayan climb, with partner Dick Renshaw; now for the descent, with a minimum of food and scarcely any fuel. Without fuel, they could not melt the snow for water; without water, their minds and bodies would go haywire. This riveting account of their delirious retreat from Dunagiri is from *Savage Arena*, the book Tasker delivered to his publisher on the eve of his departure with the British Everest Expedition of 1982. He was last seen at a height of 27,000 feet, pushing for the summit.

# JOE TASKER

# The Way Down

[Dick Renshaw and I] slept comfortably in a hollow beneath the cliff of ice where we had dumped our rucksacks on the way to the top. We had had time left to go some way down but we reasoned that the slopes as far as the top of the rock barrier were uniform and would take very little time to descend. We would best utilize the time by resting in readiness for making a big effort next day to get down as far as possible.

We used up the last of the fuel. It had lasted about the length of time we had calculated it should. The food we apportioned out, keeping a little fruit cake, a tin of sardines, a few boiled sweets, and some squares of chocolate for the next night.

The ascent had taken longer by two days than we had planned for, and now we had to descend with no fuel and a minimum of food. I wondered what had happened to my usual caution and aversion to effort, which would normally have made me seize on the unexpected difficulty and time it was taking as a short-term excuse to go down and rest, postponing the final effort until a later date when we could return refreshed and with more supplies.

I mentioned this to Dick, in self-mocking pride that for once he had not had to sustain my flagging enthusiasm with his own relentless drive.

"I can't understand why it didn't occur to me to suggest going down before we came into the rock barrier. It should have been obvious then that we would be cutting things fine. Not like me, is it?"

And Dick replied, "No, but it occurred to me that it would be more sensible for us to go down then, and come back later, but I thought you would be suggesting it at any moment, so I just carried on and you never said anything!"

Without fuel for the stove we could melt no snow for water, and without liquid we would deteriorate rapidly. We needed a minimum of eight pints of liquid each day to avoid rapid physical deterioration, and though we were surrounded by snow we had no means of melting it. The total food we had left amounted to no more than a snack, hardly enough to sustain us, but even if we had had more we could not have swallowed anything without liquid to wash it down.

Our situation was serious, but we pinned our hopes on being able to descend more rapidly than we had climbed up. We regarded the rock barrier as being the most diffi-cult stretch, but knew that we could abseil down that and any other awkward places below. Without the constant struggle upward in thin air, against the force of gravity, with heavy loads on our backs, we calculated that it should not take us more than two days to reach the bottom, where we would find water and food at our tent. We would be very weak by then, but we were confident that we could do it, and we left at morn-ing to overcome the worst obstacle, the rock barrier.

Great gaps in time exist from those days. We only reached partway down the rock barrier next day, and nothing remains in my mind of all that we did before evening came and we had to chop out a precarious ledge in some ice. The ledge was a foot wide. It was a struggle to work ourselves into the bivouac tent as shelter against the gusts of wind and showers of snow. With my head swathed in the folds of nylon, I heard the clatter of the pan lid falling as Dick shuffled into position. I thought that it didn't matter, as there was no fuel for the stove and we could not use the pan anyway. Dick told me that the pan and the stove had gone too, and still it did not seem to matter. On the contrary, they had all become surplus weight once the fuel ran out, and we had not had the wit to discard them anyway.

We ate nothing, not having the wit either to realize how weak we were becoming and that in a short while our throats would become too parched to swallow even the morsels of food which did remain. We were too cramped on the tiny ledge and too exhausted to scrape about in the bottom of our sacks among the wrappers and empty food bags on the chance of finding something edible. Sleep was merciful oblivion when it came.

We left that bivouac and continued to abseil down. I can remember only that it was difficult to find somewhere to drive the pitons from which to hang the ropes. As we slowly descended, the weather deteriorated, clouds covered the sky, and the bitter wind brought more snow. We spoke little. Any word was a curt passing only of essential information; talking took energy. We needed no words to perform maneuvers which we had rehearsed on every climb we came down from. We were mute collaborators in a performance for surviving, Siamese twins and yet strangers, muffled in now ragged garb smattered with snow.

We came of the rock barrier some distance to one side of the snow ramp by which we had entered it some days ago. An expanse of hard, blue ice separated us from the shoulder on the ridge where we had spent a night on the way up.

We pulled the ropes down from the anchor point, lost now in the mist. Dick coiled one rope and placed it over his shoulder. He fastened himself to two barbed pegs driven into the ice and stood on a tiny step he had scraped out for his feet. I had made ready the other rope and, having tied one end to my waist harness, started across the hard, brittle surface of the ice slope with Dick paying out the rope as I moved across in a horizontal line.

There was an initial area where snow covered the ice and my crampon points bit in quite well; then I was on the bare, uncompromising ice itself. After days of use, the points of my crampons had become blunted. I kicked at the ice with all the force I could muster, trying to embed the metal spikes in far enough to hold my weight, but my legs had no strength and my movements were listless, like those of someone in a nightmare trying to move faster.

My arms struck powerlessly at the surface with ax and hammer, but the ice flew off in tiny fragments and the picks skated wildly away from where they had struck. Somehow I had to cross another seventy feet of this ice before I was safe.

Dick seemed unaware of my predicament. I felt the rope tighten on my waist, pulling me off balance, as something prevented him from paying it out, then he spoke.

"Joe, can you hold on while . . ."

My patience snapped and I shouted at him in desperation, "Can I, hell? This ice is terrible," so that he would know I was in trouble.

I was weakening fast. My calves ached unendurably. I cut a small step out of the ice with my ax and stood on it while I hammered in an ice peg. I passed the rope attached to my waist through a snap link in the peg and moved on with a little more reassurance. The dreamlike state persisted. Dick became a vague silhouette eighty feet away through the mist and driving snow. I kept making the motions of driving in ax, hammer, and crampon points, moving imperceptibly farther, but my adhesion was only tenuous. Wearily and inevitable, but with surprise, I fell, banging down the ice to be stopped twenty feet below the ice peg, dangling from the end of the rope.

I had stopped, and I had no thought for the danger of the situation. Four thousand feet of mountain stretched away beneath me, and one six-inch spike of metal had held in the ice, taking my weight on the rope which I had attached to it. My brain filtered out all but the essential. I needed no concern for myself, I knew I was safe, but I called out to my partner, "Are you all right, Dick?" concerned at the shock he must have had in stopping my fall and the strain he would be feeling in holding my weight still.

"Yes, I'm all right," he shouted back in a tone which said, "It's you that's fallen off, are you all right?"

I was more surprised that I had actually been held on an ice peg than frightened and unnerved by the experience.

"Dick, I can't climb across this, I'll tension across from the peg to where the ice is better."

I had fallen to an area of even harder, steeper ice and with even less strength than before I could not kick my crampon points far enough into it. Dick held my weight on the rope, which ran through the carabiner on the peg. In delicate balance, not thinking that the peg might have been loosened by my fall, I edged across, leaning against the pull of the rope, clawed with the points of my ax and hammer, and pushed with the tips of my crampons. Fifteen feet, ten feet remaining, and then I reached the white, snow-covered, softer ice.

"How much rope, Dick?"

"Forty feet."

I advanced to where a rock buttress came down into the ice, and drove some pitons into a crack. They were really secure. I knew that Dick, as fatigued as I was, would have an equally hard time crossing the ice.

The wind was hurling the snow into my face, inside the hood of my anorak and around my neck. After an age Dick still had not moved.

"Dick," I screamed into the mist, "what's the matter?"

My throat was dry and sore from thirst.

"Just getting the pegs out. Coming now."

I drew the rope in, feeling him moving, though only vaguely seeing. I wondered what it would be like to hold on to the rope like this if Dick fell. My hands were in thick mitts, matted with ice; I was shaking with cold and hardly able to stand upright. Without warning Dick swung off, tumbled down the ice, and came to a halt dangling from the end of the rope, much as I had been some time before. It was not anything terrible to hold his weight. The rope still ran through the carabiner on the peg that had held my fall. I just felt the uncomfortable strain of holding a weight I must not let go.

"Are you all right?"

"Yes."

From the position he was now in, the rope would not be long enough for Dick to reach me. If he climbed up to release the rope from where it ran through the ice peg he would still be stranded in the middle of the dreadfully hard ice. Without the safeguard of the ice peg to take some of the strain, if he fell, all his falling weight would come onto me. I was no longer strong enough to be sure of being able to hold a fall which came directly onto me.

"Dick, you'll have to take the rope you're carrying and join it to the one you're tied to. That will give you extra length so that you can have a back rope from the ice peg to reach here. Put another ice peg in where you are while you tie the two ropes together." The effort of shouting all this exhausted me further.

He hammered in an ice peg and fiddled about uncoiling the rope he had been carrying over his shoulder. I could not quite see through the wind-driven snow and cloud, but I could sense that something was not right.

"How am I going to get this other rope to you?" he asked.

"There's no need to; just tie it to the rope you were first tied to, I'll take it in till the knot comes to the top peg, then tie yourself into that second rope; that should give you enough free rope to reach me here using it as a back rope on the higher ice peg."

"Well, what's this ice peg for here?"

Somehow Dick was not thinking straight.

"That's so you don't fall off while you're doing all this."

I was not annoyed or even impatient; it was simply essential that all this be done in the shortest possible time. There was no sarcasm in the way I spelled out all these basic maneuvers as if to a novice. It was urgent that there be no misunderstanding and that we reach the bivouac spot, on the shoulder only minutes away from me, and get into our sleeping bags out of the cold. This time he was doing it right. After those minutes of waiting which stretch into hours, Dick started to move. Then he stopped.

"What's the matter?"

"I haven't got the ice peg out."

"Stuff the ice peg."

"I'll get it tomorrow."

"All right, tomorrow." Anything to keep him moving. "But please hurry," I pleaded. I was freezing and beginning to panic at the desperation of our situation. Carefully he arrived.

"Good lad."

"That's what comes of being hassled," he spat at me as he came alongside, waving a foot. The crampon dangled loose from the boot, and I gathered that somehow he blamed me for it.

We were both suffering from an advanced state of exposure and we did not know it. Dick's lack of comprehension of the simplest instructions, slowness of reaction, and irrational behavior were classic symptoms of sustained exposure to extreme cold, which not only dulls fatally the central core of the body but affects the functioning of the brain as well. I should have recognized these telltale signs and taken control, but I, too, was so affected that I could not think beyond my own misery and felt he was only being abnormally perverse.

After twenty feet the angle of the snow slope eased off into the almost horizontal shoulder on the ridge where we had dug a shallow hole against the wind on the way up. I vacated the stance I had been in for some unconscionable time and hurried down the easy ground toward the hole. The rope came taut before I reached the chosen stopping place and I waited for Dick to free himself from the pegs and follow me. He started hammering the pegs loose. I waited and froze. He hammered and hammered. He was only dimly discernible. The cold was terrible.

"Joe, one of the pegs won't come out."

"Stuff the peg. Leave it."

"I'll get it tomorrow."

"All right, tomorrow."

At last he moved. He sat down for a rest. We moved on again at opposite ends of the taut rope.

"Another fifteen feet . . . I'm almost there . . . I'm at the bivouac, Dick."

Another step into the slight hollow remaining of our previous hole. I flung my sack to the ground, sat on it, and started to pull in the rope. Dick stopped again. After the normal interval for a rest he was still there. All I craved for was sleep. Not food, nor drink, only sleep; but there still seemed to be so many things to do before we could settle down. I sat holding the rope.

"Joe, you look after yourself. . . ."

I could not catch the next words, they were garbled in the wind and mist. Then I heard, "I'm strangling myself. Got to sort the rope out."

I realized he must have got his legs caught up in the rope, but he was nearly with me, only thirty feet away. He had reached the rounded crest of the shoulder, whose broad, almost flat top was nearly fifteen feet wide. He was safe now, so I left him to untangle himself while I made ready the hollow for us to spend the night.

I pulled out the bivouac tent, put my piece of foam mat inside, sleeping bag on top of that; duvet jacket on, crampons off, boots off, inner boots slackened, a quick photograph of Dick through the airhole of the tent, and I snuggled down into my sleeping bag. In seconds I was asleep.

"Joe, do you want something to eat?" Dick's voice came from outside through the blue folds of the tent. I had no idea how much time had passed, but there was dimness, as of twilight, outside.

"Is there a piece of cake left?" It was the only thing with any moisture in it, and I hoped that the moisture would help the food slide down the dry and inflamed tube of my throat.

A small morsel of cake appeared through the entrance. I bit into it and a filling fell out from one of my teeth. It was too much effort to eat. I put the cake to one side and fell asleep again.

"Joe, do you want any of those sardines you've got?"

"No," and in the unspoken language of the intimate rapport we had developed this meant that the sardines did not get opened. We had to do things together. If I did not eat my half of the sardines at the same time as Dick we would have the problems of carrying around the half-empty tin. It did not occur to me that I could eat them in the morning, or that they would be frozen anyway and could be easily carried.

After another unmeasured period of time, I woke again; it was dark and Dick was still not in the tent beside me.

"Dick?"

"What?"

"What are you doing?"

"Nothing. It's clear out here now. It's a three-quarter moon too. Really beautiful."

The thought never came to me that he needed help, that his mind was waning with his strength. I thought it was only his everlasting toughness and resilience which enabled him to sit out and look at the stars when all that I could think of was the oblivion of sleep. I did not know that he sat out there possessed of a strange excitement and intoxicated by a silvery landscape illuminated by the rising sliver of moon.

I simply thought that I was with a person who was tougher and who had more mental reserves than I would ever have, and I fell back to sleep.

It was morning, but the sun was not yet out, when Dick woke me.

"Joe, what do you think of these?"

I struggled to find him through the folds of the bivouac bag. He was sitting up, half outside, and he held out his hands. At any time Dick's fingers look fat or plump; now, as he thrust them toward me, they emerged from his fingerless gloves swollen and BLUE; solid, hard BLUE.

"Jesus Christ, do they hurt?"

"They're . . . I'm not sure."

"Can you use them?"

"I think so."

I was lost. It was up to him to express pain and disquiet, or to complain; he just seemed to be commenting on an extraordinary phenomenon.

There was another 4,000 feet of mountain to descend before we were back on the glacier, back on level ground, and able to walk or crawl in relative safety back to Base Camp. We had by this time been without water for two days; what little food remained was virtually impossible to swallow without any liquids. It was in trying to chew some chocolate the previous night that Dick had realized that there was something wrong with his hands. He had discovered a couple of squares of chocolate when he had finally settled into his sleeping bag and sat up while eating them. Suddenly he became aware that he had finished the chocolate and was nibbling at his own fingers, which were dark, hard, and unyielding as the chocolate had been. The ends of his fingers were senseless and frozen.

He told me how the discovery that his fingers were frostbitten had not worried him at the time and he had woken to think that it had all been part of a bad dream, until he had pulled his hands out of his sleeping bag to check.

Both hands were the same. It must have happened when he took his gloves off to hammer in the ice peg and tie the ropes together, but he had said nothing about the cold then, and after a while his hands had probably gone numb, so that he stopped feeling any pain.

We usually waited until the sun rose from behind Changabang and warmed us a little before we started to move. There was no longer the ritual of melting snow, making some tea, having breakfast, which had been the normal introduction to the day, not for the two days past. With so little intake of liquid and food we also had had no cause to delay over the intricate process of relieving ourselves, for there were no solids or fluids passing through our bodies at all.

I led most of the abseils that day. We had thought we would be able to scramble down easily, but the mountain was steeper than we remembered it. All day I prepared anchor points, hung the ropes in position, pulled them down to us when we had both slid to the end, and looked for the next anchor point to repeat the procedure. Dick seemed to be ill as well as afflicted by his frostbitten hands, but he was nonetheless apologetic.

"I'm sorry you're having to do everything for me, Joe."

"That's all right, I want to get myself off this mountain as well."

I went down the ropes to the end of a rock rib and on farther down a slope of snow to within sight of some more rocks. Dick came on down and stopped at the top of the snow slope.

"What time is it, Joe? Is it too early to stop?" he shouted down.

In the unspoken language which held most of our communication now, I knew Dick was really telling me he had to stop for the night. I was surprised; it was only 3:00 P.M. and it was unlike him to give in to himself.

"Is there a good place up beside you?" It was understood that he would not have suggested stopping without having spotted a convenient site.

"There's the start of one; one and a half places here to sit down, and one there. We'll have to dig them out."

"It had better be really good for me to climb back up there."

It was only fifty feet back up an easy snow slope, but I had to rest many times, I had to stop and pant hard for breath before I reached Dick, and experienced a wordless disappointment when I saw the two tiny, inadequate hollows on either side of a prow of rock. Futile to criticize; the decision had been made.

I hacked at the snow and ice, dislodging a rock which gave a little more space. Dick, around a corner from me, was similarly preparing his place for the night.

"This is going to be a hanging bivouac," I complained out loud.

"Sounds grim," said Dick, and I presumed he was better off around that corner.

"What's your place like?"

"All right." I could visualize him sitting in comfort.

Into the rock I hammered a couple of pegs. In a horizontal line with them I drove in an ice peg and farther along thrust my ice ax into the snow. From the rock pegs I hung my rucksack, into which I slipped my foam mat and sleeping bag, and with great exertion I inserted my legs into the sleeping bag, attached my waist to the ice peg and my chest to the ice ax. Though the ledge was only a few inches wide, the rucksack held my legs in place, and the nylon loops attached to the ice peg and ice ax held the rest of my body against the side of the mountain. I was ready for sleep.

Dick was fiddling about with something around the corner. I asked what he was doing and he said that he had found a candle in his bag and was melting some snow. Drink was the one thing we craved above all, but I thought he had dropped the pan days ago, and of course we had long since run out of petrol even if the stove had not been dropped too. He said he was using his mug. The mug was made of plastic, and from the other life, before this climb, I was sure that I had a memory that plastic melted in flame, but I thought that maybe I had been mistaken and that perhaps plastic did not melt after all. We had been on the go a long time; I could easily be wrong. No water appeared and I dozed off.

From the lethargic sleep of exhaustion I became aware that it was snowing. I pulled my hood farther down over my face so as not to be disturbed by the cold flakes, and hoped that the snow would be sufficiently dry due to the extreme cold that it would not make my sleeping bag any damper.

Dick disturbed himself from whatever his arrangements were to reach around for the bivouac tent, which was hanging unused by my feet. It did not surprise me that he did not allow himself to be affected by the lethargy which had prevented me from rigging up the tent.

I dreamed of various things, but mostly of food; hot steaming pans of vegetables and casseroles of meat.

Dick was up first, before the rays of the sun had reached us. He thrust the opened tin of sardines at me. There were three left in it, a good tin, some only had four. The volume was probably the same, but it seemed as if you were getting more.

Forced into movement, I grumbled accusatorily as I packed things away, "This was a lousy bivouac. What was yours like?"

"All right."

He was away well before me, hands in pain or not, prospecting the rocks below for the first anchor point. I glanced around the corner enviously to examine the spacious platform I had visualized him sleeping on. There was a minute ledge six inches wide and at most two feet long. The ledge was marked with indentations of crampon points and I realized now why he had stirred himself to open up the bivouac tent. He had not been able to get into his sleeping bag at all but had spent all night crouched on the ledge, had not even taken his crampons off. He had needed the tent as a cover all the more when the snow started. I knew now why he was up so early; he needed to get moving to restore his circulation. "All right," he had said it was, "all right!"

Neither of us had any idea of how many days we had been descending. Dick had recovered from the state of illness of the previous day and now it was only his hands which hindered him, apart from the gradual wasting away which was common to us both. But I lapsed into a state of weakness from which I was losing the will to emerge. I felt that I could so easily sit down and rest forever. I felt no regret for the life that was slipping away, no regret for the way of life back home and people I would be leaving behind; I only wanted the suffering to come to an end. I now, in my turn, relied on Dick. If there was one person I had ever known who would go on until he dropped in his tracks, it was Dick. I did not think I had the strength anymore to get down off this mountain but I felt I had just a little strength left with which I could follow Dick's example. I forced myself to imitate his movements and resolved to do so until the end took me.

At midday I asked him to stop for a breather; putting one foot in front of another even downhill was wearying. He scrambled about in the bottom of his rucksack and produced a polythene bag which had the remains of a portion of muesli in it and a boiled sweet. In spite of the dire straits in which we were, we still carried with us all the rubbish of food wrappers and empty bags from the time when we had had food. We had kept the rubbish deliberately, not wanting to litter this barren wilderness, but now our reward was finding once overlooked or spurned remnants of things to eat from when we had had plenty. Dick's mug was blackened and misshapen, but it had not been destroyed by his attempts to melt snow the previous night. He mixed the sprinkling of oats with snow and ground up the sweet into the mug. The result was a slightly flavored, slightly more moist slush than the snow from which it originated, and it momentarily relieved our dry and burning throats. We were surrounded by tons of snow, but it was no use to us without the means to melt it. Sucking snow or ice only very briefly alleviated our parched mouths. It took too much body heat to melt even a trickle of water in the mouth, and the cold caused our mouths to crack and chap worse than before. We needed a minimum of several pints of liquid each day to avoid physical deterioration, and for some days now we had had only a few mouthfuls of snow.

Both of us remembered the lower third of the spur, the region of the lurid, discolored rock, to be loose, but fairly easy. It was for this reason we had decided to descend this way, expecting to get down it speedily. It all took so much more time than we could ever have imagined in a nightmare. Huge, loose blocks lined the way, threatening our every step. In our fatigue we were a danger to ourselves. We were both stumbling, trailing our legs and arms along, stopping to sit down at every opportunity.

"How many more abseils do you think it is, Dick, to the col?" The col at the top of the snow gully was the end of all our ambitions. From there we reckoned we could descend without using the rope.

"About three or four."

"Do you fancy stopping for the night?"

He looked at me strangely. "I thought you were serious for a moment."

"I was, but it doesn't matter."

We did another abseil, so long and steep and devious that I could not see Dick as I slid down the ropes, hanging free away from the rock. I wondered if he had fallen off the end of the ropes. He was sitting behind a rock. It was a quarter to four.

"How many abseils now, Dick?"

"Not more than two."

"You know we won't make it to the col before dark and we can't descend that gully with the torch broken. Do you fancy stopping here and finishing the descent tomorrow? I'm knackered."

"What's the matter with you?"

"I dunno; all the spit's been knocked out of me."

We were on a shelf of shale and loose rock. We each leveled out a ledge and collected snow in polythene bags. These we were going to take into our sleeping bags to try to melt some of the snow by our own body heat in the night. I was in my sleeping bag first, as Dick was still working away at preparing his ledge. We would both be able to stretch out full length here.

"Could have chosen a better place," he was muttering, and then, as I was sinking into the torpor of rest, he spoke up.

"Joe, do you want to see a crystal vein?"

"What's a crystal vein?"

"One of the wonders of nature," he said in the tone of reverence he used for mountains and things of the earth.

I was cosily established in my sleeping bag, my leg muscles were slowly relaxing for the first time that day, crystal veins were unnecessary to me, and I had no energy for rising to look at one.

"No, it's all right."

It seemed as if we might survive after all. We were a little more relaxed with each other that night and chatted briefly.

"What do you fancy doing next, Joe?"

I knew he was thinking about that ridge on Changabang. I did not know whether to believe his persistence, and again I questioned myself as to whether I was more realistic and logical or whether I was inadequate and cowardly beside his undaunted determination.

"For me Dunagiri has given me everything I hope to get out of climbing for this year, and apart from that your hands are in a bad way. You'll have to get to hospital as soon as possible with them." This last was absolutely true, but, saying it to Dick, it somehow seemed like a lame and invalid excuse.

"I suppose you're right," he said, as if it were a new thought.

I vowed never again to get far away from the basic essentials of life. Comfort was what I promised myself forever, total self-indulgence, never far from warmth and liquid and food. A life of ease, a life of luxury, was what I wanted, and I would never put it at risk again.

What is ethical climbing? What is correct style? In this stimulating essay from *Ascent* (1967), the author delineates seven basic climbing "games" in which the contestants are guided by rules understood implicitly if at all. In making these rules explicit, he is employing the game concept in the same manner as Eric Berne in the psychological milestone *Games People Play*.

# LITO TEJADA-FLORES

# Games Climbers Play

*Reality is the apparent absence of contradiction.*
— Louis Aragon, *Le Paysage de Paris*

I

What I should like to propose in this article is not a new answer to the basically unanswerable question, "What is climbing?" but rather a new way of talking and thinking about it. Climbing is not a homogeneous sport but rather a collection of differing (though related) activities, each with its own adepts, distinctive terrain, problems and satisfactions, and perhaps most important, its own rules. Therefore, I propose to consider climbing in general as a hierarchy of climbing games, each defined by a set of rules and an appropriate field of play.

The word "game" seems to imply a sort of artificiality which is foreign to what we actually feel on a climb. The attraction of the great walls, above all, is surely that when one is climbing them one is playing "for keeps." Unlike the player in a bridge game, the climber cannot simply lay down his cards and go home. But this does not mean that climbing is any less a game. Although the player's actions have real and lasting consequences, the decision to start playing is just as gratuitous and unnecessary as the decision to start a game of chess. In fact, it is precisely because there is no necessity to climb that we can describe climbing as a *game* activity.

The obstacles one must surmount to gain the summit of Indian Rock in Berkeley or the Hand at Pinnacles National Monument are scarcely of the same order as those defending the West Face of Sentinel Rock in Yosemite or the North Face of the Eiger. And the personal satisfaction of the climber upon having solved each of these problems could hardly be the same. As a result, a handicap system has evolved to equalize the inherent challenge and maintain the climber's feeling of achievement at a high level in each of these differing situations. This handicap system is expressed through the rules of the various climbing games.

It is important to realize at the outset that these rules are negatively expressed although their aim is positive. They are nothing more than a series of "don'ts": don't use fixed ropes, belays, pitons, a series of camps, etc. The purpose of these negative rules is essentially protective or conservative. That is, they are designed to conserve the climber's feeling of personal (moral) accomplishment against the meaninglessness of a success which represents merely technological victory.

Let us take as a concrete example the most complex game in the climbing hierarchy: bouldering. It is complex by definition since it has more rules than any other climbing game, rules which prohibit nearly everything — ropes, pitons, and belayers. All that is left is the individual standing in front of a rock problem. (It should be noted that the upper belay belongs to practice climbing, that is, training for any of the climbing games.) But why so many restrictions? Only because boulders are too accessible; they don't defend themselves well enough. For example, it would be an absurdity to use a ladder to reach the top of a boulder in Fontainebleau, but to use the same ladder to bridge a crevasse in the Khumbu Icefall would be reasonable, since Everest defends itself so well that one ladder no longer tips the scales toward certain success. Thus the basic principle of a handicap is applied to maintain a degree of uncertainty as to the eventual outcome, and from this very uncertainty stems the adventure and personal satisfaction of climbing.

More generally, I discern a complete spectrum of climbing games, ranked according to the complexity (or number) of their rules. The higher one goes on the scale, the more inaccessible and formidable become the climber's goals, and, in consequence, he need apply fewer restrictions to conserve the full measure of challenge and satisfaction inherent in the climbing game he is playing. At the top of the hierarchy we find the expedition game, which, although complicated to organize and play, is, formalistically speaking, the simplest game of all, since virtually nothing is forbidden to the climber. The recent use of airplanes and helicopters exemplifies the total lack of rules in the pure expedition game.

While variant games have arisen in isolated and special circumstances in different countries, one can distinguish the following seven basic climbing games.

# THE ETHICAL CLIMBER

## 1. THE BOULDERING GAME

We have already discussed bouldering, but one should note that the basic bouldering rules eliminate not only protection but also companions. The boulderer is essentially a solo climber. In fact, when we see solo climbing at any level of difficulty, it represents the application of bouldering rules to some other climbing game. Aside from that, this game is found in every country where climbing exists, although the number of climbers who specialize in it is relatively small.

## 2. THE CRAG CLIMBING GAME

Crag climbing as a pure game form has doubtless reached its highest form of expression in the British Isles. It is practiced on cliffs of limited size — routes averaging one to three pitches in length. Because of their limited size and the large amount of time at the climber's disposal, such routes are not imposing enough to be approached with the full arsenal of the climber's tools (though they may contain moves as hard as those of any climb). Fundamentally, the game consists in climbing them free with the use of extremely well-defined and limited protection. The use of pitons is avoided or, in special cases, standardized at an absolute minimum. Pure crag climbing is scarcely practiced as a game in this country except in areas such as Pinnacles National Monument, where the rock is virtually unpitonable. There are, however, a number of areas in the States, such as the Shawangunks, where the crag game could be played with more rigor.

## 3. THE CONTINUOUS ROCK CLIMBING GAME

This is the game that most California climbers know best. It differs from the crag game in allowing the full range of rock climbing equipment to be used at the discretion of the climber as well as allowing the use of direct aid. Fundamentally, this game should be played on longer, multipitch climbs whose length puts a kind of time limit to the mechanical means that a climber can employ and still reach the top. Shorter climbs should still be approached as more complex games with stricter rules.

## 4. THE BIG-WALL GAME

This game is practiced not only on the bigger Yosemite walls but in the Dolomites and elsewhere. It is characterized by the prolonged periods of time spent on the walls and by the fact that each member of the party does not have to climb every lead (e.g., different climbers may prusik with loads on different days but are still considered to have done the entire climb). The full technical and logistic equipment range is allowed. In the modern big-wall game fixed ropes to the ground and multiple attempts to prepare the route are no longer allowed (see Part II), and a rigorous distinction is still made between free and artificial moves and pitches.

## 5.  THE ALPINE CLIMBING GAME

In Alpine climbing the player encounters for the first time the full range of hostile forces present in the mountain environment. In addition to problems of length and logistics, he meets increased objective dangers in the form of falling rock, bad weather, and extreme cold, and bad conditions such as verglas. All this leads to a further relaxation of formal rules, since success in the game may often include merely surviving. In Alpine climbing the use of pitons is avoided wherever possible because of time loss in situations where speed means safety, but where pitons are used there is a tendency to use them as holds also. Thus the rules of this game do not require one to push all leads free. The restrictions upon the player are more determined by the nature of the mountain and the route than by a set of rules which he accepts in advance.

## 6.  THE SUPER-ALPINE GAME

This is the newest climbing game to appear and is not yet completely understood. It rejects expedition techniques on terrain which would traditionally have been suitable for it. Its only restrictive rule is that the party must be self-contained. Any umbilical-like connection in the form of a series of camps, fixed ropes, etc., to a secure base is no longer permitted. This rule provides a measure of commitment that automatically increases the uncertainty of success, making victory that much more meaningful. Often the major Alpine routes under extreme winter conditions provide suitable terrain for super-Alpine climbs. Some of the early, classic super-Alpine routes were the South Face of Aconcagua, the ascent of Cerro Torre by Egger and Maestri, and the first winter ascent of the Eiger North Wall.

## 7.  THE EXPEDITION GAME

I have already mentioned the lack of rules in this game, but I wish to point that there are still differences of personal involvement on the part of the players from expedition to expedition. For example, members of the German Broad Peak expedition who packed all their own loads up the mountain were, in a sense, playing a more difficult game than the usual Himalayan expedition that moves up the mountain on the backs of its Sherpas.

It should be noted that the above ordering of climbing games is not an attempt to say that some games are better, harder, or more worthwhile in themselves than others. One remembers that the very purpose of the game structure is to equalize such value connotations from game to game so that the climber who plays any of these games by its proper set of rules should have at least a similar feeling of personal accomplishment. Of course, each type of game will still have its own proponents, its own classics, heroes, and myths.

The real purpose of ranking climbing games into such a hierarchy, however, is not to make judgments about a game or its players, but rather to have a useful scale against which to discuss climbing ethics, since unethical behavior involves a disregard of certain rules.

## II

Within our new framework we can now clear up certain misconceptions about climbing ethics. Ethical climbing merely means respecting the set of rules of the climbing game that one is playing. Conversely, unethical climbing occurs when a climber attempts to use a set of rules appropriate to a game higher up on the scale than the one he is actually playing (i.e., a less restrictive set of rules). Applying this idea to the bolt controversy that has animated ethical discussions among climbers for the last several years, we can see that there is nothing unethical about bolts per se; it is merely that their use is prohibited by the rules of certain climbing games and not by others. In certain games the question becomes meaningless, for, as Bonatti points out, on a major mixed face no amount of bolts can guarantee success, whereas an excessive number will ensure defeat through lack of time.

I have assumed so far that the rules for various climbing games were fixed. Of course, this is not the case, as both the games and their rules are undergoing a constant, if slow, evolution. The central problem of climbing ethics is really the question: Who makes the rules for these games? and secondarily: How do they change with time?

On reflection, it seems to me that the rules of various climbing games are determined by the climbing community at large, but less so by climbers approaching the two extremes of ability. One of these elements is composed of those fainthearted types who desire to overcome every new difficulty with some kind of technological means rather than at the expense of personal effort under pressure. The other group is the small nucleus of elite climbers whose basic concern is not with merely ethical climbing but with minimizing the role of technology and increasing that of individual effort in order to do climbs with better *style*. But before talking about style and the role of the elite climber in climbing evolution, I want to expand my idea that the majority of climbers are responsible for deciding the rules of a given climbing game.

No matter what their origin, a set of rules must be consecrated by usage and general acceptance. Thus, the way good climbers have always done a climb becomes the traditional way of doing it; the rules become classic and constitute an ethical minimum for the climb, defining at the same time the climbing game to which it belongs. But what of new climbs? At any moment there are relatively few members of the climbing community capable of doing significant first ascents; these will be members of the creative elite we have already mentioned. The question arises: Should the style they use on a first ascent determine the rules for succeeding ascents? I think not (although their approaches and attitudes will of course serve as guidelines for following parties). Examples of cases where the first ascent has not set the pattern for succeeding ascents are almost too numerous to list. Just because Jeff Foott made the first ascent of Patio Pinnacle solo or because Bonatti soloed the Southwest Pillar of the Drus, following climbers have felt under no obligation to stick to the difficult rules of the first ascent; or just because the first ascent of the Eiger North Wall was made in a storm, no one has seriously suggested that later parties wait for bad weather to go up the face. A kind of group prudence is at work here, rejecting individual solutions whose extremism puts them beyond the reach of the majority of competent climbers climbing at any given period.

What, then, is the role of the small minority of extremist climbers in the evolution of climbing games? To understand it we must first develop the idea of climbing style. Style may be defined as the conscious choice of a set of rules for a given climbing game. Thus, if a climber follows the accepted rules for a given game, he is climbing both in classical style and ethically. Bad style and unethical climbing are synonymous and represent the choice of rules from a simpler (higher) game, such as Alpine climbing with expedition style. On the other hand, a climber can choose to climb with better style and still will be climbing ethically by choosing rules from a game lower down in the hierarchy than that which he is playing. A fitting example would be the way John Gill has applied bouldering rules to certain crag climbing problems, doing extremely hard, unprotected moves high off the ground.

In this way the creative nucleus of elite climbers can express itself by climbing with better style than the average climber (like aristocrats playing a more demanding game than the democratic majority), which certainly provides enough room for personal expression, yet seems to avoid the traditional aristocratic role of leadership and direction. In fact, these climbers lead the majority only indirectly — their responsibility is not to determine and set ethical standards (rules) for the majority but rather to demonstrate the feasibility of new standards by climbing with consistently superior style. Thus, they stake out the possible directions for the evolution of climbing games. And this, aside from suffering the wiles of equipment-mongers, is the only way that such changes can come about.

Let me give a concrete example. The most evident is the way in which the rules of the big-wall game have evolved in Yosemite Valley under the influence of the best climbers of the day whose primary concern was to do their own climbs in the best style possible rather than to impose an arbitrary set of rules on all climbers. After the feasibility of doing the bigger Grade VI walls without siege tactics had been consistently demonstrated, climbers were impressed enough to accept this approach as a basic rule to such an extent that today even strangers to the Yosemite climbing community (such as the two Frenchmen who did the Nose of El Capitan in the spring of 1966) follow it as a matter of course.

In a less dramatic way the rules of all climbing games are changing constantly, becoming ever more restrictive in order to preserve the fundamental challenge that the climber is seeking from the inroads of a fast changing technology. The present laissez-faire of the uppermost games is disappearing slowly as the complexity of rules shifts up the spectrum. The eventual victim, of course, will be the expedition game, which will disappear completely as super-Alpine climbing takes its place. This is not only the newest but, in a sense, the most creative climbing game, since here the nature of the obstacles encountered is so severe that it will be a long, long time before technological advances even begin to encroach upon the climber's personal satisfaction. The possibilities, on the other hand, are immense. One can even visualize the day when, with ultra-modern bivouac gear, a climbing party of two sets off to do an 8,000-meter peak just as today one sets off to do a hard route on the Grand Teton or on Mont Blanc.

Here, I think, this article should end: not because speculations about the future of climbing are either futile or uninteresting, but because we have already wandered far enough from our original subject. That climbing will continue to evolve is a certainty, although it is far less certain that the idea of climbing games is the best basis for looking at this evolution. But surely this, or any, new framework for thinking and talking about what we are actually doing when we climb is at least a valid step toward the future.

There are mountains in Africa, too. This oddly Victorian — or perhaps it's simply colonial — piece is reminiscent of the scientific expeditions to the Alps which Samuel Clemens spoofed earlier in this volume. And yet it possesses a charm which has made Tilman's *Snow on the Equator* (1938), from which this excerpt is taken, a favorite among aficionados of mountaineering literature.

# H. W. TILMAN

# Kenya Mountain

Not long after our return from Kilimanjaro I heard from S. that the coffee had managed so well in his absence that he was now ready to carry out a plan which he had long had in mind. This was nothing less than a traverse of the twin peaks of Kenya by ascending the west ridge and descending by the 1929 route. I was quite agreeable, and, whether we succeeded in carrying out this ambitious plan or not, we expected to put in a very good fortnight playing about on the mountain. This time our rendezvous was Nakuru, a town 100 miles west of Nairobi, where we forgathered toward the end of July. S. brought with him one of his farm boys, named Saidi, to cook and make himself generally useful. His normal occupation was driving a tractor.

Nanyuki, our jumping-off place at the foot of the mountain, was 240 miles away, but we were anxious to get there in the day. At least one of us was, for S. was burning with impatience to be on the mountain, while I, who had to drive, would have been content to reach it in two. We left Nakuru at half-past four in the morning in rain and mist, and lost some precious time by missing the way in the fog and going for some miles down the wrong road. By the time we had breakfasted at Naivasha the weather had improved, and, as we climbed the steep, rough road up the escarpment out of the Rift Valley, the parched country looked, as was usual there, as though it did not know what rain was.

An hour was spent in Nairobi collecting some food and necessaries, but we left again at midday with 140 miles still to go. It remained dry until we pulled into Nanyuki at six o'clock, but while we were enquiring the whereabouts of the farm from which we had arranged to take transport, there was a heavy shower. The farm was only a mile or two out, but the road to it consisted mainly of two enormous ruts, out of which it was essential to keep the wheels. The rain was fatal to a safe negotiation of this atrocity, and, after several hairbreadth escapes, we landed fairly in both ruts, the car sitting firmly down on the axles. It was almost dark, so we abandoned ship and walked on to the farm, where we slept.

Next morning was a busy one. The car had to be rescued with a team of oxen, and our impedimenta made up into fifty-pound loads, but at one o'clock we started with five pack ponies, led by six boys, to carry our ten loads. The way led through homely grass glades surrounded by cedar forest, where a rhino, standing in the middle of one, looked as unreal as a dragon would have done. We had to pass within 200 yards of him, but he elected to run away instead of stampeding blindly through the caravan—a contingency that one should always be prepared for in the presence of these eccentric beasts. Having steered safely past this Scylla, we nearly got foul of Charybdis in the shape of a big bull elephant standing at the edge of the forest. The ponies got very jumpy, but he, too, moved quietly away, and allowed us to settle into our camp just inside the forest. A heavy storm just missed us, so that we spent a happy evening under the cedars sitting around a noble fire. No elephant or rhino came to disturb the peace of the night—a peace which was broken only by the distant snapping of a bamboo, where, perhaps, some elephant moved, and by the slow, shrill, long-drawn cry of the tree hyrax—that unforgettable sound which for me embodies all the mystery and charm of Africa.

Next morning our march continued through the forest zone, the Kikuyu pony men beating tins and shouting to give timely warning of our approach to any rhino, buffalo, or elephant within earshot. On the west and north side of the mountain, the forest is of a drier type than the "rain" forest of Kilimanjaro, which is found again on the wetter eastern slopes of Kenya. Cedar trees predominated among olive and podocarpus; all valuable for timber, but the first-named especially so because it is the pencil cedar.

The trees, growing scanty and stunted, yielded at length to bamboos, which in turn faded away as we reached the beginning of the moors of tussocky grass, heath, and giant groundsel. Here one of the ponies had to be relieved of its load, and, before we reached the caves which were our objective, everyone was tired and the boys mutinous. The cave which the natives annexed was very good; ours was wet; but there was no lack of groundsel, which makes an excellent fuel.

In the night two of the ponies ran away, so that some reorganization was needed before we got away at half-past ten with three ponies, one of which I now led, while S. and three of the boys carried the remaining loads. Our way lay up the broad Mackinder Valley, and as we marched we gazed at the peak, filling the head of the valley and looking like some glorious cathedral. A cloudless blue sky, with the sunlight sparkling on the glaciers, gave vigor to the black outlines of its rock.

We took up our quarters in another convenient cave near the head of the valley, at a height of about 14,000 feet. Saidi we kept with us, but the boys and the ponies we sent down to the lower camp with instructions to visit us occasionally for orders. In spite of the height, there was still plenty of senecio (giant groundsel) for fuel, and it was needed, because the night was clear and cold, with the thermometer registering some six degrees of frost.

Our first task was to reconnoiter the west ridge, and to do this we made ascents of two rock aiguilles of about 16,000 feet. The comfort and conveniences of our base had to be paid for by a rather laborious climb up a steep, dry, boulder-strewn watercourse, which had to be ascended and descended every day going to and returning from the scene of our activities. The climbing of these two rock peaks, Dutton and Peter — which, by the way, were first ascents — made a satisfying and not too difficult first day, and showed us that the west ridge could be reached from a col at its foot. The col lay at the head of the Joseph Glacier, and the problem of reaching it, and the nature of the ridge above it, were the questions to which we devoted the second day.

Leaving camp at seven, we reached the snout of the glacier at half-past eight. Some step cutting was necessary to gain a lodgment on the glacier, up which we then went as far as the foot of an ice couloir leading to our col. Here we took to some rotten and rather difficult rock on its left bank, and reached the col before midday. The col was narrow, and sitting astride it, *à cheval*, we gazed with fascination at the terrific view of the west face of the mountain. Below the almost vertical cliffs of the pinnacled west ridge were two hanging glaciers which seemed to cling there in defiance of all laws of gravity. Below them again, the rocks, which were swept by the ice falling from these glaciers, curved steeply to the Tyndall Glacier, a thousand feet below us. The little we could see of the lower part of our proposed route up the ridge was not encouraging. An upward traverse over steep ice and snow-covered rock led to a notch between what we called the Grand and Petit gendarmes, and everything depended on our ability to turn the former by a traverse on the north side, which we could not see, in order to gain the ridge above it. What lay beyond we could not tell, and it seemed doubtful whether we should get far enough to learn. . . .

We were up at 3 A.M. on this eventful morning, left camp at 4:30 A.M., and were at the foot of the Joseph Glacier at dawn. Our steps were intact, so we mounted rapidly, this time taking to the rocks on the opposite side of the ice couloir, which brought us to the col at a point nearer to the foot of the west ridge. We were there by 8 A.M., and sat on its knife-edge for a breather with our legs dangling over the Tyndall Glacier below.

We roped up and began climbing, with S. leading, as he did from here to the top. The traverse across the south flank of the Petit Gendarme took time and care. The rocks were steep, exposed, and plastered with ice and snow, which had to be chipped or scraped away before foothold could be found on the rock beneath. We moved one at a time, crossing a series of rock ribs which effectually concealed from us what lay ahead. We liked the whole thing so little that there was some talk of retreat, but we agreed that we should at least gain the notch before admitting that we had bitten off more than we could chew.

This was at length reached by an ice couloir just before midday, when the usual mists began to envelop the peak and the upper part of our ridge. A halt was called to munch some chocolate before going on to have a look at the traverse on the north side of the Grand Gendarme. As the rocks on that side were dry and free from snow, and as the memory of what we had just climbed was fresh in our minds, we both preferred going on to going back. Some difficult rock had to be overcome before we succeeded at last in turning the Grand Gendarme and gaining the ridge once more above it, and twice the leader had to accept a shoulder from the second man wedged in a crack below. We were confronted now by a succession of pinnacles, none so imposing as the Grand Gendarme, but one or two gave just as much trouble to surmount. No turning movement below these was possible, for the ridge now fell away almost sheer on both sides, so that each had to be taken as it came.

Snow began falling lightly, but, as this seemed a daily occurrence of an afternoon, we were not unduly alarmed by it; indeed, so preoccupied were we with the climbing that it passed almost unheeded. We had now got to the point where the northeast ridge abutted against the west ridge, which here turns southward toward the summit, almost horizontally. Climbing along the crest on unstable rocks, we were presently faced by a great gap in the ridge into which it was impossible to climb. Conscious that by so doing we were denying ourselves the possibility of retreat, we lowered ourselves down into it.

Crossing the icy crest of the cap, more ridge work followed, the rock being now of a hard columnar formation which was very pleasant to handle. A patch of difficult ice just below the summit delayed but did not stop us, and at 4:15 we climbed, tired but elated, on to the summit of Batian. Except for the brief halts on the col and below the Grand Gendarme, we had been climbing continuously for twelve hours.

S. was familiar with the route down on the southeast side, but there were a bare two hours of daylight left, so, allowing only time to swallow each a small tin of meat essence, we began the descent. Crossing the Gate of the Mists between Batian and Nelion, we lost much valuable time by having to cut steps in hard, sticky ice. Nelion was climbed, and, without pause, we started down the other side. Things now began to happen. First the point of my ax was twisted clean off, and then, as I was descending a rock pitch with the ax hitched in the rope around my waist, a slip, which was immediately checked, jerked the ax free and it shot down the slope bound for the Lewis Glacier. At the same time S. was attacked with violent spasms of vomiting, which could only be attributed to the meat essence. Each bout of sickness necessitated a long halt and made him progressively weaker.

Our pace slowed, the light began to fade, and the rocks became almost too cold to handle. A bivouac was suggested, for with one man axless, one sick, and both tired, it was becoming questionable whether we could continue to climb safely, but a bitter east wind springing up banished all thoughts of a bivouac, and the light of the moon, which sailed out from behind some cloud, encouraged us to persevere. Very slowly and cautiously we climbed down, using the rope to lower ourselves wherever possible. The most vivid impression that remains in my mind of this grim ordeal is how S., in the feeble state he was, not only climbed, but led the way unerringly and safeguarded his companion.

At about 9 P.M. we descended by means of a final rappel onto the frozen snow of the Lewis Glacier, whence, unroping, we began the trudge up to Point Lenana, a snow ridge which had to be crossed on the way back to our camp some four or five hours' march away. Now that the tension was over we realized how exhausted we were. The gentle slope of hard snow in front of us appeared quite insuperable, and we now remembered that there was a hut lower down the glacier near a place called the Curling Pond. For this we headed, where, on reaching it about 10 P.M., we lay and shivered until the first streak of light encouraged us to start once more for our camp. S.'s sickness had passed off, and we got there by 8 A.M., when we promptly turned in and spent the rest of the day in bed. Our return home with the milk did not seem to surprise the faithful Saidi, nor did he display much curiosity as to what we had been doing since we left camp the previous morning. What did astonish him, I think, was our hunger, which took several days to appease.

A fictional set piece, of course, but neatly done. This passage is from Trevanian's bestseller of 1972, *The Eiger Sanction*.

# TREVANIAN

# "The Surface Was Moving Beneath Him"

There was a grating sound, and Anderl realized the surface was moving beneath him. A vast scab of crusted snow had loosened from the face and was slipping down, slowly at first, and he was in the middle of the doomed island. It was no use digging in; that would be like clinging to a falling boulder. Reacting automatically, he scrambled upward, seeking firm snow. Then he was tumbling sideward. He spread his limbs to stop the deadly roll and plunged his ax into the surface, covering it with his body. And still he slipped down and sideward, a deep furrow above him from the dig of his ax.

Jonathan had been huddled with Karl and Jean-Paul in the deep step he had just cut out. His eyes were fixed on the snow before him, his mind empty, and he shivered convulsively as he had at each *étape*. At Karl's shout, a sudden squirt of adrenaline stopped the shivering instantly and, his eyes glazed with fatigue, he watched with a stupid calm the snowslide come at him.

Karl pushed Jonathan down upon the encased corpse and covered both with his body, locking his fingers around the ice ax that was their belay point. The avalanche roared over them, deafening and suffocating, clutching at them, piling up under them, and trying to tug them away from their step.

And with a sudden ringing silence, it was over.

Jonathan clawed his way up past Karl's limp body and scooped the fresh snow out of the step. Then Karl scrambled up, panting, his hands bleeding, skin still stuck to the cold ax. Jean-Paul was half covered with snow, but he was still there.

"I can't move!" The voice was not far from them.

Anderl was spread-eagled on the surface of the snow, his feet not three meters from the edge of the rock cliff. The snowslide had carried him down, then had capriciously veered aside, over the others, and left him face down, his body still covering the ax that had broken his slide. He was unhurt, but each attempt to move caused him to slip downward a few inches. He tried twice, then had the good judgment to remain still.

He was just out of reach, and the freshly uncovered snow was too unstable to be crossed. The rope from Karl to Anderl lay in a hairpin loop up toward his earlier stance and back sharply, but only the two ends of it emerged from the snow. . . .

Anderl slipped down several inches, this time without attempting to move.

Jonathan and Karl tugged and whipped the rope, trying desperately to unbury it. They dared not pull with all their strength lest it suddenly come free and precipitate them off the face.

"I feel foolish," Anderl called. And he slipped farther down.

"Shut up!" Jonathan croaked. There was nothing for an ice piton to hold on to, so he hurriedly slapped his ax and Karl's deep into the soft snow, then he laced the slack they had tugged in from Anderl's line back and forth between the two ax handles. "Lie down on that," he ordered, and Karl mutely obeyed.

Jonathan unroped himself and started up Anderl's buried line, alternately clinging to it and ripping it out of the snow. Each time he gained a little slack he lay still on the steeply inclined surface as Karl whipped the loose rope around the axes. It was all-important that there be as little slack as possible when the line came free. Once he reached the point at which the rope began to curve down toward Anderl, he had to move quickly, knowing that he must be very close to Anderl when the line came free. Movement now was most awkward, and the adrenaline that had fed Jonathan's body was burning off, leaving heavy-limbed nausea in its stead. He wrapped his legs around the rope and tugged it loose with one hand, expecting at any moment to come sliding down on top of Anderl as they both snapped to the end of their slack.

It happened when they were only ten feet apart, and fate was in a humorous mood. The line slipped slowly out of the snow and they skidded gently sideward, Jonathan atop Anderl, until they were directly below Karl and the protection of the big step, their feet overhanging the lip of the rock cliff. They scrambled up with little difficulty.

The instant he fell into the almost vertical snow cave, Jonathan collapsed from within. He crouched near Jean-Paul's body, shivering uncontrollably, limp with fatigue.

Anderl was cheerful and talkative, and Karl was obedient. Between them they widened the step, and Anderl set about making tea. The first cup he gave to Jonathan with two small red pills, heart stimulants.

"I certainly felt ridiculous out there. I wanted to laugh, but I knew that the motion would make me slip, so I bit my lip. It was wonderful the way you came out to get me, Jonathan. But in the future I wish you would not use me to ride around on like a sled. I know what you were doing. Showing off for the people down on the terrace. Right?" He babbled on, brewing tea and passing it around like a solicitous Austrian aunt.

The heart stimulant and the tea began to make inroads on Jonathan's fatigue. He practiced controlling his shivering as he stared at the maroon ooze of blood around the rips in his pants. He knew he would not be able to stand another night in open bivouac. They had to move on. His exhalations were whimpers: for him, the last stages of fatigue. He was not certain how long he could continue to wield the ice ax. The muscles of his forearms were knotted and stiff, and his grip was a thing of rusted metal. He could clamp his fist shut or release it totally, but he had no control over the middle pressures.

He knew perfectly well that, in this condition, he should not be leading. But he did not dare turn the rope over to either of the younger men. Karl had retreated into automaton depression, and Anderl's brassy chatter had a disturbing note of hysteria about it.

They collected themselves to move out. As he took the metal cup back, Anderl examined Jonathan's gray-green eyes as though seeing him for the first time. "You're very good, you know, Jonathan. I've enjoyed climbing with you."

Jonathan forced a smile. "We'll make it."

Anderl grinned and shook his head. "No, I don't think so. But we shall continue with style."

They took the cliff quickly, rappelling on a doubled rope. That which looked most daring to Eiger Birds below was in reality much less demanding than slogging down through the snowfields. Evening was setting in, so they did not waste time retrieving Anderl's rope.

Months later it could still be seen dangling there, half rotten.

One more snowfield to cross and they would be perched above the station windows. The brutal cycle began again. It was colder now with the sun going. Jonathan set his jaw and turned off his mind. He cut step after step, the shocks against the ax head traveling up his throbbing arm directly to the nape of his neck. Chop. Step down. Lean out. Chop. And shiver convulsively as the others close up. The minutes were painfully long, the hours beyond the compass of human time.

This account was written in 1862, one year after Professor Tyndall and his trusted guide J. J. Bennen had notched the first ascent of the Weisshorn. Now linked with John Lubbock in an assault upon the Jungfrau, Tyndall is about to confront disaster and the unpleasant truth about Bennen's mettle under stress. (See the piece by Philip C. Gossett earlier in this volume, "The Death of Bennen.")

# JOHN TYNDALL

# Rescue from a Crevasse

From the Rhone Glacier we proceeded down the Rhone Valley to Fiesch, whence, in the cool twilight, all three of us ascended to the Hotel Jungfrau, on the Eggishorn. This we made our headquarters for some days, and here Lubbock and I decided to ascend the Jungfrau. The proprietor of the hotel keeps guides for this excursion, but his charges are so high as to be almost prohibitory. I, however, needed no guide in addition to my faithful Bennen; but simply a porter of sufficient strength and skill to follow where he led. In the village of Laax, Bennen found such a porter — a young man named Bielander, who had the reputation of being both courageous and strong. He was the only son of his mother, and she was a widow.

This young man and a second porter we sent on with our provisions to the Grotto of the Faulberg, where we were to spend the night. Between the Eggishorn and this cave the glacier presents no difficulty which the most ordinary caution cannot overcome, and the thought of danger in connection with it never occurred to us. An hour and a half after the departure of our porters we slowly wended our way to the lake of Märjelen, which we skirted, and were soon upon the ice. The middle of the glacier was almost as smooth as a carriage road, cut here and there by musical brooks produced by the superficial ablation. To Lubbock the scene opened out with the freshness of a new revelation, as, previously to this year, he had never been among the glaciers of the Alps.

To me, though not new, the region had lost no trace of the interest with which I first viewed it. We moved briskly along the frozen incline, until, after a couple of hours' march, we saw a solitary human being standing on the lateral moraine of the glacier, near the point where we were to quit it for the cave of the Faulberg.

At first this man excited no attention. He stood and watched us, but did not come toward us, until finally our curiosity was aroused by observing that he was one of our own two men. The glacier here is always cut by crevasses, which, while they present no real difficulty, require care. We approached our porter, but he never moved; and when we came up to him he looked stupid, and did not speak until he was spoken to. Bennen addressed him in the patois of the place, and he answered in the same patois. His answer must have been more than usually obscure, for Bennen misunderstood the most important part of it. "My God!" he exclaimed, turning to us, "Walters is killed!" Walters was the guide at the Eggishorn, with whom, in the present instance, we had nothing to do. "No, not Walters," responded the man; "it is my comrade that is killed." Bennen looked at him with a wild bewildered stare. "How killed?" he exclaimed. "Lost in a crevasse," was the reply. We were all so stunned that for some moments we did not quite seize the import of the terrible statement. Bennen at length tossed his arms in the air, exclaiming, "Jesu Maria! What am I to do?" With the swiftness that some ascribe to dreams, I surrounded the fact with imaginary adjuncts, one of which was that the man had been drawn dead from the crevasse, and was now a corpse in the cave of the Faulberg, for I took it for granted that, had he been still entombed, his comrade would have run or called for our aid. Several times in succession the porter affirmed that the missing man was certainly dead. "How does he know that he is dead?" Lubbock demanded. "A man is sometimes rendered insensible by a fall without being killed." This question was repeated in German, but met with the same dogmatic response. "Where is the man?" I asked. "There," replied the porter, stretching his arm toward the glacier. "In the crevasse?" A stolid "Ja!" was the answer. It was with difficulty that I quelled an imprecation. "Lead the way to the place, you blockhead," and he led the way.

We were soon beside a wide and jagged cleft which resembled a kind of cave more than an ordinary crevasse. This cleft had been spanned by a snow bridge, now broken, and to the edge of which footsteps could be traced. The glacier at the place was considerably torn, but simple patience was the only thing needed to unravel its complexity. This quality our porter lacked, and, hoping to make shorter work of it, he attempted to cross the bridge. It gave way, and he went down, carrying an immense load of debris along with him. We looked into the hole, at one end of which the vision was cut short by darkness, while immediately under the broken bridge it was crammed with snow and shattered icicles. We saw nothing more. We listened with strained attention, and from the depths of the glacier issued a low moan. Its repetition assured us that it was no delusion — the man was still alive. Bennen from the first had been extremely excited; and the fact of his having, as a Catholic, saints and angels to appeal to, augmented his emotion. When he heard the moaning he became almost frantic. He attempted to get into the crevasse, but was obliged to recoil. It was quite plain that a second life was in danger, for my guide seemed to have lost all self-control. I placed my hand heavily upon his shoulder, and admonished him that upon his coolness depended the life of his friend. "If you behave like a man, we shall save him; if like a woman, he is lost."

A first-rate rope accompanied the party, but unhappily it was with the man in the crevasse. Coats, waistcoats, and braces were instantly taken off and knotted together. I watched Bennen while this work was going on; his hands trembled with excitement, and his knots were evidently insecure. The last junction complete, he exclaimed, "Now let me down!" "Not until each of these knots has been tested; not an inch!" Two of them gave way, and Lubbock's waistcoat also proved too tender for the strain. The debris was about forty feet from the surface of the glacier, but two intermediate prominences afforded a kind of footing. Bennen was dropped down upon one of these; I followed, being let down by Lubbock and the other porter. Bennen then descended the remaining distance, and was followed by me. More could not find room.

The shape and size of the cavity were such as to produce a kind of resonance, which rendered it difficult to fix the precise spot from which the sound issued; but the moaning continued, becoming to all appearance gradually feebler. Fearing to wound the man, the ice rubbish was cautiously rooted away; it rang curiously as it fell into the adjacent gloom. A layer two or three feet thick was thus removed; and finally, from the frozen mass, and so bloodless as to be almost as white as the surrounding snow, issued a single human hand. The fingers moved. Around it we rooted, cleared the arm, and reached the knapsack, which we cut away. We also regained our rope. The man's head was then laid bare, and my brandy flask was immediately at his lips. He tried to speak, but his words jumbled themselves to a dull moan. Bennen's feelings got the better of him at intervals; he wrought like a hero, but at times he needed guidance and stern admonition. The arms once free, we passed the rope underneath them, and tried to draw the man out. But the ice fragments around him had regelated so as to form a solid case. Thrice we essayed to draw him up, thrice we failed; he had literally to be hewn out of the ice, and not until his last foot was extricated were we able to lift him. By pulling him from above, and pushing him from below, the man was at length raised to the surface of the glacier.

For an hour we had been in the crevasse in shirt sleeves — the porter had been in it for two hours — and the dripping ice had drenched us. Bennen, moreover, had worked with the energy of madness, and now the reaction came. He shook as if he would fall to pieces; but brandy and some dry covering revived him. The rescued man was helpless, unable to stand, unable to utter an articulate sentence. Bennen proposed to carry him down the glacier toward home. Had this been attempted, the man would certainly have died upon the ice. Bennen thought he could carry him for two hours; but the guide underrated his own exhaustion and overrated the vitality of the porter. "It cannot be thought of," I said; "to the cave of Faulberg, where we must tend him as well as we can." We got him to the side of the glacier, where Bennen took him on his back; in ten minutes he sank under his load. It was now my turn, so I took the man on my back and plodded on with him as far as I was able. Helping each other thus by turns, we reached the mountain grot.

The sun had set, and the crown of the Jungfrau was embedded in amber light. Thinking that the Märjelen See might be reached before darkness, I proposed starting in search of help. Bennen protested against my going alone, and I thought I noticed moisture in Lubbock's eye. Such an occasion brings out a man's feeling if he have any. I gave them both my blessing and made for the glacier. But my anxiety to get quickly clear of the crevasses defeated its own object. Thrice I found myself in difficulty, and the light was visibly departing. The conviction deepened that persistence would be folly, and the most impressive moment of my existence was that on which I stopped at the brink of a profound fissure and looked upon the mountains and the sky. The serenity was perfect—not a cloud, not a breeze, not a sound, while the last hues of sunset spread over the solemn west.

I returned; warm wine was given to our patient, and all our dry clothes were wrapped around him. Hot water bottles were placed at his feet, and his back was briskly rubbed. He continued to groan a long time; but, finally, both this and the trembling ceased. Bennen watched him solemnly, and at length muttered in anguish, "Sir, he is dead!" I leaned over the man and found him breathing gently; I felt his pulse—it was beating tranquilly. "Not dead, dear old Bennen; he will be able to crawl home with us in the morning." The prediction was justified by the event; and two days afterward we saw him at Laax, minus a bit of his ear, with a bruise upon his cheek, and a few scars upon his hand, but without a broken bone or serious injury of any kind.

The self-denying conduct of the second porter made us forget his stupidity—it may have been stupefaction. As I lay there wet, through the long hours of that dismal night, I almost registered a vow never to tread upon a glacier again. But, like the forces in the physical world, human emotions vary with the distance from their origin, and a year afterward I was again upon the ice.

Did you ever wonder where the term "cliffhanger" came from? This 1945 novel is surely not the source, but it does serve as a model of sweaty-palm storytelling. Ullman, a first-rate climber, has contributed much to the nonfiction side of mountaineering literature as well, notably his history, *The Age of Mountaineering*.

# JAMES RAMSEY ULLMAN

# The White Tower

He was lying in the cleft, and the cleft was a gateway to the west.

There was the north wall of the Weissturm, below him and to the right, falling away in precipice after precipice into a sea of space. There were the other peaks of the Kandermatt Range, lying flattened and remote beneath the blue miles, and beyond them, sprawling wildly into the distance, the crumpled, snow-choked wilderness of the Pennines and the Oberland. They were all there before him now, the great peaks and ranges of the heart of Europe, exactly as he had seen them on so many other unforgotten mornings beneath the trembling, tapering wings of Mitchell or Marauder. The solemn crags of Monte Rosa and the Mischabel; the jutting spires of the Matterhorn, Weisshorn, Finsteraarhorn; the Jungfrau, Eiger, Mönch, Schreckhorn; and, above and beyond them all, the immense dome of Mont Blanc arching white and glittering into the stainless sky. Between the ranges, deep and hidden, were the valleys and lakes and villages that were Switzerland. Beyond them, spreading still and mist-sheathed to the farthest horizon, were the blue, distant foothills that were France.

His eyes knew the familiar contours. His tongue knew the familiar names. But they were no more real to him now than the painted patterns of a canvas cyclorama on some remote and implausible stage.

He drew his handkerchief from his pocket and held it first around one and then the other of his torn and bleeding hands. He opened his mouth wide and sucked great draughts of the thin, freezing air into his burning lungs. His eyes slowly followed the trail of footprints that led down from the gateway of the cleft along a gentle snow slope, dipped to a narrow saddle between the north and east faces of the mountain, and disappeared up an equally gentle snow slope at the base of the summit pyramid.

It is only a walk, he thought.

He leaned back against the rocks of the cleft, closing his eyes.

You should eat something, he thought.

He found a cracker in the rucksack and took a bite from it, but the dry flakes rasped like splinters in his throat, and after a moment he spat them out. Then he tried a sliver of chocolate, but it turned instantly into a thick, doughy pellet against his tongue. For a few minutes he sat bent forward, his forehead against his drawn-up knees, retching and coughing. Then he opened the canteen and took a sip of water. He did not feel the water at all in his mouth or throat, but only in his stomach, when it got there, lying cold and heavy as stone. A moment later he was retching again, coughing again.

He got up and closed the rucksack and slung it on his shoulders and wiped his hands again with the handkerchief and pulled on his inner gloves and then his outer gloves and picked up his ice ax.

"All right—let's go," he said.

He felt suddenly very strong and lightheaded and lighthearted, but when he tried to sing a snatch of song no sound came out from between his cracked lips, and when he turned to smile at Carla she was not there.

He followed the slope down, looking intently at the footprints in the snow before him. Not at the blue space on either side of him nor at the mountaintops below him nor at the mountaintop above, but only at the firm, even-spaced footprints in the snow. He followed them to the bottom of the slope, across the narrow bridgelike saddle, and up the slope on the far side. When he reached the crest and turned to look back, the shoulder and the Watchtower and the cleft between were already far beneath him, a remote and insubstantial gray silhouette superimposed upon the blue-white depths beyond. He tried to sing again, but again no sound came out. And Carla was still . . .

He shook his head sharply. This is no good, he thought. No good at all.

He sat down on the frozen snow. This time he did not lie back or close his eyes or try to eat or drink, but merely sat quietly, drawing in slow, deep breaths, sucking the oxygen from the air into his lungs and blood and brain. When he stood up again he felt steadier. He pushed back the wristlet of his mitten and looked at his watch. It was half-past eight. Holding the watch closer, he looked at the second hand circling its measured, unhurried way around the dial; then he held it to his ear, under the flap of his helmet, listening to its precise, metallic clicking. Yes, he felt steadier now. He felt very steady.

Turning, he stared up the mountainside. Directly beyond the crest on which he stood the snow flattened out into an almost level ramp for a distance of perhaps a hundred feet; then it climbed in another long slope to a second crest and, beyond that, to a third and a fourth. It was more like a sea than a mountain, he thought — a bright, sungleaming sea seen from the gunwale of a heeling boat, tilting in great frozen billows toward the sky. Beyond the fourth crest, which jutted out more steeply and boldly than the others, he could see only blue space. There might be more slopes, more crests, behind it — or there might be the walls of the Citadel. It could not be so very much farther now to the Citadel: about fifteen hundred feet, Andreas had said, from the shoulder to its base, and he was already standing a good three or four hundred above the shoulder. Suddenly he was aware that his heart had begun to pound again, but this time it was neither from exhaustion nor from fear.

He took the binoculars from the rucksack, raised them to his eyes, and swept them slowly over the white waste above. A zigzagging trail of footprints leaped into focus before him, and steep blue pitches of glare ice and granulated drifts and hummocks of snow. But there was no human figure. Nothing moved. Lowering his glasses, he slung them by their strap around his neck; then he put on his rucksack again and started up the slope.

He put one foot in front of the other. He put one foot above the other. He kicked and stepped, kicked and stepped, in slow monotonous rhythm, and the humps and cracks and ripples of the snow crept slowly and monotonously past beneath his down-turned eyes. From the crest of the second slope he could still see three crests above him. And at the crest of the third there were still three. Wave upon wave the frozen snow masses rose above him, their reflected sunglare beating down upon him with a fierce white incandescent light.

On the fourth crest he stopped and put on his snow goggles. On the sixth — or perhaps it was the seventh — he stopped again and sat down to rest, his elbows propped on his knees and his forehead resting on the cold steel head of his ax. He was tired now — very tired. His feet felt like two enormous lumps of iron on the ends of his legs, and a deep, throbbing bone ache was spreading in slow waves from his knees and thighs into every joint and cranny of his body. There is no hurry, he thought. No hurry at all. You can close your eyes and lie back in the snow a minute. For just a few minutes. . . .

He jerked himself to his feet. For a few moments he stood motionless, the upper part of his body swaying a little as he leaned for support on his ax. Then he began to climb again. He kicked, stepped, kicked, stepped. He put one foot in front of the other; one foot above the other. The white tilting billows of the mountain rolled down past him like a sea.

And as he climbed on — with the snow slipping by, and the yards and footprints and the minutes slipping by, and time and distance and the mountain and the sky all slipping silently by together — as he put his left boot before his right boot and then his right boot before his left boot, he became gradually aware that a curious thing had begun to happen to him. His body was numb now; it felt muffled and remote, scarcely any longer a part of him at all. But his mind and perceptions were growing clearer. Plodding step by step up the unending mountainside, it seemed to him as if the stainless clarity of that high, gleaming world were slowly and magically being distilled into his own brain and senses. The sky was a bluer blue than he had ever seen before, the snow a whiter white. The contours of the slope above no longer sprawled away in a confused and meaningless blur of distance, but rose up still and frozen before him in sharp-edged focus. Where before there had only been mass and height, only snow and sky, all was now substance and form, color and texture, detail upon minute detail, piled one upon the other, blending one into the other, separate from and yet a part of each other, infinitely complex and yet infinitely clear. He felt the steel of his ax through the two thicknesses of his mittens and the cold thin air against the sweat of his forehead and the tiny crunching contraction of each pinpoint of snow beneath the thick, nailed soles of his boots. He smelled the wool of his sweaters and the leather of boots and harness and his own man-smell and the fresh snow on the slope and the older snow beneath it and the ancient ice beneath them both. He saw the great lift of the snow, the structure and texture of a mountaintop of snow, and he saw too the smallness and closeness and secrecy of the snow, its humps and hollows and cracks and wind-ripples, the structure and texture of its flakes, its grains and molecules. He felt and smelled and saw these things not one after the other, but all at once, all together. He *knew* them all together. It was as if slowly, as he climbed, one veil after another were being withdrawn from between him and the apprehensible world, until all that had once been hidden was now revealed, all that had been secret was made known. He kicked and stepped, kicked and stepped. He moved slowly and steadily upward through the snow; through the white billows of the mountain; through the purity and stillness of time.

And then, presently, within the stillness . . .

He stopped and stood quite still. He stood leaning on his ice ax, his eyes narrowed, listening, but the only sounds were the faint soft crunch of snow beneath his boots and the measured rasping of his breath in his throat. His eyes moved slowly over the slope above; then he turned and stared down the slope below. There was only sky and sun and snow and the footprints in the snow. There was only silence and space.

And yet the illusion that he had heard a sound persisted; the illusion — if it *was* an illusion — that he was no longer alone. His mind went back to the night on the lower terrace when he and Radcliffe had sat listening to the distant humming of the wind; to the Englishman's description of the presence that filled the stillness on the frozen wastes of Everest. . . . *Mallory used to say it was ourselves. The selves we were trying to leave behind.* . . . He shook his head and closed his eyes, pressing the lids tightly against the balls. Opening them again, he did not look up or down the mountainside but moved his gaze slowly and deliberately from one close, tangible object to another: from the minute globules of snow on his boots to the smooth yellow wool of his mittens. He raised his arm, pushed back the wristlet of the mitten, and looked at his watch.

The hands still pointed to half-past eight.

He brought the watch closer to his goggled eyes, staring at the second hand that slanted motionless across the dial. He held it against his ear, under his helmet, and fumbled with the stem through the awkward thicknesses of his mittens. A sudden hollowness of panic filled him, and he twisted and jabbed at the stem and shook his arm violently; but the thing that was strapped to his wrist was merely an inert functionless rectangle of glass and steel. Dropping his arm to his side, he stood looking about him again at the snow and the sky. The sun was high over his left shoulder now: to the east—or was it the southeast?—or the south? He turned, circling slowly, but the sun seemed to follow him around. It seemed to be blazing down on him, not from any one point in the sky, but from the whole sky, from the snow, from everywhere.

He stood still again, staring up the slope, listening again. There was no sound. Nothing moved. He began climbing again. And the sun and the silence climbed after him.

There was the snow and the footprints in the snow. There was the slope and the crest, and the next slope and the next crest, the slope and the crest beyond. There was the smooth, ice-veined wall of the Citadel rising sheer into the sky beyond the last crest. There was a ramp of snow curving around the wall to the right, and a sharp bend in the ramp, and the ramp narrowing and steepening, and beyond the ramp the summits of the Alps and the blue valleys that were Switzerland and the blue horizon that was France. There was Siegfried Hein standing beyond the next bend in the ramp and turning and looking at him, his eyes very gray and steady in his sun-blackened face.

Ordway stopped.

You must think clearly now, he thought. His eyes moved over the muffled figure, over the torn boots and the great jagged rents at the knees and elbows, and back to the burned, stubbled face and the gray eyes. You must think and talk very clearly now.

"You have changed your mind, I see," Hein said.

He nodded.

"A long, hard climb, is it not?"

"Yes."

"But you found the footprints and the piton helpful, perhaps?"

"Yes, I found them very helpful."

He could not feel his tongue or lips moving, and the words stuck like thick lumps in his throat. Suddenly he leaned against the rock wall beside him, choking and coughing.

Hein watched him in silence. "You will excuse me if I go on now?" he said presently.

Ordway started to speak, choked again, and stood crouched with his head against the rock. Then the paroxysm passed and he turned slowly back to the German.

"On?" he repeated thickly.

"To the top."

"I'm going to the top too."

Hein shrugged. "That is up to you, of course." His eyes were still fixed on Ordway's face. "Permit me to make a suggestion, however, Herr Kapitän. Do not waste your time trying to climb the rock."

Ordway's gaze moved slowly upward over the vertical ice-sheathed wall of the Citadel.

"It's the same all around?" he asked.

"Yes, it is the same all around. I have reconnoitered it for more than an hour and made a start in two or three places; but it is unclimbable. You will forgive me, perhaps, that I was not even able to hammer in a piton for our mutual convenience."

Ordway looked at him for a long moment in silence. Very steady now, he thought. Very clear and sure and steady . . .

"And this ledge?" he asked.

"Is the one possibility."

Ordway moved forward to a point a few feet beyond the German and peered around a protruding buttress in the rock wall along the curving flange of the ramp. Only a short pitch of precipice remained above them—twenty vertical feet, perhaps, twenty-five at the most—with the ramp cutting diagonally upward across its face. It was far narrower and steeper than the section on which they stood—a mere ribbon of snow clinging to the mountainside. But it was there. It extended in an unbroken path to the top of the Citadel and ended in a broad, jutting platform of rock above.

Ordway turned back to Hein.

"It looks all right," he said.

"Yes, it does, doesn't it?"

"Let's go, then."

He took another step forward, but stopped suddenly when he saw that the other had not moved. For a moment the two men looked at each other in silence.

"I would not be quite so impatient if I were you, Herr Kapitän," said Hein quietly. "If, for example, you would take the trouble, as I did, to study the ledge ahead from various angles, you would perhaps notice something that will change your mind."

Ordway's eyes moved from Hein back to the ramp. He pressed himself in against the precipice wall and stared upward. Then he crouched and leaned outward. Digging his fingers and toes into the snow, he inched the upper part of his body out over the rim of the ledge until at last he could see what lay beyond and beneath it. And in that same instant he saw what Hein had meant. The section of the ramp on which they stood was, in effect, the sloping top of a bulge in the cliffs below, and the snow that covered it rested on a firm, if narrow, base of solid rock. But directly ahead, where the ramp steepened across the final pitch, the bulge no longer existed. The ribbon of snow that formed its surface was not a covering over rock beneath, but merely a cornice or unsupported platform, clinging of its own adhesiveness to the face of the precipice. Below it was no firm outthrust of the mountainside, but 8,000 feet of air.

Ordway stood up slowly.

"It wouldn't hold a man," he said.

Hein shook his head. "No, it would not hold a man."

"Then—"

He felt the gray eyes on his face again—the gray eyes, steady and mocking.

"Then if you will let me by, Herr Kapitän"—Hein moved past him for a step or two, stopped again and stood staring up along the ramp—"I shall be starting now."

"But how can you? Which way?"

"You have heard of a hand traverse, perhaps?"

"Yes, but —" He broke off abruptly, his eyes following Hein's along the sheer face beyond. And now for the first time he saw that there was a crack in the smooth surface of the rock. Beginning not more than two yards ahead of where they stood, it slanted upward across the precipice, roughly parallel to the snow ramp and about five feet above it, and ended where the ramp ended, at the base of the jutting platform above. It was a thin, hairline crack, far too narrow and shallow to hold a booted foot; but its lower lip seemed to curl upward and outward just enough to support the grasp of a man's tightly curved fingers.

Ordway's eyes went back to Hein.

"It's at least forty feet," he said.

"Yes."

"And a thirty-degree angle."

"Yes."

"But you think you can make it?"

"Yes, I think I can make it."

There was another silence between them. Ordway looked once again at the thin, slanting crack and the ribbon of snow beneath it and the gulf of space beyond. Then he quietly unslung his rope from his shoulder.

"All right," he said.

Hein looked at him without speaking.

"Shall we go?" asked Ordway.

The German shook his head slowly. "I am going alone," he said.

"We're going together."

"No. Whether you try to follow me or not is your own affair, although having seen your attempts at climbing I would advise most strongly against it. But I am afraid I have finished with dragging you and your companions to the top of the Weissturm."

Ordway stood straight and still, his palms flattened against the rock behind him. For a moment the only sound was the deep rasping of his breath in his throat.

"I am not asking you to help me," he said quietly.

"No? What then?"

"I'm suggesting that we help each other."

"You are under the impression then that I need your help?"

"As much as I need yours." Ordway held out the rope. "Here. Tie it on."

Hein did not move.

"Tie it on, I say!"

He heard his own voice, tiny and hoarse and straining in the silence of snow and sky. He saw the gray walls of the Citadel and the white glint of a slope above the eaves. He felt the tautness of his body, the straining of his lungs, the wild pounding of his heart.

"We've come this far together, Hein," he said. "Let's finish it together. . . ."

The German stared at him silently for a moment. The eyes in the blackened, bearded, ice-crusted face were now no longer mocking, but as cold and hard and bleak as stone. "No," he said, his voice low and even, "we will not finish it together. I will finish it alone, and you will not finish it at all. And shall I tell you why that is the way it will be, Captain Ordway? It is because I am strong and you are weak. It is because I have the courage and the skill and the will to do it, and you have not. It is because I am a German climbing for Germany, and you are not climbing for anything, but only running away."

Ordway did not speak. He did not move. He stood there, as immobile and frozen as the mountain wall behind him, the coil of rope in his extended hand.

What happened then remained in his memory afterward not as remembered reality but as the blurred images and sensations of a half-apprehended dream. There was the sudden great surge of anger rising within him; an anger such as he had never felt in his life before; an engulfing and consuming tide that was more than anger, deeper and colder and more bitter than anger. There was Hein standing in front of him, Hein turning away again and moving slowly up the ramp. There was the wild, shaken, despairing instant in which he was about to hurl himself forward upon him. . . . But he did not hurl himself forward. He still neither spoke nor moved. . . . And now, as he stood watching, Siegfried Hein approached the lower end of the unsupported snow ramp, studied the slanting crack in the rock above, and, grasping its lower lip with the fingers of both hands, swung himself out onto the face of the precipice.

With slow, measured movements the German pulled himself across and upward, his head and shoulders held close in against the line of the crack, his feet dragging without pressure along the surface of the snow below. His right hand slid forward, gripped, and pulled. Then his body moved after it as the left hand slipped forward too. He reached, gripped, pulled, reached again. After each five or six swings he rested a moment, with his hands close together in the crack and his chin resting on its outcurving lip. Then he moved on again. Presently he was halfway to the rock platform above. Perhaps a minute later he was two-thirds of the way. And still he moved on, steadily and silently. The only movement in that enormous stillness of snow and air was the slow, rhythmic motion of his hands and body. The only sound was the faint scraping of his clothing against the wall of rock.

And then suddenly, startlingly, there was another sound. . . .

With a sharp, dry crack the lip of the crevice to which Hein was clinging broke away from under his hands. For a terrible timeless instant Ordway heard the scratch of his bootnails against the rock and saw his fingers clawing at the wall. Then he was no longer clinging to the wall at all but standing on the unsupported snow ramp below. The snow trembled, seemed for a moment to be slowly buckling under his weight . . . and held.

Then there was silence again. Hein did not move. Nothing moved.

"Can you get back on the wall?" Ordway called.

The German did not answer. For a few moments he remained frozen where he stood; then very slowly and cautiously, without moving his feet, he raised his arms and groped upward to the right along the rock wall. Apparently, however, he could find no hold. Lowering his arms, he stood staring down at the snow, and Ordway could see that he was carefully shifting his weight and advancing one foot, inch by inch, in front of the other. He took one step, then a second. But he never took the third. For in the next instant the snow directly in front of him disappeared. It did not seem to break away or to fall. It was just soundlessly and magically no longer there. In the spot where Hein had been about to set his foot there was now revealed the blue sea of air that washed the 8,000-foot north face of the Weissturm.

Ordway shut his eyes, but only for a second, and when he opened them Hein was still miraculously there.

"Don't move!" he heard his voice calling. "Don't move an inch!"

And at the same moment he realized that, without having thought it or willed it, he himself had begun to move; that he had unslung his pack and dropped his ax and rope; that he was edging toward the snow ramp, grasping the crack above it with bare hands, swinging himself out onto the precipice beyond. . . .

He kept his face to the mountainside and his eyes on the gray rock creeping past them. He reached, gripped, pulled, reached again. He clung motionless to the lip of the crack, counted ten, and swung on again. When at last he turned and looked ahead he was no more than ten or twelve feet from the point where Hein stood. When he turned for the second time he was almost within arm's reach of him.

Directly ahead of him now was the section of the crack from which the lip had broken away in Hein's grasp. Slanting diagonally upward above the German's head, it was now no more than the merest fold in the vertical rock, shorn clean of all protuberances or roughnesses on which a hand or finger could secure a grip. It was not a long section — a yard across perhaps, four feet at the most — and beyond it the crack was deep and flanged again, cutting upward in its final stretch to the summit of the rock wall and the jutting platform above. But the point at which the lip began was still a foot or more beyond Hein's grasp, and between him and its granite safety was the jagged hole in the snow ramp and blue depths of space. Ordway's eyes moved back to Hein and from Hein to the point in the lower section of the crack to which he himself was clinging. Here, too, there was a distance of perhaps a foot between the German's farthest possible grasp and the nearest projection of the lip. But there was one difference. On the far side there was only one man's reach to bridge the gap, and on this side there were two.

"The crack's strong enough here to hold the two of us," Ordway said quietly. "I'm going to reach out my hand. Don't move until you're sure you have a grip on it. When I pull, jump."

He shifted his left hand to the securest grip he could find and jammed his elbow deep into the crack. Then he swiveled slowly around and extended his right hand until it was within two feet of Hein's shoulders.

"Take it," he said.

Hein did not move.

"Take it!"

But even as he spoke he knew now, with sudden and absolute certainty, that Siegfried Hein was not going to take his hand. The German stood, motionless and silent, looking at him, and Ordway looked back at him across the intervening yard of space and the arc of his extended arm. He saw the square-lined, blackened face and the tight, rigid flesh of the cheeks and jawline. He saw the snow-flecked stubble of the beard and the greased, frozen crack of the thin lips and the minute glistening beads of sweat that coursed slowly down through the grease and stubble and flecks of snow. He saw the bleak-gray unmoving eyes and the bleakness behind the eyes. And in the same instant it seemed to him that he was seeing everything that was behind the eyes. For one flashing, timeless instant on that forlorn and timeless mountainside he looked into a man's eyes, and everything that the man was was there. He saw it all now, naked and manifest before him: the frustration and bitterness and contumacy; the fear and the pride and the bottomless sterility of pride; the despairing lonely hunger of the unloving and unloved; the will to conquer and the will to die. . . .

He saw it all. And then he saw the face turning from him, Hein turning away from him, advancing one foot slowly in front of the other, reaching out with both arms toward the upper section of the crack that slanted upward toward the platform at the summit of the cliff. He saw him stop and crouch, motionless. He saw him leap toward the rock wall, hit it, grasp it, cling to it, claw at it, slip from it, fall slowly backward from it onto the snow ramp. Hein did not seem to hit the snow. He simply disappeared through it, soundlessly. In the same instant the ramp itself was gone. Then there was only silence and stillness again, and the mountain wall curving downward, and a few puffs and shreds of spindrift wreathing gently in the windless air.

Martin Ordway hung from the crack and stared dully at the wall of rock from which the snow had broken away. The ramp was gone, and in its place was space — but not only space. For along the line where the concealing snow had joined the mountainside there was now revealed a narrow but solid flange of granite, banding the smooth face of the Citadel. He lowered himself to it, edged along it, grasped the lip of the crack on the far side, pulled himself forward and upward. . . .

This deliciously absurd story is presumably true, or at the least fundamentally true. Waugh's travels on journalistic assignments in eastern Africa and southern Arabia in the 1920s included a visit to Aden, which on the whole he liked, no matter what you read here. The selection appeared in *Remote People*, a volume of essays published in 1930.

# EVELYN WAUGH

# Tricky Bits

Nothing in my earlier acquaintance with Mr. Leblanc had given me any reason to suspect what I was letting myself in for when I accepted his invitation to join him in his little walk over the rocks. He was a general merchant, commercial agent, and shipowner of importance, the only European magnate in the Settlement; they said of him that he thrived on risk and had made and lost more than one considerable fortune in his time. I met him dining at the Residency, on my first evening in Aden. He talked of Abyssinia, where he had heavy business undertakings, with keen sarcasm; he expressed his contempt for the poetry of Rimbaud; he told me a great deal of very recent gossip about people in Europe; he produced, from the pocket of his white waistcoat, a press cutting about Miss Rebecca West's marriage; after dinner he played some very new gramophone records he had brought with him. . . .

A day or two afterward he invited me to dinner at his house in Crater. A smart car with a liveried Indian chauffeur came to fetch me. We dined on the roof; a delicious dinner; iced *vin rosé* — "It is not a luxurious wine, but I am fond of it; it grows on a little estate of my own in the South of France" — and the finest Yemen coffee. With his very thin gold watch in his hand, Mr. Leblanc predicted the rising of a star — I forget which. Punctual to the second, it appeared, green and malevolent, on the rim of the hills; cigars glowing under the night sky; from below the faint murmur of the native streets; all infinitely smooth and civilized.

At this party a new facet was revealed to me in the character of my host. Mr. Leblanc the man of fashion I had seen. Here was Mr. Leblanc the patriarch. The house where we sat was the top story of his place of business; at the table sat his daughter, his secretary, and three of his "young men." The young men were his clerks, learning the business. One was French, the other two English lately down from Cambridge. They worked immensely hard—often, he told me, ten hours a day; often halfway through the night, when a ship was in. They were not encouraged to go to the club or to mix in the society of Steamer Point. They lived together in a house near Mr. Leblanc's; they lived very well and were on terms of patriarchal intimacy with Mr. Leblanc's family. "If they go up to Steamer Point, they start drinking, playing cards, and spending money. Here, they work so hard that they cannot help saving. When they want a holiday they go around the coast visiting my agencies. They learn to know the country and the people; they travel in my ships; at the end of a year or two they have saved nearly all their money and they have learned business. For exercise we take little walks over the rocks together. Tennis and polo would cost them money. To walk in the hills is free. They get up out of the town into the cool air, the views are magnificent, the gentle exercise keeps them in condition for their work. It takes their minds, for a little, off business. You must come with us one day on one of our walks."

I agreed readily. After the torpid atmosphere of Aden it would be delightful to take some gentle exercise in the cool air. And so it was arranged for the following Saturday afternoon. When I left, Mr. Leblanc lent me a copy of Gide's *Voyage au Congo*.

Mr. Leblanc the man of fashion I knew, and Mr. Leblanc the patriarch. On Saturday I met Mr. Leblanc the man of action, Mr. Leblanc the gambler.

I was to lunch first with the young men at their "mess"—as all communal *ménages* appear to be called in the East. I presented myself dressed as I had seen photographs of "hikers," with shorts, open shirt, stout shoes, woollen stockings, and large walking stick. We had an excellent luncheon, during which they told me how, one evening, they had climbed into the Parsees' death house, and what a row there had been about it. Presently one of them said, "Well, it's about time to change. We promised to be round at the old man's at half-past."

"Change?"

"Well, it's just as you like, but I think you'll find those things rather hot. We usually wear nothing except shoes and shorts. We leave our shirts in the cars. They meet us on the bathing beach. And if you've got any rubber-soled shoes I should wear them. Some of the rocks are pretty slippery." Luckily I happened to have some rubber shoes. I went back to the chaplain's house, where I was then living, and changed. I was beginning to be slightly apprehensive.

Mr. Leblanc looked magnificent. He wore newly creased white shorts, a silk openwork vest, and white *espadrilles* laced like a ballet dancer's around his ankles. He held a tuberose, sniffing it delicately. "They call it an Aden lily sometimes," he said. "I can't think why."

There was with him another stranger, a guest of Mr. Leblanc's on a commercial embassy from an oil firm. "I say, you know," he confided in me, "I think this is going to be a bit stiff. I'm scarcely in training for anything very energetic."

We set out in the cars and drove to a dead end at the face of the cliffs near the ancient reservoirs. I thought we must have taken the wrong road, but everyone got out and began stripping off his shirt. The Leblanc party went hatless; the stranger and I retained our topees.

"I should leave those sticks in the car," said Mr. Leblanc.

"But shan't we find them useful?" (I still nursed memories of happy scrambles in the Wicklow Hills.)

"You will find them a great nuisance," said Mr. Leblanc.

We did as we were advised.

Then the little walk started. Mr. Leblanc led the way with light, springing steps. He went right up to the face of the cliff, gaily but purposefully, as Moses may have approached the rocks from which he was about to strike water. There was a little crack running like fork lightning down the blank wall of stone. Mr. Leblanc stood below it, gave one little skip, and suddenly, with great rapidity and no apparent effort, proceeded to ascend the precipice. He did not climb; he rose. It was as if someone were hoisting him up from above and he had merely to prevent himself from swinging out of the perpendicular, by keeping contact with rocks in a few light touches of foot and hand.

In just the same way, one after another, the Leblanc party were whisked away out of sight. The stranger and I looked at each other. "Are you all right?" came reverberating down from very far ahead. We began to climb. We climbed for about half an hour up the cleft in the rock. Not once during that time did we find a place where it was possible to rest or even to stand still in any normal attitude. We just went on from foothold to foothold; our topees made it impossible to see more than a foot or two above our heads. Suddenly we came on the Leblanc party sitting on a ledge.

"You look hot," said Mr. Leblanc. "I see you are not in training. You will find this most beneficial."

As soon as we stopped climbing, our knees began to tremble. We sat down. When the time came to start again, it was quite difficult to stand up. Our knees seemed to be behaving as they sometimes do in dreams. . . .

"We thought it best to wait for you," continued Mr. Leblanc, "because there is rather a tricky bit here. It is easy enough when you know the way, but you need someone to show you. I discovered it myself. I often go out alone in the evenings finding tricky bits. Once I was out all night, quite stuck. I thought I should be able to find a way when the moon rose. Then I remembered there was no moon that night. It was a very cramped position."

The tricky bit was a huge overhanging rock with a crumbling flaky surface.

"It is really quite simple. Watch me and then follow. You put your right foot here"—a perfectly blank, highly polished surface of stone—"then rather slowly you reach up with your left hand until you find a hold. You have to stretch rather far . . . so. Then you cross your right leg under your left — this is the difficult part — and feel for a footing on the other side. . . . With your right hand you just steady yourself . . . so." Mr. Leblanc hung over the abyss partly out of sight. His whole body seemed prehensile and tenacious. He *stood* there like a fly on the ceiling. "That is the position. It is best to trust more to the feet than the hands — push up rather than pull down . . . you see the stone here is not always secure." By way of demonstration he splintered off a handful of apparently solid rock from above his head and sent it tinkling down to the road below. "Now all you do is to shift the weight from your left foot to your right, and swing yourself around . . . so." And Mr. Leblanc disappeared from view.

Every detail of that expedition is kept fresh in my mind by recurrent nightmares. Eventually after about an hour's fearful climb we reached the rim of the crater. The next stage was a tramp across the great pit of loose cinders; then the ascent of the other rim, to the highest point of the peninsula. Here we paused to admire the view, which was indeed most remarkable; then we climbed down to the sea. Variety was added to this last phase by the fact that we were now in the full glare of the sun which had been beating on the cliffs from noon until they were blistering hot.

"It will hurt the hands if you hang on too long," said Mr. Leblanc. "One must jump on the foot from rock to rock like the little goats."

At last, after about three hours of it, we reached the beach. Cars and servants were waiting. Tea was already spread; bathing dresses and towels laid out.

"We always bathe here, not at the club," said Mr. Leblanc. "They have a screen there to keep out the sharks — while in this bay, only last month, two boys were devoured."

We swam out into the warm sea. An Arab fisherman, hopeful of a tip, ran to the edge of the sea and began shouting to us that it was dangerous. Mr. Leblanc laughed happily and, with easy, powerful strokes, made for the deep waters. We returned to shore and dressed. My shoes were completely worn through, and there was a large tear in my shorts where I had slipped among the cinders and slid some yards. Mr. Leblanc had laid out for him in the car a clean white suit, a shirt of green crepe de chine, a bow tie, silk socks, buckskin shoes, ivory hairbrushes, scent spray, and hair lotion. We ate banana sandwiches and drank very rich China tea.

For a little additional thrill on the way back, Mr. Leblanc took the wheel of his car. I am not sure that that was not the most hair-raising experience of all.

"See that peak there, Mummy? . . . You and me have got to be up there the day after tomorrow."
So Mummykins and Sonny-boy take to the peak and confound the experts. Wells is not generally
regarded as a writer with a gift for comedy; here is the delightful exception to the rule, from his
*Collected Stories* (1927).

# H. G. WELLS

# Little Mother Up the Mörderberg

I made a kind of record at Arosa by falling down three separate crevasses on three
successive days. That was before little Mother followed me out there. When she came,
I could see at a glance she was tired and jaded and worried, and so instead of letting her
fret about in the hotel and get into a wearing tangle of gossip, I packed her and two
knapsacks up, and started off on a long, refreshing, easygoing walk northward, until a
blister on her foot stranded us at the Magenruhe Hotel on the Sneejoch. She was for
going on, blister or no blister—I never met pluck like Mother's in all my life—but I
said, "No. This is a mountaineering inn, and it suits me down to the ground—or if you
prefer it, up to the sky. You shall sit in the veranda by the telescope, and I'll prance
about among the peaks for a bit."

"Don't have accidents," she said.

"Can't promise that, little Mother," I said; "but I'll always remember I'm your only
son."

So I pranced. . . .

I need hardly say that in a couple of days I was at loggerheads with all the mountaineers in that inn. They couldn't stand me. They didn't like my neck with its strong, fine Adam's apple — being mostly men with their heads *jammed* on — and they didn't like the way I bore myself and lifted my aviator's nose to the peaks. They didn't like my being a vegetarian and the way I evidently enjoyed it, and they didn't like the touch of color, orange and green, in my rough serge suit. They were all of the dingy school — the sort of men I call gentlemanly owls — shy, correct-minded creatures, mostly from Oxford, and as solemn over their climbing as a cat frying eggs. Sage they were, great head nodders, and "I-wouldn't-venture-to-do-a-thing-like-that" -ers. They always did what the books and guides advised, and they classed themselves by their seasons; one was in his ninth season, and another in his tenth, and so on. I was a novice and had to sit with my mouth open for bits of humble pie.

My style that! Rather!

I would sit in the smoking room sucking away at a pipeful of hygienic herb tobacco — they said it smelled like burning garden rubbish — and waiting to put my spoke in and let a little light into their minds. They set aside their natural reticence altogether in their efforts to show how much they didn't like me.

"You chaps take these blessed mountains too seriously," I said. "They're larks, and you've got to lark with them."

They just slued their eyes round at me.

"I don't find the solemn joy in fussing you do. The old-style mountaineers went up with alpenstocks and ladders and light hearts. That's my idea of mountaineering."

"It isn't ours," said one red-boiled hero of the peaks, all blisters and peeling skin, and he said it with an air of crushing me.

"It's the right idea," I said serenely, and puffed at my herb tobacco.

"When you've had a bit of experience you'll know better," said another, an oldish young man with a small gray beard.

"Experience never taught *me* anything," I said.

"Apparently not," said someone, and left me one down and me to play. I kept perfectly tranquil.

"I mean to do the Mörderberg before I go down," I said quietly, and produced a sensation.

"When are you going down?"

"Week or so," I answered, unperturbed.

"It's not the climb a man ought to attempt in his first year," said the peeling gentleman.

"*You* particularly ought not to try it," said another.

"No guide will go with you."

"Foolhardy idea."

"Mere brag."

"Like to see him do it."

I just let them boil for a bit, and when they were back to the simmer I dropped in, pensively, with, "Very likely I'll take that little Mother of mine. She's small, bless her, but she's as hard as nails."

But they saw they were being drawn by my ill-concealed smile; and this time they contented themselves with a few grunts and gruntlike remarks, and then broke up into little conversations in undertones that pointedly excluded me. It had the effect of hardening my purpose. I'm a stiff man when I'm put on my mettle, and I determined that the little Mother *should* go up the Mörderberg, where half these solemn experts hadn't been, even if I had to be killed or orphaned in the attempt. So I spoke to her about it the next day. She was in a deck chair on the veranda, wrapped up in rugs and looking at the peaks.

"Comfy?" I said.

"Very," she said.

"Getting rested?"

"It's so nice."

I strolled to the rail of the veranda. "See that peak there, Mummy?"

She nodded happily, with eyes half shut.

"That's the Mörderberg. You and me have got to be up there the day after tomorrow."

Her eyes opened a bit. "Wouldn't it be rather a climb, dearest?" she said.

"I'll manage that all right," I said, and she smiled consentingly and closed her eyes.

"So long as you manage it," she said.

I went down the valley that afternoon to Daxdam to get gear and guides and porters, and I spent the next day in glacier and rock practice above the hotel. That didn't add to my popularity. I made two little slips. One took me down a crevasse — I've an extraordinary knack of going down crevasses — and a party of three which was starting for the Kinderspitz spent an hour and a half fishing me out; and the other led to my dropping my ice ax on a little string of people going for the Humpi Glacier. It didn't go within thirty inches of anyone, but you might have thought from the row they made that I had knocked out the collective brains of the party. Quite frightful language they used, and three ladies with them too!

The next day there was something very like an organized attempt to prevent our start. They brought out the landlord, they remonstrated with Mother, they did their best to blacken the character of my two guides. The landlord's brother had a first-class row with them.

"Two years ago," he said, "they lost their Herr!"

"No particular reason," I said, "why you shouldn't keep yours on, is it?"

That settled him. He wasn't up to a polyglot pun, and it stuck in his mind like a fishbone in the throat.

Then the peeling gentleman came along and tried to overhaul our equipment. "Have you got this?" it was, and "Have you got that?"

"Two things," I said, looking at his nose pretty hard, "we haven't forgotten. One's blue veils and the other Vaseline."

I've still a bright little memory of the start. There was the pass a couple of hundred feet or so below the hotel, and the hotel — all name and windows — standing out in a great, desolate, rocky place against lumpy masses of streaky green rock, flecked here and there with patches of snow and dark shelves of rhododendron, and rising perhaps a thousand feet toward the western spur of the massif. Our path ran before us, meandering among the boulders down to stepping stones over a rivulet, and then upward on the other side of the stream toward the Magenruhe Glacier, where we had to go up the rocks to the left and then across the icefall to shelves on the precipitous face on the west side. It was dawn, the sun had still to rise, and everything looked very cold and blue and vast about us. Everyone in the hotel had turned out to bear a hand in the row — some of the *déshabillés* were disgraceful — and now they stood in a silent group watching us recede. The last word I caught was "They'll have to come back."

"We'll come back all right," I answered. "Never fear."

And so we went our way, cool and deliberate, over the stream and up and up toward the steep snowfields and icy shoulder of the Mörderberg. I remember that we went in absolute silence for a time, and then how suddenly the landscape gladdened with sunrise, and in an instant, as if speech had thawed, all our tongues were babbling.

I had one or two things in the baggage that I hadn't cared for the people at the inn to see, and I had made no effort to explain why I had five porters with the load of two and a half. But when we came to the icefall I showed my hand a little, and unslung a stout twine hammock for the mater. We put her in this with a rug around her, and sewed her in with a few stitches; then we roped up in line, with me last but one and a guide front and rear, and Mummy in the middle carried by two of the porters. I stuck my alpenstock through two holes I had made in the shoulders of my jacket under my rucksack, T-shape to my body, so that when I went down a crevasse, as I did ever and again, I just stuck in its jaws and came up easy as the rope grew taut. And so, except for one or two bumps that made the mater chuckle, we got over without misadventure.

Then came the rock climb on the other side, requiring much judgment. We had to get from ledge to ledge as opportunity offered, and here the little Mother was a perfect godsend. We unpacked her after we had slung her over the big fissure — I forget what you call it — that always comes between glacier and rock — and whenever we came to a bit of ledge within eight feet of the one we were working along, the two guides took her and slung her up, she being so light, and then she was able to give a foot for the next man to hold by and hoist himself. She said we were all pulling her leg, and that made her and me laugh so much that the whole party had to wait for us.

It was pretty tiring altogether doing that bit of the climb — two hours we had of it before we got to the loose masses of rock on the top of the arête. "It's worse going down," said the elder guide.

I looked back for the first time, and I confess it did make me feel a bit giddy. There was the glacier looking quite petty, and with a black gash between itself and the rocks.

For a time it was pretty fair going up the rocky edge of the arête, and nothing happened of any importance, except that one of the porters took to grousing because he was hit on the shin by a stone I dislodged. "Fortunes of war," I said, but he didn't seem to see it, and when I just missed him with a second he broke out into a long, whining discourse in what I suppose he thought was German—I couldn't make head or tail of it.

"He says you might have killed him," said the little Mother.

"They say," I quoted. "What say they? *Let* them say."

I was for stopping and filling him up with a feed, but the elder guide wouldn't have it. We had already lost time, he said, and the traverse around the other face of the mountain would be more and more subject to avalanches as the sun got up. So we went on. As we went around the corner to the other face I turned toward the hotel—it was the meanest little oblong spot by now—and made a derisive gesture or so for the benefit of anyone at the telescope.

We did get one rock avalanche that reduced the hindmost guide to audible prayer, but nothing hit us except a few bits of snow. The rest of the fall was a couple of yards and more out from us. We were on rock just then and overhung; before and afterward we were edging along steps in an ice slope cut by the foremost guide, and touched up by the porters. The avalanche was much more impressive before it came in sight, banging and thundering overhead, and it made a tremendous uproar in the blue deeps beneath, but in actual transit it seemed a mean show—mostly of stones smaller than I am.

"All right?" said the guide.

"Toned up," I answered.

"I suppose it *is* safe, dear?" asked the little Mother.

"Safe as Trafalgar Square," I said. "Hop along, Mummykins."

Which she did with remarkable agility.

The traverse took us onto old snow at last, and here we could rest for lunch—and pretty glad we were both of lunch and rest. But here the trouble with the guides and porters thickened. They were already a little ruffled about my animating way with loose rocks, and now they kicked up a tremendous shindy because instead of the customary brandy we had brought nonalcoholic ginger cordial. Would they even try it? Not a bit of it! It was a queer little dispute, high up in that rarefied air, about food values and the advantages of making sandwiches with nuttar. They were an odd lot of men, invincibly set upon a vitiated and vitiating dietary. They wanted meat, they wanted alcohol, they wanted narcotics to smoke. You might have thought that men like these, living in almost direct contact with nature, would have liked "nature" foods, such as plasmon, protose, plobose, digestine, and so forth. Not them! They just craved for corruption. When I spoke of drinking pure water one of the porters spat in a marked, symbolic manner over the precipice. From that point onward discontent prevailed.

We started again about half-past eleven, after a vain attempt on the part of the head guide to induce us to turn back. We had now come to what is generally the most difficult part of the Mörderberg ascent, the edge that leads up to the snowfield below the crest. But here we came suddenly into a draft of warm air blowing from the southwest, and everything, the guide said, was unusual. Usually the edge is a sheet of ice over rock. Today it was wet and soft, and one could kick steps in it and get one's toes into rock with the utmost ease.

"This is where Herr Tomlinson's party fell," said one of the porters, after we'd committed ourselves to the edge for ten minutes or so.

"Some people could fall out of a four-post bed," I said.

"It'll freeze hard again before we come back," said the second guide, "and us with nothing but *verdammt* ginger inside of us."

"You keep your rope taut," said I.

A friendly ledge came to the help of Mother in the nick of time, just as she was beginning to tire, and we sewed her up all but the feet in her hammock again, and roped her carefully. She bumped a bit, and at times she was just hanging over immensity and rotating slowly, with everybody else holding like grim death.

"My dear," she said, the first time this happened, "is it *right* for me to be doing this?"

"Quite right," I said, "but if you can get a foothold presently again—it's rather better style."

"You're sure there's no danger, dear?"

"Not a scrap."

"And I don't fatigue you?"

"You're a stimulant."

"The view," she said, "is certainly becoming very beautiful."

But presently the view blotted itself out, and we were in clouds and a thin drift of almost thawing snowflakes.

We reached the upper snowfield about half-past one, and the snow was extraordinarily soft. The elder guide went in up to his armpits.

"Frog it," I said, and spread myself out flat, in a sort of swimming attitude. So we bored our way up to the crest and along it. We went in little spurts and then stopped for breath, and we dragged the little Mother after us in her hammock-bag. Sometimes the snow was so good we fairly skimmed the surface; sometimes it was so rotten we plunged right into it and splashed about. I went too near the snow cornice once and it broke under me, but the rope saved me, and we reached the summit about three o'clock without further misadventure. The summit was just bare rock with the usual cairn and pole. Nothing to make a fuss about. The drift of snow and cloudwisp had passed, the sun was blazing hot overhead, and we seemed to be surveying all Switzerland. The Magenruhe Hotel was at our toes, hidden, so to speak, by our chins. We squatted about the cairn, and the guides and porters were reduced to ginger and vegetarian ham sandwiches. I cut and scratched an inscription, saying I had climbed on simple food, and claiming a record.

Seen from the summit, the snowfields on the northeast side of the mountain looked extremely attractive, and I asked the head guide why that way up wasn't used. He said something in his peculiar German about precipices.

So far our ascent had been a fairly correct ascent in rather slow time. It was in the descent that that strain in me of almost unpremeditated originality had play. I wouldn't have the rope returning across the upper snowfield, because Mother's feet and hands were cold, and I wanted her to jump about a bit. And before I could do anything to prevent it she had slipped, tried to get up by rolling over *down* the slope instead of up, as she ought to have done, and was leading the way, rolling over and over and over, down toward the guide's blessed precipices above the lower snowfield.

I didn't lose an instant in flinging myself after her, ax up, in glissading attitude. I'm not clear what I meant to do, but I fancy the idea was to get in front of her and put on the brake. I did not succeed, anyhow. In twenty seconds I had slipped, and was sitting down and going down out of my own control altogether.

Now, most great discoveries are the result of accident, and I maintain that in that instant Mother and I discovered two distinct and novel ways of coming down a mountain.

It is necessary that there should be first a snow slope above with a layer of softish, rotten snow on the top of ice, then a precipice, with a snow-covered talus sloping steeply at first and then less steeply, then more snow slopes and precipices according to taste, ending in a snowfield or a not too greatly fissured glacier, or a reasonable, not too rocky slope. Then it all becomes as easy as chuting the chutes.

Mother hit on the sideways method. She rolled. With the snow in the adhesive state it had got into, she had made the jolliest little snowball of herself in half a minute, and the nucleus of as clean and abundant a snow avalanche as anyone could wish. There was plenty of snow going in front of her, and that's the very essence of both our methods. You must fall on your snow, not your snow on you, or it smashes you. And you mustn't mix yourself up with loose stones.

I, on the other hand, went down feet first, and rather like a snowplow; slower than she did, and if, perhaps, with less charm, with more dignity. Also I saw more. But it was certainly a tremendous rush. And I gave a sort of gulp when Mummy bumped over the edge into the empty air and vanished.

It was like a toboggan ride gone mad down the slope until I took off from the edge of the precipice, and then it was like a dream.

I'd always thought falling must be horrible. It wasn't in the slightest degree. I might have hung with my clouds and lumps of snow about me for weeks, so great was my serenity. I had an impression then that I was as good as killed — and that it didn't matter. I wasn't afraid — that's nothing! — but I wasn't a bit uncomfortable. Whack! We'd hit something, and I expected to be flying to bits right and left. But we'd only got onto the snow slope below, at so steep an angle that it was merely breaking the fall. Down we went again. I didn't see much of the view after that because the snow was all around and over my head, but I kept feet foremost and in a kind of sitting posture, and then I slowed and then I quickened again and bumped rather, and then harder, and bumped and then bumped again and came to rest. This time I was altogether buried in snow, and twisted sideways with a lot of heavy snow on my right shoulder.

I sat for a bit enjoying the stillness—and then I wondered what had become of Mother, and set myself to get out of the snow about me. It wasn't so easy as you might think; the stuff was all in lumps and spaces like a gigantic sponge, and I lost my temper and struggled and swore a good deal, but at last I managed it. I crawled out and found myself on the edge of heaped masses of snow quite close to the upper part of the Magenruhe Glacier. And far away, right up the glacier and near the other side, was a little thing like a black beetle struggling in the heart of an immense split ball of snow.

I put my hands to my mouth and let out with my version of the yodel, and presently I saw her waving her hand.

It took me nearly twenty minutes to get to her. I knew my weakness, and I was very careful of every crevasse I came near. When I got up to her, her face was anxious.

"What have you done with the guides?" she asked.

"They've got too much to carry," I said. "They're coming down another way. Did you like it?"

"Not very much, dear," she said; "but I daresay I shall get used to these things. Which way do we go now?"

I decided we'd find a snow bridge across the bergschrund—that's the word I forgot just now—and so get onto the rocks on the east side of the glacier, and after that we had uneventful going right down to the hotel. . . .

Our return evoked such a strain of hostility and envy as I have never met before or since. First they tried to make out we'd never been to the top at all, but Mother's little proud voice settled that sort of insult. And, besides, there was the evidence of the guides and porters following us down. When they asked about the guides, "They're following *your* methods," I said, "and I suppose they'll get back here tomorrow morning somewhen."

That didn't please them.

I claimed a record. They said my methods were illegitimate.

"If I see fit," I said, "to use an avalanche to get back by, what's that to you? You tell me me and Mother can't do the confounded mountain anyhow, and when we do you want to invent a lot of rules to disqualify us. You'll say next one mustn't glissade. I've made a record, and you know I've made a record, and you're about as sour as you can be. The fact of it is, you chaps don't know your own silly business. Here's a good, quick way of coming down a mountain, and you ought to know about it—"

"The chance that both of you are not killed was one in a thousand."

"Nonsense! It's the proper way to come down for anyone who hasn't a hidebound mind. You chaps ought to practice falling great heights in snow. It's perfectly easy and perfectly safe, if only you know how to set about it."

"Look here, young man," said the oldish young man with the little gray beard, "you don't seem to understand that you and that lady have been saved by a kind of miracle — "

"Theory!" I interrupted. "I'm surprised you fellows ever come to Switzerland. If I were your kind I'd just invent theoretical mountains and play for points. However, you're tired, little Mummy. It's time you had some nice warm soup and tucked yourself up in bed. I shan't let you get up for six-and-thirty hours."

But it's queer how people detest a little originality.

Whymper was an artist who received a commission from a London publisher to sketch the monuments of Europe's playground. His *Scrambles Amongst the Alps* is surely *the* classic of mountaineering literature, and this passage from that 1871 book is the sport's ultimate tale of Pyrrhic victory. After seven attempts upon the Matterhorn between 1861 and 1865, Whymper and his party of seven finally succeeded. They spent a single hour glorying in their accomplishment, then commenced the retreat that ended in tragedy and in a controversy that still provokes heated words in Alpine chalets. Climbers and nonclimbers alike would do well to take heed of Whymper's concluding sentences.

# EDWARD WHYMPER

# "But the Rope Broke"

*Had we succeeded well,*
*We had been reckoned 'mongst the wise: our minds*
*Are so disposed to judge from the event.*
—EURIPIDES

*It is a thoroughly unfair, but an ordinary custom, to praise or*
*blame designs (which in themselves may be good or bad) just*
*as they turn out well or ill. Hence the same actions are at one*
*time attributed to earnestness and at another to vanity.*
—PLINY MINOR

We started from Zermatt on the thirteenth of July 1865, at half-past five, on a brilliant and perfectly cloudless morning. We were eight in number—Croz, old Peter and his two sons, Lord F. Douglas, Hadow, Hudson and I. To ensure steady motion, one tourist and one native walked together. The youngest Taugwalder fell to my share, and the lad marched well, proud to be on the expedition, and happy to show his powers. The wine bags also fell to my lot to carry, and throughout the day, after each drink, I replenished them secretly with water, so that at the next halt they were found fuller than before! This was considered a good omen, and little short of miraculous.

On the first day we did not intend to ascend to any great height, and we mounted, accordingly, very leisurely; picked up the things which were left in the chapel at the Schwarzsee at 8:20, and proceeded thence along the ridge connecting the Hörnli with the Matterhorn. At half-past eleven we arrived at the base of the actual peak; then quitted the ridge, and clambered around some ledges, onto the eastern face. We were now fairly upon the mountain, and were astonished to find that places which from the Riffel, or even from the Furggen Glacier, looked entirely impracticable, were so easy that we could run about.

Before twelve o'clock we had found a good position for the tent, at a height of 11,000 feet. Croz and young Peter went on to see what was above, in order to save time on the following morning. They cut across the heads of the snow slopes which descended toward the Furggen Glacier, and disappeared around a corner; but shortly afterward we saw them high up on the face, moving quickly. We others made a solid platform for the tent in a well-protected spot, and then watched eagerly for the return of the men. The stones which they upset told us that they were very high, and we supposed that the way must be easy. At length, just before 3 P.M., we saw them coming down, evidently much excited. "What are they saying, Peter?" "Gentlemen, they say it is no good." But when they came near we heard a different story. "Nothing but what was good; not a difficulty, not a single difficulty! We could have gone to the summit and returned today easily!"

We passed the remaining hours of daylight—some basking in the sunshine, some sketching or collecting; and when the sun went down, giving, as it departed, a glorious promise for the morrow, we returned to the tent to arrange for the night. Hudson made tea, I coffee, and we then retired each one to his blanket bag; the Taugwalders, Lord Francis Douglas, and myself, occupying the tent, the others remaining, by preference, outside. Long after dusk the cliffs above echoed with our laughter and with the songs of the guides, for we were happy that night in camp, and feared no evil.

We assembled together outside the tent before dawn on the morning of the fourteenth, and started directly it was light enough to move. Young Peter came on with us as a guide, and his brother returned to Zermatt. We followed the route which had been taken on the previous day, and in a few minutes turned the rib which had intercepted the view of the eastern face from our tent platform. The whole of this great slope was now revealed, rising for 3,000 feet like a huge natural staircase. Some parts were more, and others were less, easy; but we were not once brought to a halt by any serious impediment, for when an obstruction was met in front it could always be turned to the right or to the left. For the greater part of the way there was, indeed, no occasion for the rope, and sometimes Hudson led, sometimes myself. At 6:20 we had attained a height of 12,800 feet, and halted for half an hour; we then continued the ascent without a break until 9:55, when we stopped for fifty minutes, at a height of 14,000 feet. Twice we struck the northeast ridge and followed it for some little distance — to no advantage, for it was usually more rotten and steep, and always more difficult than the face. Still, we kept near to it, lest stones perchance might fall.

We had now arrived at the foot of that part which, from the Riffelberg or from Zermatt, seems perpendicular or overhanging, and could no longer continue upon the eastern side. For a little distance we ascended by snow upon the arête — that is, the ridge — descending toward Zermatt, and then, by common consent, turned over to the right, or to the northern side. Before doing so, we made a change in the order of ascent. Croz went first, I followed, Hudson came third; Hadow and old Peter were last. "Now," said Croz, as he led off, "now for something altogether different." The work became difficult and required caution. In some places there was little to hold, and it was desirable that those should be in front who were least likely to slip. The general slope of the mountain at this part was *less* than forty degrees, and snow had accumulated in, and had filled up, the interstices of the rock face, leaving only occasional fragments projecting here and there. These were at times covered with a thin film of ice, produced from the melting and refreezing of the snow. It was the counterpart, on a small scale, of the upper 700 feet of the Pointe des Écrins — only there was this material difference; the face of the Écrins was about, or exceeded, an angle of fifty degrees, and the Matterhorn face was less than forty degrees. It was a place over which any fair mountaineer might pass in safety, and Mr. Hudson ascended this part, and, as far as I know, the entire mountain, without having the slightest assistance rendered to him upon any occasion. Sometimes, after I had taken a hand from Croz, or received a pull, I turned to offer the same to Hudson; but he invariably declined, saying it was not necessary. Mr. Hadow, however, was not accustomed to this kind of work, and required continual assistance. It is only fair to say that the difficulty which he found at this part arose simply and entirely from want of experience.

This solitary difficult part was of no great extent. We bore away over it at first, nearly horizontally, for a distance of about 400 feet; then ascended directly toward the summit for about 60 feet; and then doubled back to the ridge which descends toward Zermatt. A long stride around a rather awkward corner brought us to snow once more. The last doubt vanished! The Matterhorn was ours! Nothing but 200 feet of easy snow remained to be surmounted!

You must now carry your thoughts back to the seven Italians who started from Breuil on the eleventh of July. Four days had passed since their departure, and we were tormented with anxiety lest they should arrive on the top before us. All the way up we had talked of them, and many false alarms of "men on the summit" had been raised. The higher we rose, the more intense became the excitement. What if we should be beaten at the last moment? The slope eased off, at length we could be detached, and Croz and I, dashing away, ran a neck-and-neck race, which ended in a dead heat. At 1:40 P.M. the world was at our feet, and the Matterhorn was conquered. Hurrah! Not a footstep could be seen.

It was not yet certain that we had not been beaten. The summit of the Matterhorn was formed of a rudely level ridge, about 350 feet long, and the Italians might have been at its farther extremity. I hastened to the southern end, scanning the snow right and left eagerly. Hurrah! again; it was untrodden. "Where were the men?" I peered over the cliff, half-doubting, half-expectant, and saw them immediately — mere dots on the ridge, at an immense distance below. Up went my arms and my hat. "Croz! Croz!! come here!" "Where are they, Monsieur?" "There, don't you see them, down there?" "Ah! the *coquins*, they are low down." "Croz, we must make those fellows hear us." We yelled until we were hoarse. The Italians seemed to regard us — we could not be certain. "Croz, we *must* make them hear us; they *shall* hear us!" I seized a block of rock and hurled it down, and called upon my companion, in the name of friendship, to do the same. We drove our sticks in, and prized away the crags, and soon a torrent of stones poured down the cliffs. There was no mistake about it this time. The Italians turned and fled.*

Still, I would that the leader of that party could have stood with us at that moment, for our victorious shouts conveyed to him the disappointment of the ambition of a lifetime. He was *the* man, of all those who attempted the ascent of the Matterhorn, who most deserved to be the first upon its summit. He was the first to doubt its inaccessibility, and he was the only man who persisted in believing that its ascent would be accomplished. It was the aim of his life to make the ascent from the side of Italy, for the honor of his native valley. For a time he had the game in his hands: he played it as he thought best; but he made a false move, and he lost it.

The others had arrived, so we went back to the northern end of the ridge. Croz now took the tent pole, and planted it in the highest snow. "Yes," we said, "there is the flagstaff, but where is the flag?" "Here it is," he answered, pulling off his blouse and fixing it to the stick. It made a poor flag, and there was no wind to float it out, yet it was seen all around. They saw it at Zermatt — at the Riffel — in the Val Tournanche. At Breuil, the watchers cried, "Victory is ours!" They raised "bravos" for Carrel, and "vivas" for Italy, and hastened to put themselves *en fête*. On the morrow they were undeceived. "All was changed; the explorers returned sad — cast down — disheartened — confounded — gloomy." "It is true," said the men. "We saw them ourselves — they hurled stones at us! The old traditions *are* true — there are spirits on the top of the Matterhorn!"

We returned to the southern end of the ridge to build a cairn, and then paid homage to the view. The day was one of those superlatively calm and clear ones which usually precede bad weather. The atmosphere was perfectly still, and free from all clouds or vapors. Mountains fifty — nay, a hundred — miles off, looked sharp and near. All their details — ridge and crag, snow and glacier — stood out with faultless definition. Pleasant

---

*I learned afterward from J.-A. Carrel that they heard our first cries. They were then upon the southwest ridge, close to the Cravate, and *twelve hundred and fifty feet* below us; or, as the crow flies, at a distance of about one third of a mile.

thoughts of happy days in bygone years came up unbidden, as we recognized the old, familiar forms. All were revealed — not one of the principal peaks of the Alps was hidden. I see them clearly now — the great inner circles of giants, backed by the ranges, chains, and massifs. First came the Dent-Blanche, hoary and grand; the Gabelhorn and pointed Rothorn; and then the peerless Weisshorn: the towering Mischabelhörner, flanked by the Allalinhorn, Strahlhorn, and Rimpfischhorn; then Monte Rosa — with its many Spitzes — the Lyskamm, and the Breithorn. Behind were the Bernese Oberland, governed by the Finsteraarhorn; the Simplon and St. Gotthard groups; the Disgrazia and the Ortler. Toward the south we looked down to Chivasso on the plain of Piedmont, and far beyond. The Viso — 100 miles away — seemed close upon us; the Maritime Alps — 130 miles distant — were free from haze. Then came my first love — the Pelvoux; the Écrins and the Meije; the clusters of the Graians; and lastly, in the west, glowing in full sunlight, rose the monarch of all — Mont Blanc. Ten thousand feet beneath us were the green fields of Zermatt, dotted with chalets, from which blue smoke rose lazily. Eight thousand feet below, on the other side, were the pastures of Breuil. There were forests black and gloomy, and meadows bright and lively; bounding waterfalls and tranquil lakes; fertile lands and savage wastes; sunny plains and frigid *plateaux*. There were the most rugged forms, and the most graceful outlines — bold, perpendicular cliffs, and gentle undulating slopes; rocky mountains and snowy mountains, somber and solemn, or glittering and white, with walls — turrets — pinnacles — pyramids — domes — cones — and spires! There was every combination that the world can give, and every contrast that the heart could desire.

We remained on the summit for one hour —

*One crowded hour of glorious life.*

It passed away too quickly, and we began to prepare for the descent.

Hudson and I again consulted as to the best and safest arrangement of the party. We agreed that it would be best for Croz to go first,* and Hadow second; Hudson, who was almost equal to a born mountaineer in sureness of foot, wished to be third; Lord Francis Douglas was placed next, and old Peter, the strongest of the remainder, after him. I suggested to Hudson that we should attach a rope to the rocks on our arrival at the difficult bit, and hold it as we descended, as an additional protection. He approved the idea, but it was not definitely settled that it should be done. The party was being arranged in the above order while I was sketching the summit, and they had finished, and were waiting for me to be tied in line, when someone remembered that our names had not been left in a bottle. They requested me to write them down, and moved off while it was being done.

A few minutes afterward I tied myself to young Peter, ran down after the others, and

---

*If the members of the party had been more equally efficient, Croz would have been placed *last*.

caught them just as they were commencing the descent of the difficult part. Great care was being taken. Only one man was moving at a time: when he was firmly planted the next advanced, and so on. They had not, however, attached the additional rope to rocks, and nothing was said about it. The suggestion was not made for my own sake, and I am not sure that it even occurred to me again. For some little distance we two followed the others, detached from them, and should have continued so had not Lord Francis Douglas asked me, about 3 P.M., to tie on to old Peter, as he feared, he said, that Taugwalder would not be able to hold his ground if a slip occurred.

A few minutes later, a sharp-eyed lad ran into the Monte Rosa Hotel, to Seiler, saying that he had seen an avalanche fall from the summit of the Matterhorn onto the Matterhorn Glacier. The boy was reproved for telling idle stories; he was right, nevertheless, and this was what he saw.

Michel Croz had laid aside his ax, and in order to give Mr. Hadow greater security, was absolutely taking hold of his legs, and putting his feet, one by one, into their proper positions.* So far as I know, no one was actually descending. I cannot speak with certainty, because the two leading men were partially hidden from my sight by an intervening mass of rock, but it is my belief, from the movements of their shoulders, that Croz, having done as I have said, was in the act of turning around, to go down a step or two himself; at this moment Mr. Hadow slipped, fell against him, and knocked him over. I heard one startled exclamation from Croz, then saw him and Mr. Hadow flying downward; in another moment Hudson was dragged from his steps, and Lord Francis Douglas immediately after him.† All this was the work of a moment. Immediately we heard Croz's exclamation, old Peter and I planted ourselves as firmly as the rocks would permit: the rope was taut between us, and the jerk came on us both as on one man. We held; but the rope broke midway between Taugwalder and Lord Francis Douglas. For a few seconds we saw our unfortunate companions sliding downward on their

---

*Not at all an unusual proceeding, even between born mountaineers. I wish to convey the impression that Croz was using all pains, rather than to indicate inability on the part of Mr. Hadow. . . .
†At the moment of the accident, Croz, Hadow, and Hudson were close together. Between Hudson and Lord F. Douglas the rope was all but taut, and the same between all the others who were *above*. Croz was standing by the side of a rock which afforded good hold, and if he had been aware, or had suspected, that anything was about to occur, he might and would have gripped it, and would have prevented any mischief. He was taken totally by surprise. Mr. Hadow slipped off his feet on to his back, his feet struck Croz in the small of the back, and knocked him right over, head first. Croz's ax was out of his reach, and without it he managed to get his head uppermost before he disappeared from our sight. If it had been in his hand I have no doubt that he would have stopped himself and Mr. Hadow.
Mr. Hadow, at the moment of the slip, was not occupying a bad position. He could have moved either up or down, and could touch with his hand the rock of which I have spoken. Hudson was not so well placed, but he had liberty of motion. The rope was not taut from him to Hadow, and

backs, and spreading out their hands, endeavoring to save themselves. They passed from our sight uninjured, disappeared one by one, and fell from precipice to precipice on the Matterhorn Glacier below, a distance of nearly 4,000 feet in height. From the moment the rope broke it was impossible to help them.

So perished our comrades! For the space of half an hour we remained on the spot without moving a single step. The two men, paralyzed by terror, cried like infants, and trembled in such a manner as to threaten us with the fate of the others. Old Peter rent the air with exclamations of "Chamonix! Oh, what will Chamonix say?" He meant, Who would believe that Croz could fall? The young man did nothing but scream or sob, "We are lost! we are lost!" Fixed between the two, I could neither move up nor down. I begged young Peter to descend, but he dared not. Unless he did, we could not advance. Old Peter became alive to the danger, and swelled the cry, "We are lost! we are lost!" The father's fear was natural — he trembled for his son; the young man's fear was cowardly — he thought of self alone. At last old Peter summoned up courage, and changed his position to a rock to which he could fix the rope; the young man then descended, and we all stood together. Immediately we did so, I asked for the rope which had given way, and found, to my surprise — indeed, to my horror — that it was the weakest of the three ropes. It was not brought, and should not have been employed, for the purpose for which it was used. It was old rope, and, compared with the others, was feeble. It was intended as a reserve, in case we had to leave much rope behind, attached to rocks. I saw at once that a serious question was involved, and made him give me the end. It had broken in midair, and it did not appear to have sustained previous injury.

For more than two hours afterward I thought almost every moment that the next would be my last; for the Taugwalders, utterly unnerved, were not only incapable of giving assistance, but were in such a state that a slip might have been expected from them at any moment. After a time, we were able to do that which should have been done at first, and fixed rope to firm rocks, in addition to being tied together. These ropes were cut from time to time, and were left behind. Even with their assurance the men were afraid to proceed, and several times old Peter turned with ashy face and faltering limbs, and said, with terrible emphasis, "*I cannot!*"

About 6 P.M. we arrived at the snow upon the ridge descending toward Zermatt, and all peril was over. We frequently looked, but in vain, for traces of our unfortunate companions; we bent over the ridge and cried to them, but no sound returned. Con-

the two men fell ten or twelve feet before the jerk came upon him. Lord F. Douglas was not favorably placed, and could move neither up nor down. Old Peter was firmly planted, and stood just beneath a large rock which he hugged with both arms. I enter into these details to make it more apparent that the position occupied by the party at the moment of the accident was not by any means excessively trying. We were compelled to pass over the exact spot where the slip occurred, and we found — even with shaken nerves — that *it* was not a difficult place to pass. I have described the *slope generally* as difficult, and it is so undoubtedly to most persons; but it must be distinctly understood that Mr. Hadow slipped at a comparatively easy part.

vinced at last that they were neither within sight nor hearing, we ceased from our useless efforts; and, too cast down for speech, silently gathered up our things, and the little effects of those who were lost, preparatory to continuing the descent. When, lo! a mighty arch appeared, rising above the Lyskamm, high into the sky. Pale, colorless, and noiseless, but perfectly sharp and defined, except where it was lost in the clouds, this unearthly apparition seemed like a vision from another world; and, almost appalled, we watched with amazement the gradual development of two vast crosses, one on either side. If the Taugwalders had not been the first to perceive it, I should have doubted my senses. They thought it had some connection with the accident, and I, after a while, that it might bear some relation to ourselves. But our movements had no effect upon it. The spectral forms remained motionless. It was a fearful and wonderful sight, unique in my experience, and impressive beyond description, coming at such a moment.

I was ready to leave, and waiting for the others. They had recovered their appetites and the use of their tongues. They spoke in patois, which I did not understand. At length the son said in French, "Monsieur." "Yes." "We are poor men; we have lost our Herr; we shall not get paid; we can ill afford this."* "Stop!" I said, interrupting him, "that is nonsense; I shall pay you, of course, just as if your Herr were here." They talked together in their patois for a short time, and then the son spoke again. "We don't wish you to pay us. We wish you to write in the hotel book at Zermatt, and to your journals, that we have not been paid." "What nonsense are you talking? I don't understand you. What do you mean?" He proceeded — "Why, next year there will be many travelers at Zermatt, and we shall get more *voyageurs.*"

Who would answer such a proposition? I made them no reply in words, but they knew very well the indignation that I felt. They filled the cup of bitterness to overflowing, and I tore down the cliff, madly and recklessly, in a way that caused them, more than once, to inquire if I wished to kill them. Night fell; and for an hour the descent was continued in the darkness. At half-past nine a resting place was found, and upon a wretched slab, barely large enough to hold the three, we passed six miserable hours. At daybreak the descent was resumed, and from the Hörnli ridge we ran down to the chalets of Buhl, and on to Zermatt. Seiler met me at his door, and followed in silence to my room. "What is the matter?" "The Taugwalders and I have returned." He did not need more, and burst into tears; but lost no time in useless lamentations, and set to work to arouse the village. Ere long a score of men had started to ascend the Hohlicht heights, above Kalbermatt and Z'Mutt, which commanded the plateau of the Matterhorn Glacier. They returned after six hours, and reported that they had seen the bodies lying motionless on the snow. This was on Saturday; and they proposed that we should leave on Sunday evening, so as to arrive upon the plateau at daybreak on Monday. Unwilling to lose the slightest chance, the Reverend J. M'Cormick and I

*They had been traveling with, and had been engaged by, Lord F. Douglas, and so considered him their employer, and responsible to them.

resolved to start on Sunday morning. The Zermatt men, threatened with excommunication by their priests if they failed to attend the early mass, were unable to accompany us. To several of them, at least, this was a severe trial. Peter Perren declared with tears that nothing else would have prevented him from joining in the search for his old comrades. Englishmen came to our aid. The Reverend J. Robertson and Mr. J. Phillpotts offered themselves, and their guide Franz Andermatten; another Englishman lent us Joseph Marie and Alexandre Lochmatter. Frédéric Payot, and Jean Tairraz, of Chamonix, also volunteered.

We started at 2 A.M. on Sunday the sixteenth, and followed the route that we had taken on the previous Thursday as far as the Hörnli. Thence we went down to the right of the ridge, and mounted through the seracs of the Matterhorn Glacier. By 8:30 we had got to the plateau at the top of the glacier, and within sight of the corner in which we knew my companions must be. As we saw one weather-beaten man after another raise the telescope, turn deadly pale, and pass it on without a word to the next, we knew that all hope was gone. We approached. They had fallen below as they had fallen above—Croz a little in advance, Hadow near him, and Hudson some distance behind; but of Lord Francis Douglas we could see nothing. We left them where they fell; buried in snow at the base of the grandest cliff of the most majestic mountain of the Alps.

All those who had fallen had been tied with the manilla, or with the second and equally strong rope, and, consequently, there had been only one link—that between old Peter and Lord Francis Douglas—where the weaker rope had been used. This had a very ugly look for Taugwalder, for it was not possible to suppose that the others would have sanctioned the employment of a rope so greatly inferior in strength when there were more than 250 feet of the better qualities still remaining out of use. For the sake of the old guide (who bore a good reputation), and upon all other accounts, it was desirable that this matter should be cleared up; and after my examination before the court of inquiry which was instituted by the government was over, I handed in a number of questions which were framed so as to afford old Peter an opportunity of exculpating himself from the grave suspicions which at once fell upon him. The questions, I was told, were put and answered; but the answers, although promised, have never reached me.*

Meanwhile, the administration sent strict injunctions to recover the bodies, and upon the nineteenth of July, twenty-one men of Zermatt accomplished that sad and danger-

---

*This was not the only occasion upon which M. Clemenz (who presided over the inquiry) failed to give up answers that he promised. It is greatly to be regretted that he did not feel that the suppression of the truth was equally against the interests of travelers and of the guides. If the men were untrustworthy, the public should have been warned of the fact; but if they were blameless, why allow them to remain under unmerited suspicion?

Old Peter Taugwalder labored for a long time under an unjust accusation. Notwithstanding repeated denials, even his comrades and neighbors at Zermatt persisted in asserting or insinuating

ous task. Of the body of Lord Francis Douglas they, too, saw nothing; it was probably still arrested on the rocks above. The remains of Hudson and Hadow were interred upon the north side of the Zermatt Church, in the presence of a reverent crowd of sympathizing friends. The body of Michel Croz lies upon the other side, under a simpler tomb; whose inscription bears honorable testimony to his rectitude, to his courage, and to his devotion.

So the traditional inaccessibility of the Matterhorn was vanquished, and was replaced by legends of a more real character. Others will essay to scale its proud cliffs, but to none will it be the mountain that it was to its early explorers. Others may tread its summit snows, but none will ever know the feelings of those who first gazed upon its marvelous panorama; and none, I trust, will ever be compelled to tell of joy turned into grief, and of laughter into mourning. It proved to be a stubborn foe; it resisted long, and gave many a hard blow; it was defeated at last with an ease that none could have anticipated, but, like a relentless enemy — conquered but not crushed — it took terrible vengeance. The time may come when the Matterhorn shall have passed away, and nothing, save a heap of shapeless fragments, will mark the spot where the great mountain stood; for, atom by atom, inch by inch, and yard by yard, it yields to forces which nothing can withstand. That time is far distant; and, ages hence, generations unborn will gaze upon its awful precipices, and wonder at its unique form. However exalted may be their ideas, and however exaggerated their expectations, none will come to return disappointed!

The play is over, and the curtain is about to fall. Before we part, a word upon the graver teachings of the mountains. See yonder height! 'Tis far away — unbidden comes the word "Impossible!" "Not so," says the mountaineer. "The way is long, I know; it's difficult — it may be — dangerous. It's possible, I'm sure; I'll seek the way; take counsel

that he *cut* the rope which led from him to Lord Francis Douglas. In regard to this infamous charge, I say that he *could* not do so at the moment of the slip, and that the end of the rope in my possession shows that he did not do so beforehand. There remains, however, the suspicious fact that the rope which broke was the thinnest and weakest one that we had. It is suspicious, because it is unlikely that any of the four men in front would have selected an old and weak rope when there was abundance of new, and much stronger, rope to spare; and, on the other hand, because if Taugwalder thought that an accident was likely to happen, it was to his interest to have the weaker rope where it was placed.

I should rejoice to learn that his answers to the questions which were put to him were satisfactory. Not only was his act at the critical moment wonderful as a feat of strength, but it was admirable in its performance at the right time. He left Zermatt, and lived for several years in retirement in the United States; but ultimately returned to his native valley, and died suddenly on July 11, 1888, at the Lac Noir (Schwarzee).

of my brother mountaineers, and find how they have gained similar heights, and learned to avoid the dangers." He starts (all slumbering down below); the path is slippery — may be laborious, too. Caution and perseverance gain the day — the height is reached! and those beneath cry, "Incredible; 'tis superhuman!"

We who go mountain scrambling have constantly set before us the superiority of fixed purpose or perseverance to brute force. We know that each height, each step, must be gained by patient, laborious toil, and that wishing cannot take the place of working; we know the benefits of mutual aid; that many a difficulty must be encountered, and many an obstacle must be grappled with or turned, but we know that where there's a will there's a way; and we come back to our daily occupations better fitted to fight the battle of life, and to overcome the impediments which obstruct our paths, strengthened and cheered by the recollection of past labors, and by the memories of victories gained in other fields.

I have not made myself either an advocate or an apologist for mountaineering, nor do I now intend to usurp the functions of a moralist; but my task would have been ill performed if it had been concluded without one reference to the more serious lessons of the mountaineer. We glory in the physical regeneration which is the product of our exertions; we exult over the grandeur of the scenes that are brought before our eyes, the splendors of sunrise and sunset, and the beauties of hill, dale, lake, wood, and waterfall; but we value more highly the development of manliness, and the evolution, under combat with difficulties, of those noble qualities of human nature — courage, patience, endurance, and fortitude.

Some hold these virtues in less estimation, and assign base and contemptible motives to those who indulge in our innocent sport.

*Be thou as chaste as ice, as pure as snow, thou shalt not escape calumny.*

Others, again, who are not detractors, find mountaineering, as a sport, to be wholly unintelligible. It is not greatly to be wondered at — we are not all constituted alike. Mountaineering is a pursuit essentially adapted to the young or vigorous, and not to the old or feeble. To the latter, toil may be no pleasure; and it is often said by such persons, "This man is making a toil of pleasure." Let the motto on the title page be an answer, if an answer be required.* Toil he must who goes mountaineering; but out of the toil comes strength (not merely muscular energy — more than that), an awakening of all the faculties; and from the strength arises pleasure. Then, again, it is often asked, in tones which seem to imply that the answer must, at least, be doubtful, "But does it repay you?" Well, we cannot estimate our enjoyment as you measure your wine, or weigh your lead — it is real, nevertheless. If I could blot out every reminiscence, or erase

*"Toil and pleasure, in their natures opposite, are yet linked together in a kind of necessary connection" (Livy).

every memory, still I should say that my scrambles among the Alps have repaid me, for they have given me two of the best things a man can possess — health and friends.

The recollections of past pleasures cannot be effaced. Even now as I write they crowd up before me. First comes an endless series of pictures, magnificent in form, effect, and color. I see the great peaks, with clouded tops, seeming to mount up for ever and ever; I hear the music of the distant herds, the peasant's *jodel,* and the solemn church bells; and I scent the fragrant breath of the pines: and after these have passed away, another train of thoughts succeeds — of those who have been upright, brave, and true; of kind hearts and bold deeds; and of courtesies received at stranger hands, trifles in themselves, but expressive of that goodwill toward men which is the essence of charity.

Still, the last, sad memory hovers around, and sometimes drifts across like floating mist, cutting off sunshine, and chilling the remembrance of happier times. There have been joys too great to be described in words, and there have been griefs upon which I have not dared to dwell; and with these in mind I say, Climb if you will, but remember that courage and strength are naught without prudence, and that a momentary negligence may destroy the happiness of a lifetime. Do nothing in haste; look well to each step; and from the beginning think what may be the end.

This brief extract from "the climber's Bible," G. Winthrop Young's *Mountain Craft* of 1920, is a splendid summation of the principal virtue of the sport — that it provides a measure of the spirit, that which is best in the race. The author was an Alpinist of considerable achievement before World War I, and despite the amputation of one leg owing to an injury incurred in battle, he continued to climb until 1935. However, his greatest contribution to the sport consists of his books of guidance, his autobiography *On High Hills*, and his verse.

# GEOFFREY WINTHROP YOUNG

# The Measure of Courage

A leader or a last man in the Alps absolutely must not fall. We may accept the fact that daring leaders will take risks, and that accidents can happen, provided every leader is aware of the distinction between the risks which no man may allow himself to take for his party even with their consent, and the risks which he may take for himself alone, but which his friends will be ill advised if they allow him to incur.

We cannot but be grateful for the spirit, though it is but human to criticize the action, of men who find joy in a contest with forces greater than themselves. Too often the profitable by-products of successful courage are alone admitted as justifications for the spirit in which adventure is undertaken. Deaths above the clouds or under the water are taken as heroic incidents, excusable in the interests of human progress. Deaths upon rock or under snow, inspired by the like and often by an even more disinterested spirit of adventure, are condemned as folly. Mountaineering must be judged by a spiritual, not a utilitarian, standard. Courage, moral and physical, that has its source in vigorous vitality and its goal in the extension of human freedom, finds on the hills its hardiest school. It is a very wholesome emulation that leads men, as their skill and power increase, to measure them against ever increasing natural difficulties. Our competition with the mountains injures no other human competitor by our success. Our conquest of them ends only in the conquest of ourselves. During these last years by none has the sacrifice been made more willingly than by our younger climbers. Their courage was that of the races from which they sprang: to mountaineering they owed its discovery and its training. We may not reproach it to the hills if the self-reliance they teach leads, here or there, some high heart into danger, before their harder lesson, of experience, has been learned.

And having said this, I must repeat that a leader in the Alps or big ranges, before he takes a chance, must make certain that the risk will be confined to himself, supposing such certainty can ever be attained. When he has made as certain of this as he can — he must not fall!

Did Mallory and Irvine reach the summit of Everest in 1924, only to perish in their descent? This is the great mystery of mountaineering in this century, as Whymper's broken rope was for the century past. The passage below represents the penultimate chapter of Sir Francis's *The Epic of Mount Everest* (1926), in which he concludes: "Everest indeed conquered their bodies. But their spirit is undying. No man onward from now will ever climb a Himalayan peak and not think of Mallory and Irvine."

# FRANCIS YOUNGHUSBAND

# Mallory and Irvine

Fury raged in [Mallory's] soul as he was forced to return from Camp V. Fury not against the individual porters who could not be brought to go farther but against the whole set of circumstances which thus compelled him to go back at the very moment when the weather at last was favorable. But Mallory was in no mind to be finally thwarted. He would recoil but to spring higher. He was absolutely possessed with the idea of climbing Mount Everest. Climbing Everest was no incident in his life. He had made it his whole life. Perhaps he had not Somervell's large geniality and way of carrying men along with him, nor Norton's capacity for leading a whole big expedition. He was more accustomed, and more fitted, to the lesser expeditions of a few choice companions. But he was more deadly intent on the *idea* than any. If any single one was the soul of the Expedition it was Mallory. And his was not so much bull dog tenacity, or sheer hard determination to conquer, as the imagination of the artist who cannot leave his work until it is completely, neatly, and perfectly, finished. Mallory was himself the very embodiment of the "Everest spirit." And to get him away from Everest before Everest itself had hurled him back you would have had to pull him up by the very roots of his being.

With fresh plans kindling within him he passed on from Camp IV straight through on the same day to Camp III, there to examine the possibilities of an ascent with oxygen. Mallory never was a real enthusiast for oxygen. But, if it were the only way of getting up Mount Everest, use it he would. Neither was Irvine an oxygen enthusiast, and privately he told Odell that he would rather get to the final pyramid without oxygen than to the top with it—a sentiment with which most of us will assuredly agree. And so probably would Mallory. But Mallory had this to consider—that Norton and Somervell would be doing the very utmost that the present expedition could do *without* oxygen. And, if they did not succeed, then one last attempt should be made—this time *with* oxygen. He therefore, as was his wont, threw his whole soul into arrangements for an oxygen attempt. And he chose for his companion Irvine, not [Noel] Odell, because Irvine had faith in the use of oxygen which Odell had not. Another reason was that Irvine had a genius for mechanical devising and had already worked wonders on the defective apparatus—defective because no apparatus to contain a highly condensed gas and at the same time withstand the extreme changes of temperature experienced between the plains of India and the heights of Everest, could be constructed which would not need adjustment. And a third reason, and perhaps important as any, was that Irvine had originally been allotted to him to form one of the pairs for the ascent, and Mallory had instilled him with his ideas, and deliberately worked to make the two into a true pair, and create a keen *esprit de pair.*

In the light of subsequent experience we may doubt the wisdom of using oxygen on this attempt. The heavy apparatus was a colossal handicap. And it afterward proved that acclimatization had much greater effect than was then supposed. Odell, who had acclimatized slowly, afterward climbed twice to 27,000 feet—once with a twenty-pound oxygen apparatus on his back, though he did not use the oxygen after 26,000 feet, finding it did him little good. If Mallory had taken Odell and had made the final attempt without oxygen it is quite legitimate to suppose that the summit might have been reached. For Odell had not gone through the trying experience of the rescue which Norton, Somervell, and Mallory had; and he was probably by now quite fit to reach the summit.* And, exhausted as Mallory was from the effects of the rescue, yet with a fit and experienced climber beside him, with the knowledge that 28,100 feet had already actually been reached—always a great aid to endeavor—and with his spirit to spur him on, he might have kept up with Odell to the end. Or Odell and Irvine without using oxygen might have succeeded; for neither had Irvine been strained by the rescue exertions.

All this is conjecture, though. And at the time that Mallory was making his preparations he did not know that Norton had reached 28,100 feet, or how wonderfully Odell was acclimatizing. All he knew was that, so far, Odell had *not* been acclimatizing so well as the rest. And therefore the best chance of reaching the summit seemed to be by using oxygen.

---

*Four porters had been stranded at Camp IV. Norton, Somervell, and Mallory—all three ill from the effects of extreme cold and altitude—brought the porters down to Camp III in a dangerous climb which required, according to Younghusband, "the very acme of mountaineering skill."

On June 3 Mallory and Geoffrey Bruce had arrived back at Camp III straight from Camp V, and together they now examined into the possibilities of collecting sufficient porters capable of carrying up oxygen supplies to Camp VI. The men had improved in health as the result of rest and fine weather; and by dint of strong, personal persuasion, Bruce was just able to get together sufficient men. And while these negotiations were proceeding Irvine was occupied in getting the oxygen apparatus into efficient working order.

Odell at this time was with Hazard in Camp IV, while that indefatigable and determined photographer Noel was established on the North Peak, at an altitude of 23,000 feet, taking cinematograph records.

Arrangements were completed on June 3, and on the next day Mallory and Irvine climbed up to the North Col again with the new porters. The two climbers used oxygen and covered the distance in the fast time of two and a half hours. They were well pleased with the result, but Odell was more skeptical. Irvine's throat was already suffering much from the cold dry air, and Odell thinks that the discomfort was palpably aggravated by the use of oxygen.

Here on the North Col the new climbing party and the support were assembled. This Camp IV had, indeed, become a kind of advanced mountain base for the actual assaults on the mountain. Odell has given a description of it. Its peculiarity was that it was pitched on snow and not on rock, like the others, even the highest, no rock being available. Perched on an ice ledge, it had four tents: two for sahibs and two for porters. The ledge was a shelf of névé with a greatest breadth of about thirty feet. And a high wall of ice which rose above it on the western side gave comforting protection from the chilly winds which constantly blow from that direction. But for this screen the camp could never have been occupied for so long as it was: Odell himself was there no less than eleven days—a sufficiently remarkable fact considering that only a few years ago even mountaineers like Dr. Hunter Workman had thought it would not be possible to sleep at 21,000 feet.

The weather conditions at such an altitude are peculiarly interesting. On two days when the sun temperature at midday was 105°, the air temperature at the same time was only 29°. Odell is doubtful whether the air temperature there ever does exceed the freezing point. It is probable that the snow wastes away entirely by direct evaporation. It was consequently very dry and unconsolidated and there was never any running water.

Odell himself does not seem to have been adversely affected by these trying conditions. He says that after some degree of acclimatization his sensations were really quite normal. It was only when great exertions were required that he felt "like nothing on earth." Certainly the bad effect of high altitude on the mentality had been exaggerated, he thought. The speed of mental process might be slowed down; but their capacity was not impaired.

Into this camp on the same day, June 4, that Mallory and Irvine arrived up from Camp III, Norton and Somervell returned from their great climb. They had come straight back from their highest point, without halting at Camps V and VI. Somervell had as nearly as possible collapsed altogether in a choking fit. And Norton that night became totally blind from snow blindness. They were disappointed — and naturally so. But to be disappointed because you have reached *only* 28,100 feet is surely a remarkable confirmation of Einstein's theory of relativity! Only recently men who had reached an altitude as high as this camp to which Norton and Somervell had now *descended* 5,000 feet were looked upon as heroes.

However, there was the fact that they had not got to the *top*, and here was Mallory, with steam at high pressure, ready to make one last desperate effort. Norton entirely agreed with this decision, and was "full of admiration for the indomitable spirit of the man, determined in spite of his already excessive exertions, not to admit defeat while any chance remained." And such was Mallory's willpower and nervous energy that he seemed to Norton entirely adequate to the task. All Norton differed with him about was as to taking Irvine as his companion. Irvine was suffering from throat trouble and was not the experienced climber that Odell was. Moreover, Odell, though he had acclimatized slowly, was beginning to show that he was a climber of unequaled endurance and toughness. But, as Mallory had completed his plans, Norton, very rightly, made no attempt at that late stage to interfere with them.

Mallory halted one day, June 5, in camp with Norton, now in great pain from his snow blindness. And on the sixth he set out with Irvine and four porters. Who can tell his feelings? Certainly he well knew the dangers, and he set out in no rash, foolhardy spirit. This was his third expedition to Mount Everest; at the end of the first he had written that the highest of mountains is capable of "a severity so awful and so fatal that the wiser sort of men do well to think and tremble even on the threshold of their high endeavor"; and on both the second and third expeditions he had experienced to the full the severity of Everest.

He knew the dangers before him and was prepared to meet them. But he was a man of vision and imagination as well as daring. He could see all that success meant. Everest was the embodiment of the physical forces of the world. Against it he had to pit the spirit of man. He could see the joy in the faces of his comrades if he succeeded. He could imagine the thrill his success would cause among all fellow mountaineers; the credit it would bring to England; the interest all over the world; the name it would bring him; the enduring satisfaction to himself that he had made his life worthwhile. All this must have been in his mind. He had known the sheer exhilaration of the struggle in his minor climbs among the Alps. And now on mighty Everest exhilaration would be turned into exaltation — not at the time, perhaps, but later on assuredly. Perhaps he never exactly formulated it, yet in his mind must have been present the idea of "all or nothing." Of the two alternatives, to turn back a third time, or to die, the latter was for Mallory probably the easier. The agony of the first would be more than he as a man, as a mountaineer, and as an artist, could endure.

Irvine, younger and less experienced than Mallory, would not be so acutely aware of the risks. On the other hand, he would not so vividly visualize all that success would mean. But Odell has recorded that he was no less determined than Mallory upon going "all out." It had been his ambition to have "a shot at the summit." And now that the chance had come he welcomed it "almost with boyish enthusiasm."

In this frame of mind the pair set out on the morning of June 6. The sightless Norton could only press their hands and pathetically wish them good luck. Odell and Hazard (who had come up from Camp III as Somervell had gone down) had prepared them a meal of fried sardines with biscuits and plenty of hot tea and chocolate, and at 8:40 they started. Their personal loads consisted of the modified oxygen apparatus with two cylinders only and a few other small items such as wraps and a food ration for the day, in all about twenty-five pounds. The eight porters with them carried provisions, bedding, and additional oxygen cylinders, but no oxygen apparatus for their own use.

The morning was brilliant. It clouded over in the afternoon and a little snow fell in the evening; but this was not serious and four of Mallory's porters returned in the evening from Camp V with a note saying there was no wind there and that things looked hopeful. The next morning, the seventh, Mallory's party moved on to Camp VI, while Odell came up in support to Camp V. It would have been better, of course, if he could have gone with them and so made a party of three. Three is the ideal number for a mountain party. But the tiny tents held only two climbers. There were not sufficient porters to carry a second tent. And he could only follow a day behind, acting as a kind of support.

Mallory made Camp VI all right with his four porters. And this fact is another evidence of the value of Norton and Somervell's work. Through *their* having got porters up to this camp, 26,800 feet, the second lot of porters with Mallory went there almost as a matter of course. And from there they were sent back with a note from Mallory to Odell saying the weather was perfect for the job, but that the oxygen apparatus was a nasty load for climbing.

That evening as Odell from Camp V looked out of his tent the weather was most promising; and he thought of the hopeful feelings with which Mallory and Irvine would go to sleep. Success would seem to be at last within their grasp.

Of what happened after that we know little. Owing to some defect in the oxygen apparatus which required adjustment, or from some other cause, their start must have been late, for when Odell, following in rear, caught sight of them it was 12:50 P.M. and they were then only at the second rock step, which, according to Mallory's schedule, they should have reached at 8 A.M. at latest. And the day had not turned out so fine as the previous evening had promised. There was much mist about the mountain. It might have been finer up where Mallory and Irvine were, for Odell looking up from below did notice that the upper part of the mist was luminous. But there was sufficient cloud about to prevent Odell from keeping in touch with the two climbers; and through the drifting mists he had only a single glimpse of them again.

As he reached the top of a little crag, at about 26,000 feet, there was a sudden clearing above him. The clouds parted. The whole summit ridge and final pyramid was unveiled. And far away on a snow slope he noticed a tiny object moving and approach the rock step. A second object followed. And then the first climbed to the top of the step. As he stood intently watching this dramatic appearance the scene became enveloped in cloud once more. And this was the last that was ever seen of Mallory and Irvine. Beyond that all is mystery. . . .

Where and when they died we know not. But there in the arms of Mount Everest they lie for ever — lie 10,000 feet above where any man has lain in death before. Everest indeed conquered their bodies. But their spirit is undying. No man onward from now will ever climb a Himalayan peak and not think of Mallory and Irvine.

# Glossary

*Abseil:* to descend by sliding down a rope fastened from above.

*Aid climbing:* gaining rest or support by artificial means, such as ropes, pitons, or bolts; this equipment may be used in free climbing, but only for safety.

*Aiguille:* a needlelike peak.

*Arête:* a narrow, spiny ridge.

*Bat hook:* a Warren Harding invention that functions in shallow drilled holes on blank walls where otherwise a more time-consuming bolt placement would be indicated.

*Belay:* to secure a climber on a difficult passage by means of a rope attached to a projection; to take in or let out the rope in a way that will permit the belayer to check the fall of the climber who is belayed.

*Bolt:* When cracks are not present to permit the use of pitons, a hole is drilled and an expansion bolt is placed; a carabiner is attached to the bolt, and the rope run through. Generally the bolt is left for use by future climbers.

*Bouldering:* a type of rock climbing which emphasizes difficult routes at low altitude.

*Buildering:* same as above, only practiced on buildings.

*Cairn:* stones piled high to mark a summit attained or to indicate a route.

*Carabiner:* a snap link used for attaching the rope to an anchor.

*Chimney:* a rock fissure wide enough for a climber to enter; as a verb, to climb that fissure by means of pressure on both sides with hands, feet, back, and knees.

*Chock:* also called a nut; an anchor fitted with a rope sling or wire cable for attaching a carabiner; inserted in a crack without drilling and generally removed by the climbers who used them.

*Chockstone:* a mass of rock that has become wedged between the walls at the top of a chimney.

*Chop:* intentionally to break the head of a bolt, making it unusable for future climbs.

*Class:* a level of difficulty applied to a climb, according to the equipment and technique required to accomplish it. First class is the least difficult, sixth class the most. Through Class 4, belaying and anchoring are not necessary. Class 5 is free climbing, with the use of anchors for safety. Class 6 is aid climbing. The least difficult of Class 5 climbs is expressed as 5.1, the most difficult (originally) expressed as 5.9, but today's most difficult climbs are confusingly ranked 5.10 or 5.11. Class 6 or aid climbs, which are often easier than Class 5, are expressed differently, from A1 to A5.

*Col:* a high pass between two peaks.

*Couloir:* a rock cleft, or corridor, on the side of a mountain.

*Cornice:* a mass of overhanging snow or ice formed by the wind along a ridge.

*Crack:* a rock cleft too narrow to fit a person.

*Crampon:* a spiked metal frame attached with straps to the sole of the boot for use on hard snow or ice.

*Crevasse:* a fissure in a glacier, often quite deep.

*Dihedral:* the intersection, at nearly right angles, of two rock faces or walls; also called an open book.

*Face climbing:* the use of foot- and handholds and balance climbing as opposed to the techniques used where fissures exist, such as jamming, chimneying, and aid.

*Free climbing:* the opposite of aid climbing; upward progress may not be achieved with rope or hardware.

*Friction climbing:* the use of pressure on slanted foot- and handholds.

*Gendarme:* an abrupt steepening from a rock ridge to a pinnacle.

*Glissade:* an international slide on deep snow in a seated or standing position.

*Harness:* a configuration of straps, most often in the form of a seat, which secures the rope to the climber's body and distributes his weight in the event of a fall.

*Jam:* to force a body part—fingers, hand, foot—into a crack and achieve a hold.

*Jumar:* a popular brand of mechanical ascender which grips the rope on the downward pull but slides upward freely. The technique of jumaring is similar to prusiking.

*Lieback:* a technique employed most often in crack climbing, in which one hand or both hands pull to one side and the feet push in the opposite direction.

*Moraine:* the mass of stones and debris brought down by a glacier; when the ice has retreated, the moraine remains.

*Nut:* see CHOCK.

*Pendulum:* to swing or fall sideways while dangling at the end of a rope.

*Pinch hold:* a handhold achieved by squeezing the rock between the thumb and fingers.

*Piton:* a metal peg of varying size which may be hammered into the rock; a ring is attached for connecting a carabiner. Pitons, unlike chocks, will scar the rock.

*Piton runner:* a loop of nylon rope or tape which may serve instead of a piton if placed in an upward-pointing projection.

*Pitch:* a stretch of difficult climbing between ledges; also, the distance between two stances.

*Prusik:* a rope-climbing technique based on the use of the knot invented by Karl Prusik. Like the jumar, this knot will slide upward freely but locks once weight is placed on it.

*Rappel:* to descend a slope by sliding down a rope; friction across the body slows the rate of descent, making this a far less risky maneuver than it appears.

*Runner:* see PITON RUNNER.

*Scree:* see TALUS.

*Sérac:* an ice pinnacle, often fantastically carved by sun and wind.

*Siege:* to make repeated efforts on a route, lowering down from each failure to try again. As a show of character, admirable; as technique, execrable.

*Sky hook:* a small hook used for aid on a ledge where there is no crack for a piton.

*Sling* a short length of rope attached to a carabiner or chock.

*Stance:* the network of holds, ledges, and cracks where the climber halts to rest, place an anchor, or ready a rappel.

*Swami belt:* a waistband of nylon webbing which functions as a harness, distributing weight and lessening the severity of a fall.

*Talus:* an assemblage of large loose rocks; scree consists of similarly gathered rocks, though smaller and less stable.

*Traverse:* a horizontal passage across a face.

*Verglas:* a thin, slimy film of ice that forms on rock and is particularly treacherous.

*The editor wishes to acknowledge the following for permission to include the selections listed:*

The American Alpine Club, "Modern Yosemite Climbing," by Yvon Chouinard, copyright © 1963 by American Alpine Journal. Bell & Hyman Ltd., "Kenya Mountain," from *Snow on the Equator* by H. W. Tilman, copyright © 1938 by H. W. Tilman. Jonathan Cape Ltd., "Back from Annapurna," from *Annapurna* by Maurice Herzog, translated by Nea Morin and Janet Adam Smith, copyright © 1952 by Maurice Herzog. Crown Publishers Inc., "The Surface Was Moving Beneath Him," from *The Eiger Sanction* by Trevanian, copyright © 1972 by Trevanian. E. P. Dutton, Inc., "Climbing Blind," from *Climbing Blind* by Colette Richard, English translation by Norman Dale, copyright © 1966 by Hodder and Stoughton Ltd., London, and E. P. Dutton; "Back from Annapurna," from *Annapurna* by Maurice Herzog, copyright © 1952, 1980 by E. P. Dutton, Inc. John Farquharson Ltd., "Struggle for the Ice Ridge," from *Annapurna South Face* by Chris Bonington, copyright © 1974 by Chris Bonington. "Avalanches," from *On Mountains* by John Jerome, copyright © 1978 by John Jerome. Harper & Row Publishers, Inc., "Stranded in the Andes," from *Alive: The Story of the Andes Survivors* by Piers Paul Read, copyright © 1974 by Piers Paul Read. David Higham Associates Ltd., "My Last Climb," from *The Mountains of Youth* by Arnold Lunn, published by Oxford University Press, copyright © 1925 by Arnold Lunn. Hodder and Stoughton Ltd., "Nanga Parbat . . . Solo," from *Nanga Parbat Pilgrimage* by Hermann Buhl, copyright © 1956 by Hermann Buhl; "The Final Assault," from *High Adventure* by Edmund Hillary, copyright © 1955 by Edmund Hillary. Alfred A. Knopf., "The Mountaineer Despite Himself," from *Going to Extremes,* by Joe McGinniss, copyright © 1980 by Joe McGinniss. Literistic, Ltd., "Mont Blanc and the Scientists," from *Men, Myths and Mountains,* previously published by Harper & Row, copyright © 1976 by Ronald Clark. Little Brown and Company, "Tricky Bits," from *When the Going Was Good* by Evelyn Waugh. McGraw-Hill Book Company, "Struggle for the Ice Ridge," from *Annapurna South Face* by Chris Bonington, copyright © 1974 by Chris Bonington. Harold Matson Company, Inc., "The White Tower," from *The White Tower* by James Ramsey Ullmann, copyright © 1945, © renewed 1973 by Marion B. Ullman. Scott Meredith Literary Agency, Inc., "The Ledge," from *The Naked and the Dead* by Norman Mailer, copyright © 1948 by Norman Mailer; "Rescue from the Eiger," from *The Climb Up to Hell* by Jack Olsen, copyright © 1962 by Jack Olsen, reprinted by permission of the author and the author's agents, Scott Meredith Literary Agency, Inc., 845 Third Avenue, New York, NY 10022.

*Every effort has been made to locate copyright owners. Any not cited here will, upon notification of the publisher, be gladly acknowledged in the next printing.*